REMOTE ACCESS FOR
CISCO® NETWORKS

Remote Access for Cisco® Networks

Bill Burton
CCIE #1119

McGraw-Hill

New York   San Francisco   Washington, D.C.
Auckland   Bogotá   Caracas   Lisbon   London
Madrid   Mexico City   Milan   Montreal   New Delhi
San Juan   Singapore   Sydney   Tokyo   Toronto

McGraw-Hill

A Division of The McGraw-Hill Companies

ISBN 0-07-135200-7

The executive editor for this book was Steven Elliot and the production manager was Claire Stanley. It was set in New Century Schoolbook by TIPS Technical Publishing.

Printed and bound by Quebecor / Martinsburg.

 This book is printed on recycled, acid-free paper containing a minimum of 50% recycled de-inked fiber.

CONTENTS

Contents

Contents

PREFACE

Introduction

Many thanks for selecting *Remote Access for Cisco Routers*. I have brought years of hands-on experience and feedback from students in the classroom together in its pages, hoping you will find it helpful in building remote-access connectivity.

There are many examples in the book that describe commonly used best practices when building remote networks. Each example comes complete with all the configuration files and appropriate executive-level commands that help with verification and troubleshooting.

This is a practical guide that I hope you find useful as a handy reference book for day-to-day use.

What to Expect

There are many books out there whose main purpose is to assist the reader in passing the CMTD or BCRAN certification test. While this book covers the same material as those books, it goes way over to the practical side of building remote access networks.

When I started writing this book, it looked like an overwhelming task; 400 pages—where would the material come from? As I finished putting this together, the realization hit me that the material took up closer to 800 pages. Having to pick out the technology covered in this book was a difficult task, but I let my students decide. Most of the topics in this book were chosen based on which areas people needed explanations for outside of the Cisco course material.

The earlier chapters have greater background depth to pass on the basic skills knowledge, and the later chapters concentrate on using those basic skills as building blocks for more advances topics.

Chapter 1: Asynchronous Terminal Services

This chapter discusses the basics of asynchronous communication and then goes into a terminal dial-in example. This example walks us through some basic modem configurations.

Chapter 2: Advanced Terminal Services

This chapter extends the basic knowledge learned in Chapter 1 to virtual terminal sessions using **telnet**, setting up menus and using **autocommand** to simplify user access and set up some basic access security. The last section describes the process of setting up an access server as a system controller using reverse **telnet** as a means for connecting to the console ports of devices in a remote location.

Chapter 3: Point-to-Point Protocol

This chapter drills down on the components of PPP, from the physical layer through the Link Control Protocol and Authentication to the Network Control Protocols.

Chapter 4: IP Dial Access

Chapter 4 is where we first get into the TCP/IP arena, with asynchronous dial-in PPP connections. There are several examples, including an example where a PC uses two modems and creates a PPP Multilink connection to gain IP access to the network through an access server.

Chapter 5: Dial-on-Demand Routing

This chapter walks the reader through the sequence that a packet follows from the time it enters the router until it is sent out on the dial-up connection.

Chapter 6: Integrated Services Digital Network

Using the basic DDR skills learned in Chapter 5, we explore ISDN connectivity using static routes. There are examples for one-to-one BRI, one-to-many BRI, and BRI-to-PRI connections. After we cover the basics, we extend the dial-up process using dialer profiles.

Chapter 7: DDR with IP Routing Protocols

Using static routes to point the way to a destination is direct and it works, but in larger dial-up networks, this method can be an administrative nightmare. After we review router redistribution as a means of propagating static routes to the balance of the main network environment, we extend the routing protocols to the remote sites using: snapshot routing for RIP and IGRP, demand circuits for OSPF, and On-Demand Routing (ODR) for EIGRP.

Chapter 8: AS5200 High-end Access Server

Chapter 8 is where we take all the lessons learned up to this point and apply them to an AS5200 access server. Using a single ISDN PRI connection, we can accept asynchronous terminal connections, asynchronous IP/PPP connections, and regular ISDN connections. There is additional hardware required to accept incoming voice grade calls, integrated digital modems. There is an extra section on the management and troubleshooting of these internal digital modems.

Chapter 9: Fixed-facility WAN Services

This chapter reviews the basic synchronous connectivity options used in WAN connectivity: HDLC, the Cisco default encapsulation, a variation on serial links, setting up fractional T1/E1 circuits, X.25, and Frame Relay.

Chapter 10: Backing Up Fixed WAN Connections

This chapter examines the three methods of providing dial backup services: using a backup interface, floating static routes, and a new feature in version 12.0 of the IOS—Dialer Watch.

Chapter 11: Advanced Security with TACACS+ and RADIUS

Chapter 11 starts out with a brief (could be a whole book) description and guided tour of the CiscoSecure ACS product, followed by an example of AAA implementation in a Cisco AS5200. Our example uses Authentication, Authorization, and Accounting to verify and authorize access to an AS5200. The Authorization process implements multiple privilege levels for executive-level commands.

Chapter 12: Protocol Translation

How can we **telnet** to a DEC VAX, or an X.25 server? Use protocol translation. There is a review of the two-step and one-step methods for protocol translation, with some fancy X.25-to-TCP/IP and LAT-to-TCP/IP conversations.

Chapter 13: Network Address Translation

Mr. Inside and Mr. Outside, what's local and what's global? NAT terms are confusing, so the first order of business should be to define the terms. There is an example using overlapping IP addresses (both the source and destination IP addresses are the same) and a DNS server.

Chapter 14: Troubleshooting

The last chapter is a review of the troubleshooting hints that have occurred throughout the book. At the end of the chapter, there is a special DDR section, with flowcharts, devoted to the entire DDR process.

The Quality Challenge

Having a Scottish heritage, I wanted a gentle nudge to make me more quality-conscious, so I have come up with the following challenge. For every error in the book, the first person to fill in the error report form at *www.ccci.com/books* for each error will receive a certificate and a crisp new $1 bill. The errors can be anything, including typographical errors, configuration errors (for the specific IOS version used), grammatical errors, etc. I am the judge of what constitutes an error, but I do take this seriously. Errors found will be assigned a number and listed on the Web site.

Hands-on Labs

Configuring Cisco routers is a hands-on skill. With that in mind, I have worked out a deal with MentorLabs so that there will be vLabs (when this book is available in the bookstores) that duplicate most of the examples in the book. Appendix H details the cross-reference between the book examples and the vLab numbers.

You can find lab equipment requirements and configuration files on the Chesapeake Web site at *www.ccci.com/books*.

Examples

There are many examples in this book. Due to space considerations, many of the configurations detail the information needed to make the examples work but drop some of the more repetitive configuration commands that do not effect router operation. Readers are encouraged to try the examples on their own equipment or use vLab to complete the learning experience.

Router command-line output in the examples is annotated. The output sequence is kept intact, and the comments are interspersed. The router configurations appear as numbered listings so that detailed line-by-line definitions and descriptions can be shown. The equipment in the examples is varied, as are the IOS versions, just like in real life.

Conventions

In order to keep everything clear, this book uses some conventions to represent information. For router command-line session output, the book uses a `fixed pitch code font`. For router input commands imbedded in regular text, the book uses the **InlineCommand** font. If there is a need for multiple keys to be entered together on the keyboard, they will be surrounded by <> brackets. For example, <Ctrl Shift 6> is the standard escape sequence used to get the attention of the Cisco IOS. All three keys have to be pressed on the keyboard at the same time.

Thank You!

Finally, I would like to thank you again for picking this book. May you find it useful and educational.

ACKNOWLEDGMENTS

Writing and publishing a book can only be accomplished with the help and support of more people than I can name. Many of the concepts and ideas in this book came from interaction with many wonderful students while teaching CMTD and BCRAN for Chesapeake Network Solutions.

There are several people I would like to mention that helped with the compilation of this book: Karin August for her work in acquiring, from 3COM (US Robotics) and COMPAQ (Microcom), the modems needed to complete the examples in the book; Elissa Mayer for compiling and consolidating the glossary, from many different sources; my editor, Steve Elliot, from McGraw-Hill; Bob Kern and the folks at TIPS Technical Publishing, Inc. for providing the templates and layouts for this book; Jeannine Kolbush for her terrific ideas during the initial editing.

Special thanks to Larry Galvin at MentorLabs, who is adding many of the examples in this book to the terrific lab selection in their electronic learning product, vLab.

To my family and friends, all my thanks for your support.

— BILL BURTON
CCIE #1119

REMOTE ACCESS FOR CISCO® NETWORKS

Asynchronous Terminal Services

Introduction

So we start. This first chapter will give you a brief technical overview of standard asynchronous communications. Then we will examine the basic terminal services provided by Cisco routers and access servers. The labs are simple to set up and can be accomplished with any Cisco router with an auxiliary port, asynchronous/synchronous port, or asynchronous communications port. Samples of all three are shown by the end of the chapter.

Asynchronous Communication

How do asynchronous communications work? After we answer this question, some of the commands we use on Cisco routers and access servers will make a little more sense.

Asynchronous data is transmitted in a serial manner, one bit at a time. If we just sent some random bits of information, it would be difficult to receive these random bits and make sense out of them. So in asynchronous communications, we organize the transmission of data in characters.

The beginning and end of each character of data must be identified by start and stop bits. The start bit indicates when the data byte is about to begin, and the stop bit signals when it ends. The requirement to send these additional two bits causes asynchronous communications to be slightly slower than synchronous; however, it has the advantage that the processor does not have to deal with the additional idle characters.

An asynchronous line that is idle is identified with a value of 1 (also called a mark state). By using this value to indicate that no data is currently being sent, the devices are able to distinguish between an idle state and a disconnected line. When a character is about to be transmitted, a start bit is sent. A start bit has a value of 0 (also called a space state). Thus when the line switches from a value of 1 to a value of 0, the receiver is alerted that a data character is about to come down the line.

Once the start bit has been sent, the transmitter sends the actual data bits. There may either be five, six, seven, or eight data bits, depending on the number you have selected. Both the receiver and the transmitter must agree on the number of data bits, parity, and the baud rate (see below). Almost all devices transmit data using either seven or eight data bits. Note that when only seven data bits are employed, you cannot send

ASCII values greater than 127. After the data has been transmitted, a stop bit is sent. A stop bit has the value of 1 (mark state) and is 1, 1.5, or 2 bits long and can be detected correctly even if the previous data bit also had a value of 1. Character termination is accomplished by the stop bit's duration; this forces a mark state (idle) between characters.

Besides the synchronization provided by the use of start and stop bits, an additional bit called a parity bit may optionally be transmitted along with the data. A parity bit affords a small amount of error checking, to help detect data corruption that might occur during transmission. You can choose: even parity, odd parity, mark parity, space parity, or none at all. When even or odd parity is being used, the number of marks (logical 1 bits) in each data byte are counted, and a single bit is transmitted following the data bits to indicate whether the number of 1 bits just sent is even or odd. For example, when even parity is chosen, the parity bit is transmitted with a value of 0 if the number of preceding marks is an even number. For the eight-bit binary value of 0110 0011, the parity bit would be 0. If even parity were in effect and the binary number 1101 0110 were sent, then the parity bit would be 1. Odd parity is just the opposite, and the parity bit is 0 when the number of mark bits in the preceding word is an odd number. The parity rule is simple: for even parity, the number of mark bits must be even; for odd parity, the number of mark bits must be odd. The parity bit is either a mark or space to make the parity correct. Parity error checking is very basic, and while it will tell you if there is a single bit error in the character, it doesn't show which bit was received in error. If an even number of bits are in error, then the parity bit would not reflect any error at all. Mark parity means that the parity bit is always set to the mark signal condition, and the space parity always sends the parity bit in the space signal condition. Since these two parity options serve no useful purpose whatsoever, they are almost never used. Figure 1-1 shows some sample character transmissions.

FYI *The common shorthand for defining data stream characteristics is 8-N-1. First comes the number of data bits: 5, 6, 7, or 8. Second is parity: N(one), E(ven), O(dd), S(pace), or M(ark). Third is the number of stop bits: 1, 1.5, or 2.*

EXAMPLE   Sample #1 illustrates a sample bit stream of 1100 1001 if the definition we use is eight data bits, no parity, and one stop bit, or 8-N-1. At sample time 1, the line is idle or in the mark state (1). When the line state changes to a space state (0), the line detects the start bit and sets up a sampling rate based on the bits per second defined. When the next sample time comes, the line starts clocking in bits by sampling the data stream level for 1s and 0s. The stop bit(s) at the end of the character stream forces the data stream to a mark or idle condition so that the data stream will correctly identify the start of a new character with a space start bit.

■ ▬ ■

QUESTION #1   Based on the following data stream definitions for samples #2, #3, and #4, what are the characters being transmitted in binary, and are they valid characters or not? You will find answers to these questions at the end of the chapter.

Sample #2's definition is 5-E-1
Sample #3's definition is 8-E-2
Sample #4's definition is 7-O-1.5

Transmission speed is the one area that has not been discussed. Transmission speed is based on a clocking signal. When we get to cabling and physical layer signalling in Appendix A, we will see that there is no clocking signal between the two end points. How does the circuitry at each end know how fast to send the data stream? Each end must set matching speeds in bits per second to transmit and receive data correctly. There is another option when it comes to setting up the transmission speed at either end. The feature is referred to as autobaud. If there is a known character being received, and the speed is correct, then the character will be properly decoded. This only works if the bits per character and parity are correctly defined. Autobaud works by starting with the maximum speed available on the port or line, and checking to see if the known character is received. If the transmission is not decoded correctly, then the initial speed is reduced to the next lower standard speed, and the data stream is checked again. This process is repeated until the correct speed is detected.

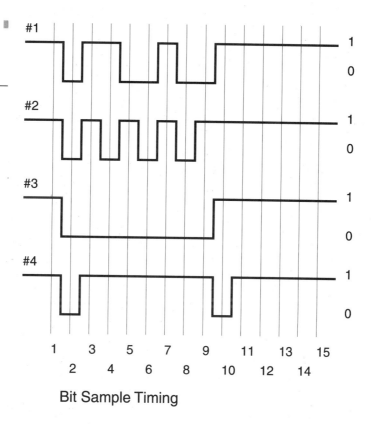

Figure 1-1
Asynchronous bit streams.

Bit Sample Timing

TIP *While autobaud appears to be a useful option, it is not as reliable as defining the actual speed of operation required.*

Table 1-1 defines the options that are available for the transmission of characters to and from Cisco routers, and are applied to an asynchronous line.

Command	Parameter	Description
databits	bits	Number of bits used to represent a single character: 5, 6, 7, 8 (default)
parity	bits	Parity bits added to the data bits for error checking each character transmitted: none (default), odd, even, space, mark.
stopbits	bits	Number of bits used to indicate the end of a transmitted character: 1, 1.5, 2 (default)
speed	bits per second	Speed of transmission in bits per second: 300 through 115200 (9600,default)

Configuring Dial Access

Now that we have covered the basics of asynchronous data streams, let's put this information to use by programming a Cisco router to accept a dial-in connection from a terminal. For this example we will use a PC with a built-in modem, a 3640 Cisco router, a 3Com 56K modem, and a Black Box 4X16 key telephone system to simulate the phone company. Figure 1-2 describes the layout of the equipment used in this example.

Figure 1-2
Dial-in equipment layout.

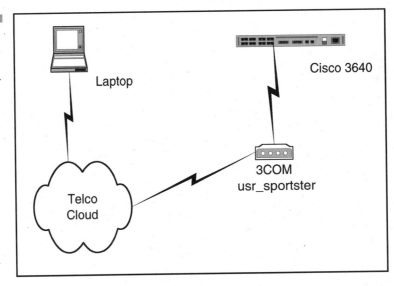

We will proceed though the initial configuration step-by-step to follow the process of building an asynchronous connection.

In order to program the Cisco access server/router for an asynchronous connection, we need to correctly identify the line number that corresponds to the physical connection. For fixed configuration routers, such as the Cisco 2511, there is a formula that is used to calculate the line number that corresponds to each physical connection. Table 1-2 provides the line assignment formula for fixed configuration Cisco routers.

The modular access servers/routers have a specific line number mapping that is defined for each possible line that could be configured within the device. Table 1-3 defines the line numbers assigned to each modular slot in the Cisco 3640. The maximum number of lines that can be defined in each slot is 32.

TABLE 1-2

Fixed configuration line assignment

Connection Type	Line Number
Console port	Line 0
Asynchronous port	Line number
Auxiliary port	Number of asynchronous ports + 1
Virtual terminals	Number of asynchronous ports + 2 is the first virtual terminal line

TABLE 1-3

Cisco 3640 line definitions

Connection Type	Line Number
Console port	Line 0
Slot 0	Lines 1– 32
Slot 1	Lines 33– 64
Slot 2	Lines 65– 96
Slot 3	Lines 97– 128
Auxiliary port	Line 129
Virtual terminals	Line 130 is the starting line number for virtual terminal sessions

There are three different access servers/routers that will be used for examples in this chapter: a Cisco 2511 access server with 16 asynchronous ports, a Cisco 3640 with asynchronous/synchronous interfaces in Slot 3, and a Cisco 1720 modular router, which will be used for our auxiliary port example.

For our first example, we are using a Cisco 3640 with an eight-port asynchronous/synchronous card in Slot 3. Looking in Table 1-3, the line numbers assigned to that slot are 97 through 128. With only eight ports available, the possible line numbers are 97 through 104. If we use interface 0 in Slot 3 for our asynchronous connection, then we will use line number 97. With the Cisco dual-purpose ports, the default mode of operation is synchronous, and to activate line 97 it is necessary to change the mode of operation to asynchronous. The initial setup commands for the router, including a connectivity **ping** test for our ethernet port, follow.

```
Router>enable
Router#conf t
Enter configuration commands, one per line.  End with CNTL/Z.
Router(config)#no ip domain-lookup
Router(config)#enable password san-fran
Router(config)#line con 0
Router(config-line)#logging synchronous
Router(config-line)#exec-timeout 0 0
Router(config-line)#host C3640
C3640(config)#int e 0/0
C3640(config-if)#ip address 172.31.200.210 255.255.255.0
C3640(config-if)#no shut
C3640(config-if)#^Z
C3640#ping 172.31.200.210
Type escape sequence to abort.
Sending 5, 100-byte ICMP Echos to 172.31.200.210, timeout is 2 seconds:
!!!!!
Success rate is 100 percent (5/5), round-trip min/avg/max = 1/1/4 ms

C3640#
```

Now we can use the **show line** command to take a look at the lines defined using the initial setup commands.

```
C3640#sho line
  Tty Typ    Tx/Rx      A Modem    Roty AccO AccI   Uses      Noise Overruns  Int
*   0 CTY               -   -       -    -    -       0         0    0/0       -
   65 TTY               - inout     -    -    -       0         0    0/0       -
   66 TTY               - inout     -    -    -       0         0    0/0       -
   67 TTY               - inout     -    -    -       0         0    0/0       -
   68 TTY               - inout     -    -    -       0         0    0/0       -
   69 TTY               - inout     -    -    -       0         0    0/0       -
   70 TTY               - inout     -    -    -       0         0    0/0       -
  129 AUX   9600/9600   -   -       -    -    -       0         0    0/0       -
```

```
130 VTY          -    -    -    -    -       0       0     0/0      -
131 VTY          -    -    -    -    -       0       0     0/0      -
132 VTY          -    -    -    -    -       0       0     0/0      -
133 VTY          -    -    -    -    -       0       0     0/0      -
134 VTY          -    -    -    -    -       0       0     0/0      -

Line(s) not in async mode -or- with no hardware support:
1-64, 71-128

C3640#
```

In the **show line** command above, we see lines 65 through 70, not the lines 97 through 104 that were expected for Slot 3. In fact, these lines represent asynchronous devices in Slot 2, MICA digital modems, which we will get to in Chapter 7. In order to get line 97 to show up, we must change the default synchronous mode of operation to asynchronous.

```
C3640#conf t
Enter configuration commands, one per line.  End with CNTL/Z.
C3640(config)#int s 3/0
C3640(config-if)#physical asynchronous
C3640(config-if)#^Z
C3640#
```

When you enter the **physical asynchronous** command, the router has to modify the internal circuit; you will notice a hesitation before the next prompt is displayed. To make sure that line 97 has been created, let's do another **show line** command.

```
C3640#show line
  Tty Typ     Tx/Rx      A Modem  Roty AccO AccI  Uses  Noise  Overruns  Int
*   0 CTY                 -   -     -    -    -      0      0     0/0      -
   65 TTY                 - inout   -    -    -      0      0     0/0      -
   66 TTY                 - inout   -    -    -      0      0     0/0      -
   67 TTY                 - inout   -    -    -      0      0     0/0      -
   68 TTY                 - inout   -    -    -      0      0     0/0      -
   69 TTY                 - inout   -    -    -      0      0     0/0      -
   70 TTY                 - inout   -    -    -      0      0     0/0      -
   97 TTY     9600/9600   -   -     -    -    -      0      0     0/0      Se3/0
  129 AUX     9600/9600   -   -     -    -    -      0      0     0/0      -
  130 VTY                 -   -     -    -    -      0      0     0/0      -
  131 VTY                 -   -     -    -    -      0      0     0/0      -
  132 VTY                 -   -     -    -    -      0      0     0/0      -
  133 VTY                 -   -     -    -    -      0      0     0/0      -
  134 VTY                 -   -     -    -    -      0      0     0/0      -

Line(s) not in async mode -or- with no hardware support:
1-64, 71-96, 98-128

C3640#
```

There are 12 columns in the **show line** command. As we will be using this command throughout this book, let's take a look at the content of each column. The first column is the line number. Second is the line type: CON (console), TTY (asynchronous), AUX (auxiliary), VTY (virtual terminal). The third column is the speed of operation, both transmit (TX) and receive (RX). The fourth column indicates Autobaud (F) or not (-). The fifth column is modem operational mode: callin, callout, CTS-req, DTR-Act, RIisCD, or inout. The sixth column is the rotary group that this line is assigned to. The seventh and eighth columns define the output (AccO) and input (AccI) access lists assigned to control access to this line. The ninth column is the number of uses since system startup. The tenth column is the number of times noise has been detected since system startup. The eleventh column is the number of hardware (UART) overruns/software buffer overflows, both defined as the number of overruns or overflows that have occurred on the specified line since the system was restarted. Hardware overruns are buffer overruns; the UART chip has received bits from the software faster than it can process them. A software overflow occurs when the software has received bits from the hardware faster than it can process them. Twelfth is the interface that corresponds to this line.

An asterisk (*) preceding the number in the Tty field means the line is currently active, running a terminal-oriented protocol. An A preceding the number indicates the line is currently active in autoselect mode. An I preceding the number indicates that the line is free and can be used for asynchronous mode because it is configured as an async mode interactive interface.

Now it is time to put in the configuration commands that program the line for the character transmission.

```
C3640#conf t
Enter configuration commands, one per line.  End with CNTL/Z.
C3640(config)#line 97
C3640(config-line)#speed 115200
C3640(config-line)#parity none
C3640(config-line)#databits 8
C3640(config-line)#stopbits 1
C3640(config-line)#^Z
C3640#
```

We have defined how our line will communicate to the external modem, so now we have to establish a connection to the modem. We will use a technique called reverse telnet. We will telnet from our console connection to one of our internal addresses inside the router, but instead of using the normal port, 23, we will use port 2097. This port number XYYY is made up of two components, X and YYY. The X defines the type of protocol translation that will take place when we connect to line number YYY. Type 2 creates an ASCII terminal session on the line defined by translating telnet packets to individual ASCII characters.

```
C3640#telnet 172.31.200.210 2097
Trying 172.31.200.210, 2097 ...
% Connection refused by remote host

C3640#
```

Connection refused? Oops, when we telnet to any target, it is necessary to supply at least a password to authenticate access to the target resource. Let's add a login process and a password to our line 97, and while we are at it, let's complete the configuration process. Flow control is typically set to hardware, but there are other options listed in the following code. The **transport input all** command is used to define which of the available protocols can be used for connections to this line. By specifying **all**, we will be able to use any protocol, including telnet.

```
C3640#conf t
Enter configuration commands, one per line.   End with CNTL/Z.
C3640(config)#line 97
C3640(config-line)#login
C3640(config-line)#password cisco
C3640(config-line)#flowcontrol ?
  NONE      Set no flow control
  hardware  Set hardware flow control
  software  Set software flow control

C3640(config-line)#flowcontrol hardware
C3640(config-line)#transport input all
C3640(config-line)#^Z
C3640#
```

This should complete our basic line configuration. Using reverse telnet, we should now be able to connect to our modem. When we issue our **telnet** command, we get a password prompt. When we enter the password correctly, we get a Password OK that lets us know we have successfully established a connection to the modem. It looks like we are dead at first, because there is no prompt or any other indication that we are connected. Entering **at** should get us a response of OK, indicating that we are connected. Help is obtained with the **at$** command (output has been deleted), and the current modem settings are displayed using the **ati4** command. We will spend more time later with modem configurations and commands.

```
C3640#telnet 172.31.200.210 2097
Trying 172.31.200.210, 2097 ... Open


User Access Verification

Password:
Password OK
at
OK
at $
HELP,   Command Quick Reference (CTRL-S to Stop, CTRL-C to Cancel)

&$      HELP, Ampersand Commands               Mn    n=0  Speaker OFF
        .

        .
        .
n=3     Hi Speaker Volume                 $ HELP,  Command Summary

OK
ati4
U.S. Robotics 56K FAX EXT Settings...

   B0  E1  F1  M1  Q0  V1  X1  Y0
   BAUD=115200   PARITY=N   WORDLEN=8
   DIAL=TONE     ON HOOK    CID=0

   &A1  &B1  &C1  &D2  &G0  &H1  &I0  &K1
   &M4  &N0  &P0  &R2  &S0  &T5  &U0  &Y1

   S00=001  S01=000  S02=043  S03=013  S04=010  S05=008  S06=002
   S07=060  S08=002  S09=006  S10=014  S11=070  S12=050  S13=000
   S15=000  S16=000  S18=000  S19=000  S21=010  S22=017  S23=019
   S25=005  S27=000  S28=008  S29=020  S30=000  S31=128  S32=002
   S33=000  S34=000  S35=000  S36=014  S38=000  S39=000  S40=001
   S41=000  S42=000

   LAST DIALED #:
OK
```

Aren't we lucky that all modems use the exact same commands, so that we have no problem programming these modems using the standard AT commands? Just kidding. We are using a USRobotics (3COM) Sportster modem, and the commands used to program the modems used in this book can be found in Appendix B.

To get out of the modem command environment, we have to break out of our telnet session and get back to the router console prompt. The escape sequence is easy to do, with a little practice. First, hold down the <control> key and the <shift> key and press the <6> key once. Second, remove all fingers from the keyboard and hit the <x> key. This sequence can be used to break out of any telnet session. More complex situations will be covered in Chapter 2. After we break out of our telnet session, we can see where we have active telnet sessions by using the **where** or **show sessions** command. The asterisk on the left-hand side indicates the last active connection, and pressing <enter> at the command prompt will reconnect you to the telnet destination. If you have multiple telnet sessions active, just type in **resume X**, or just **X**, where X is the connection number shown in the **where** command.

```
C3640#where
Conn Host                    Address              Byte   Idle Conn Name
  *   1 172.31.200.210        172.31.200.210          0     0
172.31.200.210

C3640#
```

To shut down our active telnet connection, we type in the **disconnect X** command, where X is the connection number. If we want to disconnect the active connection, we can just type in **disconnect** without the connection number. When there are multiple connections to be terminated, type in **quit**, **exit**, or **logout** to end the session and close all open telnet sessions.

```
C3640#disconnect
Closing connection to 172.31.200.210 [confirm]
C3640#
```

Typing in the **telnet** commands to get to the modem can be time-consuming when you are troubleshooting modem problems, but there is a shortcut we can set up on the router. Using a static **ip host** command, we can assign a name to an IP address and port number.

```
C3640#conf t
Enter configuration commands, one per line.  End with CNTL/Z.
C3640(config)#ip host modem0 2097 172.31.200.210
C3640(config)#^Z
C3640#
```

Now we can program the modem to operate properly with the Cisco router by typing **modem0** to establish the connection. The modem command string **at&F1&C1&B1S0=1&W** will be used later on when we talk about automating the modem initialization process later in this chapter.

```
C3640#modem0
Trying modem0 (172.31.200.210, 2097)... Open


User Access Verification

Password:
Password OK
at
OK
at&F1&C1&B1S0=1&W

OK
```

Let's break out of the modem connection and save what we have
entered up to this point.

```
C3640#copy running startup-config
Destination filename [startup-config]?
Building configuration...

C3640#
```

HyperTerminal Setup

In order to test out our configuration, we need to set up a PC with a terminal connection that can be used to dial in to our Cisco router/access server.
We will use the HyperTerminal program available with Windows 95 and
Windows 98. In Windows, open up the HyperTerminal folder under Acces-
sories (see Figure 1-3). Double click on the Hypertrm icon to get started.

Pick an icon from the bottom row and apply a name to the desktop
icon (see Figure 1-4).

Select the country, enter the area code and number, and select the connection type (see Figure 1-5).

Enter the location you wish to use for this new setup (see Figure 1-6).

Select the dial properties for this location (see Figure 1-7).

After clicking on the Dial button (see Figure 1-6), you will see the connect status window (see Figure 1-8).

After the hyperterm session is set up, then we dial in and watch how
data flows from the router console through the reverse telnet session to
the modem.

Asynchronous Terminal Services

Figure 1-3
HyperTerminal folder.

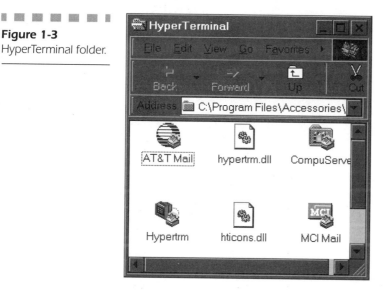

Figure 1-4
Icon definition and
identification.

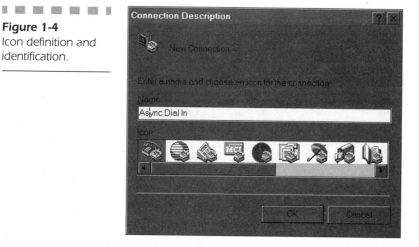

```
C3640#where
Conn Host                    Address                Byte  Idle Conn Name
*   1 modem0                 172.31.200.210            0     0 modem0

C3640#
[Resuming connection 1 to modem0 ... ]

RING

CONNECT 28800/ARQ/V34/LAPM/V42BIS
hello
```

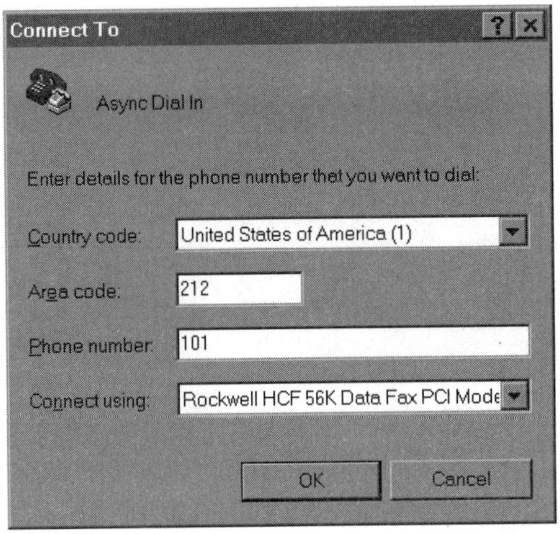

Figure 1-5
Phone number and
connection defini-
tion.

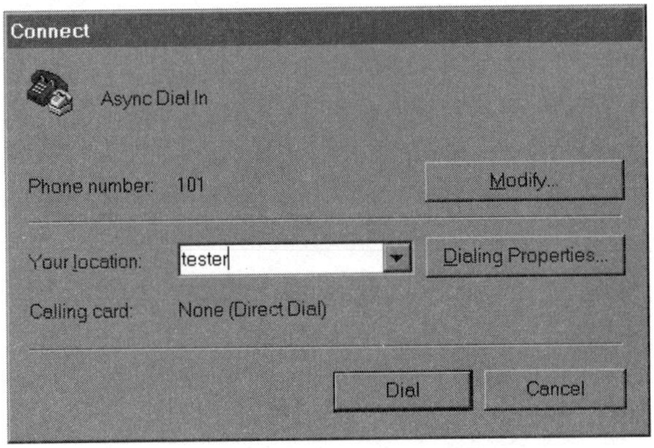

Figure 1-6
Location identifica-
tion.

Notice that in the last line above, the hello came from the other side of our connection. We couldn't log in to the router because we have a command session open from the router to the modem.

```
C3640#disconnect
Closing connection to modem0 [confirm]
C3640#
```

Now that we have disconnected the modem command session, we can attempt again to dial in to the router. We know that the modem connection is being made from our modem testing earlier. But the router did not pick up on the fact that someone had dialed in. Did we miss something?

Figure 1-7
Dialing properties.

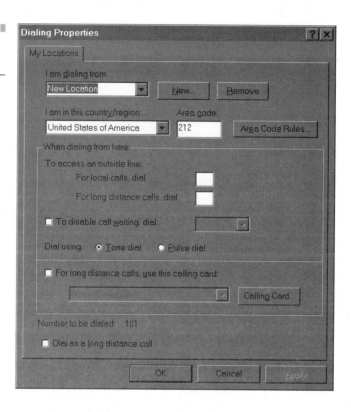

Figure 1-8
Connecting status.

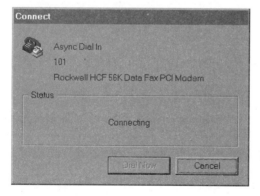

If we look at our previous **show line** command, there is no entry under the modem operation column for line 97. The MICA modems show an operational status of inout, the ability to recognize status changes from the modem, and the ability for the modem to accept commands from the router. Line 97 has no entry in this column, so let's put in the **modem inout** command and test out our connection.

```
C3640#conf t
Enter configuration commands, one per line.  End with CNTL/Z.
C3640(config)#line 97
C3640(config-line)#modem inout
C3640(config-line)#^Z
C3640#
```

If we can dial in, then we have a valid connection and can establish our executive session. It looks like we are in.

```
User Access Verification

Password:
C3640>en
Password:
C3640#
```

Let's look at the console connection and see if our message appeared.

```
C3640#


***
***
*** Message from tty97 to all terminals:
***
hello there I have dialed in!!


C3640#
```

Success! We have completed our basic dial-in connection. Let's take a look at our completed configuration for our successful dial-in connection in Code Listing 1-1. Some lines have been deleted for clarity.

Code Listing 1-1
Initial C3640 router configuration.

```
1   C3640#show run
2   Building configuration...
3
4   Current configuration:
5   !
6   version 12.0
7   !
```

Code Listing 1-1
(continued)

```
 8   hostname C3640
 9   !
10   enable password san-fran
11   !
12   ip host modem0 2097 172.31.200.210
13   !
14   interface Ethernet0/0
15    ip address 172.31.200.210 255.255.255.0
16    no ip directed-broadcast
17   !
18   interface Serial3/0
19   physical-layer async
20    no ip address
21    no ip directed-broadcast
22    shutdown
23   !
24   ip classless
25   !
26   line con 0
27    exec-timeout 0 0
28    logging synchronous
29    length 0
30    transport input none
31   line 65 70
32   line 97
33    password cisco
34    login
35    modem InOut
36    transport input all
37    stopbits 1
38    speed 115200
39    flowcontrol hardware
40   line aux 0
41   line vty 0 4
42   !
43   end
44
45   C3640#
```

Who wants to program the modem by hand? That could be tedious and prone to error, so let's automate the modem programming.

Modem Setup

To set up our modem in the previous example, it was necessary to reverse telnet to enter **AT** commands. There are two different ways to have this modem configuration take place automatically, the **modem autoconfigure** command and chat scripts.

Automatic Configuration

There are two different modes of operation for the **modem autoconfigure** command, the discovery mode and specifying the exact modem type. While it sounds like the discovery mode of operation is the easiest, it is also dangerous, as changes to the internal code of the modem could occur and the modem might no longer function properly. In our example, we will add the command to our configuration.

```
C3640#conf t
Enter configuration commands, one per line.  End with CNTL/Z.
C3640(config)#line 97
C3640(config-line)#modem autoconfigure type usr_sportster
C3640(config-line)#^Z
C3640#
```

Turn on the **debug confmodem** process to make sure that the process is running properly, and then trigger the automatic programming of the modem by clearing line 97.

```
C3640#debug confmodem
Modem Configuration Database debugging is on
C3640#clear line 97
[confirm]
 [OK]


C3640#
01:26:35: TTY97: Modem command:   --AT&F&C1&D2&H1&R2&M4&K1&B1S0=1H0--
01:26:36: TTY97: Modem configuration succeeded
01:26:37: TTY97: detection speed (115200) response ---OK---
01:26:37: TTY97: Done with modem configuration
C3640#
```

Note that there are two steps that take place, programming the modem with the **AT** commands and speed detection. Oh yes, speed detection is one of the most important keys to successful asynchronous connectivity when working with Cisco routers/access servers.

■ ■

NOTE When modems communicate across the telephone network, circuits can become noisy. When today's modems encounter a significant number of errors, they do the natural thing—they slow down the transmission speed. Cisco routers can't do this; they can't change speed. Refer to our discussion earlier in this chapter about asynchronous

character transmission to understand why a modem changing speed will interrupt communications. When the modem gets programmed, make sure the modem locks into the DTE speed.

In the preceding sample **debug** output, the **&B1** in the initialization string is the **AT** command that locks the modem into the established Cisco router transmission speed.

Modem internal commands change over time, and new models of modems are shipped before Cisco can update the modem information stored internally in the Cisco IOS.

In the example above, we used the mode type of usr_sportster, but how did we know this modem is supported by the Cisco router? We use the **show modemcap** command to look at all the entries built into the current version of Cisco IOS.

```
C3640#show modemcap
default
codex_3260
usr_courier
usr_sportster
hayes_optima
global_village
viva
telebit_t3000
microcom_hdms
microcom_server
nec_v34
nec_v110
nec_piafs
cisco_v110
mica
C3640#
```

Sure enough, usr_sportster is one of the entries in the database. What settings are being used to program the modem? We use the show **modemcap usr_sportster** command to see the details.

```
C3640#show modemcap usr_sportster
Modemcap values for usr_sportster
Factory Defaults (FD):  &F
Autoanswer (AA):  S0=1
Carrier detect (CD):  &C1
Drop with DTR (DTR):  &D2
Hardware Flowcontrol (HFL):  &H1&R2
Lock DTE speed (SPD):  &B1
DTE locking speed (DTE):  [not set]
Best Error Control (BER):  &M4
Best Compression (BCP):  &K1
No Error Control (NER):  &M0
```

```
No Compression (NCP):  &K0
No Echo (NEC):  E0
No Result Codes (NRS):  Q1
Software Flowcontrol (SFL):  [not set]
Caller ID (CID):  [not set]
On-hook (ONH):  H0
Off-hook (OFH):  H1
Miscellaneous (MSC):  [not set]
Template entry (TPL):  usr_courier
Modem entry is built-in.

C3640#
```

But what if we need to change these defaults? The following sequence uses the **modemcap edit** command to create a new modemcap entry, usr_new. All the available parameters we can change are shown when we use our helpful **?**.

```
C3640#conf t
Enter configuration commands, one per line.  End with CNTL/Z.
C3640(config)#modemcap edit usr_new ?
  autoanswer             Edit entry for autoanswer
  best-compression       Edit entry for best compression
  best-error-control     Edit entry for best error control
  caller-id              Edit entry for Caller ID
  carrier-detect         Edit entry for carrier-detect
  dtr                    Edit entry for DTR
  factory-default        Edit entry for factory default
  hardware-flowcontrol   Edit entry for hardware flowcontrol
  miscellaneous          Edit entry for miscellaneous commands
  no-compression         Edit entry for no compression
  no-echo                Edit entry for no echo
  no-error-control       Edit entry for no error control
  no-results             Edit entry for no results (quiet mode)
  software-flowcontrol   Edit entry for software flowcontrol
  speed                  Edit entries for locking modem speed
  template               Specify modemcap entry to use as a template

C3640(config)#
```

Rather than re-enter all the individual commands, we can use all the same parameters from an existing entry in our modemcap database by specifying an existing entry in the database as the template.

```
C3640(config)#modemcap edit usr_new template usr_sportster
```

Now we can override the factory default setting, &F, that we saw in our debug confmodem and show modemcap usr_sportster samples above. After we make the change, we check the creation of our new entry, usr_new, with the **show modemcap** command.

```
C3640(config)#modemcap edit usr_new factory-default &F1
C3640(config)#^Z
C3640#show modemcap
default
codex_3260
usr_courier
usr_sportster
hayes_optima
global_village
viva
telebit_t3000
microcom_hdms
microcom_server
nec_v34
nec_v110
nec_piafs
cisco_v110
mica
usr_new

C3640#
```

Our new entry has been added to the list, and we can verify the new factory default setting by using the **show modemcap usr_new** command.

```
C3640#showmodemcap usr_new
Modemcap values for usr_new
Factory Defaults (FD):  &F1
Autoanswer (AA):  S0=1
Carrier detect (CD):  &C1
Drop with DTR (DTR):  &D2
Hardware Flowcontrol (HFL):  &H1&R2
Lock DTE speed (SPD):  &B1
DTE locking speed (DTE):  [not set]
Best Error Control (BER):  &M4
Best Compression (BCP):  &K1
No Error Control (NER):  &M0
No Compression (NCP):  &K0
No Echo (NEC):  E0
No Result Codes (NRS):  Q1
Software Flowcontrol (SFL):  [not set]
Caller ID (CID):  [not set]
On-hook (ONH):  H0
Off-hook (OFH):  H1
Miscellaneous (MSC):  [not set]
Template entry (TPL):  usr_sportster
C3640#
```

Now we can test out the process to see if it works by clearing line 97 and examining the debug confmodem output.

```
C3640#clear line 97
[confirm]
 [OK]
C3640#
01:33:50: TTY97: Modem command:   --AT&F1&C1&D2&H1&R2&M4&K1&B1S0=1H0--
01:33:51: TTY97: Modem configuration succeeded
01:33:52: TTY97: detection speed (115200) response ---OK---
01:33:52: TTY97: Done with modem configuration
C3640#
```

This is a standard method for insuring that the modem is always programmed properly. Each time the line is reset through a **clear line** command, or when a dial-in connection is closed, the autoconfigure process runs. The engineers at the Technical Assistance Center do not always trust this automatic process and may recommend the use of chat scripts for initializing the modem at system startup. Chat script initialization is the next topic covered in this chapter.

Code Listing 1-2 shows the router configuration for the modem autoconfigure process. Some lines have been deleted for clarity. Please note the format of creating the modemcap entry usr_new on line 13. The application of the modemcap entry usr_new is shown in line 38.

Code Listing 1-2

```
1    C3640#show running
2    Building configuration...
3
4    Current configuration:
5    !
6    version 12.0
7    !
8    hostname C3640
9    !
10   enable password san-fran
11   !
12   ip host modem0 2097 172.31.200.210
13   modemcap entry usr_new:FD=&F1:TPL=usr_sportster
14   !
15   interface Ethernet0/0
16     ip address 172.31.200.210 255.255.255.0
17     no ip directed-broadcast
18   !
19   interface Serial3/0
20     physical-layer async
21     no ip address
22     no ip directed-broadcast
23     shutdown
24   !
25   ip classless
26
27   !
28   line con 0
29   exec-timeout 0 0
```

Code Listing 1-2
(continued)

```
30    logging synchronous
31    length 0
32    transport input none
33  line 65 70
34  line 97
35    password cisco
36  login
37    modem InOut
38    modem autoconfigure type usr_new
39    transport input all
40    stopbits 1
41    speed 115200
42    flowcontrol hardware
43  line aux 0
44  line vty 0 4
45    login
46  !
47  end
48
49  C3640#
```

Chat Scripts

Chat scripts are used for initializing modems, providing asynchronous dialing instructions, and logging on to remote systems.

The format of the command is chat-script NAME expect-string1 send-string1[expect-string2 send-string2 [expect-string3 send-string3. . . .]]. The **expect-string/send-string** combo is repeated as many times as needed.

Table 1-4 details the special escape sequences that are used to insert special characters, or provide for telephone number insertion with \T.

There are two other special strings that are used when building a chat script, ABORT and TIMEOUT. The ABORT string sequence is used to terminate the chat script operation if the word defined as string is detected. For example, the ABORT BUSY sequence will terminate the chat script if the word BUSY is returned by the modem. The TIMEOUT time sets the time to wait for input, in seconds, before terminating the chat script. The default is 5 seconds, which may not be sufficient for standard modem communications.

In later chapters we will be using chat scripts extensively, so let's test your knowledge by giving you an example, then asking you to decode some additional samples.

TABLE 1-4
Chat script escape
sequences

Escape Sequence	Description
""	Expect a null string
EOT	Send an end-of-transmission character
BREAK	Cause a BREAK. This sequence is sometimes simulated with line speed changes and null characters. It may not work on all systems.
\c	Suppress new line at the end of the send string. In other words, do nothing.
\d	Delay for 2 seconds
\K	Insert a BREAK
\n	Send a newline or linefeed character
\p	Pause for 1/4 second
\r	Send a return
\s	Send a space character
\t	Send a table character
\\	Send a backslash (\) character
\T	Replaced by phone number
\q	Reserved

EXAMPLE

```
chat-script dial ABORT BUSY "" AT OK "ATDT 5551212" TIMEOUT 30 CONNECT \c
```

The name we will reference for this chat script is dial. If the word BUSY is returned by the modem, we will abort the chat script. Next, we wait for "" (a null string), or nothing, and immediately send an AT. We wait for an OK and then send ATDT 5551212. The quotes around the command and the number tell the chat script to treat everything between the double quotes as a single string. After the dial string is sent, we wait for 30 seconds for the word CONNECT to be returned. When it is, we send nothing and terminate the chat script with the **\c**.

QUESTION #2 *Interpret the following chat scripts and determine if each chat script works.*

Sample #1

```
chat-script dialit ABORT busy ABORT "no carrier" ""
"ATDT5551234" TIMEOUT 30 CONNECT\c
```

Sample #2

```
chat-script initmodem "" AT OK "AT&F1&C1&B1S0=1&W"
```

Now that we have defined chat script operation, let's use this technique to program the modem at system startup. First we will program in the chat script `initmodem` using the hardware flow control factory default &F1, follow carrier detect &C1, and lock DTE speed &B1. Lastly, we store this configuration in the modem with &W.

```
C3640#conf t
Enter configuration commands, one per line.  End with CNTL/Z.
C3640(config)#chat-script initmodem "" "AT&F1&C1&B1S0=1&W"
C3640(config)#
```

Now we need to activate this chat script by configuring line 97. There are many different options for script activation shown below. We will select the startup option so that it only has to execute once when the router/access server starts up.

```
C3640(config)#line 97
C3640(config-line)#script ?
  activation     chat script to run whenever line is activated
  arap-callback  chat script to run on line whenever ARAP callback is initiated
  callback       chat script to run on line whenever callback is initiated
  connection     chat script to run whenever connection is made to the line
  dialer         chat script to run whenever dialer makes an outgoing call
  reset          chat script to run whenever line is reset
  startup        chat script to run at system startup

C3640(config-line)#script startup initmodem
C3640(config-line)#^Z

C3640#
```

To see if this works, let's reset the router and check it out. The initial startup messages have been removed for clarity.

```
C3640#wr
Building configuration...

C3640#reload
Proceed with reload? [confirm]

System Bootstrap, ...

Press RETURN to get started!


C3640>en
C3640#who
     Line       User       Host(s)                 Idle Location
*   0 con 0                idle                      0
C3640#
```

Now we dial in and see if we have an incoming connection on line 97.

```
C3640#who
     Line       User       Host(s)                 Idle Location
*   0 con 0                idle                      0
   97 tty 97              idle                      0

C3640#
```

Success! But can we be sure? Let's use a simple technique to test the chat script initmodem. Let's activate the chat script initmodem when the line is reset. See the script ? options above.

```
C3640#conf t
Enter configuration commands, one per line.  End with CNTL/Z.
C3640(config)#line 97
C3640(config-line)#script reset initmodem
C3640(config-line)#^Z
C3640#
```

Turn on debugging with the **debug chat line 97** command to watch the chat script execute when the line is reset. If the modem still works with the router, then we will be all set.

```
C3640#debug chat ?
  line  Single TTY line to debug scripts
  <cr>

C3640#debug chat line 97
```

```
Chat scripts activity debugging is on for line number 97
C3640#clear line 97
[confirm]
 [OK]
C3640#
00:03:01: CHAT97: Attempting line reset script
00:03:01: CHAT97: Matched chat script initmodem to string initmodem
00:03:01: CHAT97: Asserting DTR
00:03:01: CHAT97: Chat script initmodem started
00:03:01: CHAT97: Sending string: AT&F1&C1&B1S0=1&W
00:03:02: CHAT97: Chat script initmodem finished, status = Success
C3640#
```

So we are done, right? Maybe we should take a quick review of the current configuration for line 97 to make absolutely sure.

```
line 97
 password cisco
 script startup initmodem
 script reset initmodem
 login
 modem InOut
 modem autoconfigure type usr_new
 transport input all
 stopbits 1
 speed 115200
 flowcontrol hardware
```

Wow, we have three different methods of programming the modem! Let's check out that **modem autoconfigure** command to see if it executes when the **script reset initmodem** has been configured. Check out the debug status with the **show debug** command, then activate the **debug confmodem** command.

```
C3640#show debug
Chat Scripts:
  Chat scripts activity debugging is on for line number 97
C3640#debug confmodem
Modem Configuration Database debugging is on
C3640#
```

If we **clear line 97**, then we can watch the debug output to see what happens. It looks like both commands execute, chat script first, then the autoconfigure process.

```
C3640#clear line 97
[confirm]
 [OK]
C3640#
```

```
00:04:11: CHAT97: Attempting line reset script
00:04:11: CHAT97: Matched chat script initmodem to string initmodem
00:04:11: CHAT97: Asserting DTR
00:04:11: CHAT97: Chat script initmodem started
00:04:11: CHAT97: Sending string: AT&F1&C1&B1S0=1&W
00:04:12: CHAT97: Chat script initmodem finished, status = Success
C3640#
00:04:19: TTY97: Modem command:   --AT&F1&C1&D2&H1&R2&M4&K1&B1S0=1H0--
00:04:19: TTY97: Modem configuration succeeded
00:04:21: TTY97: detection speed (115200) response ---OK---
00:04:21: TTY97: Done with modem configuration
C3640#
```

Now let's get rid of the **modem autoconfigure** command and test out our chat script by clearing line 97.

```
C3640#conf t
Enter configuration commands, one per line.  End with CNTL/Z.
C3640(config)#line 97
C3640(config-line)#no modem autoconfigure
C3640(config-line)#^Z
C3640#clear line 97
[confirm]
 [OK]
C3640#
00:04:56: CHAT97: Attempting line reset script
00:04:56: CHAT97: Matched chat script initmodem to string initmodem
00:04:56: CHAT97: Asserting DTR
00:04:56: CHAT97: Chat script initmodem started
00:04:56: CHAT97: Sending string: AT&F1&C1&B1S0=1&W
00:04:57: CHAT97: Chat script initmodem finished, status = Success
C3640#
```

It looks good, so let's clean up line 97 by removing the **script reset** command.

```
C3640#conf t
Enter configuration commands, one per line.  End with CNTL/Z.
C3640(config)#line 97
C3640(config-line)#no script reset initmodem
C3640(config-line)#^Z
C3640#
```

Let's take a look at the completed configuration in Code Listing 1-3. Some lines have been deleted for clarity.

Code Listing 1-3

```
1    C3640#showrun
2    Building configuration...
3
4    Current configuration:
5    !
6    version 12.0
7    hostname C3640
8    !
9    enable password san-fran
10   !
11   ip host modem0 2097 172.31.200.210
12   chat-script initmodem "" "AT&F1&C1&B1S0=1&W"
13   modemcap entry usr_new:FD=&F1:TPL=usr_sportster
14   !
15   interface Ethernet0/0
16    ip address 172.31.200.210 255.255.255.0
17    no ip directed-broadcast
18   !
19   interface Serial3/0
20    physical-layer async
21    no ip address
22    no ip directed-broadcast
23    shutdown
24   !
25   line con 0
26    exec-timeout 0 0
27    logging synchronous
28    length 0
29    transport input none
30   line 65 70
31   line 97
32    password cisco
33    script startup initmodem
34    login
35    modem InOut
36    transport input all
37    stopbits 1
38    speed 115200
39    flowcontrol hardware
40   line aux 0
41   line vty 0 4
42    login
43   !
44   end
45
46   C3640#
```

The example above uses the Cisco 3640 router, but there are two other examples of asynchronous dial-in connections to review.

The first is the use of a Cisco 1720 router's auxiliary port. Code Listing 1-4 has the complete router configuration. Lines 47 through 55 define our auxiliary port as a dial-in connection.

Code Listing 1-4

```
1    RO1720#show run
2    Building configuration...
3
4    Current configuration:
5    !
6    version 12.0
7    service timestamps debug uptime
8    service timestamps log uptime
9    no service password-encryption
10   !
11   hostname RO1720
12   !
13   enable password san-fran
14   !
15   memory-size iomem 25
16   ip subnet-zero
17   no ip domain-lookup
18   !
19    interface Serial0
20    no ip address
21    no ip directed-broadcast
22    no ip mroute-cache
23    shutdown
24   !
25   interface Serial1
26    no ip address
27    no ip directed-broadcast
28    shutdown
29   !
30   interface BRI0
31    no ip address
32    no ip directed-broadcast
33    shutdown
34   !
35   interface FastEthernet0
36    ip address 172.31.200.205 255.255.255.0
37    no ip directed-broadcast
38   !
39   ip classless
40   no ip http server
41   !
42   line con 0
43    exec-timeout 0 0
44    logging synchronous
45    length 0
46    transport input none
47   line aux 0
48    password cisco
49    login
50    modem InOut
51    modem autoconfigure type usr_courier
52    transport input all
53    stopbits 1
54    speed 115200
55    flowcontrol hardware
56   line vty 0 4
57    login
58   !
```

■ ■

Code Listing 1-4
(continued)

```
59   no scheduler allocate
60   end
61
62   RO1720#
```

Let's take a look at our lines with the **show line** command. Please note that our auxiliary line shows up as line 5. Because the 1720 is a modular router, and the two WAN Interface Card slots can be set up with dual asynchronous/synchronous cards, lines 1 through 4 are reserved for the possibility of these ports' existence. The 1720 IOS has some additional information at the end of each line, indicating line state.

```
RO1720#show line
    Tty Typ     Tx/Rx     A Modem  Roty AccO AccI  Uses  Noise  Overruns   Int
*     0 CTY                -   -    -    -    -      1     1      0/0  - Ready
      5 AUX 115200/115200- inout   -    -    -      1     2      13/0 - Idle
      6 VTY                -   -    -    -    -      0     0      0/0  - Idle
      7 VTY                -   -    -    -    -      0     0      0/0  - Idle
      8 VTY                -   -    -    -    -      0     0      0/0  - Idle
      9 VTY                -   -    -    -    -      0     0      0/0  - Idle
     10 VTY                -   -    -    -    -      0     0      0/0  - Idle

Line(s) not in async mode -or- with no hardware support:
1-4

RO1720#
```

In order to check out the modem operation on the 1720, let's turn on **debug modem** and **debug confmodem** commands.

```
RO1720#show debug
General OS:
  Modem control/process activation debugging is on
Modem Autoconfig:
  Modem Configuration Database debugging is on
RO1720#


RO1720#
00:25:08: TTY5: CTS came up on IDLE line
00:25:08: TTY5: autoconfigure probe started
00:25:11: TTY5: detection speed (115200) response ---OK---
00:25:11: TTY5: Modem command:   --AT&F&C1&D2&H1&R2&M4&K1&B1S0=1H0--
00:25:12: TTY5: Modem configuration succeeded
00:25:13: TTY5: detection speed (115200) response ---OK---
00:25:13: TTY5: Done with modem configuration
00:27:02: TTY5: DSR came up
00:27:02: tty5: Modem: IDLE->(unknown)
00:27:02: TTY5: EXEC creation
00:27:02: TTY5: set timer type 10, 30 seconds
00:27:05: TTY5: create timer type 1, 600 seconds
00:27:08: TTY5: set timer type 10, 30 seconds
RO1720#
```

Now let's log in from the PC and send a message.

```
***
***
*** Message from tty5 to all terminals:
***
hello, I have logged in
```

The **who** command should show us that line 5 is up and running.

```
RO1720#who
       Line      User      Host(s)             Idle Location
*   0 con 0                idle                0
    5 aux 0                idle                0

    Interface  User       Mode                Idle Peer Address

RO1720#
```

Now we disconnect from line 5 and watch the sequence that takes place when the line is reset.

```
RO1720#
00:28:14: TTY5: Line reset by "Exec"
00:28:14: TTY5: Modem: (unknown)->HANGUP
00:28:14: TTY5: destroy timer type 0
00:28:14: TTY5: destroy timer type 1 (OK)
00:28:14: TTY5: destroy timer type 3
00:28:14: TTY5: destroy timer type 4
00:28:14: TTY5: destroy timer type 2
00:28:14: TTY5: dropping DTR, hanging up
00:28:14: TTY5: Set DTR to 0
00:28:14: tty5: Modem: HANGUP->IDLE
RO1720#
00:28:17: TTY5: restoring DTR
00:28:17: TTY5: Set DTR to 1
00:28:17: TTY5: autoconfigure probe started
00:28:17: TTY5: Modem command:   --AT&F&C1&D2&H1&R2&M4&K1&B1S0=1H0--
00:28:18: TTY5: Modem configuration succeeded
RO1720#
00:28:19: TTY5: detection speed (115200) response ---OK---
00:28:19: TTY5: Done with modem configuration
RO1720#
```

Now we take a look at the Cisco 2511 Access Server. First we put in our basic system commands.

```
Router>en
Router#conf t
Enter configuration commands, one per line.  End with CNTL/Z.
Router(config)#host Dial2511
Dial2511(config)#line con 0
Dial2511(config-line)#enable password san-fran
Dial2511(config)#no ip domain-lookup
```

```
Dial2511(config)#line con 0
Dial2511(config-line)#length 0
Dial2511(config-line)#logging synchronous
Dial2511(config-line)#exec-timeout 0 0
Dial2511(config-line)#int e 0
Dial2511(config-if)#ip address 172.31.200.215 255.255.255.0
Dial2511(config-if)#no shutdown
Dial2511(config-if)#^Z
Dial2511#
```

Now let's use the **show line** command to take a look at the lines defined in our access server. There are fixed TTY lines 1 through 16 built into this access server. There is no need to set the ports to asynchronous, they are asynchronous by default.

```
Dial2511#show line
  Tty Typ     Tx/Rx      A Modem  Roty AccO AccI  Uses   Noise  Overruns
*   0 CTY                 -   -     -    -    -      0      0      0/0
    1 TTY   9600/9600     -   -     -    -    -      0      0      0/0
    2 TTY   9600/9600     -   -     -    -    -      0      0      0/0
    3 TTY   9600/9600     -   -     -    -    -      0      1      0/0
    4 TTY   9600/9600     -   -     -    -    -      0      0      0/0
    5 TTY   9600/9600     -   -     -    -    -      0      0      0/0
    6 TTY   9600/9600     -   -     -    -    -      0      0      0/0
    7 TTY   9600/9600     -   -     -    -    -      0      0      0/0
    8 TTY   9600/9600     -   -     -    -    -      0      0      0/0
    9 TTY   9600/9600     -   -     -    -    -      0      0      0/0
   10 TTY   9600/9600     -   -     -    -    -      0      0      0/0
   11 TTY   9600/9600     -   -     -    -    -      0      0      0/0
   12 TTY   9600/9600     -   -     -    -    -      0      0      0/0
   13 TTY   9600/9600     -   -     -    -    -      0      0      0/0
   14 TTY   9600/9600     -   -     -    -    -      0      0      0/0
   15 TTY   9600/9600     -   -     -    -    -      0      0      0/0
   16 TTY   9600/9600     -   -     -    -    -      0      0      0/0
   17 AUX   9600/9600     -   -     -    -    -      0      0      0/0
   18 VTY                 -   -     -    -    -      0      0      0/0
   19 VTY                 -   -     -    -    -      0      0      0/0
   20 VTY                 -   -     -    -    -      0      0      0/0
   21 VTY                 -   -     -    -    -      0      0      0/0
   22 VTY                 -   -     -    -    -      0      0      0/0
```

Now we program line 1 for modem operation using our 3COM USRobotics Courier modem. When we set the speed below, we get a strange message,— Failed to change line 1's speed —because after we set up a line for autoconfiguration, the speed will be negotiated during the autoconfigure process.

```
Dial2511#conf t
Enter configuration commands, one per line.  End with CNTL/Z.
Dial2511(config)#line 1
Dial2511(config-line)# password cisco
Dial2511(config-line)# login
```

```
Dial2511(config-line)# modem InOut
Dial2511(config-line)# modem autoconfigure type usr_courier
Dial2511(config-line)# transport input all
Dial2511(config-line)# stopbits 1
Dial2511(config-line)# speed 115200
Failed to change line 1's speed
Dial2511(config-line)# flowcontrol hardware
Dial2511(config-line)#^Z
Dial2511#
```

Now let's look at our **show line** output to make sure that the programming was in effect.

```
Dial2511#show line
 Tty Typ     Tx/Rx         A Modem  Roty AccO AccI  Uses    Noise    Overruns
*  0 CTY                   -  -       -    -    -      0       0        0/0
   1 TTY 115200/115200     - inout    -    -    -      0       0        0/0
   2 TTY    9600/9600      -  -       -    -    -      0       0        0/0
   3 TTY    9600/9600      -  -       -    -    -      0       0        0/0
   4 TTY    9600/9600      -  -       -    -    -      0       0        0/0
   5 TTY    9600/9600      -  -       -    -    -      0       0        0/0
   6 TTY    9600/9600      -  -       -    -    -      0       0        0/0
   7 TTY    9600/9600      -  -       -    -    -      0       0        0/0
   8 TTY    9600/9600      -  -       -    -    -      0       0        0/0
   9 TTY    9600/9600      -  -       -    -    -      0       0        0/0
  10 TTY    9600/9600      -  -       -    -    -      0       0        0/0
  11 TTY    9600/9600      -  -       -    -    -      0       0        0/0
  12 TTY    9600/9600      -  -       -    -    -      0       0        0/0
  13 TTY    9600/9600      -  -       -    -    -      0       0        0/0
  14 TTY    9600/9600      -  -       -    -    -      0       0        0/0
  15 TTY    9600/9600      -  -       -    -    -      0       0        0/0
  16 TTY    9600/9600      -  -       -    -    -      0       0        0/0
  17 AUX    9600/9600      -  -       -    -    -      0       0        0/0
  18 VTY                   -  -       -    -    -      0       0        0/0
  19 VTY                   -  -       -    -    -      0       0        0/0
  20 VTY                   -  -       -    -    -      0       0        0/0
  21 VTY                   -  -       -    -    -      0       0        0/0
  22 VTY                   -  -       -    -    -      0       0        0/0

Dial2511#
```

For more detail about line 1, we can use the **show line 1** command. We can see that the modem hardware state shows noDSR, meaning that the modem has not been activated.

```
Dial2511#show line 1
 Tty Typ     Tx/Rx         A Modem  Roty AccO AccI  Uses    Noise    Overruns
   1 TTY 115200/115200     - inout    -    -    -      0       0        0/0

Line 1, Location: "", Type: ""
Length: 24 lines, Width: 80 columns
Baud rate (TX/RX) is 115200/115200, no parity, 1 stopbits, 8 databits
Status: No Exit Banner, Modem Detected
Capabilities: Hardware Flowcontrol In, Hardware Flowcontrol Out
```

```
    Modem Callout, Modem RI is CD, Modem Autoconfigure
Modem state: Idle
Group codes:    0
Modem hardware state: CTS noDSR  DTR RTS, Modem Configured
Special Chars: Escape  Hold  Stop  Start  Disconnect  Activation
               ^^x     none   -     -       none
 Timeouts:      Idle EXEC      Idle Session    Modem Answer  Session   Dispatch
               00:10:00          never                        none    not set
                               Idle Session Disconnect Warning
                                 never
                               Login-sequence User Response
                               00:00:30
                               Autoselect Initial Wait
                                 not set
Modem type is usr_courier.
Session limit is not set.
Time since activation: never
Editing is enabled.
History is enabled, history size is 10.
DNS resolution in show commands is enabled
Full user help is disabled
Allowed transports are lat pad v120 mop telnet rlogin nasi.  Preferred is lat.
No output characters are padded
No special data dispatching characters

Dial2511#
```

The PC dials into the access server. We can verify the incoming call using the **who** command to see if line 1 is active.

```
Dial2511#who
      Line      User      Host(s)               Idle Location
 *  0 con 0               idle              07:16:42
    1 tty 1               idle              00:00:20

Dial2511#
```

The **show line 1** command shows us that the connection is up by checking the Modem state for DSR, and checking the Status for ready and active.

```
Dial2511#showline 1
  Tty Typ      Tx/Rx      A Modem  Roty AccO AccI  Uses   Noise   Overruns
 *  1 TTY 115200/115200 - inout     -    -    -     0       0       0/0

Line 1, Location: "", Type: ""
Length: 24 lines, Width: 80 columns
Baud rate (TX/RX) is 115200/115200, no parity, 1 stopbits, 8 databits
Status: Ready, Active, No Exit Banner, Modem Detected
Capabilities: Hardware Flowcontrol In, Hardware Flowcontrol Out
  Modem Callout, Modem RI is CD, Modem Autoconfigure
Modem state: Ready
Group codes:    0
Modem hardware state: CTS DSR  DTR RTS, Modem Configured
```

```
Special Chars: Escape  Hold  Stop  Start  Disconnect  Activation
               ^^x     none   -     -     none
Timeouts:      Idle EXEC     Idle Session    Modem Answer  Session   Dispatch
               00:10:00         never                        none     not set
                              Idle Session Disconnect Warning
                                 never
                              Login-sequence User Response
                              00:00:30
                              Autoselect Initial Wait
                                 not set
Modem type is usr_courier.
Session limit is not set.
Time since activation: 00:01:14
Editing is enabled.
History is enabled, history size is 10.
DNS resolution in show commands is enabled
Full user help is disabled
Allowed transports are lat pad v120 mop telnet rlogin nasi.  Preferred is lat.
No output characters are padded
No special data dispatching characters
Dial2511#
```

After the PC terminal session is established, the user sends a message to all terminals, including the console connection.

```
Dial2511#

***
***
*** Message from tty1 to all terminals:
***
logged in successfully
Dial2511#
```

If we want to force a logged-in user off the system, we can do that with the **clear line XXX** command, where **XXX** is the individual line number to be cleared.

```
Dial2511#clear line 1
[confirm]
 [OK]
Dial2511#who
    Line      User      Host(s)                Idle Location
 *  0 con 0             idle                   07:19:27

Dial2511#
```

Code Listing 1-5 shows the configuration for the Cisco 2511.

Code Listing 1-5

```
1    Current configuration:
2    !
3    version 11.3
4    service timestamps debug uptime
5    service timestamps log uptime
6    no service password-encryption
7    !
8    hostname Dial2511
9    !
10   enable password san-fran
11   !
12   no ip domain-lookup
13   !
14   interface Ethernet0
15    ip address 172.31.200.215 255.255.255.0
16   !
17   interface Serial0
18    no ip address
19   shutdown
20   !
21   interface Serial1
22    no ip address
23    shutdown
24   !
25   ip classless
26   !
27   line con 0
28    exec-timeout 0 0
29    logging synchronous
30    length 0
31   line 1
32    password cisco
33    login
34    modem InOut
35    modem autoconfigure type usr_courier
36    transport input all
37    stopbits 1
38    speed 115200
39    flowcontrol hardware
40   line 2 16
41   line aux 0
42   line vty 0 4
43    login
44   !
45   end
```

Summary

In this chapter, we took a look at the very basic form of asynchronous communication from a dial-in terminal or PC to Cisco routers and access servers. In the next chapter, we will extend this process to include more advanced features for asynchronous dial-in and virtual terminal sessions.

Questions and Answers

1. *Based on the following data stream definitions for samples #2, #3, and #4, what are the characters being transmitted, and are they valid characters or not?*

    Sample #2's definition is 5-E-1. The data stream is 10101. With even parity, the parity bit should be set to mark, but it is set to space instead—indicating that there was a transmission error.

    Sample #3's definition is 8-E-2. The data stream is 00000001, with the parity bit at sample time 11 set to mark to even up the number of mark bits.

    Sample #4's definition is 7-O-1.5. The data stream is 1111111, with the parity bit at sample time 10 set to space to make the number of mark bits odd.

2. *Interpret the following chat scripts and determine if each chat script works.*

    Sample #1

    ```
    chat-script dialit ABORT busy ABORT "no carrier" ""
       "ATDT5551234" TIMEOUT 30 CONNECT\c
    ```

    The name of the script is `dialit`. The script will abort if the called party is busy (ABORT busy), or carrier is lost (ABORT "no carrier"). It will not wait for a modem response ("") before dialing 555123 ("ATDT 555123"). It will timeout after 30 seconds (TIMEOUT 30) if it doesn't receive a connection indication (CONNECT\c). Watch out! CONNECT\c is not a valid response from the modem. Mis-typed chat scripts are very difficult to find, but the **debug chat** command is a terrific tool.

    Sample #2

    ```
    chat-script initmodem "" AT OK "AT&F1&C1&B1S0=1&W"
    ```

    The name of the chat script is `initmodem`. The script will wait for nothing (""), send **AT** and wait for OK, and then send **AT&F1&C1&B1S0=1&W** to initialize the modem.

Advanced Terminal Services

The first chapter introduced you to basic asynchronous dial-in services. In this chapter, we explore some of the more advanced features of terminal operations. We start by looking at virtual terminal sessions created by telnet access to the router. We will expand the authorization process to include user names and passwords. There are other advanced features—such as: menu creation, automatically executing commands on login, and restricting telnet access—that enhance both dial-in and virtual terminal operations.

The lab equipment used for this chapter includes the following Cisco routers/access servers: 3640, 1720, and 2511. Figure 2-1 shows the equipment layout for most examples in this chapter.

Virtual Terminal Sessions

In the last chapter, we dealt with straight VT100 terminals or PCs running a terminal program like HyperTerminal that dialed in through the telephone network and connected to our Cisco routers for basic communications. We can also establish terminal access through the LAN side of the network using virtual terminal (VTY) access based on Telnet. When the Cisco router/access servers are initially configured, there are five default virtual terminal sessions created. The line section below comes from the 3640 we used in the last chapter, and the last entry—line vty 0 4—defines these five default VTY sessions.

```
line con 0
 exec-timeout 0 0
 logging synchronous
 transport input none
line 65 70
line 97
 password cisco
 login
 transport input all
 stopbits 1
 speed 115200
 flowcontrol hardware
line aux 0
line vty 0 4
```

With all telnet access, there is a security requirement that at least a password is required to establish connectivity. We could use the same technique used on line 97 in the preceding code and put in a simple password for access control, or we could upgrade our security by having indi-

Figure 2-1
Chapter 2 equip-
ment layout.

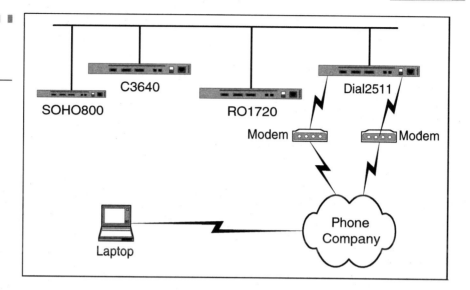

vidual users log in to the router. If we have individual users log in, then
we can control the access that each user has using the `autocommand` and
`menu` features. Let's set up several users on the 3640 and try the features
out.

```
C3640#conf t
Enter configuration commands, one per line.   End with CNTL/Z.
C3640(config)#username user1 password pass1
C3640(config)#username user2 password pass2
C3640(config)#username user3 password pass3
C3640(config)#^Z
C3640#
```

We have created our local username and password database in the
3640 and now we have to apply this database to the VTY sessions.

```
C3640#conf t
Enter configuration commands, one per line.   End with CNTL/Z.
C3640(config)#line vty 0 4
C3640(config-line)#login local
C3640(config-line)#^Z
C3640#
```

Now that we have created a local database and assigned the database
to our virtual terminal sessions, let's test it out from another device on
the network.

```
Dial2511>telnet 172.31.200.210
Trying 172.31.200.210 ... Open


User Access Verification

Username: user2
Password:
C3640>
```

We logged in as `user2` with password `pass2`, but how can we verify the connection? We can use the **who** or **systat** command to verify the connection. Sure enough, line 130 shows up with `user2` to verify that the connection was made.

```
C3640>who
      Line       User      Host(s)                Idle Location
    0 con 0                idle                 2
 *130 vty 0      user2     idle                 0 172.31.200.215

C3640>quit

[Connection to 172.31.200.210 closed by foreign host]
Dial2511>
```

Now let's telnet in twice, leaving both sessions open using the **<ctrl><shft>6 x** escape sequence to maintain the first session for user1.

```
Dial2511>telnet 172.31.200.210
Trying 172.31.200.210 ... Open


User Access Verification

Username: user1
Password:
C3640><ctrl><shft>6 x
Dial2511>telnet 172.31.200.210
Trying 172.31.200.210 ... Open


User Access Verification

Username: user2
Password:
C3640>who
      Line       User      Host(s)                Idle Location
    0 con 0                idle                 17
  130 vty 0      user1     idle                 0 172.31.200.215
 *131 vty 1      user2     idle                 0 172.31.200.215

C3640>
```

The **who** command shows which sessions are open, which user is logged in, the source where the session was initiated, and an * next to the current active session (our second connection for user2). We can use the escape sequence to go back to the initiating device, Dial2511, and use the **where** command to check out the active telnet sessions.

```
<ctrl><shft>6 x
Dial2511#where
Conn Host                 Address           Byte  Idle Conn Name
    1 172.31.200.210      172.31.200.210       0     3 172.31.200.210
*   2 172.31.200.210      172.31.200.210       0     0
Dial2511#
```

Let's disconnect our second active connection to C3640 and verify the action using the **where** command. We are back to a single connection to C3640.

```
Dial2511#disconnect
Closing connection to 172.31.200.210 [confirm]
Dial2511#
Dial2511#where
Conn Host                 Address           Byte  Idle Conn Name
*   1 172.31.200.210      172.31.200.210       0     0 172.31.200.210

Dial2511#
```

Now let's connect to another router, RO1720, on the network. This router requires only a password for incoming telnet sessions.

```
Dial2511#telnet 172.31.200.205
Trying 172.31.200.205 ... Open


User Access Verification

Password:
RO1720>
```

We are logged into two different devices. To verify that we have established these connections, use the escape sequence to return to Dial2511, our starting point. The **where** command shows us the two active sessions. Session 2 has an * next to it, indicating that it is the current active connection. To resume the session 2 connection, just press **<enter>**.

```
<ctrl><shft>6 x
Dial2511#where
Conn Host                    Address            Byte  Idle Conn Name
    1 172.31.200.210         172.31.200.210        0     2 172.31.200.210
  * 2 172.31.200.205         172.31.200.205        0     0 172.31.200.205

Dial2511#<enter>
[Resuming connection 2 to 172.31.200.205 ... ]

RO1720>
```

If you want to bounce around between sessions for debugging or troubleshooting purposes, all you have to enter is the session number to resume a connection. Break out of the RO1740 session with the escape sequence and connect to C3640 by entering a 1. Note that the * has moved to session 1.

```
<ctrl><shft>6 x
Dial2511#1
[Resuming connection 1 to 172.31.200.210 ... ]

C3640>
<ctrl><shft>6 x
Dial2511#where
Conn Host                    Address            Byte  Idle Conn Name
  * 1 172.31.200.210         172.31.200.210        0     0 172.31.200.210
    2 172.31.200.205         172.31.200.205        0     1 172.31.200.205

Dial2511#
```

To terminate session 2, all we have to do is use the **disconnect 2** command. To verify the session is terminated, use the **where** command.

```
Dial2511#disconnect 2
Closing connection to 172.31.200.205 [confirm]
Dial2511#where
Conn Host                    Address            Byte  Idle Conn Name
  * 1 172.31.200.210         172.31.200.210        0     2 172.31.200.210

Dial2511#
```

Telnet sessions are great for accessing routers across the network because direct console connections require a local presence. If you intend to use debugging commands, you will need a few extra commands. To see debugging information, use the **terminal monitor** command— but don't forget to go into configuration mode and turn off console debugging so you don't get a nasty phone call from the target router site.

```
Dial2511#telnet 172.31.200.210
Trying 172.31.200.210 ... Open


User Access Verification

Username: user1
Password:
C3640>en
Password:
C3640#debug ip packet
IP packet debugging is on
C3640#conf t
Enter configuration commands, one per line.  End with CNTL/Z.
C3640(config)#no logging console
C3640(config)#^Z
C3640#term mon
C3640#
02:39:44: IP: s=172.31.200.215 (Ethernet0/0),,,
02:39:44: IP: s=172.31.200.210 (local)...
02:39:44: IP: s=172.31.200.215 (Ethernet0/0)...
C3640#
```

Make sure you turn console logging back on when you finish trouble-shooting. Note that the help response to **logging console ?** is misleading. Instead of presenting the information in order from most important to least important, it presents the information in alphabetical order. See Table 2-1 for the priority levels in descending sequence.

```
C3640#conf t
Enter configuration commands, one per line.  End with CNTL/Z.
C3640(config)#logging console ?
  alerts        Immediate action needed
  critical      Critical conditions
  debugging     Debugging messages
  emergencies   System is unusable
  errors        Error conditions
  informational Informational messages
  notifications Normal but significant conditions
  warnings      Warning conditions
  <cr>

C3640(config)#logging console debugging
C3640(config)#^Z
02:41:00: %SYS-5-CONFIG_I: Configured from console by user1 on vty0 (172.31.200.215)
C3640#quit

[Connection to 172.31.200.210 closed by foreign host]
Dial2511#
```

TABLE 2-1

Level	Command	Description
0	emergencies	System is unusable
1	alerts	Immediate action needed
2	critical	Critical conditions
3	errors	Error conditions
4	warnings	Warning conditions
5	notifications	Normal but significant conditions
6	informational	Informational messages
7	debugging	Debugging messages

Now that we have covered both asynchronous dial-in and telnet virtual terminal connections, let's add to the basics.

Menus

Telnet into a router, log in, and get presented with a command line to start communicating. Many users start sweating and get cold and clammy hands when presented with this situation. Other users may be kept from the access server's command line interface altogether for security reasons. In this section, we will show you how to build a menu to relieve both users' and security officers' nightmares. As this menu process is most often used on access servers, let's set up our menu on Dial2511.

First let's look at the options available for creating menus on a Cisco router/access server.

```
Dial2511#conf t
Enter configuration commands, one per line.  End with CNTL/Z.
Dial2511(config)#menu linemenu ?
  clear-screen  Use termcap database to clear screen
  command       Set menu command
  default       Item number to use for RETURN
  line-mode     require <enter> after typing selection
  options       Set per-item options
  prompt        Set prompt string
  single-space  single-space menu entries on display
  status-line   Display user status at top of screen
  text          Set text of menu line
  title         Set menu title

Dial2511(config)#
```

The two primary options used to build a menu are **text** and **command**. Use the **text** option to define the selection character and the displayed text of a single menu item. Use the **command** option to provide the executive level command that gets executed when the selection character is entered.

When there are nine or less **text/command** pairs in the menu, you operate the menu by pressing the identifying character without pressing the **<enter>** key. In order to force the use of the **<enter>** key for nine or less **text/command pairs**, use the **line-mode** option. If operating in **line-mode**, then we can activate a prompt for use during the selection process. We will use all of the above options in the menu sample below.

If you wish to modify the way a **text/command** pair operates, then use the **options** parameter. You can either require a separate **login** to protect sensitive commands, or force a **pause** after the command runs to let the user view the screen. The **help** command is shown below.

```
Dial2511(config)#menu linemenu options 3 ?
  login  Login required before command
  pause  pause after command, before redrawing menu
  <cr>

Dial2511(config)#^Z
Dial2511#
```

Now we enter our configuration commands to build the menu.

```
Dial2511#conf t
Enter configuration commands, one per line.  End with CNTL/Z.
Dial2511(config)#menu linemenu title /
Enter TEXT message.  End with the character '/'.



        Test Line Menu

/
Dial2511(config)#menu linemenu text 1 Telnet to C3640
Dial2511(config)#menu linemenu command 1 telnet 172.31.200.210
Dial2511(config)#menu linemenu text 2 Telnet to RO1720
Dial2511(config)#menu linemenu command 2 telnet 172,31,200.205
Dial2511(config)#menu linemenu text 3 Show IP Route
Dial2511(config)#menu linemenu command 3 show ip route
Dial2511(config)#menu linemenu options 3 pause
Dial2511(config)#menu linemenu text 4 Menu Exit
Dial2511(config)#menu linemenu command 4 logout
Dial2511(config)#menu linemenu clear-screen
Dial2511(config)#menu linemenu single-space
Dial2511(config)#menu linemenu line-mode
Dial2511(config)#menu linemenu status-line
Dial2511(config)#menu linemenu default 4
```

```
Dial2511(config)#menu linemenu prompt /
Enter TEXT message.  End with the character '/'.

Enter Menu Number:/
Dial2511(config)#^Z
Dial2511#
```

Let's test out this menu from the command line. All line numbers refer to Code Listing 2-1.

Line 1 is where we execute the menu from the command line.

Line 2 is the status line, showing the host name, line number, and terminal type.

Lines 3 through 17 are the output of our menu commands. Lines 10-13 are the four **text/command** pairs we defined in our menu configuration. Line 17 is the prompt that gets used when we are in **line-mode**.

On line 17 we enter a **1** and initiate a telnet session to C3640 (172.31.200.210).

After logging in, we quit the telnet session and get returned back to the menu, as displayed with lines 28 through 43.

Next we enter a **2** and initiate a telnet to RO1720 (172.31.200.205).

After logging in, we quit the telnet session and get returned back to the menu, as displayed with lines 53 through 68.

Next we enter a **3** and get the start of a **show ip route** command on lines 69 through 80. The menu comes back on lines 81 through 96 only after we hit any key (where is that pesky **any** key) to end the **pause** option that we applied to the **text/command** pair defined for selection 3.

On line 96 we just press the **<enter>** key and take the default menu selection, **4**, which exits the menu process by logging us out of the executive session.

Code Listing 2-1

```
1    Dial2511#menu linemenu
2    Server "Dial2511"    Line 0    Terminal-type (unknown)
3
4
5
6
7        Test Line Menu
8
9
10    1        Telnet to C3640
11    2        Telnet to RO1720
12    3        Show IP Route
13    4        Menu Exit
14
15
16
```

Code Listing 2-1
(continued)

```
17   Enter Menu Number:1
18   Trying 172.31.200.210 ... Open
19
20
21   User Access Verification
22
23   Username: user1
24   Password:
25   C3640>quit
26
27   [Connection to 172.31.200.210 closed by foreign host]
28   Server "Dial2511"    Line 0    Terminal-type (unknown)
29
30
31
32
33        Test Line Menu
34
35
36        1              Telnet to C3640
37        2              Telnet to RO1720
38        3              Show IP Route
39        4              Menu Exit
40
41
42
43   Enter Menu Number:2
44   Trying 172.31.200.205 ... Open
45
46
47   User Access Verification
48
49   Password:
50   RO1720>quit
51
52   [Connection to 172.31.200.205 closed by foreign host]
53   Server "Dial2511"    Line 0    Terminal-type (unknown)
54
55
56
57
58        Test Line Menu
59
60
61        1              Telnet to C3640
62        2              Telnet to RO1720
63        3              Show IP Route
64        4              Menu Exit
65
66
67
68   Enter Menu Number:3
69   Codes: C - connected, S - static, I - IGRP, R - RIP, M - mobile, B - BGP
70   D - EIGRP, EX - EIGRP external, O - OSPF, IA - OSPF inter area
71   N1 - OSPF NSSA external type 1, N2 - OSPF NSSA external type 2
72   E1 - OSPF external type 1, E2 - OSPF external type 2, E - EGP
73   i - IS-IS, L1 - IS-IS level-1, L2 - IS-IS level-2, * - candidate
     default
```

```
74   U - per-user static route, o - ODR
75
76   Gateway of last resort is not set
77
78        172.31.0.0/24 is subnetted, 1 subnets
79   C        172.31.200.0 is directly connected, Ethernet0
80   --More--
81   Server "Dial2511"    Line 0    Terminal-type (unknown)
82
83
84
85
86        Test Line Menu
87
88
89       1              Telnet to C3640
90       2              Telnet to RO1720
91       3              Show IP Route
92       4              Menu Exit
93
94
95
96   Enter Menu Number:
97
98   .
99   .
100  .
101
102  Dial2511 con0 is now available
103
104
105  Press RETURN to get started.
```

Below is the final output of our menu definition, as extracted from our **show running-config** command.

```
!
menu linemenu title ^C



        Test Line Menu-

^C
menu linemenu prompt ^C

Enter Menu Number:^C
menu linemenu text 1 Telnet to C3640
menu linemenu command 1 telnet 172.31.200.210
menu linemenu text 2 Telnet to RO1720
menu linemenu command 2 telnet 172.31.200.205
menu linemenu text 3 Show IP Route
menu linemenu command 3 show ip route
menu linemenu options 3 pause
menu linemenu text 4 Menu Exit
```

```
menu linemenu command 4 logout
menu linemenu clear-screen
menu linemenu status-line
menu linemenu default 4
menu linemenu line-mode
menu linemenu single-space
!
```

We have completed our menu programming but have not applied this menu to our router processing. We will do this using the **autocommand** command.

Autocommand Process

The **autocommand** command can be executed on a line-by-line basis, or on a user-by-user basis.

On a line-by-line basis, we can execute any **exec** command. This is great for environments where every user who logs into the specific access server line performs the same tasks.

```
Dial2511(config)#line 1
Dial2511(config-line)#autocommand ?
  LINE  Appropriate EXEC command

Dial2511(config-line)#
```

The other option is to define the **exec** command that will be executed when a specific user logs in. When we built our local authentication database before, we used the username and password combination to create each entry. By adding in the **autocommand** parameter, we will execute the **exec** command defined by **<WORD>** when we define the user (see below).

```
Dial2511(config)#username user1 password pass1
Dial2511(config)#username user1 autocommand <WORD>
```

Let's give this a go, by first setting up a second line on the Dial2511 access server, then setting up line 1 to perform a direct telnet to C3640 at login time. Then set up line 2 to use the local database for logging users in, user1 to use the linemenu menu, and user2 to be provided regular access to Dial2511.

Let's configure Dial2511. First, define our usernames and passwords.

```
Dial2511#conf t
Enter configuration commands, one per line.  End with CNTL/Z.
Dial2511(config)#username user1 password pass1
Dial2511(config)#username user1 autocommand menu linemenu
Dial2511(config)#username user2 password 0 pass2
Dial2511(config)#^z
Dial2511#
```

Second, add **autocommand telnet 172.31.200.210** to `line 1`, and the **login local** command on `line 2` to direct the access process to our local username and password database.

```
Dial2511#conf t
Enter configuration commands, one per line.  End with CNTL/Z.
Dial2511(config)#line 1
Dial2511(config)#autocommand telnet 172.31.200.210
Dial2511(config)#line 2
Dial2511(config)#login local
Dial2511(config)#modem InOut
Dial2511(config)#modem autoconfigure type usr_sportster
Dial2511(config)#transport input all
Dial2511(config)#stopbits 1
Dial2511(config)#speed 115200
Dial2511(config)#flowcontrol hardware
Dial2511(config)#^Z
Dial2511#
```

Let's take a look at the current debug commands in place with the **show debug** command. Modem control and process activation will help us determine when the dial in circuits are activated.

```
Dial2511#show debug
General OS:
  Modem control/process activation debugging is on
Dial2511#
```

Our first test will be `user2` dialing in to `line 2`. Based on our configuration, we have to log in using the local database, and `user2` has direct access to Dial2511's command line.

```
User Access Verification

Username: user2
Password:
Dial2511>quit
```

Let's track the same sequence on Dial2511. Data Set Ready (DSR) came up indicating the modem has answered an incoming call, changing the modem state from idle to ready. After logging in, an EXEC creation takes place, indicating a command line user is now active. We can use the **who** command to verify that user2 logged into line 2. When the dial-in user enters **quit**, then the exec session resets the line, the modem hangs up, the router drops Data Terminal Ready (DTR), the modem goes idle, and the router restores DTR to prepare for the next incoming call.

```
Dial2511#
1d10h: TTY2: DSR came up
1d10h: tty2: Modem: IDLE->READY
1d10h: TTY2: EXEC creation
Dial2511#who
     Line      User       Host(s)                    Idle Location
*   0 con 0                idle                       1d10h
    2 tty 2    user2       idle                     00:00:17

Dial2511#
1d10h: TTY2: Line reset by "Exec"
1d10h: TTY2: Modem: READY->HANGUP
1d10h: TTY2: dropping DTR, hanging up
1d10h: tty2: Modem: HANGUP->IDLE
1d10h: TTY2: restoring DTR
```

Next, let's test line 2 with user1, who has been configured to use the linemenu menu. User1 logs in, the menu is displayed, and we test the menu by entering option **3**. Success! Then we use option **4** to exit from the access server.

```
User Access Verification

Username: user1
Password:


Server "Dial2511"    Line 2    Terminal-type (unknown)



     Test Line Menu


   1            Telnet to C3640
   2            Telnet to RO1720
   3            Show IP Route
   4            Menu Exit


Enter Menu Number:3
```

```
Codes: C - connected, S - static, I - IGRP, R - RIP, M - mobile, B - BGP
       D - EIGRP, EX - EIGRP external, O - OSPF, IA - OSPF inter area
       N1 - OSPF NSSA external type 1, N2 - OSPF NSSA external type 2
       E1 - OSPF external type 1, E2 - OSPF external type 2, E - EGP
       i - IS-IS, L1 - IS-IS level-1, L2 - IS-IS level-2, * - candidate default
       U - per-user static route, o - ODR

Gateway of last resort is not set

     172.31.0.0/24 is subnetted, 1 subnets
C       172.31.200.0 is directly connected, Ethernet0
--More--

Server "Dial2511"    Line 2    Terminal-type (unknown)



        Test Line Menu


    1           Telnet to C3640
    2           Telnet to RO1720
    3           Show IP Route
    4           Menu Exit



Enter Menu Number:4
```

Let's look at the same test from the Dial2511 console port. After the dial in connection is established, we use the **who** command to verify that user1 has in fact logged in to line 2.

```
1d10h: TTY2: DSR came up
1d10h: tty2: Modem: IDLE->READY
1d10h: TTY2: EXEC creation
Dial2511#who
     Line      User      Host(s)              Idle Location
*  0 con 0               idle                 1d10h
   2 tty 2    user1      idle             00:00:14

Dial2511#
1d10h: TTY2: Line reset by "Exec"
1d10h: TTY2: Modem: READY->HANGUP
1d10h: TTY2: dropping DTR, hanging up
1d10h: tty2: Modem: HANGUP->IDLE
1d10h: TTY2: restoring DTR
```

Lastly, we will test a user dialing in to line 1. We only have to enter a password to get access to Dial2511, but then the **autocommand** command kicks in and we immediately telnet to 172.31.200.210 (C3640) and are presented with the login process for C3640. We use the **who** command to see which user is logged in and to verify that we arrived on a virtual terminal connection. The location has the source IP address of the incoming telnet connection.

```
User Access Verification

Password:

Trying 172.31.200.210 ... Open


User Access Verification

Username: user3
Password:
C3640>who
     Line     User      Host(s)                   Idle Location
     0 con 0            idle              1d10h
  *130 vty 0   user3    idle                 0 172.31.200.215

C3640>quit
[Connection to 172.31.200.210 closed by foreign host]
```

Let's look at the same test from Dial2511. After the dial-in connection is made, we use the **who** command to verify that line 1 is being used and that we have an active connection to C3640 (172.31.200.210). Even though there is an active telnet connection to C3640, we see no active connections when we use the **where** command. The **where** command shows only external connections from the current session—in this case, the console port.

```
Dial2511#
1d10h: TTY1: DSR came up
1d10h: tty1: Modem: IDLE->READY
1d10h: TTY1: EXEC creation
Dial2511#who
     Line     User      Host(s)                   Idle Location
  *  0 con 0            idle              1d10h
     1 tty 1            172.31.200.210    00:00:15

Dial2511#where
% No connections open
Dial2511#
```

Code Listing 2-2 shows the complete configuration for all of the sections we have configured to this point.

Lines 12 through 14 define our local username/password database.

Lines 22 through 45 define our menu operation.

Lines 52 through 61 define our line 1 operation. Lines 53 and 54 define our login access as a simple password. Line 57 automatically starts a telnet session upon successful login on this line.

Lines 62 through 69 define our line 2 operation. Line 63 defines our login access as the local database of usernames and passwords. There are no **autocommand** commands on the line; the process is controlled by the local user database.

Code Listing 2-2

```
1    Dial2511#show run
2    Building configuration...
3
4    Current configuration:
5    !
6    version 11.3
7    !
8    hostname Dial2511
9    !
10   enable password san-fran
11   !
12   username user2 password 0 pass2
13   username user1 password 0 pass1
14   username user1 autocommand menu linemenu
15   no ip domain-lookup
16   !
17   interface Ethernet0
18    ip address 172.31.200.215 255.255.255.0
19   !
20   ip classless
21   !
22   menu linemenu title ^C
23
24
25
26            Test Line Menu
27
28   ^C
29   menu linemenu prompt ^C
30
31   Enter Menu Number:^C
32   menu linemenu text 1 Telnet to C3640
33   menu linemenu command 1 telnet 172.31.200.210
34   menu linemenu text 2 Telnet to RO1720
35   menu linemenu command 2 telnet 172.31.200.205
36   menu linemenu text 3 Show IP Route
37   menu linemenu command 3 show ip route
38   menu linemenu options 3 pause
39   menu linemenu text 4 Menu Exit
40   menu linemenu command 4 logout
41   menu linemenu clear-screen
42   menu linemenu status-line
43   menu linemenu default 4
44   menu linemenu line-mode
45   menu linemenu single-space
46   !
```

Code Listing 2-2
(continued)

```
47   !
48   line con 0
49    exec-timeout 0 0
50    logging synchronous
51    length 0
52   line 1
53    password cisco
54    login
55    modem InOut
56    modem autoconfigure type usr_courier
57    autocommand telnet 172.31.200.210
58    transport input all
59    stopbits 1
60    speed 115200
61    flowcontrol hardware
62   line 2
63    login local
64    modem InOut
65    modem autoconfigure type usr_sportster
66    transport input all
67    stopbits 1
68    speed 115200
69    flowcontrol hardware
70   line 3 16
71   line aux 0
72   line vty 0 4
73    login
74   !
75   end
76
77   Dial2511#
```

Access-Class

Now for some additional security for our terminal access using the **access-class** command. Output access lists are great for filtering traffic flowing through the router, but they can't filter traffic that starts from a router exec session. This presents a security risk, as anyone who breaks into the router can telnet to any reachable IP address. Cisco recognized this security hole and added input access lists to prevent unwanted access to the routers. However, input access lists require the router to examine every incoming packet to see if it is permitted to enter the router. This can have a negative impact on router performance. The **access-class** command modifies terminal operations by assigning an access list to either incoming or outgoing telnet sessions.

We will use C3640 as our test bed for filtering incoming and outgoing telnet requests.

The **access-list 1** command below specifically permits and denies the two addresses we will use for testing incoming telnet connections. The **access-list 2** command permits and denies the two addresses we will use for testing outgoing telnet connections. We will assign these access lists to our VTY connections with our **access-class** commands.

```
C3640#conf t
Enter configuration commands, one per line.  End with CNTL/Z.
C3640(config)#access-list 1 permit 172.31.200.205 0.0.0.0 log
C3640(config)#access-list 1 deny 172.31.200.210 0.0.0.0 log
C3640(config)#access-list 2 permit 172.31.200.215 0.0.0.0
C3640(config)#access-list 2 deny 172.31.200.205 0.0.0.0
C3640(config)#line vty 0 4
C3640(config-line)#access-class 1 in
C3640(config-line)#access-class 2 out
C3640(config-line)#^Z
C3640#
```

To make sure the **access-list** commands are set up properly, we use the **show access-list** command.

```
C3640#show access-list
Standard IP access list 1
    deny   172.31.200.210 log
    permit 172.31.200.205 log
Standard IP access list 2
    permit 172.31.200.215
    deny   172.31.200.205
C3640#
```

To make sure that the **access-class** commands have been applied to our virtual terminal sessions, we use the **show line** command. If we examine lines 130 through 134, we see the **access-class** commands are in effect.

```
C3640>show line
  Tty Typ      Tx/Rx     A Modem  Roty AccO AccI   Uses   Noise  Overruns    Int
*   0 CTY                -   -      -    -    -      0      0      0/0         -
   65 TTY                - inout   -    -    -      0      0      0/0         -
   66 TTY                - inout   -    -    -      0      0      0/0         -
   67 TTY                - inout   -    -    -      0      0      0/0         -
   68 TTY                - inout   -    -    -      0      0      0/0         -
   69 TTY                - inout   -    -    -      0      0      0/0         -
   70 TTY                - inout   -    -    -      0      0      0/0         -
   97 TTY 115200/115200- inout     -    -    -      0      0      0/0       Se3/0
  129 AUX    9600/9600   -   -      -    -    -      0      0      0/0         -
*130 VTY                -   -      -    2    1     23      0      0/0         -
  131 VTY                -   -      -    2    1      1      0      0/0         -
  132 VTY                -   -      -    2    1      0      0      0/0         -
  133 VTY                -   -      -    2    1      0      0      0/0         -
```

```
134 VTY            -    -    -   2    1    0     0    0/0      -
Line(s) not in async mode -or- with no hardware support:
1-64, 71-96, 98-128

C3640>
```

Time for testing our configuration. First we will check out the outgoing telnet filters. When we try to connect to Dial2511 (172.31.200.215), we are successful; but when we try to connect to RO1720, we are told that connections to that host are not permitted.

```
C3640#telnet 172.31.200.215
Trying 172.31.200.215 ... Open


User Access Verification

Password:
Dial2511>quit

[Connection to 172.31.200.215 closed by foreign host]
C3640#telnet 172.31.200.205
Trying 172.31.200.205 ...
% Connections to that host not permitted from this terminal
C3640#
```

Now we test our incoming telnet connections. When we try to connect from Dial2511 (172.31.200.215), our connection request is refused; and when we try to connect from RO1720 (172.31.200.205), we are successful.

```
Dial2511#telnet 172.31.200.210
Trying 172.31.200.210 ...
% Connection refused by remote host

Dial2511#

RO1720>telnet 172.31.200.210
Trying 172.31.200.210 ... Open


User Access Verification

Username: user1
Password:
C3640>
```

Now that we have finished testing our access list control of telnet sessions, let's look at our complete configuration in Code Listing 2-3.

■ ■

Code Listing 2-3

```
1   C3640#show running
2   Building configuration...
3
4   Current configuration:
5   !
6   version 12.0
7   service timestamps debug uptime
8   service timestamps log uptime
9   no service password-encryption
10  !
11  hostname C3640
12  !
13  logging buffered 4096 debugging
14  enable password san-fran
15  !
16  username test password 0 cisco
17  username user1 password 0 pass1
18  username user2 password 0 pass2
19  username user3 password 0 pass3
20  ip subnet-zero
21  no ip domain-lookup
22  ip host modem0 2097 172.31.200.210
23  chat-script initmodem "" "AT&F1&C1&B1S0=1&W"
24  modemcap entry usr_new:FD=&F1:TPL=usr_sportster
25  !
26  interface Ethernet0/0
27   ip address 172.31.200.210 255.255.255.0
28   no ip directed-broadcast
29  !
30  interface Serial3/0
31   physical-layer async
32   ip unnumbered Ethernet0/0
33   no ip directed-broadcast
34   encapsulation ppp
35   async mode dedicated
36   peer default ip address pool mypool
37   ppp authentication chap pap
38  !
39  ip local pool mypool 172.31.200.10 172.31.200.20
40  ip classless
41  !
42  logging trap debugging
43  access-list 1 deny    172.31.200.210 log
44  access-list 1 permit 172.31.200.205 log
45  access-list 2 permit 172.31.200.215
46  access-list 2 deny    172.31.200.205
47  !
48  line con 0
49   exec-timeout 0 0
50   logging synchronous
51   length 0
52   transport input none
53  line 65 70
54  line 97
55   password cisco
56   script startup initmodem
57   login
58   modem InOut
```

Code Listing 2-3
(continued)

```
59   transport input all
60    stopbits 1
61    speed 115200
62    flowcontrol hardware
63   line aux 0
64   line vty 0 4
65    access-class 1 in
66    access-class 2 out
67    login local
68   !
69   end
70
71   C3640#
```

There is another technique we can use to connect to multiple devices in a remote location—using an access server as a system controller.

System Controllers

An access server can also take on the role of a system controller for remote sites. We can plug the asynchronous ports into the console ports of a series of routers and switches, and then use the reverse telnet technique used for modem programming in Chapter 1 to establish connections. We will extend this process using the **ip alias** and **ip host** commands.

Figure 2-2 shows the network layout for this operation.

First we will look at the Dial2511 configuration in Code Listing 2-4. Since this is a complete configuration, let's pick out the lines that apply to our system controller configuration.

Lines 19 through 22 are the **ip host** commands that define names for our asynchronous ports using the `ethernet 0` address. These commands can be used to provide named access to the devices on the asynchronous ports.

Lines 38 through 41 are the **ip alias** commands which the access server will use to connect an external network device as it telnets to one of the specified addresses. The access server will respond to the ARP request for the specified IP address, and establish a translation from the incoming telnet request to the asynchronous port defined.

Lines 93 through 97 define `line 5` through `line 8` as standard asynchronous connections to router/switch console ports.

```
1    Dial2511#show run
2    Building configuration...
3
4    Current configuration:
5    !
6    version 11.3
7    service timestamps debug uptime
8    service timestamps log uptime
9    no service password-encryption
10   !
11   hostname Dial2511
12   !
13   enable password san-fran
14   !
15   username user2 password 0 pass2
16   username user1 password 0 pass1
17   username user1 autocommand menu linemenu
18   no ip domain-lookup
19   ip host SOHO800 2005 172.31.200.215
20   ip host RO1720 2006 172.31.200.215
21   ip host Dial2511 2007 172.31.200.215
22   ip host C3640 2008 172.31.200.215
23   !
24   !
25   !
26   interface Ethernet0
27     ip address 172.31.200.215 255.255.255.0
28   !
29   interface Serial0
30     no ip address
31   shutdown
32   !
33   interface Serial1
34     no ip address
35     shutdown
36   !
37   ip classless
38   ip alias 172.31.200.219 2008
39   ip alias 172.31.200.218 2007
40   ip alias 172.31.200.217 2006
41   ip alias 172.31.200.216 2005
42   !
43   !
44   menu linemenu title ^C
45
46
47
48          Test Line Menu
49
50   ^C
51   menu linemenu prompt ^C
52
53   Enter Menu Number:^C
54   menu linemenu text 1 Telnet to C3640
55   menu linemenu command 1 telnet 172.31.200.210
56   menu linemenu text 2 Telnet to RO1720
57   menu linemenu command 2 telnet 172.31.200.205
58   menu linemenu text 3 Show IP Route
```

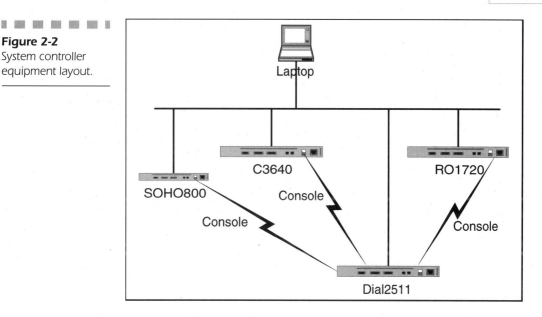

Figure 2-2
System controller
equipment layout.

Code Listing 2-4
(continued)

```
59    menu linemenu command 3 show ip route
60    menu linemenu options 3 pause
61    menu linemenu text 4 Menu Exit
62    menu linemenu command 4 logout
63    menu linemenu clear-screen
64    menu linemenu status-line
65    menu linemenu default 4
66    menu linemenu line-mode
67    menu linemenu single-space
68    !
69    !
70    line con 0
71      exec-timeout 0 0
72      logging synchronous
73      length 0
74    line 1
75      password cisco
76      login
77      modem InOut
78      modem autoconfigure type usr_courier
79      autocommand telnet 172.31.200.210
80      transport input all
81      stopbits 1
82      speed 115200
83      flowcontrol hardware
84    line 2
85      login local
86      modem InOut
87      modem autoconfigure type usr_sportster
88      transport input all
```

■ ■

Code Listing 2-4
(continued)

```
 89   stopbits 1
 90    speed 115200
 91    flowcontrol hardware
 92   line 3 4
 93   line 5 8
 94    password access
 95    login
 96    transport input all
 97   stopbits 1
 98   line 9 16
 99   line aux 0
100   line vty 0 4
101    password cisco
102    login
103   !
104   end
105   Dial2511#
```

Let's look at our local testing, through our console port, to see if our **ip host** commands work. We can use the host name to start telnet sessions, our escape sequence (**<ctrl><shft>6 x**) to return to a Dial2511 console prompt, and the **where** command to make sure that all the connections are there.

```
Dial2511#soho800
Trying SOHO800 (172.31.200.215, 2005)... Open


User Access Verification

Password:
Password OK

SOHO800#
<ctrl><shft>6 x
Dial2511#ro1720
Trying RO1720 (172.31.200.215, 2006)... Open


User Access Verification

Password:
Password OK

RO1720#
<ctrl><shft>6 x
Dial2511#c3640
Trying C3640 (172.31.200.215, 2008)... Open


User Access Verification

Password:
Password OK
```

```
C3640#
<ctrl><shft>6 x
Dial2511#where
Conn Host             Address            Byte  Idle Conn Name
    1 soho800         172.31.200.215       0     0 soho800
    2 ro1720          172.31.200.215       0     0 ro1720
*   3 c3640           172.31.200.215       0     0 c3640

Dial2511#
```

Now for our second test, the **ip alias** commands, to make sure we can telnet to the alias addresses and establish connectivity. Note that there is an alias for Dial2511, which is also part of the test.

```
Dial2511>
Dial2511>telnet 172.31.200.216
Trying 172.31.200.216 ... Open


User Access Verification

Password:
Password:
Password OK

SOHO800#<ctrl><shft>6 x
Dial2511>telnet 172.31.200.217
Trying 172.31.200.217 ... Open


User Access Verification

Password:
Password OK

RO1720#<ctrl><shft>6 x
Dial2511>telnet 172.31.200.218
Trying 172.31.200.218 ... Open


User Access Verification

Password:
Password OK

Dial2511#!telnet to dial2511 then dial to alias
Dial2511#<ctrl><shft>6 x
Dial2511>telnet 172.31.200.219
Trying 172.31.200.219 ... Open


User Access Verification

Password:
Password OK
```

```
C3640#<ctrl><shft>6 x
Dial2511>where
Conn Host                  Address              Byte  Idle Conn Name
     1 172.31.200.216      172.31.200.216         0     1 172.31.200.216
     2 172.31.200.217      172.31.200.217         0     1 172.31.200.217
     3 172.31.200.218      172.31.200.218         0     0 172.31.200.218
*    4 172.31.200.219      172.31.200.219         0     0 172.31.200.219

Dial2511>quit
  (You have open connections) [confirm]
Closing: 172.31.200.216 !
Closing: 172.31.200.217 !
Closing: 172.31.200.218 !
Closing: 172.31.200.219 !
```

Summary

In this chapter, we expanded our discussion of basic asynchronous terminal dial-in operation to include some advanced information on virtual terminal sessions and their management.

Point-to-Point Protocol

This is a foundation chapter that will define the most commonly used wide-area dial-up data transmission protocol, PPP. We will review two different functions: managing the physical link operation with Link Control Protocol (LCP), and managing data transmission protocols and processes—such as IP, Compression, and CDP—using Network Control Protocols (NCP).

The Point-to-Point Protocol (PPP) is a standards-based protocol used to encapsulate multiple data transmission protocols' datagrams over a single point-to-point link.

The Not Invented Here (NIH) syndrome occurred in the past and made our job, as network administrators, a place of great opportunities. Networking Ethernet is fairly easy; each protocol we will run has a standard protocol ID assigned by Internet Assigned Numbers Authority (IANA). If only manufacturers in the past had agreed to use this same protocol ID when it came to point-to-point WAN connectivity! Cisco uses this technique for the standard point-to-point HDLC synchronous communications, which is covered in Chapter 8.

At this point I could give you a list of RFCs for some light reading, and we could go on to the next chapter. However, this chapter is designed to give you a plain language description of the way PPP operates. If you wish to review the RFCs, there is an RFC list in the back of the book in Appendix C.

■ ▬ ■

FYI Rather than cover every option, code, and vendor nuance of PPP, this chapter is designed to provide a thorough understanding of the processes involved to aid you in troubleshooting PPP connections.

Physical Layer

RFC 1549 defines physical layer connectivity. It provides for PPP framing over both bit-oriented and octet-oriented synchronous links, and asynchronous links with eight bits of data and no parity. These links must be full-duplex, but can be either dedicated or circuit-switched.

Link Control Protocol (LCP)

Link Control Protocol (LCP) is the key to successful PPP communications. LCP operation is referenced in RFC 1661 and RFC 1570. The LCP negotiates the options used to transport information and multiplex traffic across our point-to-point link. RFC 1661 defines the operation of the LCP for establishing, configuring, and testing the data-link connection.

After the data-link protocol has been established, the LCP takes over and begins the negotiation process to establish the encapsulation format and packet sizes, detect looped links, establish compression, and manage link termination. During the negotiation, if authentication is selected, the LCP manages the authentication process, which we will review later in this chapter.

Next we will review the state changes that take place in the LCP from link startup to link shutdown. For leased lines, this happens the first time the link is activated, but for dial-in connections, it takes place every time a connection is established.

We will use an asynchronous dial-in session to track the state changes that take place during a typical session. The state changes are shown in Figure 3-1. It is a simplified state diagram that will give us an overall picture that ties in to our debugging output in Chapter 4.

Figure 3-1
LCP link state diagram.

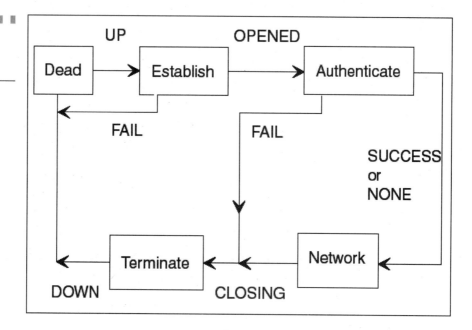

Let's review this state diagram, because when it comes to trouble-shooting dial-in services using PPP, a good understanding of the process will speed up problem correction.

LCP Dead State The link starts out in the Dead state, meaning the physical connection is down. In asynchronous communication, when the modem detects a carrier (CD/DSR) and the physical link comes UP, the link goes into the Establishing state.

LCP Establishing State This is the moment when PPP starts negotiating with its peer on the other side of the point-to-point link. If you have ever seen a PPP link connect, and then hang up after about twenty seconds, it is probably a misconfiguration on one side or the other that prevents the two sides of the point-to-point link from correctly establishing a PPP LCP connection. If the LCP sends out configuration requests without getting a response, the LCP times out and sends out another configuration request. The next chapter has examples of this type of failure from both the Cisco side and the Windows 95/98 side.

Negotiation takes place when each side sends out configuration requests and gets configuration acknowledgments, negative acknowledgments, or LCP packet rejects to determine which features to use to manage the link. Each configuration request will have several options used to define the operation of the link. See Table 3-1 for the definition of the basic LCP options.

TABLE 3-1

Code	Option	Description
1	Maximum-Receive-Unit	Defines the maximum number of octets that can be transmitted
3	Authentication Protocol	Defines the specific authentication method to use to authenticate the requestor
4	Quality Protocol	Defines specific method for monitoring link quality
5	Magic-Number	Defines a random unique number to identify each side of a point-to-point link
6	Protocol-Field-Compression	Reduces PPP Protocol field from two octets to one octet for low-speed links
7	Address-and-Control-Field-Compression	Eliminates frame Address and Control fields from data transmissions not used in most point-to-point links

NOTE *During negotiation the Magic Number option has an important function, loop detection. Each peer in our point-to-point link picks a random number used to identify itself. If you send out your Magic Number in a request, and it is reflected back to you, the point-to-point circuit is looped.*

The preceding options are used in the configuration negotiation process. Table 3-2 defines the list of basic LCP Packet Codes used during the negotiation phase.

Let's use an example to get a better understanding of how the configuration negotiation process operates. Our example will use two peers named Left and Right and is described in Figure 3-2.

TABLE 3-2

Code	Type	Description
1	Configure-Request	Required request for negotiation of link options; link options detailed in Table 3.1
2	Configure-Ack	Required response to configuration requests with valid options
3	Configure-Nak	Required response to configuration requests with valid but unacceptable option values
4	Configure-Reject	Required response to configuration requests with unrecognized options
5	Terminate-Request	Request by one side to terminate the PPP connection
6	Terminate-Ack	Required response to a Terminate-Request
7	Code-Reject	Required response when an unrecognized LCP code is received; usually indicates peer is operating with a different version of PPP
8	Protocol-Reject	Required when an NCP protocol is requested after LCP state changes to OPEN and the NCP protocol is not defined on the device issuing this packet
9	Echo-Request	Request for peer response
10	Echo-Reply	Required response to Echo-Request
11	Discard-Request	One-way local-to-remote transmission for debugging and performance testing

Figure 3-2
LCP negotiation
example.

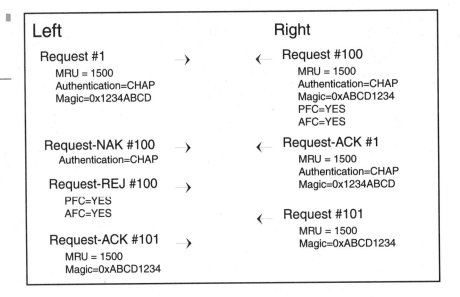

In our example, both Left and Right send out configuration requests. When Right receives Left's request, Right agrees to the options requested and sends back an acknowledgment (ACK). When Left receives Right's request, Left sends back a negative acknowledgment (NAK) for authentication using Challenge Handshake Authentication Protocol (CHAP), as Left doesn't do CHAP. Left sends back a configuration reject (REJ), as Left is not allowed to do PFC and AFC. After the NAK and REJ are sent back to Right, Right sends out a new request with those options known to be acceptable to Left and then waits for Left to ACK this second request. This negotiation process may go back and forth several times, as both sides modify their requests based on their peer's feedback, or response delays.

LCP Authentication State Once we have successfully negotiated our options for communicating across the link, it is time to authenticate the connection. In our example, Right will use CHAP to authenticate Left, and Left will not authenticate Right, which is typical for dial-in connections. (There is an in-depth authentication section coming next.) After the authentication process is completed, the link is considered open, and we begin the individual NCP negotiations.

LCP Network State In the Network state, each NCP configured negotiates appropriate parameters and begins data communications. If an

NCP fails to negotiate with its peer, then the specific NCP is not operational—but it does not necessarily mean that the PPP connection is terminated. This can be very frustrating during the troubleshooting process. The link is up, but there is no data communication. We have an example of this type of NCP failure in Chapter 4.

LCP Terminate State PPP can initiate link termination due to loss of carrier for asynchronous communications, authentication failure, link quality failure, idle line timeout, or administrative shutdown of the link. When a terminate acknowledgment is received back, or after a reasonable wait time, the LCP state goes to Dead.

LCP Dead State We have completed the LCP state cycle defined in Figure 3-1, and the peer is waiting for a new connection.

Authentication

There are two primary methods for authenticating PPP connections, Password Authentication Protocol (PAP) and Challenge Handshake Authentication Protocol (CHAP).

PAP comes from simpler times when hackers and viruses had nothing to do with computers. When the link becomes open, a peer that wishes to be authenticated with PAP asks the other side to validate the connection. When the physical link is up, the username and password are sent in plain text. The authenticator looks up the information in the appropriate database. If there is a match in the database, then authentication is complete, and we move on to NCP processing. If there is no match, then the link is terminated.

CHAP is more complex because it uses a technique that never sends passwords between peers. Instead, it uses an MD5 encryption process for authentication. Rather than username and password, think of the information used by PPP CHAP as a username and encryption key. Figure 3-3 will visually walk you through this process.

After the LCP negotiation is completed and the link is open, both sides check the authentication method picked and initiate the selected process. Right picks out a random number, assigns an ID to the challenge, and sends it off to Left. Left takes the ID number and the random number generated by Right, applies the encryption key samepass to the two numbers, and calculates a hashed number using MD5 encryption. Left returns the hashed number in a packet to Right using the same ID number, so that Right can match the response with the original challenge. Left includes its name in the response, so that Right can look up the responder in its database. Right looks up Left in the database to find the encryption key to use. After finding the encryption key, the challenger duplicates the MD5 encryption with the original ID, random number, and samepass to calculate its own hash number. If the calculated hash number on the Right matches the hash number sent by Left, then Left is sent a message indicating that the response was authenticated. If there is no match, then Left is sent a message saying the response is rejected, and Right initiates link termination.

Figure 3-3
CHAP authentication
process.

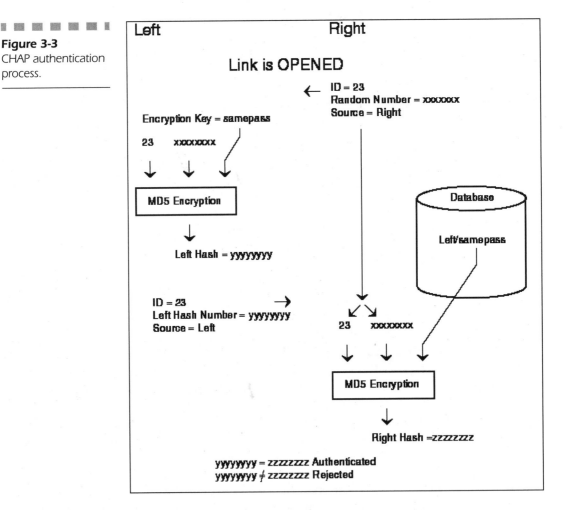

After the authentication process has successfully finished, then the LCP is considered fully open and operational. Now the NCP negotiation process begins.

NOTE *While most Cisco implementations use two way CHAP authentication, with both sides challenging, most dial-in connections have CHAP authentication initiated by the Cisco router / access server.*

Network Control Protocol (NCP)

NCP operates after LCP has opened and authenticated the peers on a point-to-point link. NCPs use the same PPP Packet Codes used to negotiate at the LCP level, but only Codes 1 through 7 (Configure-Request, Configure-Ack, Configure-Nak, Configure-Reject, Terminate-Request, Terminate-Ack, and Code-Reject). Table 3-2 has more details on these negotiation codes.

Instead of covering all NCPs, we will cover the three desktop protocols—IP, IPX, and AppleTalk—not in great detail, but enough to recognize the most common options for future debugging and troubleshooting.

IP Control Protocol (IPCP)

TCP/IP is the most common protocol transported across PPP, and there are two options in common use: assignment of IP addresses, and compression.

First, let's take a look at IP addressing, which by default assigns no IP address. This option provides a way to negotiate the IP address used on the local end of the link. It allows the local-side peer to state which IP address it desires, or to request that the remote peer provide the information. The remote peer can provide this information by sending a NAK when the IP address requested by the local peer is unacceptable, and will subsequently return a valid IP address to the local peer's next request.

If negotiating the remote IP address is required, and the remote peer did not provide the option in its original configuration request, the IP address negotiation option should be appended to the NAK response to let the other side know that the option is required. If the IP address sent by the local peer to the remote peer is not acceptable, the remote peer needs to provide the correct IP address.

Now let's look at IP compression options. Van Jacobson TCP/IP header compression reduces the size of the TCP/IP headers to as few as three bytes. This can be a significant improvement on slow serial lines, particularly for interactive traffic. Think of Telnet character-by-character transmission; each character typed on the terminal generates three packets, all with IP and TCP headers. The compression option is used to indicate the ability to receive compressed packets. Each end of the link must separately request this option if bidirectional compression is desired. Even with compression turned on, it will only compress header information for those packets that will benefit from compression.

AppleTalk Control Protocol (ATCP)

The AppleTalk protocol is still widely used, and there are seven options we can use for PPP NCP negotiation: AppleTalk addressing, routing protocol, broadcast suppression, compression, server information, zone information, and the default router address.

First, let's look at AppleTalk addressing, which, by default, assigns no AppleTalk address. This option provides a way to negotiate the Apple-Talk network and node number to use on the local end of the link. It allows the local peer to state which AppleTalk-address it desires, or to request that the remote peer provide the information. The remote peer can provide the information by sending a NAK to the local peer and returning a valid AppleTalk address. In all cases, if addresses are used, both sides must have a common network number and different node numbers (that kind of makes sense; duplicates are bad).

If the local peer sends a request for addressing with a network or node number specified as zero, the remote peer interprets it as a request to supply an AppleTalk address. If the remote peer sends an ACK with the network or node number specified as zero, then no address is the correct setting. Two peers with no addresses will create a link made up of two half-routers. I guess they mean bridging?

The next option is to select the AppleTalk routing protocol used to exchange information; the default is the Routing Table Maintenance Protocol (RTMP). The four options are: none, RTMP, AURP, or ABGP.

Next we have broadcast suppression, which by default is not active. In a large AppleTalk network, the extensive use of the Name Binding Protocol (NBP) requests could flood our link and interfere with communications. This option is asymmetric so that the local peer can still issue NBP requests for network services, while the remote peer blocks broadcasts directed to the local peer.

The next PPP NCP negotiation option, is AppleTalk protocol compression, which is off by default.

Next is an option that allows the local peer to get the AppleTalk name of the remote peer.

Then comes the option that allows the local peer to identify the Zone assigned to the PPP link.

Last is the option to get the address of the seed router used to supply network and zone information on the PPP link. RTMP updates received by the local peer will override this option.

IPX Control Protocol (IPXCP)

Lastly, we will look at the IPX protocol for establishing Novell services across the PPP link. PPP does not distinguish between normal IPX encapsulation and IPXWAN encapsulation. IPXWAN is just another IPX protocol. The options in this NCP are: IPX network number, node number, compression, routing protocol, and a special configuration complete option—to support IPXWAN.

First comes the IPX network number option, which by default is set to no network number. If there is no need to include the PPP link in a routing process, no network number is required. Both sides must agree on a network number, or, if one peer sets a network number to zero, the other peer will supply the network number for the link. If the network numbers do not match, the NCP will not open for IPX traffic.

Next is the node number, which must be unique to each peer if an IPX network number is assigned; no duplicates allowed.

Next is the compression option that each peer is willing to accept.

Next is the routing protocol option, which by default is Novell's combination of Routing Information Protocol (RIP) and Service Advertising Protocol (SAP). The other options are None or Novell Link Services Protocol (NLSP). None must stand alone, but NLSP and RIP/SAP can coexist.

The last option is configuration complete. This option does not have to be used, but when IPXWAN is also configured on this link, detection of a configuration complete response will negate the need for the extra overhead required to run IPXWAN.

Multilink PPP

In order to establish communications over a point-to-point link, each end of the PPP link must first send LCP packets to configure the data link during the Link Establishment phase. After the link has been established, PPP provides for an Authentication phase in which the authentication protocols can be used to determine identifiers associated with each system connected by the link.

The goal of the multilink operation is to coordinate multiple independent links between a fixed pair of systems, providing a logical link with greater bandwidth than any individual link. The aggregate link, or bundle, is named by the pair of identifiers for the two systems connected across the multiple links. A system identifier is usually the user or host name provided during PPP Authentication. The bundled links can be different physical links, as in multiple asynchronous lines, but may also be instances of multiplexed links, such as ISDN, X.25, or Frame Relay. The links may also be of different kinds, such as dial-up asynchronous links, ISDN links, and leased synchronous links.

Not all packets travelling across a virtual link or bundle are segmented so that the segments can travel in parallel across the multiple links. Some control packets, or packets that are so small that segmentation makes no sense, are sent across an individual link unchanged. The segmentation and reassembly of packets takes place in such a manner as to be transparent to the NCP hand-off process at both ends of our point-to-point link.

Note that network protocols that are not sent using multilink headers cannot be sequenced (and consequently will be delivered in any convenient way).

Summary

In this chapter, we reviewed the operation of the Point-to-Point Protocol and its components, the Link Control Protocol, and a few Network Control Protocols. By having a better understanding of the principles behind PPP negotiation, we can troubleshoot PPP connections more effectively.

IP Dial Access

This chapter puts together our first three topics to create end-user IP connectivity. A workstation with dial-in access and a TCP/IP stack will use the PPP protocol to run TCP/IP applications by dialing in to a Cisco router/access server to access the network.

In this chapter, we will establish a basic dial-in connection from a Windows 95/98 PC into our Cisco router environment. Instead of a general purpose router like the 3640, we will use a Cisco 2511 access server. Figure 4-1 shows the equipment layout for most examples in this chapter.

Windows 95/98 Dial-In Setup

Let's walk through the setup for Dial-Up Networking in the Windows 95/98 environment. First we will select the Make New Connection icon in the Dial-Up Networking window (see Figure 4-2).

The next window, shown in Figure 4-3, is used to define the icon name. Make sure you use a significant name for easier access.

In Figure 4-4 we enter the phone number to use to dial in to our access server.

Figure 4-1
Equipment layout.

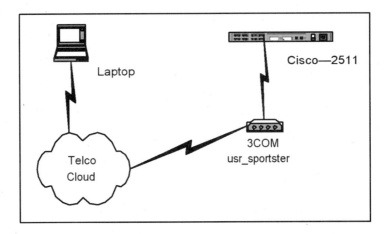

Figure 4-2
Dial-up networking—
make a new connec-
tion.

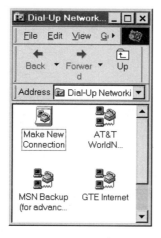

Figure 4-3
New connection
name.

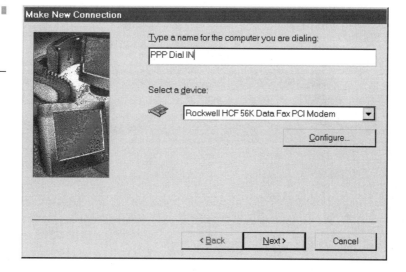

Figure 4-5 shows us the created dial-in connection. However, the standard parameters may not support our requirements, so next we will look at the default properties of the connection.

Select the new connection from the Dial-Up Networking window (see Figure 4-6), and then click the right button on the mouse and select properties.

First we look at the General information in Figure 4-7 to verify that our dial properties are correct.

Figure 4-4
New connection
phone number.

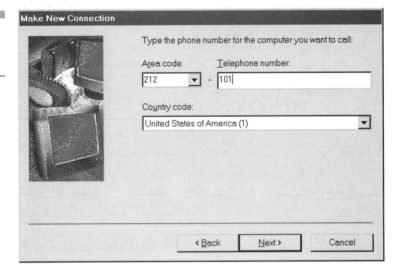

Figure 4-5
Completed new con-
nection.

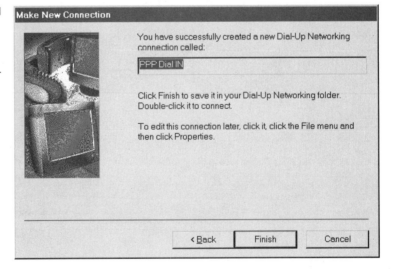

In Figure 4-8 we look at the Server Types and get set up for the sim-
plest IP connectivity available (no need for NetBEUI or IPX/SPX). Log
onto network, enable software compression, and TCP/IP are the only
options we will check.

Now we check our TCP/IP settings in Figure 4-9 to make sure we are
set up properly to use the settings passed to us from the access server.

Figure 4-6
Select the new con-
nection.

Figure 4-7
PPP dial IN, proper-
ties—General.

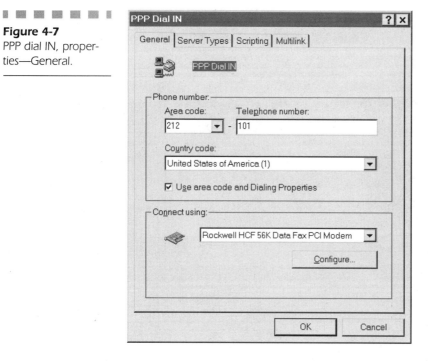

Next let's see what it looks like when we successfully connect to the host using PPP in Figure 4-10.

When we click on the Connect button, the process moves to a status screen that takes us through the three steps used to make a connection: first, dialing; then, verifying user name and password; and last, logging on to the network. This sequence is shown in Figure 4-11.

When a connection is successful the first time, a special window pops up and informs us about status-checking capabilities. Figure 4-12 shows the details concerning status-checking the active connection.

Figure 4-13 shows the window that pops up if we click on the two-computer icon in the lower right corner of the screen: we get the current status of the connection and are given the option of disconnecting.

This is the way a normal dial-in connection is set up and connects. In the next section, we will take a look at some of the error message windows that pop up and explain why these message windows appear.

Figure 4-8
PPP dial IN, properties—server types.

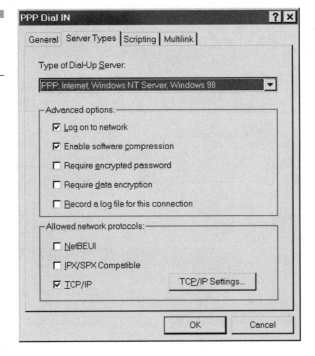

Figure 4-9
PPP dial IN, proper-
ties—TCP/IP Settings.

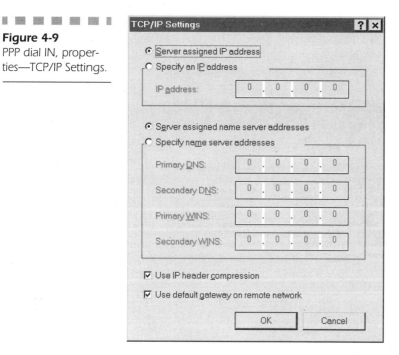

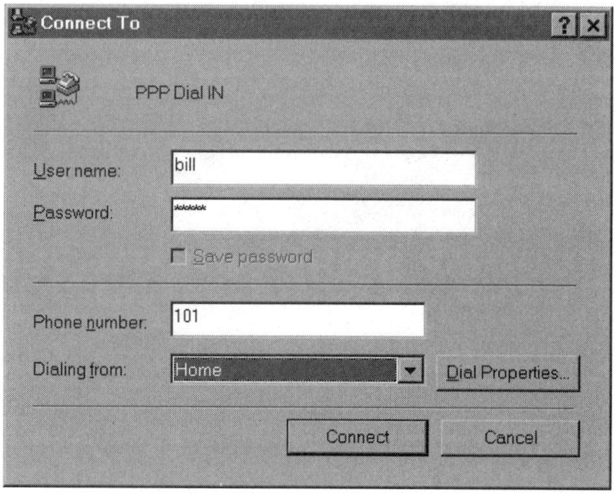

Figure 4-10
PPP dial IN, initial
screen.

Figure 4-11
PPP dial IN, standard
connection
sequence.

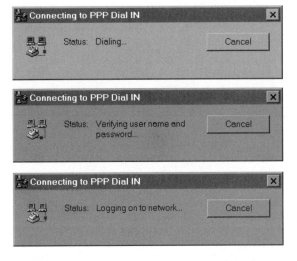

Figure 4-12
PPP dial IN, first con-
nection window.

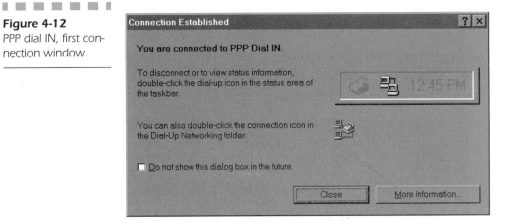

Figure 4-13
Current connection
status window.

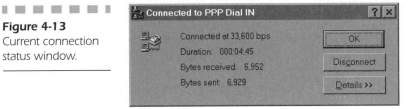

Programming the Cisco Router/ Access Server

Now for the good part, programming the Cisco router/access server to accept our PPP dial-in connection. Let's look at an extract of the AS2511 configuration used for straight asynchronous dial-in to see what is currently active.

```
hostname AS2511
!
enable password san-fran
!
modemcap entry usr_new:FD=&F1:TPL=usr_sportster
!
interface Ethernet0
 ip address 172.31.200.210 255.255.255.0
!
ip classless
!
line con 0
 exec-timeout 0 0
 logging synchronous
 length 0
line 1
 password cisco
 login
 modem InOut
 modem autoconfigure type usr_sportster
 transport input all
 stopbits 1
 speed 115200
 flowcontrol hardware
line 2 16
line aux 0
line vty 0 4
 password cisco
 login
!
end
```

There is no interface defined for a PPP connection. If we try a PPP dial-in connection, it will fail. Let's take a look, in Figure 4-14, at the message that pops up when we try a dial-in PPP connection.

Well, the message is correct—we are not prepared for an incoming PPP connection. Let's get to it—PPP connectivity coming right up. We will now create an ASYNC interface and program it to carry PPP traffic. Code Listing 4-1 shows the commands.

Line 3 creates an asynchronous interface that corresponds to line 1.

Line 4 sets up for PPP encapsulation.

Figure 4-14
Router/access server
not programmed for
PPP dial-in.

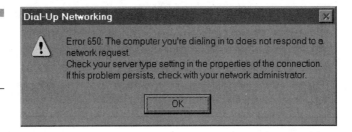

Lines 5 through 7 show us the authentication options available with
this version of the Cisco IOS.

Line 9 selects PAP for our first test.

Line 10 is a quick check to see if there are any more options that can
be used for PPP authentication. It looks like we can extend authentication to use multiple methods depending on negotiation with the incoming
PPP request.

Line 17 sets up interface async 1 to process IP traffic, but instead of
using up an IP subnet for our dial-in link, we will borrow the IP address
from our Ethernet 0 interface for all IP packets sourced from the router
to our dial-in site.

Lines 18 through 23 define the mechanism that will assign an IP
address to the dial-in peer across the PPP link. We will use both the
pool and dhcp options in more advanced configurations. Line 23 sets up
a specific address for the remote peer.

Lines 24 through 28 show us the two options for asynchronous communications, dedicated to either PPP or SLIP, or interactive so that
regular asynchronous dial-in connections as well as PPP or SLIP connections can be started. More on these options later when we modify this
basic PPP dial-in connection to provide both PPP and asynchronous connectivity.

Line 28 sets the interface to be dedicated for PPP or SLIP connections.

Code Listing 4-1
Initial PPP configura-
tion commands.

```
1    AS2511#conf t
2    Enter configuration commands, one per line.  End with CNTL/Z.
3    AS2511(config)#int async 1
4    AS2511(config-if)#encapsulation ppp
5    AS2511(config-if)#ppp authentication ?
6    chap  Challenge Handshake Authentication Protocol (CHAP)
7    pap   Password Authentication Protocol (PAP)
8
9    AS2511(config-if)#ppp authentication pap
10   AS2511(config-if)#ppp authentication pap ?
```

■ ■

Code Listing 4-1
(continued)

```
11   callin     Authenticate remote on incoming call only
12   chap       Challenge Handshake Authentication Protocol (CHAP)
13   if-needed  Do not negotiate PAP or CHAP if user has already
     authenticated
14   <cr>
15
16   AS2511(config-if)#ppp authentication pap
17   AS2511(config-if)#ip unnumbered ethernet 0
18   AS2511(config-if)#peer default ip address ?
19   A.B.C.D  Default IP address for remote end of this interface
20   dhcp     Use DHCP proxy client mechanism to allocate a peer IP
     address
21   pool     Use IP pool mechanism to allocate a peer IP address
22
23   AS2511(config-if)#peer default ip address 172.31.200.100
24   AS2511(config-if)#async mode ?
25   dedicated    Line is dedicated as an async interface
26   interactive  Line may be switched between interactive use and
     async interface
27
28   AS2511(config-if)#async mode dedicated
29   AS2511(config-if)#^Z
30   AS2511#
```

Let's dial in again and see how our connection works. We get another error message when we dial in from our PC (the window is shown in Figure 4-15).

It looks like we have had a failure. Let's go through the troubleshooting steps and check out this problem.

Let's look at the asynchronous debugging command options first and then the generated output. In all the following debug output, we see As1, Async 1, and TTY1, indicating which interface is being processed.

```
AS2511#debug async ?
  framing  Packet framing
  packet   Packet I/O
  state    Interface state changes

AS2511#
```

■ ■ ■ ■ ■ ■ ■

Figure 4-15
PPP dial IN, password failure message window.

First, we will check out state changes. We see `Async Protocol Mode` being started for the remote peer, followed immediately by a reset.

```
AS2511#debug async state
Async interface state changes debugging is on
AS2511#
03:04:58: As1 PPP: Async Protocol Mode started for 172.31.200.100
03:05:00: %LINK-5-CHANGED: Interface Async1, changed state to reset
03:05:04: Async1: Async protocol mode stopped for 172.31.200.100
03:05:06: %LINK-3-UPDOWN: Interface Async1, changed state to down
AS2511#
```

After we turn off all debugging, we try the command **debug async framing** to see if we get any more information.

```
AS2511#undebug all
All possible debugging has been turned off
AS2511#debug async framing
Async interface framing debugging is on
03:09:52: Async1: Setup PPP framing on TTY1
03:09:52: As1 PPP: Processed packet cached during autoselect
03:09:54: %LINK-3-UPDOWN: Interface Async1, changed state to up
03:09:54: Async1: Enabling PPP framing in UART's Microcode on line TTY1
03:09:56: %LINK-5-CHANGED: Interface Async1, changed state to reset
03:09:59: Async1: Reset PPP framing on TTY1
AS2511#
```

The incoming PPP packet is recognized, and hardware framing is turned on, but the process of activating the link is reset.

NOTE *This is our standard troubleshooting process: first check out the physical layer, and when proper operation is verified, move up to the data-link layer.*

Let's look at the **debug** options available in this version of IOS for troubleshooting PPP.

```
AS2511#debug ppp ?
  authentication  CHAP and PAP authentication
  bap             BAP protocol transactions
  error           Protocol errors and error statistics
  multilink       Multilink activity
  negotiation     Protocol parameter negotiation
  packet          Low-level PPP packet dump
```

The command **debug PPP negotiation** is the best place to start, as the LCP layer goes to the `establishing` state as soon as the physical link is up and running.

```
AS2511#debug ppp negotiation
PPP protocol negotiation debugging is on
AS2511#
03:35:09: %LINK-3-UPDOWN: Interface Async1, changed state to up
03:35:09: As1 PPP: Treating connection as a dedicated line
03:35:09: As1 PPP: Phase is ESTABLISHING, Active Open
```

AS2511 sends out a configuration request with Asynchronous Control Character Mapping (ACCM), PAP authentication, our Magic Number, Protocol Field Compression (PFC), and Address and Control Field Compression (ACFC). The last two options will reduce the normal PPP framing overhead.

```
03:35:09: As1 LCP: O CONFREQ [Closed] id 5 len 24
03:35:09: As1 LCP:    ACCM 0x000A0000 (0x0206000A0000)
03:35:09: As1 LCP:    AuthProto PAP (0x0304C023)
03:35:09: As1 LCP:    MagicNumber 0x1140E529 (0x05061140E529)
03:35:09: As1 LCP:    PFC (0x0702)
03:35:09: As1 LCP:    ACFC (0x0802)
```

AS2511 gets a configuration acknowledgment accepting the AS2511 PPP request (id 5).

```
03:35:10: As1 LCP: I CONFACK [REQsent] id 5 len 24
03:35:10: As1 LCP:    ACCM 0x000A0000 (0x0206000A0000)
03:35:10: As1 LCP:    AuthProto PAP (0x0304C023)
03:35:10: As1 LCP:    MagicNumber 0x1140E529 (0x05061140E529)
03:35:10: As1 LCP:    PFC (0x0702)
03:35:10: As1 LCP:    ACFC (0x0802)
```

The AS2511 gets a configuration request from the dial-in device that matches up with our configuration, with the exception of a callback request.

```
03:35:10: As1 LCP: I CONFREQ [ACKrcvd] id 2 len 23
03:35:10: As1 LCP:    ACCM 0x000A0000 (0x0206000A0000)
03:35:10: As1 LCP:    MagicNumber 0x01232702 (0x050601232702)
03:35:10: As1 LCP:    PFC (0x0702)
03:35:10: As1 LCP:    ACFC (0x0802)
03:35:10: As1 LCP:    Callback 6 (0x0D0306)
```

As we did not set up to process a PPP callback, we will reject this option only and let the dial-in device resubmit its configuration request.

```
03:35:10: As1 LCP: O CONFREJ [ACKrcvd] id 2 len 7
03:35:10: As1 LCP:     Callback 6  (0x0D0306)
```

Here comes the resubmission. This time the dial-in device has dropped the callback request, and since the AS2511 agrees, a configuration acknowledgment is returned.

```
03:35:10: As1 LCP: I CONFREQ [ACKrcvd] id 3 len 20
03:35:10: As1 LCP:     ACCM 0x000A0000 (0x0206000A0000)
03:35:10: As1 LCP:     MagicNumber 0x01232702 (0x050601232702)
03:35:10: As1 LCP:     PFC (0x0702)
03:35:10: As1 LCP:     ACFC (0x0802)
03:35:10: As1 LCP: O CONFACK [ACKrcvd] id 3 len 20
03:35:10: As1 LCP:     ACCM 0x000A0000 (0x0206000A0000)
03:35:10: As1 LCP:     MagicNumber 0x01232702 (0x050601232702)
03:35:10: As1 LCP:     PFC (0x0702)
03:35:10: As1 LCP:     ACFC (0x0802)
```

Both sides in our PPP connection have agreed on the parameters, and now the LCP state is open.

```
03:35:10: As1 LCP: State is Open
```

The first order of business after the link is fully operational is to process authentication. If no authentication has been negotiated, then we will proceed directly to NCP negotiation. In this example, PAP was negotiated, and the next step details the authentication process. First, we see that only this end of the conversation is authenticating, which is normal in a dial-in configuration. The messages in this debug stream indicate that PPP is using the PAP authentication process, but it has failed.

```
03:35:10: As1 PPP: Phase is AUTHENTICATING, by this end
03:35:10: As1 PAP: I AUTH-REQ id 1 len 15 from "bill"
03:35:10: As1 PAP: Authenticating peer bill
03:35:10: As1 PAP: O AUTH-NAK id 1 len 27 msg is "Authentication failure"
```

Nuts—I knew we forgot something. Perhaps a local database that has bill in it would help us make a connection. The termination process follows, shutting down LCP and waiting for a new connection.

```
03:35:10: As1 PPP: Phase is TERMINATING
03:35:10: As1 LCP: O TERMREQ [Open] id 6 len 4Username bill not found
03:35:10: As1 LCP: I TERMACK [TERMsent] id 6 len 4
03:35:10: As1 LCP: State is Closed
```

```
03:35:10: As1 PPP: Phase is DOWN
03:35:10: As1 PPP: Phase is ESTABLISHING, Passive Open
03:35:10: As1 LCP: State is Listen
03:35:12: %LINK-5-CHANGED: Interface Async1, changed state to reset
03:35:12: As1 LCP: State is Closed
03:35:12: As1 PPP: Phase is DOWN
03:35:12: As1 IPCP: Remove route to 172.31.200.100
03:35:17: %LINK-3-UPDOWN: Interface Async1, changed state to down
03:35:17: As1 LCP: State is Closed
03:35:17: As1 PPP: Phase is DOWN
AS2511#
```

If you look in the above output we see that the NCP, IPCP, was jumping the gun a little by allocating the IP address for the dial-in device and inserting the address in the access server IP routing table.

We know what the first problem is, so let's add the username and password for bill to our local AS2511 database.

```
AS2511#conf t
Enter configuration commands, one per line.  End with CNTL/Z.
AS2511(config)#username bill password cisco
AS2511(config)#^Z
AS2511#
```

Let's try that dial-in again. We will go right back to the same spot where we failed in our last attempt, LCP open.

```
04:39:06: As1 LCP: State is Open
04:39:06: As1 PPP: Phase is AUTHENTICATING, by this end
04:39:06: As1 PAP: I AUTH-REQ id 1 len 15 from "bill"
04:39:06: As1 PAP: Authenticating peer bill
04:39:06: As1 PAP: O AUTH-ACK id 1 len 5
04:39:06: As1 PPP: Phase is UP
```

Hooray—we are in. Now we start the next phase, the negotiation and activation of our NCPs.

The sequence below is our AS2511 trying to start several NCPs, TCP/IP, Cisco Discovery Protocol (CDP), Logical Link Control 2 (LLC2), and Advanced Peer-to-Peer Networking Automatic Node Routing (APPNANR). These are NCP options that the Cisco routers attempt to activate, by default, as we just configured TCP/IP.

```
04:39:06: As1 IPCP: O CONFREQ [Closed] id 3 len 10
04:39:06: As1 IPCP:    Address 172.31.200.210 (0x0306AC1FC8D2)
04:39:06: As1 CDPCP: O CONFREQ [Closed] id 2 len 4
04:39:06: As1 LLC2CP: O CONFREQ [Closed] id 2 len 4
04:39:06: As1 APPNANRCP: O CONFREQ [Closed] id 2 len 4
```

Next we get a request from our dial-in device for IP information—the only option we are ready to hand out is an IP address, so we reject all the compression, DNS, and WINS options.

```
04:39:06: As1 IPCP: I CONFREQ [REQsent] id 1 len 40
04:39:06: As1 IPCP:    CompressType VJ 15 slots CompressSlotID (0x0206002D0F01)
04:39:06: As1 IPCP:    Address 0.0.0.0 (0x030600000000)
04:39:06: As1 IPCP:    PrimaryDNS 0.0.0.0 (0x810600000000)
04:39:06: As1 IPCP:    PrimaryWINS 0.0.0.0 (0x820600000000)
04:39:06: As1 IPCP:    SecondaryDNS 0.0.0.0 (0x830600000000)
04:39:06: As1 IPCP:    SecondaryWINS 0.0.0.0 (0x840600000000)
04:39:06: As1 IPCP: O CONFREJ [REQsent] id 1 len 34
04:39:06: As1 IPCP:    CompressType VJ 15 slots CompressSlotID (0x0206002D0F01)
04:39:06: As1 IPCP:    PrimaryDNS 0.0.0.0 (0x810600000000)
04:39:06: As1 IPCP:    PrimaryWINS 0.0.0.0 (0x820600000000)
04:39:06: As1 IPCP:    SecondaryDNS 0.0.0.0 (0x830600000000)
04:39:06: As1 IPCP:    SecondaryWINS 0.0.0.0 (0x840600000000)
```

Next, the dial-in device wants to try Microsoft Point-to-Point Compression (MPPC or MS-PPC). We are not set up for MPPC over the Compression Control Protocol NCP, so LCP rejects that protocol.

```
04:39:06: As1 CCP: I CONFREQ [Not negotiated] id 1 len 15
04:39:06: As1 CCP:    MS-PPC supported bits 0x00000001 (0x120600000001)
04:39:06: As1 CCP:    Stacker history 1 check mode EXTENDED (0x1105000104)
04:39:06: As1 LCP: O PROTREJ [Open] id 14 len 21 protocol CCP
04:39:06: As1 LCP:    (0x80FD0101000F12060000000111050001)
04:39:06: As1 LCP:    (0x04)
```

We finally get a response back from the dial-in device accepting our IP address request.

```
04:39:06: As1 IPCP: I CONFACK [REQsent] id 3 len 10
04:39:06: As1 IPCP:    Address 172.31.200.210 (0x0306AC1FC8D2)
```

We can assume that the other device is not a Cisco device or does not wish to use Cisco Discovery Protocol (CDP), as our request is rejected along with LLC2CP and APPNANR.

```
04:39:06: As1 LCP: I PROTREJ [Open] id 4 len 10 protocol CDPCP (0x820701020004)
04:39:06: As1 CDPCP: State is Closed
04:39:06: As1 LCP: I PROTREJ [Open] id 5 len 10 protocol LLC2CP (0x804B01020004)
04:39:06: As1 LLC2CP: State is Closed
04:39:06: As1 LCP: I PROTREJ [Open] id 6 len 10 protocol APPNANRCP (0x804D01020004)
04:39:06: As1 APPNANRCP: State is Closed
```

LCP has finally noted that the link is up and running. Perhaps our debugging has impacted the router's ability to process information in a timely manner.

```
04:39:06: %LINEPROTO-5-UPDOWN: Line protocol on Interface Async1, changed state to up
```

CDP has still been processing in the background, and with all the debug activity, IPCP has timed out waiting for a good response.

```
04:39:06: As1 PPP: Unsupported or un-negotiated protocol. Link cdp
04:39:06: As1 PPP: Trying to negotiate NCP for Link cdp
04:39:06: As1 CDPCP: State is Closed
04:39:07: As1 CDPCP: TIMEout: Time 0xFF888D State Closed
04:39:07: As1 CDPCP: State is Listen
04:39:08: As1 IPCP: TIMEout: Time 0xFF8E98 State ACKrcvd
```

With all the other options out of the picture, the AS2511 has time to successfully negotiate the IPCP options, all the way down to handing out an IP address to the dial-in device.

```
04:39:08: As1 IPCP: O CONFREQ [ACKrcvd] id 4 len 10
04:39:08: As1 IPCP:    Address 172.31.200.210 (0x0306AC1FC8D2)
04:39:08: As1 IPCP: I CONFACK [REQsent] id 4 len 10
04:39:08: As1 IPCP:    Address 172.31.200.210 (0x0306AC1FC8D2)
04:39:09: As1 IPCP: I CONFREQ [ACKrcvd] id 2 len 34
04:39:09: As1 IPCP:    Address 0.0.0.0 (0x030600000000)
04:39:09: As1 IPCP:    PrimaryDNS 0.0.0.0 (0x810600000000)
04:39:09: As1 IPCP:    PrimaryWINS 0.0.0.0 (0x820600000000)
04:39:09: As1 IPCP:    SecondaryDNS 0.0.0.0 (0x830600000000)
04:39:09: As1 IPCP:    SecondaryWINS 0.0.0.0 (0x840600000000)
04:39:09: As1 IPCP: O CONFREJ [ACKrcvd] id 2 len 28
04:39:09: As1 IPCP:    PrimaryDNS 0.0.0.0 (0x810600000000)
04:39:09: As1 IPCP:    PrimaryWINS 0.0.0.0 (0x820600000000)
04:39:09: As1 IPCP:    SecondaryDNS 0.0.0.0 (0x830600000000)
04:39:09: As1 IPCP:    SecondaryWINS 0.0.0.0 (0x840600000000)
04:39:09: As1 IPCP: I CONFREQ [ACKrcvd] id 3 len 10
04:39:09: As1 IPCP:    Address 0.0.0.0 (0x030600000000)
04:39:09: As1 IPCP: O CONFNAK [ACKrcvd] id 3 len 10
04:39:09: As1 IPCP:    Address 172.31.200.100 (0x0306AC1FC864)
04:39:09: As1 IPCP: I CONFREQ [ACKrcvd] id 4 len 10
04:39:09: As1 IPCP:    Address 172.31.200.100 (0x0306AC1FC864)
04:39:09: As1 IPCP: O CONFACK [ACKrcvd] id 4 len 10
04:39:09: As1 IPCP:    Address 172.31.200.100 (0x0306AC1FC864)
04:39:09: As1 IPCP: State is Open
04:39:09: As1 IPCP: Install route to 172.31.200.100
AS2511#
```

The route to our dial-in device is installed, and TCP/IP communications is established. Our dial-in device can now communicate with the balance of our TCP/IP network.

Let's change the authentication to CHAP and add in another option, `callin`, to see if it affects our router operation.

```
AS2511#conf t
Enter configuration commands, one per line.  End with CNTL/Z.
AS2511(config)#int async 1
AS2511(config-if)#ppp authentication CHAP callin
AS2511(config-if)#^Z
AS2511#
```

No change occurs using `callin` as an authentication option, but that is expected in a dial-in situation. The AS2511 challenges our dial-in device, gets a response back, and validates the dial-in device. For a review on PAP and CHAP, please see Chapter 3.

```
AS2511#debug ppp authentication
PPP authentication debugging is on
AS2511#
05:38:44: %LINK-3-UPDOWN: Interface Async1, changed state to up
05:38:44: As1 PPP: Treating connection as a dedicated line
05:38:46: As1 PPP: Phase is AUTHENTICATING, by this end
05:38:46: As1 CHAP: O CHALLENGE id 3 len 27 from "AS2511"
05:38:46: As1 CHAP: I RESPONSE id 3 len 25 from "bill"
05:38:46: As1 CHAP: O SUCCESS id 3 len 4
05:38:46: %LINEPROTO-5-UPDOWN: Line protocol on Interface Async1, changed state to up
AS2511#
```

We are almost finished with our configuration, but we have left our AS2511 in a PPP-only mode, and our asynchronous dial-in connection to create `exec` sessions won't work. Let's add those commands into our line and interface configurations. Applying **async mode interactive** to the interface, let's start an executive session if the first character that shows up on the link is a carriage return. If the first character that shows up on the interface is the start of a PPP, SLIP, or ARAP connection, and we have defined the corresponding `autoselect` operation on the associated `line`, then the appropriate protocol will be activated. In this case, we want only `exec` sessions or PPP sessions to start. The `during-login` option allows the user to receive a username and/or password prompt without pressing the return key. After the user logs in, the autoselect function begins.

```
AS2511#conf t
Enter configuration commands, one per line.  End with CNTL/Z.
AS2511(config)#int async 1
AS2511(config-if)#async mode interactive
AAS2511(config-if)#line 1
```

```
AS2511(config-line)#autoselect ppp
AS2511(config-line)#autoselect during-login
AS2511(config-line)#^Z
AS2511#
```

We now have a fully functioning access-server connection that permits both asynchronous terminal sessions for router management, and dial-in TCP/IP sessions to gain access to the rest of the network.

To test our active PPP connection, let's **telnet** to the Ethernet 0 IP address 172.31.22.210. In Windows 95/98, select Start and then Run to activate the test (see Figure 4-16).

The complete Cisco 2511 configuration for PPP dial-in and asynchronous terminal dial-in follows in Code Listing 4-2.

Code Listing 4-2
AS2511 configured for asynchronous and PPP connections.

```
1    AS2511#sho run
2    Building configuration...
3
4    Current configuration:
5    !
6    version 11.3
7    service timestamps debug uptime
8    service timestamps log uptime
9    no service password-encryption
10   !
11   hostname AS2511
12   !
13   enable password san-fran
14   !
15   username bill password 0 cisco
16   modemcap entry usr_new:FD=&F1:TPL=usr_sportster
17   !
18   !
19   !
```

Figure 4-16
Telnet activation in Windows 95/98.

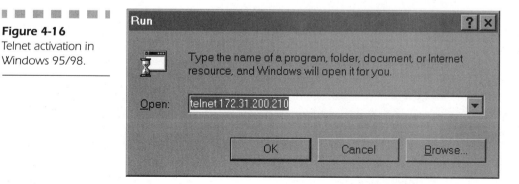

```
20  interface Ethernet0
21   ip address 172.31.200.210 255.255.255.0
22  shutdown
23  !
24  interface Serial0
25   no ip address
26   no ip mroute-cache
27   shutdown
28  !
29  interface Serial1
30   no ip address
31   shutdown
32  !
33  interface Async1
34   ip unnumbered Ethernet0
35   encapsulation ppp
36   async mode interactive
37   peer default ip address 172.31.200.100
38   ppp authentication chap callin
39  !
40  ip classless
41  !
42  !
43  !
44  line con 0
45   exec-timeout 0 0
46   logging synchronous
47   length 0
48  line 1
49   password cisco
50   autoselect during-login
51   autoselect ppp
52   login
53   modem InOut
54   modem autoconfigure type usr_sportster
55   transport input all
56   stopbits 1
57   speed 115200
58   flowcontrol hardware
59  line 2 16
60  line aux 0
61  line vty 0 4
62   password cisco
63   login
64  !
65  end
```

PPP Multilink

PPP Multilink is a terrific way for the remote user to increase the throughput for dial-in users. Adding a second modem to the dial-in process can double the normal dial-in throughput. In the Dial-Up Networking window (see Figure 4-17), select the icon that will be used for PPP Multilink. We will select PPP Dial IN from the icons displayed. An external COMPAQ Microcom 415 modem with a built-in speakerphone is used in this example. This is a great option for folks with a home office, as the second line can be used for regular voice calls while the primary line is on a data call.

When the dial-in access icon is selected, press the right mouse button and select Properties from the menu displayed. When the Properties window pops up, select the Multilink section to add in our Microcom modem (see Figure 4-18). Select Use additional devices, and then add the additional device from the list of available devices. If there are additional devices available, you can extend this Multilink process by adding more modems.

Code Listing 4-3 shows our PPP Multilink configuration on the Cisco 2511. Let's take a look at the significant parts of the configuration.

Line 10 is one of the keys to successful operation, the authentication information, where `bill` is the user logging in with a password of `cisco`.

There are three different components of our PPP multilink connection: `line 1` and `line 2` for the physical connection characteristics, interfaces `async1` and `async 2` as the logical interfaces to be assigned to our third component, and `interface dialer1`.

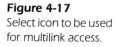

Figure 4-17
Select icon to be used for multilink access.

Figure 4-18
Adding a second
modem to the PPP
dial IN connection.

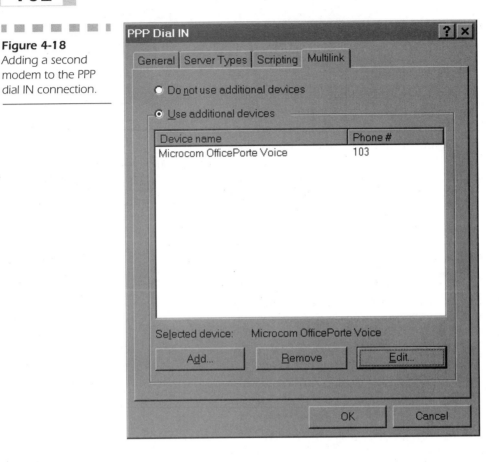

Figure 4-19
PPP multilink equip-
ment layout.

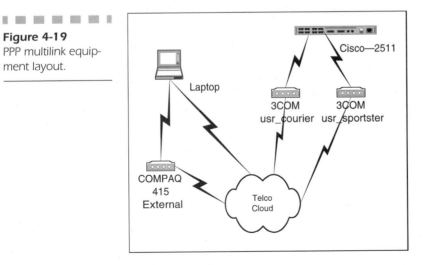

Lines 63 through 84 define the two lines that define the physical connection characteristics used to connect our two modems into the Cisco 2511.

Lines 19 through 37 define the two asynchronous interfaces used to create our multilink access. Lines 23 and 37 define these interfaces as a member of rotary-group 1. Notice that, except for `autoselect ppp` in lines 66 and 77, there is no indication that we will be creating a PPP multilink connection.

Lines 39 through 51 define `interface Dialer1`, the focus of our rotary-group commands defined in our asynchronous interfaces.

Line 40 eliminates the use of a specific IP address for this interface and lets the Cisco 2511 borrow the IP address of the Ethernet interface when sourcing IP packets from the dialer interface.

Lines 40, 50, and 51 define our PPP environment for encapsulation, authentication, and multilink.

Line 44, `dialer in-band`, is the key to making sure that any modem signaling is recognized by the dialer interface.

FYI *The command* **dialer in-band** *must be applied to any interface that does not have direct access to an out-of-band signaling method such as ISDN Basic or Primary Rate Interface.*

Line 46 defines the threshold level, 10, and traffic direction, either, used to trigger a second circuit on our PPP multilink connection. The threshold level of 10 means that 10/255 is applied to the bandwidth of the dialer interface. For example, if the bandwidth of the dialer interface is defined as 64,000 bits per second, the threshold level of 10 will trigger a call when the traffic in either direction reaches 2,510 bits per second (64000 * 10/255 = 2510).

Line 47, `dialer-group 1`, will be covered in Chapter 5.

Line 48 defines the method used for assigning IP addresses to dial-in clients, a local pool of IP addresses.

Line 53 sets up our pool of IP addresses. These addresses get used in an unusual way, as we will see later on in this example.

Code Listing 4-3

```
1    version 11.3
2    service timestamps debug uptime
3    service timestamps log uptime
4    no service password-encryption
5    !
6    hostname AS2511
7    !
8    enable password san-fran
9    !
10   username bill password 0 cisco
11   no ip domain-lookup
12   ip host AS2511 172.31.200.210
13   modemcap entry usr_new:FD=&F1:TPL=usr_sportster
14   !
15   interface Ethernet0
16    ip address 144.251.100.101 255.255.255.0 secondary
17    ip address 172.31.200.210 255.255.255.0
18   !
19   interface Async1
20    ip unnumbered Ethernet0
21    encapsulation ppp
22    dialer in-band
23    dialer rotary-group 1
24    dialer-group 1
25    async mode interactive
26    no fair-queue
27    no cdp enable
28   !
29   interface Async2
30    ip unnumbered Ethernet0
31    encapsulation ppp
32    dialer in-band
33    dialer rotary-group 1
34    dialer-group 1
35    async mode interactive
36    no fair-queue
37    no cdp enable
38   !
39   interface Dialer1
40    ip unnumbered Ethernet0
41    encapsulation ppp
42    no ip route-cache
43    no ip mroute-cache
44    dialer in-band
45    dialer string 116
46    dialer load-threshold 10 either
47    dialer-group 1
48    peer default ip address pool asyncpool
49    no cdp enable
50    ppp authentication chap callin
51    ppp multilink
52   !
53   ip local pool asyncpool 172.31.200.100 172.31.200.110
54   ip classless
55   !
56   logging buffered 64000 debugging
57   dialer-list 1 protocol ip permit
58   !
```

```
59  line con 0
60    exec-timeout 0 0
61    logging synchronous
62    length 0
63  line 1
64    password cisco
65    autoselect during-login
66    autoselect ppp
67    login
68    modem InOut
69    modem autoconfigure type usr_sportster
70    transport input all
71    stopbits 1
72    speed 115200
73    flowcontrol hardware
74  line 2
75    password cisco
76    autoselect during-login
77    autoselect ppp
78    login
79    modem InOut
80    modem autoconfigure type usr_courier
81    transport input all
82    stopbits 1
83    speed 115200
84    flowcontrol hardware
85  line 3 16
86  line aux 0
87  line vty 0 4
88    exec-timeout 0 0
89    password cisco
90    login
91  !
92  end
```

Let's take a look at the output of **debug PPP negotiation** to see how PPP multilink becomes active.

The first difference shows up right away: 172.31.200.105 is being assigned to dialer 1 as our Async2 (As2) interface becomes active, even though this is not the first address in our address pool (more on this later).

```
AS2511#
00:32:46: Di1 IPCP: Install route to 172.31.200.105
00:32:48: %LINK-3-UPDOWN: Interface Async2, changed state to up
```

The call is being processed as a callin, and the Cisco 2511 is waiting for initial negotiations from the dial-in client.

```
00:32:48: As2 PPP: Treating connection as a callin
00:32:48: As2 PPP: Phase is ESTABLISHING, Passive Open
00:32:48: As2 LCP: State is Listen
```

The first attempt at negotiation from the client looks similar to our previous encounters with PPP, with the exception of MRRU 1500. This is the option that identifies a request for PPP multilink and specifies the Maximum Transport Unit (MTU) that it can process. Both sides must agree to multilink in order to activate this feature.

```
00:32:49: As2 LCP: I CONFREQ [Listen] id 3 len 46
00:32:49: As2 LCP:    ACCM 0x000A0000 (0x0206000A0000)
00:32:49: As2 LCP:    MagicNumber 0x00BF0743 (0x050600BF0743)
00:32:49: As2 LCP:    PFC (0x0702)
00:32:49: As2 LCP:    ACFC (0x0802)
00:32:49: As2 LCP:    Callback 6 (0x0D0306)
00:32:49: As2 LCP:    MRRU 1500 (0x110405DC)
00:32:49: As2 LCP:    EndpointDisc 1 Local
00:32:49: As2 LCP:    (0x131301300373C14207BF00F0C661C13A)
00:32:49: As2 LCP:    (0x0B0000)
```

We also need to send out our PPP negotiation options to the dial-in client, including our MRRU, to indicate PPP multilink and define our MTU.

```
00:32:49: As2 LCP: O CONFREQ [Listen] id 3 len 38
00:32:49: As2 LCP:    ACCM 0x000A0000 (0x0206000A0000)
00:32:49: As2 LCP:    AuthProto CHAP (0x0305C22305)
00:32:49: As2 LCP:    MagicNumber 0x1099F5BF (0x05061099F5BF)
00:32:49: As2 LCP:    PFC (0x0702)
00:32:49: As2 LCP:    ACFC (0x0802)
00:32:49: As2 LCP:    MRRU 1524 (0x110405F4)
00:32:49: As2 LCP:    EndpointDisc 1 Local (0x130901415332353131)
```

The Cisco 2511 rejects the dial-in client's request for callback.

```
00:32:49: As2 LCP: O CONFREJ [Listen] id 3 len 7
00:32:49: As2 LCP:    Callback 6 (0x0D0306)
```

The dial-in client responds to our configuration request with an acknowledgment.

```
00:32:49: As2 LCP: I CONFACK [REQsent] id 3 len 38
00:32:49: As2 LCP:    ACCM 0x000A0000 (0x0206000A0000)
00:32:49: As2 LCP:    AuthProto CHAP (0x0305C22305)
00:32:49: As2 LCP:    MagicNumber 0x1099F5BF (0x05061099F5BF)
00:32:49: As2 LCP:    PFC (0x0702)
00:32:49: As2 LCP:    ACFC (0x0802)
```

```
00:32:49: As2 LCP:      MRRU 1524 (0x110405F4)
00:32:49: As2 LCP:      EndpointDisc 1 Local (0x130901415332353131)
```

After we reject the callback option, the dial-in client sends back a new
configuration request without the callback option.

```
00:32:49: As2 LCP: I CONFREQ [ACKrcvd] id 4 len 43
00:32:49: As2 LCP:      ACCM 0x000A0000 (0x0206000A0000)
00:32:49: As2 LCP:      MagicNumber 0x00BF0743 (0x050600BF0743)
00:32:49: As2 LCP:      PFC (0x0702)
00:32:49: As2 LCP:      ACFC (0x0802)
00:32:49: As2 LCP:      MRRU 1500 (0x110405DC)
00:32:49: As2 LCP:      EndpointDisc 1 Local
00:32:49: As2 LCP:        (0x131301300373C14207BF00F0C661C13A)
00:32:49: As2 LCP:        (0x0B0000)
```

As the Cisco 2511 has no objections, it acknowledges the configuration
request.

```
00:32:49: As2 LCP: O CONFACK [ACKrcvd] id 4 len 43
00:32:49: As2 LCP:      ACCM 0x000A0000 (0x0206000A0000)
00:32:49: As2 LCP:      MagicNumber 0x00BF0743 (0x050600BF0743)
00:32:49: As2 LCP:      PFC (0x0702)
00:32:49: As2 LCP:      ACFC (0x0802)
00:32:49: As2 LCP:      MRRU 1500 (0x110405DC)
00:32:49: As2 LCP:      EndpointDisc 1 Local
00:32:49: As2 LCP:        (0x131301300373C14207BF00F0C661C13A)
00:32:49: As2 LCP:        (0x0B0000)
```

LCP negotiation is complete, and the Cisco 2511 moves to the open
state and begins the authentication process. The authentication is successful, and we move to the next phase in our multilink process.

```
00:32:49: As2 LCP: State is Open
00:32:49: As2 PPP: Phase is AUTHENTICATING, by this end
00:32:49: As2 CHAP: O CHALLENGE id 3 len 27 from "AS2511"
00:32:50: As2 CHAP: I RESPONSE id 3 len 25 from "bill"
00:32:50: As2 CHAP: O SUCCESS id 3 len 4
```

This is where we step into new territory. Instead of the normal NCP
negotiation phase, PPP begins processing the multilink process. As the
call to Async2 is the first connection in our multilink process, we need to
establish a bundle based on the user who dialed in. We will build a Virtual Access interface that will tie together all the individual calls
arriving at the Cisco 2511 into a single call.

```
00:32:50: As2 PPP: Phase is VIRTUALIZED
00:32:50: Vi1 PPP: Phase is DOWN, Setup
00:32:50: %LINK-3-UPDOWN: Interface Virtual-Access1, changed state to up
00:32:50: Vi1 PPP: Treating connection as a callin
00:32:50: Vi1 PPP: Phase is ESTABLISHING, Passive Open
00:32:50: Vi1 LCP: State is Listen
00:32:50: Vi1 PPP: Phase is UP
```

Interface Virtual-Access1 is active through the authentication phase and is ready to negotiate the NCPs.

For clarity, we will examine only the output generated by the IP Control Protocol (IPCP). We start negotiating our IP addressing by sending out our IP address (the IP address of our Ethernet interface).

```
00:32:50: Vi1 IPCP: O CONFREQ [Closed] id 1 len 10
00:32:50: Vi1 IPCP:    Address 172.31.200.210 (0x0306AC1FC8D2)
```

PPP assigned an IP address to Async2 during the startup phase, but as we have built a virtual interface, we need to remove this address from the routing table before we negotiate the IP address that will be used for our multilink connection.

```
00:32:50: Di1 IPCP: Remove route to 172.31.200.105
```

Now we start the IPCP negotiation by getting a request from the dial-in client for IP addressing.

```
00:32:50: Vi1 IPCP: I CONFREQ [REQsent] id 1 len 40
00:32:50: Vi1 IPCP:    CompressType VJ 15 slots CompressSlotID (0x0206002D0F01)
00:32:50: Vi1 IPCP:    Address 0.0.0.0 (0x030600000000)
00:32:50: Vi1 IPCP:    PrimaryDNS 0.0.0.0 (0x810600000000)
00:32:50: Vi1 IPCP:    PrimaryWINS 0.0.0.0 (0x820600000000)
00:32:50: Vi1 IPCP:    SecondaryDNS 0.0.0.0 (0x830600000000)
00:32:50: Vi1 IPCP:    SecondaryWINS 0.0.0.0 (0x840600000000)
```

The address request that the virtual interface will respond to is a request for an address of 0.0.0.0, not the full DHCP setup above. The dialer interface assigned the local address pool asyncpool to hand out IP addresses to dial-in clients. The address 172.31.200.101 has been assigned to our multilink connection.

```
00:32:50: Vi1 IPCP: Using pool 'asyncpool'
00:32:50: Vi1 IPCP: Pool returned 172.31.200.101
```

The Cisco 2511 rejects the dial-in request for IP address assignment.

```
00:32:50: Vi1 IPCP: O CONFREJ [REQsent] id 1 len 34
00:32:50: Vi1 IPCP:    CompressType VJ 15 slots CompressSlotID (0x0206002D0F01)
00:32:50: Vi1 IPCP:    PrimaryDNS 0.0.0.0 (0x810600000000)
00:32:50: Vi1 IPCP:    PrimaryWINS 0.0.0.0 (0x820600000000)
00:32:50: Vi1 IPCP:    SecondaryDNS 0.0.0.0 (0x830600000000)
00:32:50: Vi1 IPCP:    SecondaryWINS 0.0.0.0 (0x840600000000)
```

Then the dial-in client requests Microsoft PPP Compression, but compression is not supported by the Cisco 2511. With the asynchronous connections, compression is used to achieve the higher throughput of modern modems, and additional compression will not significantly improve performance.

```
00:32:50: Vi1 CCP: I CONFREQ [Not negotiated] id 1 len 15
00:32:50: Vi1 CCP:    MS-PPC supported bits 0x00000001(0x120600000001)
00:32:50: Vi1 CCP:    Stacker history 1 check mode EXTENDED (0x1105000104)
00:32:50: Vi1 LCP: O PROTREJ [Open] id 1 len 21 protocol CCP
00:32:50: Vi1 LCP:    (0x80FD0101000F12060000000111050001)
00:32:50: Vi1 LCP:    (0x04)
```

The dial-in client acknowledges the original IP address request made by the Cisco 2511.

```
00:32:50: Vi1 IPCP: I CONFACK [REQsent] id 1 len 10
00:32:50: Vi1 IPCP:    Address 172.31.200.210 (0x0306AC1FC8D2)
```

The following messages let us know that the LCP phase of PPP has been recorded by the Cisco 2511, and interfaces `Async2` and `Virtual-Access1` are up at the data-link layer. Note that the `Dialer1` interface does not figure into this equation; it is used as a template for building the `Virtual-Access` interface.

```
00:32:52: %LINEPROTO-5-UPDOWN: Line protocol on Interface Async2, changed state to up
00:32:52: %LINEPROTO-5-UPDOWN: Line protocol on Interface Virtual-Access1, changed state
   to up
```

We have run out of time negotiating IPCP, so we must now start all over again.

```
00:32:53: Vi1 IPCP: TIMEout: Time 0x1E19B0 State ACKrcvd
```

First, we send out our address to the dial-in client, and it is accepted.

```
00:32:53: Vi1 IPCP: O CONFREQ [ACKrcvd] id 2 len 10
00:32:53: Vi1 IPCP:    Address 172.31.200.210 (0x0306AC1FC8D2)
00:32:53: Vi1 IPCP: I CONFACK [REQsent] id 2 len 10
00:32:53: Vi1 IPCP:    Address 172.31.200.210 (0x0306AC1FC8D2)
```

Next, we get the dial-in request for DHCP information that we reject in favor of a simple IP address.

```
00:32:53: Vi1 IPCP: I CONFREQ [ACKrcvd] id 2 len 34
00:32:53: Vi1 IPCP:    Address 0.0.0.0 (0x030600000000)
00:32:53: Vi1 IPCP:    PrimaryDNS 0.0.0.0 (0x810600000000)
00:32:53: Vi1 IPCP:    PrimaryWINS 0.0.0.0 (0x820600000000)
00:32:53: Vi1 IPCP:    SecondaryDNS 0.0.0.0 (0x830600000000)
00:32:53: Vi1 IPCP:    SecondaryWINS 0.0.0.0 (0x840600000000)
00:32:53: Vi1 IPCP: O CONFREJ [ACKrcvd] id 2 len 28
00:32:53: Vi1 IPCP:    PrimaryDNS 0.0.0.0 (0x810600000000)
00:32:53: Vi1 IPCP:    PrimaryWINS 0.0.0.0 (0x820600000000)
00:32:53: Vi1 IPCP:    SecondaryDNS 0.0.0.0 (0x830600000000)
00:32:53: Vi1 IPCP:    SecondaryWINS 0.0.0.0 (0x840600000000)
```

At last, the dial-in client has figured it out, and we get our request for an IP address. A request to recognize an IP address of 0.0.0.0 is a request for address assignment.

```
00:32:53: Vi1 IPCP: I CONFREQ [ACKrcvd] id 3 len 10
00:32:53: Vi1 IPCP:    Address 0.0.0.0 (0x030600000000)
```

In the negative acknowledgment (NAK) for recognition of address 0.0.0.0, the Cisco 2511 feeds back the address assigned from the local pool asyncpool.

```
00:32:53: Vi1 IPCP: O CONFNAK [ACKrcvd] id 3 len 10
00:32:53: Vi1 IPCP:    Address 172.31.200.101 (0x0306AC1FC865)
```

When the dial-in client comes back with the address the Cisco 2511 sent out in the NAK, then we accept the address 172.31.200.101.

```
00:32:53: Vi1 IPCP: I CONFREQ [ACKrcvd] id 4 len 10
00:32:53: Vi1 IPCP:    Address 172.31.200.101 (0x0306AC1FC865)
00:32:53: Vi1 IPCP: O CONFACK [ACKrcvd] id 4 len 10
00:32:53: Vi1 IPCP:    Address 172.31.200.101 (0x0306AC1FC865)
```

IPCP negotiation is now complete and becomes operational, and the dial-in address is added to the routing table.

```
00:32:53: Vi1 IPCP: State is Open
00:32:53: Di1 IPCP: Install route to 172.31.200.101
```

The first link in our multilink connection is now up and running. Either side in the multilink connection can trigger additional links to be bundled in with this first active link.

The dial-in client has called in on a second link, so let's follow the process of adding another link to our original multilink bundle.

Just as in our first link activation, we install a route and assign a temporary address through the `Dialer1` interface. Since the balance of the PPP negotiation goes much like the original link as we bring up interface `Async1`, let's pick up the display starting with authentication. Authentication is the key to identifying an existing PPP multilink bundle.

```
00:33:19: Di1 IPCP: Install route to 172.31.200.106
00:33:21: %LINK-3-UPDOWN: Interface Async1, changed state to up
00:33:21: As1 PPP: Treating connection as a callin
00:33:21: As1 PPP: Phase is ESTABLISHING, Passive Open
00:33:21: As1 LCP: State is Listen
00:33:22: As1 LCP: I CONFREQ [Listen] id 3 len 46
.
. Output deleted for clarity.
.
00:33:23: As1 LCP:      (0x0B0000)
00:33:23: As1 LCP: State is Open
00:33:23: As1 PPP: Phase is AUTHENTICATING, by this end
00:33:23: As1 CHAP: O CHALLENGE id 3 len 27 from "AS2511"
00:33:23: As1 CHAP: I RESPONSE id 3 len 25 from "bill"
00:33:23: As1 CHAP: O SUCCESS id 3 len 4
```

With successful authentication we attach the new link to our virtual interface and remove the temporary route to `172.31.200.106`; the `Async1` interface changes state to up. There is nothing else that lets us know what is happening.

```
00:33:23: As1 PPP: Phase is VIRTUALIZED
00:33:23: Di1 IPCP: Remove route to 172.31.200.106
00:33:24: %LINEPROTO-5-UPDOWN: Line protocol on Interface Async1, changed state to up
```

We can use the **debug ppp multilink events** command to watch each individual step of multilink operation. See Code Listing 4-4 for the details.

Lines 4 and 5 show the process of cloning the Virtual-Access1 interface from the Dialer1 interface we created in the Cisco 2511 configuration.

Line 7 shows us that the first active link for this multilink (MLP) connection is `Async2`, with the bundle `bill`.

Lines 11 and 12 show a second connection from Async1 being added to the existing multilink bundle bill.

■ ■

Code Listing 4-4

```
1   AS2511#debug ppp multilink events
2   Multilink events debugging is on
3   AS2511#
4   0:43:05: Vi1 MLP: Added to huntgroup Di1
5   00:43:05: Vi1 MLP: Clone from Di1
6   00:43:05: %LINK-3-UPDOWN: Interface Virtual-Access1, changed
    state to up
7   00:43:05: As2 MLP: bill, multilink up, first link
8   00:43:05: %LINEPROTO-5-UPDOWN: Line protocol on Interface Async2,
    changed state to up
9   00:43:05: %LINEPROTO-5-UPDOWN: Line protocol on Interface
    Virtual-Access1, changed state to up
10  00:43:36: %LINK-3-UPDOWN: Interface Async1, changed state to up
11  00:43:37: As1 MLP: Multilink up event pending
12  00:43:37: As1 MLP: bill, multilink up
13  00:43:38: %LINEPROTO-5-UPDOWN: Line protocol on Interface Async1,
    changed state to up
```

The following is the continuation of the call above and documents the multilink events as the connection is terminated.

```
00:44:05: bill MLP: Bundle reset
00:44:05: As1 MLP: Multilink down event pending
00:44:05: As1 MLP: Multilink down event pending
00:44:05: As2 MLP: Multilink down event pending
00:44:05: As2 MLP: Multilink down event pending
00:44:05: As1 MLP: Removing link from bill
00:44:05: As2 MLP: Removing link from bill
00:44:05: bill MLP: Removing bundle
00:44:05: %LINK-3-UPDOWN: Interface Virtual-Access1, changed state to down
00:44:05: %LINEPROTO-5-UPDOWN: Line protocol on Interface Async1, changed state to down
00:44:05: %LINEPROTO-5-UPDOWN: Line protocol on Interface Async2, changed state to down
00:44:05: %LINEPROTO-5-UPDOWN: Line protocol on Interface Virtual-Access1, changed state
    to down
00:44:07: %LINK-5-CHANGED: Interface Async2, changed state to reset
00:44:07: %LINK-5-CHANGED: Interface Async1, changed state to reset
00:44:12: %LINK-3-UPDOWN: Interface Async2, changed state to down
00:44:12: %LINK-3-UPDOWN: Interface Async1, changed state to down
AS2511#
```

Next we need to take a look at the how the data gets transmitted over the multilink connection with single and multiple pathways. To see multilink in operation, we will use the **debug ppp multilink fragments** command. There will be quite a lot of debug output, so make sure that you limit the use of this command in a production environment.

```
AS2511#debug ppp multilink fragments
Multilink fragments debugging is on
00:44:54: %LINK-3-UPDOWN: Interface Async2, changed state to up
00:44:55: %LINK-3-UPDOWN: Interface Virtual-Access1, changed state to up
00:44:56: %LINEPROTO-5-UPDOWN: Line protocol on Interface Async2, changed state to up
00:44:56: %LINEPROTO-5-UPDOWN: Line protocol on Interface Virtual-Access1, changed state
    to up
```

The first link is up, and we see a series of incoming messages (pings) coming from our dial-in client, but not one outgoing message. In this case, none of the messages we need to send back are considered candidates for the fragmentation being performed by the Microsoft dial-in client. Microsoft deals with PPP multilink in a different manner than Cisco does. Microsoft takes a stream of data heading out an interface and aggregates the messages into packets. Cisco does not perform any special function for packets below a certain size.

```
00:45:00: As2 MLP: I seq C0000000 size 34
00:45:00: As2 MLP: I seq C0000001 size 102
00:45:00: As2 MLP: I seq C0000002 size 102
00:45:00: As2 MLP: I seq C0000003 size 102
00:45:01: As2 MLP: I seq C0000004 size 102
00:45:01: As2 MLP: I seq C0000005 size 102
00:45:01: As2 MLP: I seq C0000006 size 102
00:45:02: As2 MLP: I seq C0000007 size 102
00:45:02: As2 MLP: I seq C0000008 size 102
00:45:02: As2 MLP: I seq C0000009 size 102
00:45:03: As2 MLP: I seq C000000A size 34
00:45:03: As2 MLP: I seq C000000B size 102
00:45:03: As2 MLP: I seq C000000C size 102
00:45:03: As2 MLP: I seq C000000D size 102
00:45:07: As2 MLP: I seq C000000E size 34
```

Now let's add in a second link to our multilink connection and see what happens. All of a sudden we are seeing individual packets coming in and being responded to over each of the active links in our multilink bundle.

```
00:45:42: As2 MLP: I seq C000000F size 66
00:45:42: As2 MLP: O seq C0000000 size 70
00:45:43: As1 MLP: I seq C0000010 size 66
00:45:43: As1 MLP: O seq C0000001 size 70
        .
        . Sequence deleted for clarity
        .
00:45:51: As1 MLP: I seq C0000018 size 66
00:45:51: As1 MLP: O seq C0000009 size 70
```

■ ■

FYI A quick word on the PPP multilink sequence numbers: All the sequence numbers start with a "C", which should be explained. Hex "C" is 1100 in binary. In multilink packets, the first hex digit is BEXX, where the B bit indicates the first fragment in a sequence of fragments, and the E bit indicates the last fragment in a sequence of fragments. Both bits set to one in the same sequence number indicates that beginning and ending fragments exist in the same transmission. Microsoft fragments always have a sequence starting with a "C".

Let's throw in a mix of large and small packets and see how the Cisco router deals with the traffic mix. We start with small-sized packets and add larger packets later.

```
00:46:39: As2 MLP: I seq C0000000 size 34
00:46:41: As2 MLP: I seq C0000001 size 102
00:46:41: As2 MLP: I seq C0000002 size 102
       .
       .
       .
00:46:43: As2 MLP: I seq C000000D size 102
00:46:46: As2 MLP: I seq C000000E size 34
```

Now the large packets start, and the second link comes up midstream. Notice that Cisco does not start fragmenting packets until the second link comes up. Again, Microsoft marks each packet as complete—with B and E bits both set—but Cisco marks packets with B, E, or both.

```
00:47:08: %LINK-3-UPDOWN: Interface Async1, changed state to up
00:47:09: As2 MLP: I seq C000000F size 578
00:47:09: As2 MLP: I seq C0000010 size 578
00:47:09: As2 MLP: I seq C0000011 size 430
00:47:09: %LINEPROTO-5-UPDOWN: Line protocol on Interface Async1, changed state to up
00:47:10: As2 MLP: I seq C0000012 size 578
00:47:10: As2 MLP: I seq C0000013 size 578
00:47:10: As1 MLP: I seq C0000014 size 430
00:47:10: As2 MLP: O seq 80000000 size 758
00:47:10: As1 MLP: O seq 40000001 size 760
00:47:10: As2 MLP: O seq C0000002 size 58
00:47:11: As2 MLP: I seq C0000015 size 578
00:47:11: As1 MLP: I seq C0000016 size 578
00:47:11: As1 MLP: I seq C0000017 size 430
00:47:11: As1 MLP: O seq 80000003 size 758
00:47:11: As2 MLP: O seq 40000004 size 760
00:47:11: As1 MLP: O seq C0000005 size 58
00:47:12: As2 MLP: I seq C0000018 size 578
00:47:12: As1 MLP: I seq C0000019 size 578
00:47:12: As1 MLP: I seq C000001A size 430
00:47:12: As2 MLP: O seq 80000006 size 758
```

```
00:47:12: As1 MLP: O seq 40000007 size 760
00:47:12: As2 MLP: O seq C0000008 size 58
```

Let's add **debug ip icmp** to the mix and watch a short sample of the output when the client pings the Cisco 2511. Note the mix of traffic going across the two active links.

```
AS2511#debug ip icmp
ICMP packet debugging is on
00:55:30: As2 MLP: I seq C0000025 size 66
00:55:30: ICMP: echo reply sent, src 172.31.200.210, dst 172.31.200.101
00:55:30: As2 MLP: O seq C0000016 size 70
00:55:31: As1 MLP: I seq C0000026 size 66
00:55:31: ICMP: echo reply sent, src 172.31.200.210, dst 172.31.200.101
00:55:31: As1 MLP: O seq C0000017 size 70
00:55:32: As2 MLP: I seq C0000027 size 66
00:55:32: ICMP: echo reply sent, src 172.31.200.210, dst 172.31.200.101
00:55:32: As2 MLP: O seq C0000018 size 70
.
. Output deleted for clarity.
.
00:55:41: As2 MLP: I seq C000002F size 578
00:55:41: As1 MLP: I seq C0000030 size 578
00:55:41: As1 MLP: I seq C0000031 size 430
00:55:41: ICMP: echo reply sent, src 172.31.200.210, dst 172.31.200.101
00:55:41: As2 MLP: O seq 80000020 size 758
00:55:41: As1 MLP: O seq 40000021 size 760
00:55:41: As2 MLP: O seq C0000022 size 58
00:55:42: As2 MLP: I seq C0000032 size 578
00:55:42: As1 MLP: I seq C0000033 size 578
00:55:42: As1 MLP: I seq C0000034 size 430
00:55:42: ICMP: echo reply sent, src 172.31.200.210, dst 172.31.200.101
00:55:42: As1 MLP: O seq 80000023 size 758
00:55:42: As2 MLP: O seq 40000024 size 760
00:55:42: As1 MLP: O seq C0000025 size 58
```

There are many **show** commands that can help us see what components are active with our PPP multilink connection.

The **show ppp multilink** command output follows. The master link that controls the multilink connection is Virtual-Access1, a dynamic interface cloned from the Dialer1 interface created in our Cisco 2511. The bundle created from the dial-in client is bill, and there are two active links, Async1 and Async2.

```
AS2511#show ppp multilink

Bundle bill, 2 members, Master link is Virtual-Access1
Dialer Interface is Dialer1
  0 lost fragments, 0 reordered, 0 unassigned, sequence 0x3F/0x11 rcvd/sent
  0 discarded, 0 lost received, 1/255 load
```

```
Member Links: 2 (max not set, min not set)
Async1
Async2
AS2511#
```

The **show dialer** command output follows. It shows the status of each of the links, Async1 and Async2, the rotary group, their status as multilink members, and which bundle they were a part of. Interface Dialer1 is our template for building the virtual access interface and details the threshold that will trigger additional calls.

```
AS2511#show dialer

Async1 - dialer type = IN-BAND ASYNC NO-PARITY
Rotary group 1, priority 0
Idle timer (120 secs), Fast idle timer (20 secs)
Wait for carrier (30 secs), Re-enable (15 secs)
Dialer state is multilink member
Current call connected never
Connected to 116 (bill)

Async2 - dialer type = IN-BAND ASYNC NO-PARITY
Rotary group 1, priority 0
Idle timer (120 secs), Fast idle timer (20 secs)
Wait for carrier (30 secs), Re-enable (15 secs)
Dialer state is multilink member
Current call connected never
Connected to 116 (bill)

Dialer1 - dialer type = IN-BAND SYNC NO-PARITY
Load threshold for dialing additional calls is 10
Idle timer (120 secs), Fast idle timer (20 secs)
Wait for carrier (30 secs), Re-enable (15 secs)

Dial String      Successes   Failures   Last called   Last status
116              0           1          never     -    Default
```

Next we have the **show ip route** command output. The following identifies the dial-in client using a host route to the dial-in client through the Dialer1 interface.

```
AS2511#show ip route
Codes: C - connected, S - static, I - IGRP, R - RIP, M - mobile, B - BGP
       D - EIGRP, EX - EIGRP external, O - OSPF, IA - OSPF inter area
       N1 - OSPF NSSA external type 1, N2 - OSPF NSSA external type 2
       E1 - OSPF external type 1, E2 - OSPF external type 2, E - EGP
       i - IS-IS, L1 - IS-IS level-1, L2 - IS-IS level-2, * - candidate default
       U - per-user static route, o - ODR

Gateway of last resort is not set

     172.31.0.0/16 is variably subnetted, 2 subnets, 2 masks
```

```
C        172.31.200.101/32 is directly connected, Dialer1
C        172.31.200.0/24 is directly connected, Ethernet0
     144.251.0.0/24 is subnetted, 1 subnets
C        144.251.100.0 is directly connected, Ethernet0
```

This is the starting point for PPP multilink, and we will explore this more when we start configuring Integrated Service Digital Network (ISDN).

Troubleshooting Techniques

There are two major areas that will be troubleshooting targets when configuring dial-in PPP connections on a Cisco router/access server: IP address assignment and authentication.

Make sure when allocating an IP address that the address space used for dial-in connections is part of the normal intranetwork address space. If devices in the network have no routes in their routing table to the dial-in addresses, the dial-in clients will be able to establish a connection to the access server but not be able to connect to network services.

Authentication is one of the areas in which it is easy to encounter problems. Later in the book we will review the use of TACACS+ and RADIUS servers to provide centralized authentication.

You can successfully troubleshoot both of these areas with the **debug ppp negotiation** command.

The other area where problems can occur is the configuration of the dial-in client software. In this chapter, we reviewed the server-type misconfiguration and authentication errors.

Summary

In this chapter, we explored dial-in PPP connections. These dial-in connections are the first IP connections we have explored in the book, and are among the most common connections used today in dial-in IP networking.

Dial-on-Demand Routing

Dial-on-demand routing (DDR) uses some of the lessons we learned in earlier chapters as a basis for establishing router-to-router communications to transport IP traffic across dial connections as needed. While the last chapter dealt with IP addresses at the edge of the network, Dial-on-Demand routing gets us right into the core.

This is the chapter where we begin the process of connecting remote sites to our central or core network. In later chapters we will use other techniques, but for now we are going to stick with basic asynchronous communications to provide remote routed network connectivity. Most people look at asynchronous communications as a very slow method for communicating, but in many areas in the United States and many countries outside the United States, there are no other options.

Most of the texts and courses start discussing the DDR process after the packet in question has arrived at the interface where the dialing connection is to take place; but it starts one step earlier with packet routing. Don't forget that DDR starts with one important concept, routing.

Routing

The use of dynamic routing protocols is common in most corporate networks, but these dynamic protocols require constant communications between peers. Hmmm, constant communications and dial-on-demand—two terms that don't seem to go together. Static routes may be more appropriate to handle dial-on-demand processing. If we look at a routing table, the way to reach a destination network has two components: the router exit interface and the next hop address. This is one of the most overlooked points when problems arise in DDR configurations. Table 5-1 defines the three methods used to define static routes.

Remember that remote sites need access to central or core services anywhere on the network. The best way to set up the remote site for access to the rest of the network is to use a default static route. Use the appropriate format of static route from Table 5-1 to direct all traffic to the core network using a destination network of 0.0.0.0 with a mask of 0.0.0.0.

TABLE 5-1

Command	Description
ip route 172.31.200.0 255.255.255.0 Async1	Sends all packets with a destination IP address on the 172.31.200.0 network to the Async1 interface
ip route 172.31.200.0 255.255.255.0 172.31.222.2	Sends all packets with a destination IP address on the 172.31.200.0 network to the next hop address, 172.31.222.2
ip route 172.31.200.0 255.255.255.0 Async1 172.31.222.2	This is a combination command that provides both pieces of information needed to reach destination network 172.31.200.0, the exit interface, and next hop address.

Interesting Traffic

Once traffic is directed to an interface, it is now time to decide whether the traffic headed out that interface is interesting enough to trigger a call. Interesting traffic is defined using two commands: **dialer-list**, which contains the rules; and **dialer-group**, which assigns the rules to an interface. These same commands keep track of the interesting traffic traveling across the dial connection, in order to keep the circuit up. Both sides of a dial connection must agree on the set of rules used to complete and maintain calls. If the two sides do not agree, then communications may be interrupted. Table 5-2 describes the command formats.

TABLE 5-2

Command	Description
dialer-list 1 protocol ip permit	This format is terrific for testing dial access, because all protocol traffic is interesting.
dialer-list 1 protocol ip permit list 101	This format defines the specific traffic to be used to trigger calls for IP traffic.
dialer-list 1 list 101	This format is an older version of the preceding command.
dialer-group 1	This command assigns the rules to an interface.

Address Resolution

This function in DDR is performed statically. It would be great if we could Address Resolution Protocol (ARP) for a telephone number across the telephone network, but it would only work if we could call all the possible telephone numbers world-wide and ask each connection if it was the next hop address. The command used to perform this function is **dialer map**. Table 5-3 defines the options and format used.

A misconception about the **dialer map** command is that it maps the final protocol destination to a telephone number—not so! The **dialer map** command maps the next hop address to a telephone number. In order to reinforce how this works, we will run an experiment with static routes over Ethernet connections to illustrate the importance of next hop addresses. Figure 5-1 shows the network layout for this experiment.

Let's take a look at the AS2511-2 configuration in Code Listing 5-1. The loopback address 192.168.1.1 is going to be our target for this test. Line 9 is key to our test, as it disables the proxy arp feature activated by default in Cisco routers/access servers. Without this line, AS2511-2 would see an ARP request from AS2511-2 for 192.168.1.1 and respond with its own MAC address, as it knows how to reach our target.

TABLE 5-3

Command	Option	Description
dialer map	**protocol** *type next-hop*	*type* is the protocol, ip, ipx, appletalk, etc. *next-hop* is the network address of the destination router to dial to reach the destination.
	name *next-hop-name*	*next-hop-name* is the host name of the destination router. More on this later.
	broadcast	All dial interfaces belong to Non-Broadcast Multi-Access networks. In order for broadcasts to be transmitted across this connection, this option must be present.
	phone-number	Telephone number to reach the destination.

Figure 5-1
ARP experiment
equipment layout.

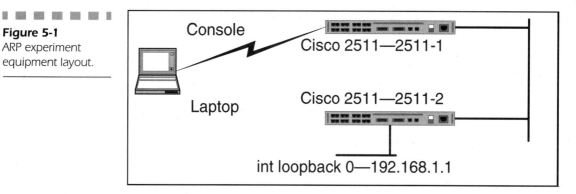

Console
Cisco 2511—2511-1

Laptop

Cisco 2511—2511-2

int loopback 0—192.168.1.1

Code Listing 5-1

```
1    !
2    hostname AS2511-2
3    !
4    interface Loopback0
5     ip address 192.168.1.1 255.255.255.0
6    !
7    interface Ethernet0
8     ip address 172.31.200.100 255.255.255.0
9     no ip proxy-arp
10   !
11   line con 0
12   line 1 16
13   line aux 0
14   line vty 0 4
15   !
16   end
```

Now let's look at the configuration for AS2511-1, the source system for our test, in Code Listing 5-2.

Code Listing 5-2

```
1    !
2    hostname AS2511-1
3    !
4    interface Ethernet0
5     ip address 172.31.200.110 255.255.255.0
6    !
7    line con 0
8    line 1 16
9    line aux 0
10   line vty 0 4
11   !
12   end
```

To see if we have a route to the target address of 192.168.1.1, use the **show ip route** command.

```
AS2511-1#show ip route
Codes: C - connected, S - static, I - IGRP, R - RIP, M - mobile, B - BGP
       D - EIGRP, EX - EIGRP external, O - OSPF, IA - OSPF inter area
       N1 - OSPF NSSA external type 1, N2 - OSPF NSSA external type 2
       E1 - OSPF external type 1, E2 - OSPF external type 2, E - EGP
       i - IS-IS, L1 - IS-IS level-1, L2 - IS-IS level-2, * - candidate default
       U - per-user static route, o - ODR

Gateway of last resort is not set

     172.31.0.0/24 is subnetted, 1 subnets
C       172.31.200.0 is directly connected, Ethernet0
AS2511-1#
```

There is no pathway to our target address, but let's try to **ping** the darn thing anyway.

```
AS2511-1#ping 192.168.1.1

Type escape sequence to abort.
Sending 5, 100-byte ICMP Echos to 192.168.1.1, timeout is 2 seconds:
.....
Success rate is 0 percent (0/5)
AS2511-1#
```

No, it didn't make it. The **show arp** command may help us out, so let's take a look.

```
AS2511-1#show arp
Protocol  Address          Age (min)  Hardware Addr   Type   Interface
Internet  172.31.200.110        -     0010.7be7.a085  ARPA   Ethernet0
Internet  172.31.200.100        3     0010.7be7.a080  ARPA   Ethernet0
AS2511-1#
```

There is nothing about our target address here, but we can reach AS2511-2 at 172.31.200.100. If we use the **debug ip packet** command, we can see why the **ping** packets are not reaching the target. Ah, it's unroutable. That makes sense—there is no entry in the routing table.

```
AS2511-1#debug ip packet
IP packet debugging is on
AS2511-1#ping 192.168.1.1

Type escape sequence to abort.
Sending 5, 100-byte ICMP Echos to 192.168.1.1, timeout is 2 seconds:
```

```
00:30:49: IP: s=172.31.200.110 (local), d=192.168.1.1, len 100, unroutable.
00:30:51: IP: s=172.31.200.110 (local), d=192.168.1.1, len 100, unroutable.
00:30:53: IP: s=172.31.200.110 (local), d=192.168.1.1, len 100, unroutable.
00:30:55: IP: s=172.31.200.110 (local), d=192.168.1.1, len 100, unroutable.
00:30:57: IP: s=172.31.200.110 (local), d=192.168.1.1, len 100, unroutable.
Success rate is 0 percent (0/5)
AS2511-1#
```

If we add a static route that points to `ethernet 0` we should be able to reach the target address.

```
AS2511-1#conf t
Enter configuration commands, one per line.  End with CNTL/Z.
AS2511-1(config)#ip route 192.168.1.0 255.255.255.0 ethernet 0
AS2511-1(config)#^Z
AS2511-1#
```

The **show ip route** command will show us if we have a pathway defined to the target address.

```
AS2511-1#show ip route
Codes: C - connected, S - static, I - IGRP, R - RIP, M - mobile, B - BGP
       D - EIGRP, EX - EIGRP external, O - OSPF, IA - OSPF inter area
       N1 - OSPF NSSA external type 1, N2 - OSPF NSSA external type 2
       E1 - OSPF external type 1, E2 - OSPF external type 2, E - EGP
       i - IS-IS, L1 - IS-IS level-1, L2 - IS-IS level-2, * - candidate default
       U - per-user static route, o - ODR

Gateway of last resort is not set

     172.31.0.0/24 is subnetted, 1 subnets
C       172.31.200.0 is directly connected, Ethernet0
S    192.168.1.0/24 is directly connected, Ethernet0
AS2511-1#
```

There is a pathway now, so we should be able to get to our target address. Let's **ping** away. The **debug ip packet** command is still active, so we should see success!

```
AS2511-1#ping 192.168.1.1

Type escape sequence to abort.
Sending 5, 100-byte ICMP Echos to 192.168.1.1, timeout is 2 seconds:

00:31:53: IP: s=172.31.200.110 (local), d=192.168.1.1 (Ethernet0), len 100, sending
00:31:53: IP: s=172.31.200.110 (local), d=192.168.1.1 (Ethernet0), len 100, encapsulation
    failed.
00:31:55: IP: s=172.31.200.110 (local), d=192.168.1.1 (Ethernet0), len 100, sending
00:31:55: IP: s=172.31.200.110 (local), d=192.168.1.1 (Ethernet0), len 100, encapsulation
    failed.
00:31:57: IP: s=172.31.200.110 (local), d=192.168.1.1 (Ethernet0), len 100, sending
```

```
00:31:57: IP: s=172.31.200.110 (local), d=192.168.1.1 (Ethernet0), len 100, encapsulation
  failed.
00:31:59: IP: s=172.31.200.110 (local), d=192.168.1.1 (Ethernet0), len 100, sending
00:31:59: IP: s=172.31.200.110 (local), d=192.168.1.1 (Ethernet0), len 100, encapsulation
  failed.
00:32:01: IP: s=172.31.200.110 (local), d=192.168.1.1 (Ethernet0), len 100, sending
00:32:01: IP: s=172.31.200.110 (local), d=192.168.1.1 (Ethernet0), len 100, encapsulation
  failed.
Success rate is 0 percent (0/5)
AS2511-1#
```

We failed again. There is a route to our destination, but when we tried to resolve the destination address with ARP, we failed and could not put our IP packets into a MAC frame. The **show arp** command still shows our original two partners on the Ethernet segment.

```
AS2511-1#show arp
Protocol  Address            Age (min)  Hardware Addr   Type   Interface
Internet  172.31.200.110            -    0010.7be7.a085  ARPA   Ethernet0
Internet  172.31.200.100            6    0010.7be7.a080  ARPA   Ethernet0
AS2511-1#
```

If we review the **show ip route** command above, we see that we have an exit interface to reach our destination, but there is no next hop address in the routing table. Let's make sure that we can still reach our next hop router with a **ping**. We sure can. Perhaps we should modify our static route entry.

```
AS2511-1#ping 172.31.200.100
Type escape sequence to abort.
Sending 5, 100-byte ICMP Echos to 172.31.200.100, timeout is 2 seconds:
!!!!!
Success rate is 100 percent (5/5), round-trip min/avg/max = 8/10/12 ms
AS2511-1#
00:32:48: IP: s=172.31.200.110 (local), d=172.31.200.100 (Ethernet0), len 100, sending
00:32:48: IP: s=172.31.200.100 (Ethernet0), d=172.31.200.110 (Ethernet0), len 100, rcvd 3
00:32:48: IP: s=172.31.200.110 (local), d=172.31.200.100 (Ethernet0), len 100, sending
00:32:48: IP: s=172.31.200.100 (Ethernet0), d=172.31.200.110 (Ethernet0), len 100, rcvd 3
00:32:48: IP: s=172.31.200.110 (local), d=172.31.200.100 (Ethernet0), len 100, sending
00:32:48: IP: s=172.31.200.100 (Ethernet0), d=172.31.200.110 (Ethernet0), len 100, rcvd 3
00:32:48: IP: s=172.31.200.110 (local), d=172.31.200.100 (Ethernet0), len 100, sending
00:32:48: IP: s=172.31.200.100 (Ethernet0), d=172.31.200.110 (Ethernet0), len 100, rcvd 3
00:32:48: IP: s=172.31.200.110 (local), d=172.31.200.100 (Ethernet0), len 100, sending
00:32:48: IP: s=172.31.200.100 (Ethernet0), d=172.31.200.110 (Ethernet0), len 100, rcvd 3
AS2511-1#
```

Instead of using the ethernet 0 interface as the target for the static route, we can use the next hop router's IP address.

```
AS2511-1#conf t
Enter configuration commands, one per line.  End with CNTL/Z.
AS2511-1(config)#ip route 192.168.1.0 255.255.255.0 172.31.200.100
AS2511-1(config)#^Z
AS2511-1#
```

We look at the **show ip route** command after the change to see if the route to our target IP address has changed. It has—instead of just the target interface in the routing table, we also have the next hop address of AS2511-2. Both the next hop address and the exit interface show up in the routing table, because the next hop address has an entry in the routing table.

```
AS2511-1#show ip route
Codes: C - connected, S - static, I - IGRP, R - RIP, M - mobile, B - BGP
       D - EIGRP, EX - EIGRP external, O - OSPF, IA - OSPF inter area
       N1 - OSPF NSSA external type 1, N2 - OSPF NSSA external type 2
       E1 - OSPF external type 1, E2 - OSPF external type 2, E - EGP
       i - IS-IS, L1 - IS-IS level-1, L2 - IS-IS level-2, * - candidate default
       U - per-user static route, o - ODR

Gateway of last resort is not set

     172.31.0.0/24 is subnetted, 1 subnets
C       172.31.200.0 is directly connected, Ethernet0
S    192.168.1.0/24 [1/0] via 172.31.200.100, Ethernet0
AS2511-1#
```

It's **ping** time. We should be successful now that we have both components in place to reach our destination: exit interface, and next hop address.

```
AS2511-1#ping 192.168.1.1

Type escape sequence to abort.
Sending 5, 100-byte ICMP Echos to 192.168.1.1, timeout is 2 seconds:
!!!!!
Success rate is 100 percent (5/5), round-trip min/avg/max = 8/10/12 ms
AS2511-1#
00:33:54: IP: s=172.31.200.110 (local), d=192.168.1.1 (Ethernet0), len 100, sending
00:33:54: IP: s=192.168.1.1 (Ethernet0), d=172.31.200.110 (Ethernet0), len 100, rcvd 3
00:33:54: IP: s=172.31.200.110 (local), d=192.168.1.1 (Ethernet0), len 100, sending
00:33:54: IP: s=192.168.1.1 (Ethernet0), d=172.31.200.110 (Ethernet0), len 100, rcvd 3
00:33:54: IP: s=172.31.200.110 (local), d=192.168.1.1 (Ethernet0), len 100, sending
00:33:54: IP: s=192.168.1.1 (Ethernet0), d=172.31.200.110 (Ethernet0), len 100, rcvd 3
00:33:54: IP: s=172.31.200.110 (local), d=192.168.1.1 (Ethernet0), len 100, sending
00:33:54: IP: s=192.168.1.1 (Ethernet0), d=172.31.200.110 (Ethernet0), len 100, rcvd 3
00:33:54: IP: s=172.31.200.110 (local), d=192.168.1.1 (Ethernet0), len 100, sending
00:33:54: IP: s=192.168.1.1 (Ethernet0), d=172.31.200.110 (Ethernet0), len 100, rcvd 3
AS2511-1#
```

Success! All pings are successful. Because we did not use ARP to resolve the target address, we should not see our target address in the ARP table. That's correct, there is no ARP resolution.

```
AS2511-1#show arp
Protocol  Address            Age (min)  Hardware Addr   Type   Interface
Internet  172.31.200.110        -       0010.7be7.a085  ARPA   Ethernet0
Internet  172.31.200.100        7       0010.7be7.a080  ARPA   Ethernet0
AS2511-1#
```

Let's use our third format of static route, where we define both the exit interface and the next hop address. The last form of the **static route** command will become very useful later on when we configure dial access using the **ip unnumbered** command.

Look at the output of the **show ip route** command and test the results with a **ping** to see that our experiment is successful.

```
AS2511-1#conf t
Enter configuration commands, one per line.  End with CNTL/Z.
AS2511-1(config)#ip route 192.168.1.0 255.255.255.0 ethernet 0 172.31.200.100
AS2511-1(config)#^Z
AS2511-1#


AS2511-1#show ip route
Codes: C - connected, S - static, I - IGRP, R - RIP, M - mobile, B - BGP
       D - EIGRP, EX - EIGRP external, O - OSPF, IA - OSPF inter area
       N1 - OSPF NSSA external type 1, N2 - OSPF NSSA external type 2
       E1 - OSPF external type 1, E2 - OSPF external type 2, E - EGP
       i - IS-IS, L1 - IS-IS level-1, L2 - IS-IS level-2, * - candidate default
       U - per-user static route, o - ODR

Gateway of last resort is not set

     172.31.0.0/24 is subnetted, 1 subnets
C       172.31.200.0 is directly connected, Ethernet0
S    192.168.1.0/24 [1/0] via 172.31.200.100, Ethernet0
AS2511-1#

AS2511-1#ping 192.168.1.1

Type escape sequence to abort.
Sending 5, 100-byte ICMP Echos to 192.168.1.1, timeout is 2 seconds:
!!!!!
Success rate is 100 percent (5/5), round-trip min/avg/max = 4/4/4 ms
AS2511-1#
```

Authentication

Authentication is a very important part of DDR. When providing DDR connectivity with remote sites, it would be negligent of us as network administrators to leave an insecure access point into the network. Most times, the CHAP protocol is used for authentication. For more details on authentication, see Chapter 3.

Authentication provides each device participating in a DDR connection with another important piece of information, the name of the other connection. Why is this so important? If an incoming call comes into a router, and the router can't store the connection information, then the return traffic cannot be identified with the existing call from the originator. The result is that the called router tries to start a new call to the originator in order to return the traffic. An example of this behavior appears later in this chapter.

Putting It All Together

Now we are going to configure two Cisco 2511 routers to communicate using DDR and asynchronous connections. Figure 5-2 shows the equipment layout.

In this example, we will do some side-by-side comparisons of the events taking place on the two access servers involved. To differentiate the two, there will be an identification tag in the margin to indicate which router is being discussed.

AS2511-1

First we will discuss the configuration for AS2511-1, shown in Code Listing 5-3. This configuration has unused portions removed.

First, in line 7 we have the username and password combination used to validate our other router when CHAP authentication is activated.

The next significant line in this configuration is line 9, where we define the generic dialer script, `dial`, used to make phone calls when interesting packets are directed out the asynchronous connection. This script is referenced in line 32.

Lines 11 and 12 define the internal target address we will use for testing DDR.

Lines 31 through 38 define our physical connectivity for interface `Async 1` on its associated line, `line 1`.

Figure 5-2
Asynchronous DDR
equipment layout.

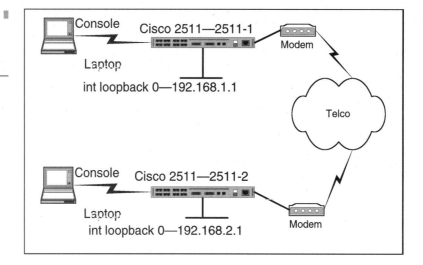

Line 32 defines the chat-script `dial` as the script to use when dial requests are being processed by `Async 1`.

Line 33 defines modem operation as capable of handling both incoming and outgoing calls.

Line 34 sets up our modem to be automatically configured from our `modemcap` database.

Lines 36 through 38 define the physical transmission characteristics used to communicate with the modem.

With `line 1` defined, we move on to the `Async1` interface defined in lines 14 through 22.

Line 15 is the IP address assigned to this interface.

Lines 16 and 22 define PPP encapsulation and CHAP authentication.

In Line 17, we must enter **dialer in-band** before we can add in any other dialer commands. This command must be used on any dial-access interface that does not have a direct out-of-band signaling channel such as ISDN BRI and PRI.

Line 18 is our **dialer map** command that will be used to perform dial-connection address resolution. The command has several options to fill in: protocol—IP, next hop address—172.31.100.2, next hop host name—as2511-2, and phone number—103.

Line 19 assigns the rules defined in `dialer-list 1` to the `async 1` interface.

Line 20 defines the way we will deal with our network layer addressing. When we specify **async dynamic address**, the assumption is that the peer on the other side of our asynchronous link will provide the network address.

Line 21 limits our asynchronous operation to either PPP or SLIP communications. It will not be possible to connect to this router/access server as an ASCII terminal when **async mode dedicated** is configured.

■ ■

Code Listing 5-3

```
1    Current configuration:
2    !
3    version 11.3
4    !
5    hostname AS2511-1
6    !
7    username AS2511-2 password 0 samepass
8    no ip domain-lookup
9    chat-script dial ABORT BUSY "" AT OK "ATDT \T" TIMEOUT 30 CONNECT
\c
10   !
11   interface Loopback0
12    ip address 192.168.1.1 255.255.255.0
13   !
14   interface Async1
15    ip address 172.31.100.1 255.255.255.0
16    encapsulation ppp
17    dialer in-band
18    dialer map ip 172.31.100.2 name as2511-2 103
19    dialer-group 1
20    async dynamic address
21    async mode dedicated
22    ppp authentication chap
23   !
24   ip classless
25   !
26   dialer-list 1 protocol ip permit
27   !
28   !
29   line con 0
30    length 0
31   line 1
32    script dialer dial
33    modem InOut
34    modem autoconfigure type usr_sportster
35    transport input all
36    stopbits 1
37    speed 115200
38    flowcontrol hardware
39   line 2 16
40   line aux 0
41   line vty 0 4
42   !
43   end
```

Code Listing 5-4 contains the configuration of our second router in this example, AS2511-2. AS2511-2 is almost a mirror image of AS2511-1, with changes appropriate to addressing and remote host names.

■ |

Code Listing 5-4

```
1    Current configuration:
2    !
3    version 11.3
4    !
5    hostname AS2511-2
6    !
7    username AS2511-1 password 0 samepass
8    no ip domain-lookup
9    chat-script dial ABORT BUSY "" AT OK "ATDT \T" TIMEOUT 30 CONNECT
\c
10   !
11   interface Loopback0
12    ip address 192.168.2.1 255.255.255.0
13   !
14   interface Async1
15    ip address 172.31.100.2 255.255.255.0
16    encapsulation ppp
17    dialer in-band
18    dialer map ip 172.31.100.1 name as2511-1 101
19    dialer-group 1
20    async dynamic address
21    async mode dedicated
22    ppp authentication chap
23   !
24   ip classless
25   !
26   dialer-list 1 protocol ip permit
27   !
28   line con 0
29    length 0
30   line 1
31    script dialer dial
32    modem InOut
33    modem autoconfigure type usr_courier
34    transport input all
35    stopbits 1
36    speed 115200
37    flowcontrol hardware
38   line 2 16
39   line aux 0
40   line vty 0 4
41   !
42   end
```

Let's take a look at what happens when the initial dial test is performed.

AS2511-1

For our first test, we will use the **debug dialer** command to watch the progress of our DDR attempt, which will be a **ping** to the `async 1` interface on AS2511-2.

```
AS2511-1#debug dialer
Dial on demand events debugging is on
AS2511-1#ping 172.31.100.2

Type escape sequence to abort.
Sending 5, 100-byte ICMP Echos to 172.31.100.2, timeout is 2 seconds:
```

We start out with the dialing trigger, which is an IP packet destined to the address across the asynchronous link. Then, because a dialer event has been directed to our local `async1` interface and its associated `line 1`, the dial string, `103`, is directed to the chat script `dial` defined in our configuration. There is no system script in this operation (more on this later). The chat script is successful.

```
12:26:32: Async1: Dialing cause ip (s=172.31.100.1, d=172.31.100.2)
12:26:32: Async1: Attempting to dial 103
12:26:32: CHAT1: Attempting async line dialer script
12:26:32: CHAT1: Dialing using Modem script: dial  & System script: none
12:26:32: CHAT1: process started
12:26:32: CHAT1: Asserting DTR
12:26:32: CHAT1: Chat script dial started.....
12:26:47: CHAT1: Chat script dial finished, status = Success
12:26:49: %LINK-3-UPDOWN: Interface Async1, changed state to up
```

Our `async1` interface came up and proceeded with the CHAP authentication, which was successful. Wait a minute, the message says we have no matching `dialer map` statement. I'm sure we put one in. This shouldn't matter, since we have called in and been authenticated. The next **ping** should work correctly.

```
12:26:50: Async1: Authenticated host AS2511-2 with no matching dialer map
12:26:50: dialer Protocol up for As1
12:26:50: dialer Protocol up for As1
12:26:50: dialer Protocol up for As1
12:26:51: %LINEPROTO-5-UPDOWN: Line protocol on Interface Async1, changed state to up
```

The connection looks good, so let's try that **ping** again. By the way, the reason the last **ping** was not successful is easy to spot if we examine our timestamps on the left-hand side of the messages. It was `12:26:32` when the dial process was initiated, and 19 seconds later at `12:36:51`, the line protocol came up on `Async1`. We only get ten seconds to send out our ping packets and get a response, so this is pretty normal for asynchronous communications.

```
AS2511-1#ping 172.31.100.2

Type escape sequence to abort.
Sending 5, 100-byte ICMP Echos to 172.31.100.2, timeout is 2 seconds:
.....
Success rate is 0 percent (0/5)
```

The **ping** packets are going out the Async1 interface because we have completed the connection process. Let's see what the **show dialer** command output has in the way of information. Something is wrong. It looks like the interface is on the way down; we are not connected!! It does show us that the last call to 103 was successful. Sure enough, as soon as the command output appears on the screen, the Async1 interface goes down.

```
AS2511-1#show dialer

Async1 - dialer type = IN-BAND ASYNC NO-PARITY
Idle timer (120 secs), Fast idle timer (20 secs)
Wait for carrier (30 secs), Re-enable (15 secs)
Dialer state is enabling
Time until interface enabled 11 secs

Dial String      Successes    Failures    Last called    Last status
103                      1           0    00:00:56        successful
AS2511-1#
12:27:30: %LINK-3-UPDOWN: Interface Async1, changed state to down
12:27:45: Async1: re-enable timeout
```

AS2511-2

Time to take a look at what is happening on the other side of the connection, AS2511-2. All looks well on this side—Async1 changes state to up. Hold on, I see a fly in the ointment—authenticated AS2511-1 with no matching dialer map. It seems that both sides have properly completed the authentication process, and the circuit is up and running. So why is the **ping** unsuccessful?

```
AS2511-2#
12:24:45: %LINK-3-UPDOWN: Interface Async1, changed state to up
12:24:45: Async1: Dialer received incoming call from <unknown>
12:24:45: Async1: Authenticated host AS2511-1 with no matching dialer map
12:24:45: dialer Protocol up for As1
12:24:45: dialer Protocol up for As1
12:24:45: dialer Protocol up for As1
12:24:46: %LINEPROTO-5-UPDOWN: Line protocol on Interface Async1, changed state to up
AS2511-2#
```

Here's something different—we are getting a message from Async1 telling us that there is `no free dialer`, and we are starting a `fast idle timer`. The `fast idle timer` is activated when a dial interface has traffic to send but there are no circuits available; in other words, there is a busy signal. Why should we have to worry about a busy signal if our peer across the asynchronous link just called us? It is kind of obvious that these fast idle timers correspond to our ping attempt from AS2511-1; five pings result in five fast idle timer starts.

```
AS2511-2#
12:24:56: Async1: No free dialer - starting fast idle timer
12:24:56: As1:starting fast idle timer 20000 ticks
12:24:58: Async1: No free dialer - starting fast idle timer
12:25:00: Async1: No free dialer - starting fast idle timer
12:25:02: Async1: No free dialer - starting fast idle timer
12:25:04: Async1: No free dialer - starting fast idle timer
AS2511-2#
```

The fast idle timer is set to `20000 ticks`. If we look at the **show dialer** command below, we see that `Fast idle timer` is set to 20 seconds, which means each tick is one millisecond.

As we use our **show dialer** command to determine if there is any additional information that will help us solve this puzzle, the `Async1` interface goes down due to the fast idle timer expiring.

```
AS2511-2#show dialer
12:25:16: Async1: fast idle timeout
12:25:16: Async1: disconnecting call

Async1 - dialer type = IN-BAND ASYNC NO-PARITY
Idle timer (120 secs), Fast idle timer (20 secs)
Wait for carrier (30 secs), Re-enable (15 secs)
Dialer state is call being disconnected

Dial String      Successes    Failures   Last called   Last status
101                      0            0   never                   -
AS2511-2#
12:25:17: %LINEPROTO-5-UPDOWN: Line protocol on Interface Async1, changed state to down
12:25:18: %LINK-5-CHANGED: Interface Async1, changed state to reset
12:25:23: %LINK-3-UPDOWN: Interface Async1, changed state to down
12:25:38: Async1: re-enable timeout
AS2511-2#
```

Just in case the problem only exists on one side of our asynchronous link and not the other, let's try the same process starting from AS2511-2. **ping** brings up the circuit just as before, and everything looks correct.

We still have that pesky "no dialer map" problem, but I know the dialer maps are in Code Listings 5-3 and 5-4!!

```
AS2511-2#ping 172.31.100.1

Type escape sequence to abort.
Sending 5, 100-byte ICMP Echos to 172.31.100.1, timeout is 2 seconds:

12:26:29: Async1: Dialing cause ip (s=172.31.100.2, d=172.31.100.1)
12:26:29: Async1: Attempting to dial 101
12:26:29: CHAT1: Attempting async line dialer script
12:26:29: CHAT1: Dialing using Modem script: dial  & System script: none
12:26:29: CHAT1: process started
12:26:29: CHAT1: Asserting DTR
12:26:29: CHAT1: Chat script dial started.....
Success rate is 0 percent (0/5)
AS2511-2#
12:26:43: CHAT1: Chat script dial finished, status = Success
12:26:46: %LINK-3-UPDOWN: Interface Async1, changed state to up
12:26:48: Async1: Authenticated host AS2511-1 with no matching dialer map
12:26:49: dialer Protocol up for As1
12:26:49: dialer Protocol up for As1
12:26:49: dialer Protocol up for As1
12:26:49: %LINEPROTO-5-UPDOWN: Line protocol on Interface Async1, changed state to up
```

Before we try anything else, we should look at the **show dialer** command output, since it may indicate that there is an error. Some new information has appeared. The link is up, the dial connection was activated by the **ping** packet destined to AS2511-1, and our time to disconnect is 110 seconds. The output shows us that we have connected to AS2511-1 using phone number 101. This looks just fine!

```
AS2511-2#show dialer

Async1 - dialer type = IN-BAND ASYNC NO-PARITY
Idle timer (120 secs), Fast idle timer (20 secs)
Wait for carrier (30 secs), Re-enable (15 secs)
Dialer state is data link layer up
Dial reason: ip (s=172.31.100.2, d=172.31.100.1)
Time until disconnect 110 secs
Connected to 101 (AS2511-1)

Dial String       Successes   Failures    Last called   Last status
101                       1          0     00:00:26      successful
AS2511-2#
```

Let's **ping** our peer, AS2511-1. I am sure that the packets will go through this time.

```
AS2511-2#ping 172.31.100.1

Type escape sequence to abort.
Sending 5, 100-byte ICMP Echos to 172.31.100.1, timeout is 2 seconds:
..
12:27:58: %LINEPROTO-5-UPDOWN: Line protocol on Interface Async1, changed state to down
12:28:00: %LINK-5-CHANGED: Interface Async1, changed state to reset...
Success rate is 0 percent (0/5)
AS2511-2#
12:28:05: %LINK-3-UPDOWN: Interface Async1, changed state to down
12:28:20: Async1: re-enable timeout
AS2511-2#
```

Wow, after only two **ping** packets got to the other side, the connection is shut down. Perhaps these **ping** packets are bad, and they are taking down the connection.

AS2511-1   Let's take a look back on our peer, AS2511-1, and see what effect these ping packets have had. Just as before, the asynchronous circuit seems to activate just fine.

```
12:28:51: %LINK-3-UPDOWN: Interface Async1, changed state to up
12:28:51: Async1: Dialer received incoming call from <unknown>
12:28:53: Async1: Authenticated host AS2511-2 with no matching dialer map
12:28:53: dialer Protocol up for As1
12:28:53: dialer Protocol up for As1
12:28:53: dialer Protocol up for As1
12:28:54: %LINEPROTO-5-UPDOWN: Line protocol on Interface Async1, changed state to up
```

The **show dialer** command output looks good, the data link layer is up, the time until disconnect is 100 seconds, and the peer across the asynchronous link is AS2511-1. There is no Dial reason on this side, so we look at the other side of a dial connection to see the Dial reason. You will always find the Dial reason on the side that initiated the call.

```
AS2511-1#show dialer

Async1 - dialer type = IN-BAND ASYNC NO-PARITY
Idle timer (120 secs), Fast idle timer (20 secs)
Wait for carrier (30 secs), Re-enable (15 secs)
Dialer state is data link layer up
Time until disconnect 100 secs (AS2511-2)

Dial String     Successes    Failures    Last called    Last status
103                     1           0     00:02:38       successful
AS2511-1#
```

It happened again! We have been disconnected by a fast idle timer expiring, but this time we only get one millisecond. In the **show dialer** command output above, I do recall seeing that the idle timeout starts at 120 seconds, and the time until disconnect is 100 seconds. It appears that the fast idle timer takes into account the current time that the circuit has been idle when calculating the amount of time to use for fast idle. In our earlier example, where the fast idle timer was set to 20000 ticks, the circuit must have had active traffic when the timer was started.

```
12:30:00: Async1: No free dialer - starting fast idle timer
12:30:00: As1:starting fast idle timer 1 ticks
12:30:00: Async1: fast idle timeout
12:30:00: Async1: disconnecting call
12:30:01: %LINEPROTO-5-UPDOWN: Line protocol on Interface Async1, changed state to down
12:30:02: %LINK-5-CHANGED: Interface Async1, changed state to reset
12:30:07: %LINK-3-UPDOWN: Interface Async1, changed state to down
12:30:22: Async1: re-enable timeout
AS2511-1#
```

That "no dialer map" message still bothers me. Perhaps we could use the **show dialer map** command to verify that the configuration is correct. It seems all right to me. Wait a second—in all our messages to this point, the host names are all showing up as AS2511-2 not as2511-2. Could these names be case-sensitive? Duh!

```
AS2511-1#show dialer map
Static dialer map ip 172.31.100.2 name as2511-2  (103) on Async1
AS2511-1#
```

AS2511-2

Could we have made the same mistake twice? Let's take a look at the AS2511-2 **show dialer map** command output and see. Sure enough, it's lower case, not upper case. We made a simple typographical error, but look at the results: no connectivity.

```
AS2511-2#show dialer map
Static dialer map ip 172.31.100.1 name as2511-1  (101) on Async1
AS2511-2#
```

We need to fix this problem before we move on to our real challenge, getting true DDR connectivity working.

```
AS2511-2#conf t
Enter configuration commands, one per line.  End with CNTL/Z.
AS2511-2(config)#int async 1
```

```
AS2511-2(config-if)#no dialer map ip 172.31.100.1 name as2511-1 101
AS2511-2(config-if)#dialer map ip 172.31.100.1 name AS2511-1 101
AS2511-2(config-if)#^Z
AS2511-2#
```

AS2511-1
Make sure to correct the other side, the AS2511-1, as well. Because we may have multiple dialer maps for multiple destinations, it is necessary to remove any incorrect dialer maps from the interface configuration.

```
AS2511-1#conf t
Enter configuration commands, one per line.  End with CNTL/Z.
AS2511-1(config)#int async1
AS2511-1(config-if)#no dialer map ip 172.31.100.2 name as2511-2 103
AS2511-1(config-if)#dialer map ip 172.31.100.2 name AS2511-2 103
AS2511-1(config-if)#^Z
AS2511-1#
```

AS2511-2
Both sides have been corrected, so if we initiate a **ping** from AS2511-2, we should see the asynchronous link become active and our ping packets eventually be successful. The **extended ping** will be used for this test. When we check out the last line of the **ping** command output, it shows us that we only achieved a 90/100 success rate. That means it took 10 ping packet failures with a two-second timeout for each failure, or twenty seconds, for the asynchronous dial connection to be established. The **extended ping** is a useful tool to calculate average connection times.

```
AS2511-2#ping
Protocol [ip]:
Target IP address: 172.31.100.1
Repeat count [5]: 100
Datagram size [100]:
Timeout in seconds [2]:
Extended commands [n]:
Sweep range of sizes [n]:
Type escape sequence to abort.
Sending 100, 100-byte ICMP Echos to 172.31.100.1, timeout is 2 seconds:

12:35:39: Async1: Dialing cause ip (s=172.31.100.2, d=172.31.100.1)
12:35:39: Async1: Attempting to dial 101
12:35:39: CHAT1: Attempting async line dialer script
12:35:39: CHAT1: Dialing using Modem script: dial  & System script: none
12:35:39: CHAT1: process started
12:35:39: CHAT1: Asserting DTR
12:35:39: CHAT1: Chat script dial started.......
12:35:53: CHAT1: Chat script dial finished, status = Success.
12:35:55: %LINK-3-UPDOWN: Interface Async1, changed state to up..!
12:35:58: dialer Protocol up for As1
12:35:58: dialer Protocol up for As1
12:35:58: dialer Protocol up for As1!!!!!!!!
12:35:58: %LINEPROTO-5-UPDOWN: Line protocol on Interface Async1, changed state to
```

```
up!!!!!!!!!!!!!!!!!!!!!!!!!!!!!!!!!!!!!!!!!!!!!!!!!!!!!!!!!!!!!!
!!!!!!!!!!!!!!!!!!!!!!!!!!!!!!!!!!
Success rate is 90 percent (90/100), round-trip min/avg/max = 116/126/148 ms
AS2511-2#
```

A quick review of the **show dialer** command options is in order. The first example, **show dialer int async 1**, provides information on a single dialer interface. The second example, **show dialer**, provides information on all dialer interfaces. The third example, **show dialer map**, shows us all static and dynamic dialer maps currently in effect.

Don't forget to turn off debugging before going on to the next step or after you finish a troubleshooting task, as some **debug** commands generate extensive messages.

```
AS2511-2#show dialer int async 1

Async1 - dialer type = IN-BAND ASYNC NO-PARITY
Idle timer (120 secs), Fast idle timer (20 secs)
Wait for carrier (30 secs), Re-enable (15 secs)
Dialer state is data link layer up
Dial reason: ip (s=172.31.100.2, d=172.31.100.1)
Time until disconnect 51 secs
Connected to 101 (AS2511-1)

Dial String      Successes     Failures     Last called    Last status
101                       1            0     00:02:03       successful
AS2511-2#show dialer

Async1 - dialer type = IN-BAND ASYNC NO-PARITY
Idle timer (120 secs), Fast idle timer (20 secs)
Wait for carrier (30 secs), Re-enable (15 secs)
Dialer state is data link layer up
Dial reason: ip (s=172.31.100.2, d=172.31.100.1)
Time until disconnect 47 secs
Connected to 101 (AS2511-1)

Dial String      Successes     Failures     Last called    Last status
101                       1            0     00:02:07       successful
AS2511-2#show dialer map
Static dialer map ip 172.31.100.1 name AS2511-1   (101) on Async1
AS2511-2#undebug all
All possible debugging has been turned off
AS2511-2#
```

AS2511-1

We are almost finished, but we should check out AS2511-1 to make sure that traffic going the other way will operate correctly. When the link comes up, we can ping the other side, and all three options of the **show dialer** command will show appropriate information.

```
12:38:00: %LINK-3-UPDOWN: Interface Async1, changed state to up
12:38:00: Async1: Dialer received incoming call from <unknown>
12:38:03: dialer Protocol up for As1
12:38:03: dialer Protocol up for As1
12:38:03: dialer Protocol up for As1
12:38:03: %LINEPROTO-5-UPDOWN: Line protocol on Interface Async1, changed state to up
AS2511-1#
AS2511-1#ping 172.31.100.2

Type escape sequence to abort.
Sending 5, 100-byte ICMP Echos to 172.31.100.2, timeout is 2 seconds:
!!!!!
Success rate is 100 percent (5/5), round-trip min/avg/max = 120/125/128 ms
AS2511-1#show dialer

Async1 - dialer type = IN-BAND ASYNC NO-PARITY
Idle timer (120 secs), Fast idle timer (20 secs)
Wait for carrier (30 secs), Re-enable (15 secs)
Dialer state is data link layer up
Time until disconnect 101 secs
Connected to 103 (AS2511-2)

Dial String      Successes   Failures    Last called    Last status
103                      0          0    never                    -
AS2511-1#
AS2511-1#show dialer int async 1

Async1 - dialer type = IN-BAND ASYNC NO-PARITY
Idle timer (120 secs), Fast idle timer (20 secs)
Wait for carrier (30 secs), Re-enable (15 secs)
Dialer state is data link layer up
Time until disconnect 60 secs
Connected to 103 (AS2511-2)

Dial String      Successes   Failures    Last called    Last status
103                      0          0    never                    -
AS2511-1#
AS2511-1#show dialer map
Static dialer map ip 172.31.100.2 name AS2511-2  (103) on Async1
AS2511-1#undebug all
All possible debugging has been turned off
AS2511-1#
```

Connectivity has been established, and now it is time to complete our DDR processing by communicating between two end points that are not part of our asynchronous link.

AS2511-1

Starting with AS2511-1, let's see if we can reach our target destination by checking out our IP routing table with the **show ip route** command. The only IP addresses we can reach are on networks 172.31.100.0/24 and 192.168.1.0/24.

```
AS2511-1#show ip route
Codes: C - connected, S - static, I - IGRP, R - RIP, M - mobile, B - BGP
       D - EIGRP, EX - EIGRP external, O - OSPF, IA - OSPF inter area
       N1 - OSPF NSSA external type 1, N2 - OSPF NSSA external type 2
       E1 - OSPF external type 1, E2 - OSPF external type 2, E - EGP
       i - IS-IS, L1 - IS-IS level-1, L2 - IS-IS level-2, * - candidate default
       U - per-user static route, o - ODR

Gateway of last resort is not set

     172.31.0.0/24 is subnetted, 1 subnets
C        172.31.100.0 is directly connected, Async1
C    192.168.1.0/24 is directly connected, Loopback0
AS2511-1#
```

When we try a **ping** to the loopback IP address of our peer across the asynchronous link, it fails to trigger a call, as expected.

Remember the first rule in DDR processing: there must be a route to the destination.

```
AS2511-1#ping 192.168.2.1

Type escape sequence to abort.
Sending 5, 100-byte ICMP Echos to 192.168.2.1, timeout is 2 seconds:
.....
Success rate is 0 percent (0/5)
AS2511-1#
```

AS2511-2

Let's perform the same check on AS2511-2 and see if the same deficiencies exist. Yes, there is no route to the destination, and the **ping** doesn't trigger an asynchronous connection.

```
AS2511-2#show ip route
Codes: C - connected, S - static, I - IGRP, R - RIP, M - mobile, B - BGP
       D - EIGRP, EX - EIGRP external, O - OSPF, IA - OSPF inter area
       N1 - OSPF NSSA external type 1, N2 - OSPF NSSA external type 2
       E1 - OSPF external type 1, E2 - OSPF external type 2, E - EGP
       i - IS-IS, L1 - IS-IS level-1, L2 - IS-IS level-2, * - candidate default
       U - per-user static route, o - ODR

Gateway of last resort is not set

     172.31.0.0/24 is subnetted, 1 subnets
C        172.31.100.0 is directly connected, Async1
C    192.168.2.0/24 is directly connected, Loopback0
AS2511-2#ping 192.168.1.1

Type escape sequence to abort.
Sending 5, 100-byte ICMP Echos to 192.168.1.1, timeout is 2 seconds:
.....
Success rate is 0 percent (0/5)
AS2511-2#
```

There is only one way to go, the `Async1` interface, so let's set up a static route to our peer's loopback interface. After the static route is defined, then the **show ip route** command indicates that we have a static route.

```
AS2511-2#conf t
Enter configuration commands, one per line.  End with CNTL/Z.
AS2511-2(config)#ip route 192.168.1.0 255.255.255.0 async 1
AS2511-2(config)#^Z
AS2511-2#show ip route
Codes: C - connected, S - static, I - IGRP, R - RIP, M - mobile, B - BGP
       D - EIGRP, EX - EIGRP external, O - OSPF, IA - OSPF inter area
       N1 - OSPF NSSA external type 1, N2 - OSPF NSSA external type 2
       E1 - OSPF external type 1, E2 - OSPF external type 2, E - EGP
       i - IS-IS, L1 - IS-IS level-1, L2 - IS-IS level-2, * - candidate default
       U - per-user static route, o - ODR

Gateway of last resort is not set

     172.31.0.0/24 is subnetted, 1 subnets
C       172.31.100.0 is directly connected, Async1
S    192.168.1.0/24 is directly connected, Async1
C    192.168.2.0/24 is directly connected, Loopback0
AS2511-2#
```

AS2511-1

Let's add the static route to AS2511-1 and make sure that the IP routing table is correct.

```
AS2511-1#conf t
Enter configuration commands, one per line.  End with CNTL/Z.
AS2511-1(config)#ip route 192.168.2.0 255.255.255.0 async1
AS2511-1(config)#^Z
AS2511-1#show ip route
Codes: C - connected, S - static, I - IGRP, R - RIP, M - mobile, B - BGP
       D - EIGRP, EX - EIGRP external, O - OSPF, IA - OSPF inter area
       N1 - OSPF NSSA external type 1, N2 - OSPF NSSA external type 2
       E1 - OSPF external type 1, E2 - OSPF external type 2, E - EGP
       i - IS-IS, L1 - IS-IS level-1, L2 - IS-IS level-2, * - candidate default
       U - per-user static route, o - ODR

Gateway of last resort is not set

     172.31.0.0/24 is subnetted, 1 subnets
C       172.31.100.0 is directly connected, Async1
C    192.168.1.0/24 is directly connected, Loopback0
S    192.168.2.0/24 is directly connected, Async1
AS2511-1#
```

AS2511-2

Now let's go back to AS2511-2 to test out our updated configuration.

Try the **ping** again; surely it will work now. Not again—nothing happened!

```
AS2511-2#ping 192.168.1.1

Type escape sequence to abort.
Sending 5, 100-byte ICMP Echos to 192.168.1.1, timeout is 2 seconds:
.....
Success rate is 0 percent (0/5)
AS2511-2#
```

The **debug dialer** command should shed some light on the cause of
the problems with the dial connection. The **ping** packet to our destination triggers a call to take place, but we get the message No dialer
string, dialing cannot occur. What is the matter? Everything
seems to be in order, and we have a route to our destination. If we look
carefully at the **show ip route** command output above, we see there is a
line in the routing table that directs traffic to our peer's loopback interface through interface Async1.

```
S    192.168.1.0/24 is directly connected, Async1
```

There is one piece missing from this line, the next hop address. When
we are sending a packet to a destination that is not directly connected to
the router/access server it requires a method to resolve that next hop
address for all outgoing requests. In this case, the next hop address is the
IP address of the Async1 interface of our peer, and we have a **dialer
map** that resolves the next hop address to a phone number. What we
don't have is a route to our destination that directs traffic to the next hop
address.

```
AS2511-2#debug dialer
Dial on demand events debugging is on
AS2511-2#
AS2511-2#ping 192.168.1.1

Type escape sequence to abort.
Sending 5, 100-byte ICMP Echos to 192.168.1.1, timeout is 2 seconds:

12:49:18: Async1: Dialing cause ip (s=172.31.100.2, d=192.168.1.1)
12:49:18: Async1: No dialer string, dialing cannot occur.
12:49:20: Async1: Dialing cause ip (s=172.31.100.2, d=192.168.1.1)
12:49:20: Async1: No dialer string, dialing cannot occur.
12:49:22: Async1: Dialing cause ip (s=172.31.100.2, d=192.168.1.1)
12:49:22: Async1: No dialer string, dialing cannot occur.
12:49:24: Async1: Dialing cause ip (s=172.31.100.2, d=192.168.1.1)
12:49:24: Async1: No dialer string, dialing cannot occur.
12:49:26: Async1: Dialing cause ip (s=172.31.100.2, d=192.168.1.1)
12:49:26: Async1: No dialer string, dialing cannot occur.
Success rate is 0 percent (0/5)
AS2511-2#show dialer map
Static dialer map ip 172.31.100.1 name AS2511-1  (101) on Async1
AS2511-2#
```

Change the static route by deleting the existing and adding in a new static route that uses the next hop address, not the interface `Async1`. When we check out the **show ip route** command output after the change, we see the next hop address, not the interface. Now we can resolve our next hop address to a phone number. How do we know which interface to use to reach the destination? There is a directly connected route to `172.31.100.0/24` via interface `Async1`.

```
AS2511-2#conf t
Enter configuration commands, one per line.  End with CNTL/Z.
AS2511-2(config)#no ip route 192.168.1.0 255.255.255.0 async 1
AS2511-2(config)#ip route 192.168.1.0 255.255.255.0 172.31.100.1
AS2511-2(config)#^Z
AS2511-2#show ip route
Codes: C - connected, S - static, I - IGRP, R - RIP, M - mobile, B - BGP
       D - EIGRP, EX - EIGRP external, O - OSPF, IA - OSPF inter area
       N1 - OSPF NSSA external type 1, N2 - OSPF NSSA external type 2
       E1 - OSPF external type 1, E2 - OSPF external type 2, E - EGP
       i - IS-IS, L1 - IS-IS level-1, L2 - IS-IS level-2, * - candidate default
       U - per-user static route, o - ODR

Gateway of last resort is not set

     172.31.0.0/24 is subnetted, 1 subnets
C       172.31.100.0 is directly connected, Async1
S    192.168.1.0/24 [1/0] via 172.31.100.1
C    192.168.2.0/24 is directly connected, Loopback0
AS2511-2#
```

A repeat of the ping test should trigger a call, and as we still have the **debug dialer** command active, we can watch the progress.

```
AS2511-2#ping 192.168.1.1

Type escape sequence to abort.
Sending 5, 100-byte ICMP Echos to 192.168.1.1, timeout is 2 seconds:

12:53:45: Async1: Dialing cause ip (s=172.31.100.2, d=192.168.1.1)
12:53:45: Async1: Attempting to dial 101
12:53:45: CHAT1: Attempting async line dialer script
12:53:45: CHAT1: Dialing using Modem script: dial  & System script: none
12:53:45: CHAT1: process started
12:53:45: CHAT1: Asserting DTR
12:53:45: CHAT1: Chat script dial started.....
Success rate is 0 percent (0/5)
AS2511-2#
12:54:00: CHAT1: Chat script dial finished, status = Success
12:54:02: %LINK-3-UPDOWN: Interface Async1, changed state to up
12:54:02: dialer Protocol up for As1
12:54:02: dialer Protocol up for As1
12:54:02: dialer Protocol up for As1
12:54:03: %LINEPROTO-5-UPDOWN: Line protocol on Interface Async1, changed state to up
AS2511-2#
```

Now that a connection has been established we should be able to **ping** the other side. Hooray, problem solved.

```
AS2511-2#ping 192.168.1.1

Type escape sequence to abort.
Sending 5, 100-byte ICMP Echos to 192.168.1.1, timeout is 2 seconds:
!!!!!
Success rate is 100 percent (5/5), round-trip min/avg/max = 128/132/140 ms
AS2511-2#
```

AS2511-1

Now let's take a look at the other side of the connection, AS2511-1. To make sure that we are processing the **ping** requests properly we activate the **debug ip packet** processing.

```
AS2511-1#debug ip packet
IP packet debugging is on
AS2511-1#
12:56:07: %LINK-3-UPDOWN: Interface Async1, changed state to up
12:56:08: %LINEPROTO-5-UPDOWN: Line protocol on Interface Async1, changed state to up
12:56:15: IP: s=172.31.100.2 (Async1), d=192.168.1.1, len 100, rcvd 4
12:56:15: IP: s=192.168.1.1 (local), d=172.31.100.2 (Async1), len 100, sending
12:56:15: IP: s=172.31.100.2 (Async1), d=192.168.1.1, len 100, rcvd 4
12:56:15: IP: s=192.168.1.1 (local), d=172.31.100.2 (Async1), len 100, sending
12:56:16: IP: s=172.31.100.2 (Async1), d=192.168.1.1, len 100, rcvd 4
12:56:16: IP: s=192.168.1.1 (local), d=172.31.100.2 (Async1), len 100, sending
12:56:16: IP: s=172.31.100.2 (Async1), d=192.168.1.1, len 100, rcvd 4
12:56:16: IP: s=192.168.1.1 (local), d=172.31.100.2 (Async1), len 100, sending
12:56:16: IP: s=172.31.100.2 (Async1), d=192.168.1.1, len 100, rcvd 4
12:56:16: IP: s=192.168.1.1 (local), d=172.31.100.2 (Async1), len 100, sending
AS2511-1#
```

Just to make sure all problems are corrected, **ping** the loopback on AS2511-2 to verify full operation. Traffic going the opposite way did not work. Looking at the **debug ip packet** command output, we see the router/access server start the sending process, but when address resolution is attempted, we get an `encapsulation failed` message. For traffic originating in AS2511-1, heading to the loopback interface on AS2511-2, we still need to resolve the next hop address to a phone number. Why did our **ping** work when it came from AS2511-2? If we look at the source address of our initial test, we will see that the source address for those pings is 172.31.100.2, an address that can be reached via our directly connected network.

```
AS2511-1#ping 192.168.2.1

Type escape sequence to abort.
Sending 5, 100-byte ICMP Echos to 192.168.2.1, timeout is 2 seconds:

12:56:49: IP: s=172.31.100.1 (local), d=192.168.2.1 (Async1), len 100, sending
12:56:49: IP: s=172.31.100.1 (local), d=192.168.2.1 (Async1), len 100, encapsulation
   failed.
12:56:51: IP: s=172.31.100.1 (local), d=192.168.2.1 (Async1), len 100, sending
12:56:51: IP: s=172.31.100.1 (local), d=192.168.2.1 (Async1), len 100, encapsulation
   failed.
12:56:53: IP: s=172.31.100.1 (local), d=192.168.2.1 (Async1), len 100, sending
12:56:53: IP: s=172.31.100.1 (local), d=192.168.2.1 (Async1), len 100, encapsulation
   failed.
12:56:55: IP: s=172.31.100.1 (local), d=192.168.2.1 (Async1), len 100, sending
12:56:55: IP: s=172.31.100.1 (local), d=192.168.2.1 (Async1), len 100, encapsulation
   failed.
12:56:57: IP: s=172.31.100.1 (local), d=192.168.2.1 (Async1), len 100, sending
12:56:57: IP: s=172.31.100.1 (local), d=192.168.2.1 (Async1), len 100, encapsulation
   failed.
Success rate is 0 percent (0/5)
AS2511-1#
```

Let's correct the routing process by replacing the static route to the loopback interface on AS2511-2.

```
AS2511-1#conf t
Enter configuration commands, one per line.  End with CNTL/Z.
AS2511-1(config)#no ip route 192.168.2.0 255.255.255.0 Async1
AS2511-1(config)#ip route 192.168.2.0 255.255.255.0 172.31.100.2
AS2511-1(config)#^Z
AS2511-1#
```

We have complete success; the **ping** works just fine.

After the asynchronous link is down, initiate a **ping** test to verify that DDR works from the AS2500-1 side. Due to the asynchronous connection time, all the pings fail because the link is not up.

```
AS2511-1#ping 192.168.2.1

Type escape sequence to abort.
Sending 5, 100-byte ICMP Echos to 192.168.2.1, timeout is 2 seconds:

13:00:29: IP: s=172.31.100.1 (local), d=192.168.2.1 (Async1), len 100, sending
13:00:29: IP: s=172.31.100.1 (local), d=192.168.2.1 (Async1), len 100, encapsulation
   failed.
13:00:31: IP: s=172.31.100.1 (local), d=192.168.2.1 (Async1), len 100, sending
13:00:31: IP: s=172.31.100.1 (local), d=192.168.2.1 (Async1), len 100, encapsulation
   failed.
13:00:33: IP: s=172.31.100.1 (local), d=192.168.2.1 (Async1), len 100, sending
13:00:33: IP: s=172.31.100.1 (local), d=192.168.2.1 (Async1), len 100, encapsulation
   failed.
13:00:35: IP: s=172.31.100.1 (local), d=192.168.2.1 (Async1), len 100, sending
```

```
13:00:35: IP: s=172.31.100.1 (local), d=192.168.2.1 (Async1), len 100, encapsulation
    failed.
13:00:37: IP: s=172.31.100.1 (local), d=192.168.2.1 (Async1), len 100, sending
13:00:37: IP: s=172.31.100.1 (local), d=192.168.2.1 (Async1), len 100, encapsulation
    failed.
Success rate is 0 percent (0/5)
AS2511-1#
```

When the asynchronous link is finally active, let's try the **ping** again to make sure we have completed two-way communications. The **debug ip packet** shows each of the successful pings.

```
13:00:46: %LINK-3-UPDOWN: Interface Async1, changed state to up
13:00:49: %LINEPROTO-5-UPDOWN: Line protocol on Interface Async1, changed state to up
AS2511-1#ping 192.168.2.1

Type escape sequence to abort.
Sending 5, 100-byte ICMP Echos to 192.168.2.1, timeout is 2 seconds:
!!!!!
Success rate is 100 percent (5/5), round-trip min/avg/max = 128/132/144 ms
AS2511-1#
13:00:55: IP: s=172.31.100.1 (local), d=192.168.2.1 (Async1), len 100, sending
13:00:55: IP: s=192.168.2.1 (Async1), d=172.31.100.1 (Async1), len 100, rcvd 3
13:00:55: IP: s=172.31.100.1 (local), d=192.168.2.1 (Async1), len 100, sending
13:00:56: IP: s=192.168.2.1 (Async1), d=172.31.100.1 (Async1), len 100, rcvd 3
13:00:56: IP: s=172.31.100.1 (local), d=192.168.2.1 (Async1), len 100, sending
13:00:56: IP: s=192.168.2.1 (Async1), d=172.31.100.1 (Async1), len 100, rcvd 3
13:00:56: IP: s=172.31.100.1 (local), d=192.168.2.1 (Async1), len 100, sending
13:00:56: IP: s=192.168.2.1 (Async1), d=172.31.100.1 (Async1), len 100, rcvd 3
13:00:56: IP: s=172.31.100.1 (local), d=192.168.2.1 (Async1), len 100, sending
13:00:56: IP: s=192.168.2.1 (Async1), d=172.31.100.1 (Async1), len 100, rcvd 3
AS2511-1#
```

Now that we have completed our end-to-end DDR connectivity, a complete set of router listings is in order.

Code Listing 5-5 shows the complete configuration for AS2511-1, and Code Listing 5-6 shows the complete configuration for AS2511-2.

Code Listing 5-5
AS2511-1 configuration.

```
1   AS2511-1#show run
2   Building configuration...
3
4   Current configuration:
5   !
6   version 11.3
7   service timestamps debug uptime
8   service timestamps log uptime
9   no service password-encryption
10  !
11  hostname AS2511-1
12  !
13  !
```

```
14   username AS2511-2 password 0 samepass
15   no ip domain-lookup
16   chat-script dial ABORT BUSY "" AT OK "ATDT \T" TIMEOUT 30 CONNECT
     \c
17   !
18   !
19   !
20   interface Loopback0
21    ip address 192.168.1.1 255.255.255.0
22   !
23   interface Ethernet0
24    no ip address
25    shutdown
26   !
27   interface Serial0
28    no ip address
29    shutdown
30   !
31   interface Serial1
32    no ip address
33    shutdown
34   !
35   interface Async1
36    ip address 172.31.100.1 255.255.255.0
37    encapsulation ppp
38    dialer in-band
39    dialer map ip 172.31.100.2 name AS2511-2 103
40    dialer-group 1
41    async dynamic address
42    async mode dedicated
43    ppp authentication chap
44   !
45   ip classless
46   ip route 192.168.2.0 255.255.255.0 172.31.100.2
47   !
48   dialer-list 1 protocol ip permit
49   !
50    line con 0
51    length 0
52   line 1
53    script dialer dial
54    modem InOut
55    modem autoconfigure type usr_sportster
56    transport input all
57    stopbits 1
58    speed 115200
59    flowcontrol hardware
60   line 2 16
61   line aux 0
62   line vty 0 4
63   !
64   end
```

Code Listing 5-6

AS2511-2 configuraiton.

```
1    AS2511-2#show run
2    Building configuration...
3
4    Current configuration:
5    !
6    version 11.3
7    service timestamps debug uptime
8    service timestamps log uptime
9    no service password-encryption
10   !
11   hostname AS2511-2
12   !
13   !
14   username AS2511-1 password 0 samepass
15   no ip domain-lookup
16   chat-script dial ABORT BUSY "" AT OK "ATDT \T" TIMEOUT 30 CONNECT
\c
17   !
18   !
19   !
20   interface Loopback0
21    ip address 192.168.2.1 255.255.255.0
22   !
23   interface Ethernet0
24    no ip address
25    no ip proxy-arp
26    shutdown
27   !
28   interface Serial0
29    no ip address
30    no ip mroute-cache
31    shutdown
32   !
33   interface Serial1
34    no ip address
35    shutdown
36   !
37   interface Async1
38    ip address 172.31.100.2 255.255.255.0
39    encapsulation ppp
40    dialer in-band
41    dialer map ip 172.31.100.1 name AS2511-1 101
42    dialer-group 1
43    async dynamic address
44    async mode dedicated
45    ppp authentication chap
46   !
47   ip classless
48   ip route 192.168.1.0 255.255.255.0 172.31.100.1
49   !
50   dialer-list 1 protocol ip permit
51   !
52   !
53   line con 0
54    length 0
55   line 1
56    script dialer dial
57    modem InOut
```

```
58    modem autoconfigure type usr_courier
59    transport input all
60    stopbits 1
61    speed 115200
62    flowcontrol hardware
63   line 2 16
64   line aux 0
65   line vty 0 4
66   !
67   end
```

Troubleshooting Techniques

While dial-on-demand routing has many components, we can simplify the troubleshooting process if we follow this formula:

1. Creating routing table entries for each destination to be reached, with the ability to resolve the next hop address to an exit interface.

2. Using **dialer map** commands that map the next hop address to a phone number and contain the name option that exactly (case-sensitive) matches the host name of the target address.

3. Using **dialer-list** commands that correctly set the rules for defining the interesting traffic used for call control.

4. Making sure that a **dialer-group** command is assigned to each `dial-access` interface to apply the call control rules defined in the **dialer-list** commands.

In Chapter 6, we will examine ISDN as another option for dial-access circuits, and we will extend these basic troubleshooting techniques.

Lab

All Cisco routers with an auxiliary port can be configured to support asynchronous DDR routing. Take two external modems using an analog key (PBX) system with extension-to-extension dialing, an analog line simulator (best source is BlackBox), or two regular phone connections. Use standard RS232 cabling to hook up two routers to the modems, and configure dial-on-demand routing between them.

Summary

This chapter introduced the reader to the world of dial-on-demand routing. Routing is the start; if there is no route to the destination, there is no DDR. Interesting traffic is defined to manage call control. Interesting traffic directed to a dial-access interface triggers a call, and continued interesting traffic will keep the dial circuit active.

We have just scratched the surface. In Chapter 6, ISDN will be used to describe advanced dial-access connectivity.

Integrated Services Digital Network

This chapter deals with the mechanism of communicating in a dial-access environment using Integrated Services Digital Network (ISDN), Basic Rate Interface (BRI), and Primary Rate Interface (PRI). This method of communicating provides a separate out-of-band signaling or D-channel, and 64-kilobits-per-second bearer or B-channels.

ISDN is the first Digital Subscriber Link (DSL)—yes, I said DSL—to be implemented. ISDN has been around for a while but has only caught on in the last five years. ISDN uses digital multiplexing to combine a signaling channel with multiple 64 Kbps bearer channels and transmit this information over a single transmission circuit. These bearer channels can carry any type of information: data, voice, or video. In this chapter, we will concentrate on configuration options and troubleshooting for data transmission, not on the nuts and bolts of how ISDN works during transmission.

Table 6-1 shows the breakdown of the capabilities for the three transmission options for ISDN: Basic Rate Interface (BRI), T1 Primary Rate Interface (PRI), and E1 Primary Rate Interface (PRI).

In Table 6-1 the only differences are the speed of the D-channel for BRI and the number of bearer channels for interface type. In this chapter, we will stick with ISDN BRI ports. (They are less expensive to purchase and to buy test gear for). In future chapters, we will deal with channelized T1 connections.

TABLE 6-1

Interface Type	Channel Type/ Speed in Kbps	Number of Channels	Encapsulation
Basic Rate Interface (BRI)	D-signaling/16	1	LAPD, Q921, Q931
	B-bearer/64	2	HDLC, PPP, Frame Relay, X.25
T1 Primary Rate Interface (PRI)	D-signaling/64	1	LAPD, Q921, Q931
	B-bearer/64	23	HDLC, PPP, Frame Relay, X.25
E1 Primary Rate Interface (PRI)	D-signaling/64	1	LAPD, Q921, Q931
	B-bearer/64	30	HDLC, PPP, Frame Relay, X.25

With ISDN connections, there is a separate signaling channel that is a direct connection between the router and the switch. The BRI method of communicating between the customer premise equipment and the local telephone company switch is the local loop. This connection is referred to as the U interface and communicates over a single pair of wires. Once the local loop reaches the customer premise, the Network Terminal 1 converts two-wire local loop communications into four-wire, two-pair communications. This four-wire communications consists of two pairs, one for transmit and one for receive, and is referred to as the S/T interface. The only time that the S and T interfaces operate independently is when an ISDN-capable PBX is placed between the NT1 and the Terminal Endpoint (TE). There are two Terminal End Point types: TE1, which communicates using the ISDN protocols to the central office switch; and TE2, which uses non-ISDN protocols to connect to a Terminal Adapter (TA) using the R interface. The TA converts non-ISDN communications to standard ISDN multiplexing. Most TAs have a built-in NT1, and Cisco router products can also have built-in NT1s. Figure 6-1 lays out the standard ISDN BRI connection options.

Figure 6-1
ISDN connections, devices, and interfaces.

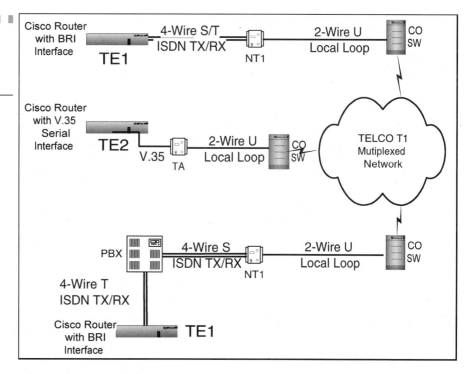

If you are looking for an in-depth discussion of each and every bit in the ISDN frames, and the voltage levels, see Appendix C for further reading. This chapter is about how to make ISDN work and how to fix it when it is broken, so let's get started with the basics.

One-to-One Basic Connectivity Using Static Routes

Figure 6-2 shows two Cisco 3620 routers, each with an ISDN BRI S/T interface. The switch used is an ADTRAN Atlas 800 with ISDN BRI U ports.

What does the diagram need to provide correct connectivity? If you determined that S/T and U ports don't mix, then you know that the missing component is an NT1.

Code Listing 6-1 shows the configuration for NewYork. Let's examine the relevant components before we start our testing.

Line 3 defines the user name and encryption key for CHAP authentication.

Line 4 defines the central office switch type; in this case it will use the basic-ni identifier. Basic-ni is an emerging standard for command structures between edge devices and central office switches. The switch, which could be a Lucent 5ESS or a Nortel DMS 100, determines the format of one of the most crucial components in ISDN connectivity, Service Profile IDs (SPIDs). You'll find more on SPIDs later in this chapter, and Appendix D provides some general SPID guidelines by service provider.

Figure 6-2
Basic ISDN connectivity equipment layout.

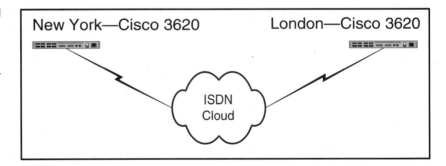

Lines 6 and 7 create our target IP address on the loopback interface.

Lines 9 through 19 define how the ISDN interface will operate for our basic testing.

Line 10 is the IP address on this end of our ISDN link.

Line 11 defines PPP encapsulation. Remember that this is the primary encapsulation method used by ISDN, due to enhanced authentication, but it can be HDLC, Frame Relay, or X.25.

Lines 12 and 13 statically map the next hop IP address, `172.31.100.2`, to the telephone numbers for London, `5552002` and `5552003`.

Line 14 ties the dial-control rules defined in `dialer-list 1` to the `BRI 0/0` interface.

Line 15 represents a feature that is new in IOS version 11.3, ISDN switch type. Older versions of the Cisco IOS permitted a single global ISDN switch type to be defined in a router; because of the BRI and PRI signaling to the central office switch, only one ISDN type could be active in a router. The Cisco 3620 in this example is more than capable of handling both types of connections.

Lines 16 and 17 are the two SPIDs. Two SPIDs? Oh yes, we have two different 64 Kbps circuits available, and each circuit to the phone company gets its own phone number and SPID. If the SPIDs are wrong, then the associated bearer channels will not operate.

NOTE *Lucent has an upgrade for their 5ESS switch that provides an ISDN connection with one phone number (a hunt group) and no SPIDs! Look for this feature to start working its way into normal production.*

Line 18 sets up CHAP authentication on this PPP link.

Line 19, `hold queue 75 in`, defines the incoming message queue as a maximum of 75 unprocessed messages.

Line 22 shows us the way to our next-door neighbor. It identifies the next hop address over the ISDN link as the path to follow to reach the loopback address on London.

Last but not least, line 24 is the command that makes it all happen. The **dialer-list** command defines the interesting traffic used for call setup and call takedown.

Code Listing 6-1
BRI to BRI—NewYork
configuration.

```
1    hostname NewYork
2    !
3    username London password 0 cisco
4    isdn switch-type basic-ni
5    !
6    interface Loopback0
7     ip address 192.168.1.1 255.255.255.0
8    !
9    interface BRI0/0
10    ip address 172.31.100.1 255.255.255.0
11    encapsulation ppp
12    dialer map ip 172.31.100.2 name London 5552002
13    dialer map ip 172.31.100.2 name London 5552003
14    dialer-group 1
15    isdn switch-type basic-ni
16    isdn spid1 21255520000101
17    isdn spid2 21255520010101
18    ppp authentication chap
19    hold-queue 75 in
20    !
21   ip classless
22   ip route 192.168.2.0 255.255.255.0 172.31.100.2
23   !
24   dialer-list 1 protocol ip permit
25   !
26   line con 0
27    exec-timeout 0 0
28    length 0
29   line aux 0
30   line vty 0 4
31    password bb
32    login
33   !
34   end
```

Code Listing 6-2 shows the configuration for London. The relevant components are the same as for NewYork, but please look at it before we start our testing sequence.

Code Listing 6-2
BRI to BRI—London
configuration.

```
1    hostname London
2    !
3    username NewYork password 0 cisco
4    isdn switch-type basic-ni
5    !
6    interface Loopback0
7     ip address 192.168.2.1 255.255.255.0
8    !
9    interface BRI0/0
10    ip address 172.31.100.2 255.255.255.0
11    encapsulation ppp
12    dialer map ip 172.31.100.1 name NewYork 5552000
13    dialer map ip 172.31.100.1 name NewYork 5552001
14    dialer-group 1
```

Code Listing 6-2
(continued)

```
15    isdn switch-type basic-ni
16    isdn spid1 21255520020101
17    isdn spid2 21255520030101
18    ppp authentication chap
19    hold-queue 75 in
20    !
21  ip classless
22  ip route 192.168.1.0 255.255.255.0 172.31.100.1
23  !
24  dialer-list 1 protocol ip permit
25  !
26  line con 0
27    exec-timeout 0 0
28    length 0
29  line aux 0
30  line vty 0 4
31    password bb
32    login
33  !
34  end
```

A good place to start is the beginning (Yogi Berra could have said that). The **show isdn status** command gives us an overall picture of the ISDN interface. The switch type is set; if there is no switch type, no communication can take place. Layer 1 is deactivated, and this cannot be a good thing. Until the connection is up, the rest of the information is informative, but not useful.

```
NewYork#show isdn status
Global ISDN Switchtype = basic-ni
ISDN BRI0/0 interface
   dsl 0, interface ISDN Switchtype = basic-ni
    Layer 1 Status:
   DEACTIVATED
    Layer 2 Status:
   Layer 2 NOT Activated
    Spid Status:
   TEI Not Assigned, ces = 1, state = 1(terminal down)
       spid1 configured, no LDN, spid1 NOT sent, spid1 NOT valid
   TEI Not Assigned, ces = 2, state = 1(terminal down)
       spid2 configured, no LDN, spid2 NOT sent, spid2 NOT valid
    Layer 3 Status:
   0 Active Layer 3 Call(s)
    Activated dsl 0 CCBs = 0
    Total Allocated ISDN CCBs = 0
NewYork#
```

There is way too much information in the **debug isdn q921** command output to go into detail here. See Appendix E for this example and a complete description of each field. Inserting some one-liners in the output that follows will give you the highlights in this **debug** command.

After we turn on the **debug** command, we power up the ISDN switch to create the following output. You may not be able to get your service provider to power off the switch, but reloading the router with no ISDN cable should give you the same results.

```
debug isdn q921
ISDN Q921 packets debugging is on
NewYork#
00:06:01: ISDN BR0/0: TX ->  IDREQ  ri = 86  ai = 127
00:06:03: ISDN BR0/0: TX ->  IDREQ  ri = 1463  ai = 127
00:06:05: ISDN BR0/0: TX ->  IDREQ  ri = 24872  ai = 127
00:06:07: ISDN BR0/0: TX ->  IDREQ  ri = 29609  ai = 127
```

Once the physical connection is active, the router sends out an ID request (IDREQ) with an Action indicator of 127, or broadcast (ai=127). Each IDREQ sent by the router is assigned a new Reference number (ri), picked at random, until an IDASSN message is received with the Terminal Endpoint Identifier (tei) in the Action indicator field (ai = 64).

```
00:06:07: ISDN BR0/0: RX <-  IDASSN  ri = 29609  ai = 64
```

Now that we have the tei for B-channel 1, we can send the SPID and make the channel active.

```
00:06:07: ISDN BR0/0: TX ->  SABMEp sapi = 0  tei = 64
00:06:07: ISDN BR0/0: RX <-  UAf sapi = 0  tei = 64
00:06:07: %ISDN-6-LAYER2UP: Layer 2 for Interface BR0/0, TEI 64 changed to up
```

The next line is our SPID being sent to the switch. If we decode the hex into ASCII, the last twenty hex digits are 21255520000101. The following messages complete the initialization of B-channel 1.

```
00:06:07: ISDN BR0/0: TX ->  INFOc sapi = 0  tei = 64  ns = 0  nr = 0  i =
   0x08007B3A0E3231323535353230303030313031
00:06:07: ISDN BR0/0: RX <-  RRr sapi = 0  tei = 64  nr = 1
00:06:07: ISDN BR0/0: RX <-  INFOc sapi = 0  tei = 64  ns = 0  nr = 1  i =
   0x08007B3B02F081
00:06:07: ISDN BR0/0: TX ->  RRr sapi = 0  tei = 64  nr = 1
```

The same sequence is followed for B-channel 2.

```
00:06:07: ISDN BR0/0: TX ->  IDREQ  ri = 44602  ai = 127
00:06:07: ISDN BR0/0: RX <-  IDASSN  ri = 44602  ai = 65
00:06:07: ISDN BR0/0: TX ->  SABMEp sapi = 0  tei = 65
00:06:07: ISDN BR0/0: RX <-  UAf sapi = 0  tei = 65
00:06:07: %ISDN-6-LAYER2UP: Layer 2 for Interface BR0/0, TEI 65 changed to up
```

```
00:06:07: ISDN BR0/0: TX ->  INFOc sapi = 0  tei = 65  ns = 0  nr = 0  i =
   0x08007B3A0E32313235353532303031303131
00:06:07: ISDN BR0/0: RX <-  RRr sapi = 0  tei = 65  nr = 1
00:06:07: ISDN BR0/0: RX <-  INFOc sapi = 0  tei = 65  ns = 0  nr = 1  i =
   0x08007B3B02F082
00:06:07: ISDN BR0/0: TX ->  RRr sapi = 0  tei = 65  nr = 1
```

The next four messages occur every ten seconds—can you say keep-alive? There is an RRp (Receiver Ready poll) and RRf (Receiver Ready final) for each B-channel to verify that the switch is active, can talk to the end points, and can process information.

```
00:06:17: ISDN BR0/0: RX <-  RRp sapi = 0  tei = 64 nr = 1
00:06:17: ISDN BR0/0: TX ->  RRf sapi = 0  tei = 64  nr = 1
00:06:17: ISDN BR0/0: RX <-  RRp sapi = 0  tei = 65 nr = 1
00:06:17: ISDN BR0/0: TX ->  RRf sapi = 0  tei = 65  nr = 1
```

Once the circuit is up, the **show isdn status** command output looks much better, with all layers up and running and the SPID processing validated. The two B-channels have teis assigned, and State = MULTIPLE_FRAME_ESTABLISHED means we are ready to place calls and use the B-channels.

```
NewYork#show isdn status
Global ISDN Switchtype = basic-ni
ISDN BRI0/0 interface
   dsl 0, interface ISDN Switchtype = basic-ni
   Layer 1 Status:
   ACTIVE
   Layer 2 Status:
   TEI = 64, Ces = 1, SAPI = 0, State = MULTIPLE_FRAME_ESTABLISHED
   TEI = 65, Ces = 2, SAPI = 0, State = MULTIPLE_FRAME_ESTABLISHED
   Spid Status:
   TEI 64, ces = 1, state = 5(init)
      spid1 configured, no LDN, spid1 sent, spid1 valid
      Endpoint ID Info: epsf = 0, usid = 70, tid = 1
   TEI 65, ces = 2, state = 5(init)
      spid2 configured, no LDN, spid2 sent, spid2 valid
      Endpoint ID Info: epsf = 0, usid = 70, tid = 2
   Layer 3 Status:
   0 Active Layer 3 Call(s)
   Activated dsl 0 CCBs = 0
   Total Allocated ISDN CCBs = 0
NewYork#
```

Now that the ISDN connection is up and running, it is time to place our first call. We accomplish call processing by sending messages across the existing link to the switch using the Q931 protocol. Turning on

debug isdn q931 will give us detailed information about this call process. We will follow this process all through the way through the call.

```
NewYork#debug isdn q931
ISDN Q931 packets debugging is on
```

To start the call we use a **ping** to the loopback interface of London.

```
NewYork#ping 192.168.1 2.1

Type escape sequence to abort.
Sending 5, 100-byte ICMP Echos to 192.168.2.1, timeout is 2 seconds:
```

First a SETUP message is sent to the switch. More detail on this command is available in Appendix E. The key here is the phone number, 5552003.

```
00:08:36: ISDN BR0/0: TX ->  SETUP pd = 8  callref = 0x01
00:08:36:            Bearer Capability i = 0x8890
00:08:36:            Channel ID i = 0x83
00:08:36:            Keypad Facility i = '5552003'
```

The router receives a call proceeding (CALL_PROC) message from the switch.

```
00:08:36: ISDN BR0/0: RX <-  CALL_PROC pd = 8  callref = 0x81
00:08:36:            Channel ID i = 0x89
```

Next the router gets a connect (CONNECT) message indicating that the called party has gone off-hook (answered the call).

```
00:08:36: ISDN BR0/0: RX <-  CONNECT pd = 8  callref = 0x81
00:08:36:            Channel ID i = 0x89
```

The BRI 0/0 interface changes state to up, and the router sends a connection acknowledgment (CONNECT_ACK) back to the switch so that data transmission can start. Our interface comes up, and our PPP connection is established.

```
00:08:36: %LINK-3-UPDOWN: Interface BRI0/0:1, changed state to up
00:08:36: ISDN BR0/0: TX ->  CONNECT_ACK pd = 8  callref = 0x01
00:08:37: %LINEPROTO-5-UPDOWN: Line protocol on Interface BRI0/0:1, changed state to up
00:08:42: %ISDN-6-CONNECT: Interface BRI0/0:1 is now connected to 5552003 London


.!!!!
Success rate is 80 percent (4/5), round-trip min/avg/max = 32/34/36 ms
NewYork#
```

Ah, sweet success. Look at how fast the call to London was completed. With only one failure in our **ping** output, it must have completed the circuit within two seconds. Having only one switch and short distances makes this example look good, but these results may not be indicative of actual field results. Later in this book we will create a scenario that requires two separate ISDN connections to work, and that does take longer to complete the end-to-end call and **ping** successfully.

If we look at the **show isdn status** command output under the Layer 3 section, we see that there is an active call on B-channel 1.

```
NewYork#show isdn status
Global ISDN Switchtype = basic-ni
ISDN BRI0/0 interface
    dsl 0, interface ISDN Switchtype = basic-ni
    Layer 1 Status:
    ACTIVE
    Layer 2 Status:
    TEI = 64, Ces = 1, SAPI = 0, State = MULTIPLE_FRAME_ESTABLISHED
    TEI = 65, Ces = 2, SAPI = 0, State = MULTIPLE_FRAME_ESTABLISHED
    Spid Status:
    TEI 64, ces = 1, state = 5(init)
        spid1 configured, no LDN, spid1 sent, spid1 valid
        Endpoint ID Info: epsf = 0, usid = 70, tid = 1
    TEI 65, ces = 2, state = 5(init)
        spid2 configured, no LDN, spid2 sent, spid2 valid
        Endpoint ID Info: epsf = 0, usid = 70, tid = 2
    Layer 3 Status:
    1 Active Layer 3 Call(s)
    Activated dsl 0 CCBs = 1
    CCB:callid=0x8001, sapi=0x0, ces=0x1, B-chan=1
    Total Allocated ISDN CCBs = 1
NewYork#
```

Many **show** commands are very useful for looking at call statistics and reviewing ISDN operations.

The **show dialer** command output follows. In our example, there is only one interface, but if more were installed in the router, there would be more interfaces shown.

For interface BRI0/0 there is an overall section that globally defines the dial strings mapped for this interface, successes, failures, last called, and the status of our last call. Then we have the detail for each B-channel.

The next section of code details the first B-channel, BRI0/0:1. Information includes timer values and the current data-link layer state. If the data-link layer is up, then there will be additional information: dial reason when this interface initiated the call, time until disconnect, and the phone number and host on the other end of the connection.

The details for the second B-channel, BRI0/0:2, follow the details for the first B-channel. This second B-channel is idle.

```
NewYork#show dialer

BRI0/0 - dialer type = ISDN

Dial String     Successes    Failures    Last called    Last status
5552004               0           0       never                  -
5552003               1           0       00:01:11        successful
0 incoming call(s) have been screened.
0 incoming call(s) rejected for callback.

BRI0/0:1 - dialer type = ISDN
Idle timer (120 secs), Fast idle timer (20 secs)
Wait for carrier (30 secs), Re-enable (15 secs)
Dialer state is data link layer up
Dial reason: ip (s=172.31.100.1, d=192.168.2.1)
Time until disconnect 50 secs
Connected to 5552003 (London)

BRI0/0:2 - dialer type = ISDN
Idle timer (120 secs), Fast idle timer (20 secs)
Wait for carrier (30 secs), Re-enable (15 secs)
Dialer state is idle
NewYork#
```

The **show dialer map** command details the address resolution for destination address by interface.

```
NewYork#show dialer map
Static dialer map ip 172.31.100.2 name London  (5552003) on BRI0/0
Static dialer map ip 172.31.100.2 name London  (5552004) on BRI0/0
NewYork#
```

The **show interface** command works a little differently for ISDN interfaces. Each ISDN interface has two components: the D, or signaling, channel; and multiple B, or bearer, channels.

To see the information about the D-channel, we use the command **show interface bri 0/0**. We add the channel number or numbers to the end of this command to look at the actual communications pathways.

An interesting section in the following **show isdn interface bri 0/0 1** command output deals with our encapsulation method of PPP. We see that the LCP state is open and we have two NCPs: IPCP and CDPCP. IP is certainly set up, but what about CDP? Of course, two Cisco routers are connected together and have established Cisco Discovery Protocol (CDP) communications.

```
NewYork#show isdn int bri 0/0 1
BRI0/0:1 is up, line protocol is up
  Hardware is QUICC BRI
  MTU 1500 bytes, BW 64 Kbit, DLY 20000 usec,
     reliability 255/255, txload 1/255, rxload 1/255
  Encapsulation PPP, loopback not set, keepalive set (10 sec)
  Time to interface disconnect:  idle 00:00:03
  LCP Open
  Open: IPCP, CDPCP
  Last input 00:00:02, output 00:00:02, output hang never
  Last clearing of "show interface" counters never
  Input queue: 0/75/0 (size/max/drops); Total output drops: 0
  Queueing strategy: weighted fair
  Output queue: 0/1000/64/0 (size/max total/threshold/drops)
     Conversations  0/1/256 (active/max active/max total)
     Reserved Conversations 0/0 (allocated/max allocated)
  5 minute input rate 0 bits/sec, 0 packets/sec
  5 minute output rate 0 bits/sec, 0 packets/sec
     37 packets input, 952 bytes, 0 no buffer
     Received 37 broadcasts, 0 runts, 0 giants, 0 throttles
     0 input errors, 0 CRC, 0 frame, 0 overrun, 0 ignored, 0 abort
     37 packets output, 954 bytes, 0 underruns
     0 output errors, 0 collisions, 0 interface resets
     0 output buffer failures, 0 output buffers swapped out
     2 carrier transitions
NewYork#
```

After the **ping** test is completed, the interface goes idle after 122 seconds. Going back to the **show dialer** command above, we see that the idle timer is set for 120 seconds, so shutdown should take place 120 seconds after the last interesting traffic goes across the interface. In the following sequence we see that the call lasts 122 seconds, which looks correct. But in the **show interface** command above, CDP is active and sends out a packet to its neighbor every 60 seconds. Why does the call terminate? The **dialer-list** command defines our set of rules for call control, and according to the rules on line 24 of Code Listing 6-1, only IP packets are used for call setup and disconnect decisions. CDP can run over the interface, but will not trigger a call or prevent a call from disconnecting.

The call disconnect sequence sends out a disconnect request, gets a release message back from the switch, and acknowledges the release to complete the circuit shutdown process.

```
00:10:38: %ISDN-6-DISCONNECT: Interface BRI0/0:1  disconnected from 5552003 London, call
    lasted 122 seconds
00:10:38: ISDN BR0/0: TX ->  DISCONNECT pd = 8  callref = 0x01
00:10:38:          Cause i = 0x8090 - Normal call clearing
00:10:38: ISDN BR0/0: RX <-  RELEASE pd = 8  callref = 0x81
00:10:38: %LINK-3-UPDOWN: Interface BRI0/0:1, changed state to down
00:10:38: ISDN BR0/0: TX ->  RELEASE_COMP pd = 8  callref = 0x01
00:10:39: %LINEPROTO-5-UPDOWN: Line protocol on Interface BRI0/0:1, changed state to down
NewYork#
```

We have paid a great deal of attention to NewYork up to this point. Now let's look at the same sequence from across the pond in London.

Activate **debug isdn q931** to see the call control messages. A SETUP message is received with Alerting on and London's B-channel 1 phone number showing up as the Called Party Number. A CONNECT message is sent out, indicating that the call is being answered, and a CONNECT_ACK comes back from the ISDN switch, indicating that the circuit on B-channel 1 has been activated. The router indicates that this circuit is established and also identifies the phone number and host name of the calling device.

```
London#debug isdn q931
ISDN Q931 packets debugging is on
London#
04:29:18: ISDN BR0/0: RX <-  SETUP pd = 8  callref = 0x01
04:29:18:          Bearer Capability i = 0x8890
04:29:18:          Channel ID i = 0x89
04:29:18:          Signal i = 0x40 - Alerting on - pattern 0
04:29:18:          Called Party Number i = 0xC1, '5552003'
04:29:18: %LINK-3-UPDOWN: Interface BRI0/0:1, changed state to up
04:29:18: ISDN BR0/0: TX -> CONNECT pd = 8  callref = 0x81
04:29:18:          Channel ID i = 0x89
04:29:18: ISDN BR0/0: RX <-  CONNECT_ACK pd = 8  callref = 0x01
04:29:18: %LINEPROTO-5-UPDOWN: Line protocol on Interface BRI0/0:1, changed state to up
04:29:24: %ISDN-6-CONNECT: Interface BRI0/0:1 is now connected to 5552000 NewYork
```

Because our connection is up and running, the **show isdn status** command shows us an operating interface with an active call on B-channel 1.

```
London#show isdn status
Global ISDN Switchtype = basic-ni
ISDN BRI0/0 interface
   dsl 0, interface ISDN Switchtype = basic-ni
    Layer 1 Status:
    ACTIVE
    Layer 2 Status:
    TEI = 64, Ces = 1, SAPI = 0, State =MULTIPLE_FRAME_ESTABLISHED
    TEI = 65, Ces = 2, SAPI = 0, State =MULTIPLE_FRAME_ESTABLISHED
    Spid Status:
```

```
      TEI 64, ces = 1, state = 5(init)
          spid1 configured, no LDN, spid1 sent, spid1 valid
          Endpoint ID Info: epsf = 0, usid = 70, tid = 1
      TEI 65, ces = 2, state = 5(init)
          spid2 configured, no LDN, spid2 sent, spid2 valid
          Endpoint ID Info: epsf = 0, usid = 70, tid = 2
      Layer 3 Status:
    1 Active Layer 3 Call(s)
      Activated dsl 0 CCBs = 1
    CCB:callid=0x3, sapi=0x0, ces=0x1, B-chan=1
      Total Allocated ISDN CCBs = 1
```

The **show dialer** command indicates that we have a current call in progress but have not initiated any calls from London.

```
London#show dialer

BRI0/0 - dialer type = ISDN

Dial String      Successes    Failures    Last called    Last status
5552001              0            0        never              -
5552000              0            0        never              -
0 incoming call(s) have been screened.
0 incoming call(s) rejected for callback.

BRI0/0:1 - dialer type = ISDN
Idle timer (120 secs), Fast idle timer (20 secs)
Wait for carrier (30 secs), Re-enable (15 secs)
Dialer state is data link layer up
Time until disconnect 78 secs
Connected to 5552000 (NewYork)

BRI0/0:2 - dialer type = ISDN
Idle timer (120 secs), Fast idle timer (20 secs)
Wait for carrier (30 secs), Re-enable (15 secs)
Dialer state is idle
```

The **show dialer map** command output shows the address resolution for our connection to NewYork.

```
London#show dialer map
Static dialer map ip 172.31.100.1 name NewYork  (5552000) on BRI0/0
Static dialer map ip 172.31.100.1 name NewYork  (5552001) on BRI0/0
```

The **show interface bri 0/0 1** command gives us the details of our BRI channel 1 operation.

```
London#show int bri 0/0 1
BRI0/0:1 is up, line protocol is up
  Hardware is QUICC BRI
  MTU 1500 bytes, BW 64 Kbit, DLY 20000 usec,
```

```
        reliability 255/255, txload 1/255, rxload 1/255
    Encapsulation PPP, loopback not set, keepalive set (10 sec)
    Time to interface disconnect:  idle 00:00:17
    LCP Open
    Open: IPCP, CDPCP
    Last input 00:00:01, output 00:00:01, output hang never
    Last clearing of "show interface" counters never
    Input queue: 0/75/0 (size/max/drops); Total output drops: 0
    Queueing strategy: weighted fair
    Output queue: 0/1000/64/0 (size/max total/threshold/drops)
      Conversations  0/1/256 (active/max active/max total)
      Reserved Conversations 0/0 (allocated/max allocated)
    5 minute input rate 0 bits/sec, 0 packets/sec
    5 minute output rate 0 bits/sec, 0 packets/sec
      86 packets input, 2255 bytes, 0 no buffer
      Received 86 broadcasts, 0 runts, 0 giants, 0 throttles
      0 input errors, 0 CRC, 0 frame, 0 overrun, 0 ignored, 0 abort
      86 packets output, 2251 bytes, 0 underruns
      0 output errors, 0 collisions, 0 interface resets
      0 output buffer failures, 0 output buffers swapped out
      9 carrier transitions
London#
```

When the interesting traffic stops flowing between NewYork and London, the call is terminated. As both sides of the conversation use the same set of rules, it is normal for both sides to simultaneously initiate a disconnect sequence. This is what happens in the following example; London issues a DISCONNECT and receives one from the switch before completing the RELEASE process.

```
04:31:20: %ISDN-6-DISCONNECT: Interface BRI0/0:1  disconnected from 5552000 NewYork, call
   lasted 122 seconds
04:31:20: ISDN BR0/0: TX -> DISCONNECT pd = 8  callref = 0x81
04:31:20:         Cause i = 0x8090 - Normal call clearing
04:31:20: ISDN BR0/0: RX <- DISCONNECT pd = 8  callref = 0x01
04:31:20:         Cause i = 0x8290 - Normal call clearing
04:31:20: ISDN BR0/0: TX -> RELEASE pd = 8  callref = 0x81
04:31:20: ISDN BR0/0: RX <- RELEASE pd = 8  callref = 0x01
04:31:20: %LINK-3-UPDOWN: Interface BRI0/0:1, changed state to down
04:31:20: ISDN BR0/0: RX <- RELEASE_COMP pd = 8  callref = 0x01
04:31:20: %LINEPROTO-5-UPDOWN: Line protocol on Interface BRI0/0:1, changed state to down
London#undebug all
All possible debugging has been turned off
London#
```

We are not finished yet with our debugging marathon. There are two more useful debug sequences to review.

The **debug isdn events** command is the next command for review. We will switch to London to initiate the connection sequence. The fact that NewYork can connect to London does not mean that London can connect to its peer, NewYork.

```
London#debug isdn events
ISDN events debugging is on
London#ping 192.168.1.1

Type escape sequence to abort.
Sending 5, 100-byte ICMP Echos to 192.168.1.1, timeout is 2 seconds:

04:34:30: ISDN BR0/0: Outgoing call id = 0x8003
04:34:30: ISDN BR0/0: Event: Call to 5552000 at 64 Kb/s
04:34:30: ISDN BR0/0: received HOST_PROCEEDING call_id 0x8003
04:34:30: ISDN BR0/0: received HOST_CONNECT call_id 0x8003
04:34:30: %LINK-3-UPDOWN: Interface BRI0/0:1, changed state to up
04:34:30: ISDN BR0/0: Event: Connected to 5552000 on B1 at 64 Kb/s

.!!!!
Success rate is 80 percent (4/5), round-trip min/avg/max = 32/33/36 ms
London#

04:34:31: %LINEPROTO-5-UPDOWN: Line protocol on Interface BRI0/0:1, changed state to up
04:34:36: %ISDN-6-CONNECT: Interface BRI0/0:1 is now connected to 5552000 NewYork
04:36:32: ISDN BR0/0: Event: Hangup call to call id 0x8003  ces = 1
04:36:32: %ISDN-6-DISCONNECT: Interface BRI0/0:1  disconnected from 5552000 NewYork, call
    lasted 122 seconds
04:36:32: ISDN BR0/0: received HOST_DISCONNECT_ACK call_id 0x8003
04:36:32: %LINK-3-UPDOWN: Interface BRI0/0:1, changed state to down
04:36:33: %LINEPROTO-5-UPDOWN: Line protocol on Interface BRI0/0:1, changed state to down
London#u all
All possible debugging has been turned off
London#
```

Look at that last test from the New York side.

```
NewYork#debug isdn events
ISDN events debugging is on
NewYork#
00:13:48: ISDN BR0/0: Incoming call id = 0x1
00:13:48: ISDN BR0/0: received HOST_INCOMING_CALL call_id 0x1
00:13:48: ISDN BR0/0: Event: Received a call from <unknown> on B1 at 64 Kb/s
00:13:48: ISDN BR0/0: Event: Accepting the call id = 0x1
00:13:48: %LINK-3-UPDOWN: Interface BRI0/0:1, changed state to up
00:13:48: ISDN BR0/0: received HOST_CONNECT call_id 0x1
00:13:48: ISDN BR0/0: Event: Connected to <unknown> on B1 at 64 Kb/s
00:13:49: %LINEPROTO-5-UPDOWN: Line protocol on Interface BRI0/0:1, changed state to up
00:13:54: %ISDN-6-CONNECT: Interface BRI0/0:1 is now connected to 5552003 London
00:15:50: ISDN BR0/0: Event: Hangup call to call id 0x1  ces = 1
00:15:50: %ISDN-6-DISCONNECT: Interface BRI0/0:1  disconnected from 5552003 London, call
    lasted 122 seconds
00:15:50: ISDN BR0/0: received HOST_DISCONNECT_ACK call_id 0x1
00:15:50: %LINK-3-UPDOWN: Interface BRI0/0:1, changed state to down
00:15:51: %LINEPROTO-5-UPDOWN: Line protocol on Interface BRI0/0:1, changed state to down
NewYork#
```

Now let's look at the **debug dialer** output from NewYork.

```
NewYork#debug dialer
Dial on demand events debugging is on
NewYork#ping 192.168.2.1

Type escape sequence to abort.
Sending 5, 100-byte ICMP Echos to 192.168.2.1, timeout is 2 seconds:

00:16:41: BRI0/0: Dialing cause ip (s=172.31.100.1, d=192.168.2.1)
00:16:41: BRI0/0: Attempting to dial 5552003
00:16:41: %LINK-3-UPDOWN: Interface BRI0/0:1, changed state to up
00:16:42: dialer Protocol up for BR0/0:1
00:16:42: %LINEPROTO-5-UPDOWN: Line protocol on Interface BRI0/0:1, changed state to up
.!!!!
Success rate is 80 percent (4/5), round-trip min/avg/max = 32/34/36 ms
NewYork#
00:16:47: %ISDN-6-CONNECT: Interface BRI0/0:1 is now connected to 5552003 London
00:18:43: BRI0/0:1: idle timeout
00:18:43: BRI0/0:1: disconnecting call
00:18:43: %ISDN-6-DISCONNECT: Interface BRI0/0:1  disconnected from 5552003 London, call
   lasted 122 seconds
00:18:44: %LINK-3-UPDOWN: Interface BRI0/0:1, changed state to down
00:18:44: BRI0/0:1: disconnecting call
00:18:44: %LINEPROTO-5-UPDOWN: Line protocol on Interface BRI0/0:1, changed state to down
NewYork#
```

London's **debug dialer** output comes next.

```
London#debug dialer
Dial on demand events debugging is on
London#
04:37:23: %LINK-3-UPDOWN: Interface BRI0/0:1, changed state to up
04:37:24: dialer Protocol up for BR0/0:1
04:37:24: %LINEPROTO-5-UPDOWN: Line protocol on Interface BRI0/0:1, changed state to up
04:37:29: %ISDN-6-CONNECT: Interface BRI0/0:1 is now connected to 5552000 NewYork
04:39:26: BRI0/0:1: idle timeout
04:39:26: BRI0/0:1: disconnecting call
04:39:26: %ISDN-6-DISCONNECT: Interface BRI0/0:1  disconnected from 5552000 NewYork, call
   lasted 122 seconds
04:39:26: %LINK-3-UPDOWN: Interface BRI0/0:1, changed state to down
04:39:26: BRI0/0:1: disconnecting call
04:39:26: %LINEPROTO-5-UPDOWN: Line protocol on Interface BRI0/0:1, changed state to down
```

This completes our first basic ISDN DDR example.

One-to-Many Basic Connectivity Using Static Routes

This next example describes how to set up a single router with the ability to connect to multiple dial-in targets. Each ISDN connection has multiple bearer channels, so we should be able to connect to multiple sites, or attach to a single remote site using PPP multilink. Figure 6-3 shows the equipment layout for this example.

The configuration in Code Listing 6-3 details the setup of the starting point for our one-to-many example.

In order to provide CHAP authentication, we need to build a local authentication database. Lines 5 through 7 define our local database, where each remote site we will connect to has a specific encryption key. This is a good security practice.

Line 11 sets our global switch type to `basic-ni` for our BRI interface.

Lines 17 through 34 define our ISDN BRI connectivity. Lines 21 through 26 define our static address resolution to the three remote sites. Because there are two telephone numbers for the two B-channels at the destination, we need two **dialer map** commands, one for each channel. If a call is made to a busy channel, then the originator looks for another number to call by scanning the **dialer map** commands. When there is only one **dialer map** command, the originator attempts a second call

Figure 6-3
One-to-many ISDN DDR equipment layout.

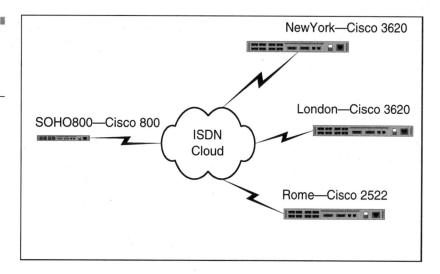

using the single telephone number. Line 29 defines the ISDN switch type for this interface. This command is generated automatically when the global switch type is entered. Lines 30 and 31 define the SPIDs required to activate the BRI connection. Lines 20, 27, 32, and 33 define our PPP operation. Lines 33 and 27 work together to provide multiple channels for this dial-up connection. Line 33 activates multilink, and line 27 sets the threshold for activating a second channel to 25/255*bandwidth, or in this case, approximately 10%. Last, but most important, is the **dialer-group 1** command on line 28. This command ties the dialing rules defined in `dialer-list 1` to this interface. No **dialer-group** command, no calls.

Line 41 defines the interesting traffic to be all valid IP packets. This includes any packets with a valid IP header, regardless of content. This is a great test methodology, and it can be used at the passive end of a dial-up connection. You will find more on this topic in Chapters 8 and 10.

Lines 37 through 39 define the static routes to the loopback interface IP addresses across the ISDN cloud. Without a valid route to our destination, we won't even try to send packets to the BRI interface.

Code Listing 6-3
One-to-many ISDN DDR—SOHO800 configuration.

```
1    version 12.0
2    !
3    hostname SOHO800
4    !
5    username NewYork password 0 pass1
6    username London password 0 pass2
7    username Rome password 0 pass3
8    !
9    ip subnet-zero
10   !
11   isdn switch-type basic-ni
12   !
13   interface Ethernet0
14     ip address 192.168.200.1 255.255.255.0
15     no ip directed-broadcast
16   !
17   interface BRI0
18     ip address 172.31.200.4 255.255.255.0
19     no ip directed-broadcast
20     encapsulation ppp
21     dialer map ip 172.31.200.1 name NewYork 5552000
22     dialer map ip 172.31.200.1 name NewYork 5552001
23     dialer map ip 172.31.200.2 name London 5552002
24     dialer map ip 172.31.200.2 name London 5552003
25     dialer map ip 172.31.200.3 name Rome 5552004
26     dialer map ip 172.31.200.3 name Rome 5552005
27     dialer load-threshold 25 either
28     dialer-group 1
29     isdn switch-type basic-ni
30     isdn spid1 21255520060101
```

```
31    isdn spid2 21255520070101
32    ppp authentication chap
33    ppp multilink
34    hold-queue 75 in
35    !
36    ip classless
37    ip route 192.168.1.0 255.255.255.0 172.31.200.1
38    ip route 192.168.2.0 255.255.255.0 172.31.200.2
39    ip route 192.168.3.0 255.255.255.0 172.31.200.3
40    !
41    dialer-list 1 protocol ip permit
42    !
43    line con 0
44     exec-timeout 0 0
45     logging synchronous
46     length 0
47     transport input none
48     stopbits 1
49    line vty 0 4
50     password ci
51     login
52    !
53    end
```

Using this configuration, let's take a look at the **show ip route** command to verify that our static routes are in place and that we can identify both the next hop address and the exit interface. Yes, we have three static routes to next hop addresses 172.31.200.1, 172.31.200.2, and 172.31.200.3, which can be reached by sending packets to the 171.168.200.0/24 subnet directly connected on interface BRI0. We have both components required to route packets to the correct interface.

```
SOHO800#show ip route
Codes: C - connected, S - static, I - IGRP, R - RIP, M - mobile, B - BGP
       D - EIGRP, EX - EIGRP external, O - OSPF, IA - OSPF inter area
       N1 - OSPF NSSA external type 1, N2 - OSPF NSSA external type 2
       E1 - OSPF external type 1, E2 - OSPF external type 2, E - EGP
       i - IS-IS, L1 - IS-IS level-1, L2 - IS-IS level-2, * - candidate default
       U - per-user static route, o - ODR
       T - traffic engineered route

Gateway of last resort is not set

     172.31.0.0/24 is subnetted, 1 subnets
C       172.31.200.0 is directly connected, BRI0
C    192.168.200.0/24 is directly connected, Ethernet0
S    192.168.1.0/24 [1/0] via 172.31.200.1, BRI0
S    192.168.2.0/24 [1/0] via 172.31.200.2, BRI0
S    192.168.3.0/24 [1/0] via 172.31.200.3, BRI0
SOHO800#
```

When we take a look at our BRI interface with the **show interface bri 0** command, we take a look at the D-channel (signaling). While we do not make active data connections to destinations using the D-channel, it must be active and connected to the Central Office (CO) switch. On the first output line, we see the word (spoofing) to indicate that the IP address is active in the routing table and that we are communicating to the CO switch. Packet activity on this display is limited to traffic between the router and the switch on the D-channel.

```
SOHO800#show interface bri 0

BRI0 is up, line protocol is up (spoofing)
  Hardware is BRI with U interface and POTS
  Internet address is 172.31.200.4/24
  MTU 1500 bytes, BW 64 Kbit, DLY 20000 usec,
     reliablility 255/255, txload 1/255, rxload 1/255
  Encapsulation PPP, loopback not set
  Last input 00:00:03, output 00:00:03, output hang never
  Last clearing of "show interface" counters never
  Input queue: 0/75/0 (size/max/drops); Total output drops: 0
  Queueing strategy: weighted fair
  Output queue: 0/1000/64/0 (size/max total/threshold/drops)
    Conversations  0/1/256 (active/max active/max total)
    Reserved Conversations 0/0 (allocated/max allocated)
  5 minute input rate 0 bits/sec, 0 packets/sec
  5 minute output rate 0 bits/sec, 0 packets/sec
    62 packets input, 286 bytes, 0 no buffer
    Received 2 broadcasts, 0 runts, 0 giants, 0 throttles
    0 input errors, 0 CRC, 0 frame, 0 overrun, 0 ignored, 0 abort
    68 packets output, 376 bytes, 0 underruns
    0 output errors, 0 collisions, 1 interface resets
    0 output buffer failures, 0 output buffers swapped out
    1 carrier transitions
```

Let's turn on the **debug dialer** command to watch the dialer events take place as we try to communicate with our three targets. We also will use the **debug PPP multilink events** to see if the traffic generated activates a second B-channel.

```
SOHO800#debug dialer
Dial on demand events debugging is on
SOHO800#debug ppp multilink events
Multilink events debugging is on
SOHO800#
```

Now it's time to **ping** our target destination and verify that we have configured our ISDN DDR options correctly.

```
SOHO800#ping 192.168.1.1

Type escape sequence to abort.
Sending 5, 100-byte ICMP Echos to 192.168.1.1, timeout is 2 seconds:
.!!!!
Success rate is 80 percent (4/5), round-trip min/avg/max = 32/38/48 ms
```

The **debug dialer** command output comes next. The first **ping** is an IP packet; based on our rules that all IP packets are good, we initiate a call. Great, B-channel 1 came up to connect us to our first target.

```
SOHO800#
00:30:39: BRI0: Dialing cause ip (s=172.31.200.4, d=192.168.1.1)
00:30:39: BRI0: Attempting to dial 5552000
00:30:39: %LINK-3-UPDOWN: Interface BRI0:1, changed state to up
00:30:39: dialer Protocol up for BR0:1
SOHO800#
00:30:40: %LINEPROTO-5-UPDOWN: Line protocol on Interface BRI0:1, changed state to up
```

Let's **ping** our second target and see what happens. Success again! Now we are connected to two different remote sites over our single ISDN BRI interface.

```
SOHO800#ping 192.168.2.1

Type escape sequence to abort.
Sending 5, 100-byte ICMP Echos to 192.168.2.1, timeout is 2 seconds:
.!!!!
Success rate is 80 percent (4/5), round-trip min/avg/max = 32/34/36 ms
SOHO800#
```

Our **debug dialer** command output is the same as last time but it also shows a connection being established to our second target.

```
SOHO800#
00:31:25: BRI0: Dialing cause ip (s=172.31.200.4, d=192.168.2.1)
00:31:25: BRI0: Attempting to dial 5552002
00:31:25: %LINK-3-UPDOWN: Interface BRI0:2, changed state to up
00:31:25: dialer Protocol up for BR0:2
00:31:26: %LINEPROTO-5-UPDOWN: Line protocol on Interface BRI0:2, changed state to up
```

Check out PPP multilink. I thought we activated this feature on our BRI interface. There doesn't seem to be any multilink activity at this time. When we check out the target systems, we may discover why.

```
SOHO800#show ppp multilink
No active bundles
```

With both connections up, we should look at our dialer interfaces with the **show dialer** command. On the master interface, BRI 0, we see the available phone numbers, how many successes and failures, last called, and status of last call. The master interface is followed by the individual B-channels. Each B-channel shows the current active timer values, the status of the data link layer, the dial cause (if this device called), the time until disconnect, and both the phone number and host name of whom we are connected to.

```
SOHO800#show dialer

BRI0 - dialer type = ISDN

Dial String      Successes    Failures    Last called    Last status
5552005              0           0         never              -
5552004              2           0         00:20:55       successful
5552003              0           0         never              -
5552002              1           0         00:00:56       successful
5552001              0           0         never              -
5552000              1           0         00:01:43       successful
0 incoming call(s) have been screened.
0 incoming call(s) rejected for callback.

BRI0:1 - dialer type = ISDN
Idle timer (120 secs), Fast idle timer (20 secs)
Wait for carrier (30 secs), Re-enable (15 secs)
Dialer state is data link layer up
Dial reason: ip (s=172.31.200.4, d=192.168.1.1)
Time until disconnect 18 secs
Connected to 5552000 (NewYork)

BRI0:2 - dialer type = ISDN
Idle timer (120 secs), Fast idle timer (20 secs)
Wait for carrier (30 secs), Re-enable (15 secs)
Dialer state is data link layer up
Dial reason: ip (s=172.31.200.4, d=192.168.2.1)
Time until disconnect 64 secs
Connected to 5552002 (London)
SOHO800#
```

The NewYork call is about to disconnect, so let's watch the **debug dialer** command output for the NewYork call.

```
00:32:41: BRI0:1: idle timeout
00:32:41: BRI0:1: disconnecting call
00:32:180388626431: %ISDN-6-DISCONNECT: Interface BRI0:1  disconnected from 5552000
   NewYork, call lasted 121 seconds
00:32:41: %LINK-3-UPDOWN: Interface BRI0:1, changed state to down
00:32:41: BRI0:1: disconnecting call
00:32:42: %LINEPROTO-5-UPDOWN: Line protocol on Interface BRI0:1, changed state to down
SOHO800#ping 192.168.3.1
```

Continuing our test, let's **ping** our third target. Again we have successfully completed our connection.

```
SOHO800#ping 192.168.3.1

Type escape sequence to abort.
Sending 5, 100-byte ICMP Echos to 192.168.3.1, timeout is 2 seconds:
.!!!!
Success rate is 80 percent (4/5), round-trip min/avg/max = 36/44/64 ms
SOHO800#
```

Back to our **debug** output. When we look at the **debug** output, we see some significant differences from the previous two connections. Instead of activating a specific B-channel, we have successfully negotiated PPP multilink, and we have to create a Virtual Access interface 1 (Vi1). Because more than one B-channel can join a multilink connection, it is necessary to dynamically create this Vi1 interface and associate it with a bundle of circuits, basing the bundle name on the authenticated remote host. The **debug ppp multilink event (MLP)** command output below indicates whether this link being added to the multilink bundle is the first link added.

```
00:33:07: BRI0: Dialing cause ip (s=172.31.200.4, d=192.168.3.1)
00:33:07: BRI0: Attempting to dial 5552004
00:33:07: %LINK-3-UPDOWN: Interface BRI0:1, changed state to up
00:33:07: BR0:1 MLP: Multilink up event pending
00:33:07: Vi1 MLP: Added to huntgroup BR0
00:33:07: Vi1 MLP: Clone from BR0
00:33:07: %LINK-3-UPDOWN: Interface Virtual-Access1, changed state to up
00:33:07: BR0:1 MLP: Rome, multilink up, first link
00:33:07: dialer Protocol up for Vi1
00:33:08: %LINEPROTO-5-UPDOWN: Line protocol on Interface BRI0:1, changed state to up
00:33:08: %LINEPROTO-5-UPDOWN: Line protocol on Interface Virtual-Access1, changed state
   to up
```

Our London call has timed out, and B-channel 2 has been disconnected and is now available for us to check out PPP Multilink.

```
SOHO800#
00:33:27: BRI0:2: idle timeout
00:33:27: BRI0:2: disconnecting call
00:33:120259084287: %ISDN-6-DISCONNECT: Interface BRI0:2  disconnected from 5552002
   London, call lasted 121 seconds
00:33:27: %LINK-3-UPDOWN: Interface BRI0:2, changed state to down
00:33:27: BRI0:2: disconnecting call
00:33:28: %LINEPROTO-5-UPDOWN: Line protocol on Interface BRI0:2, changed state to down
```

Let's test PPP multilink by using the extended **ping** command to generate data. The data generated is 1,000 packets, 1,000 bytes each. With our low threshold of 25/255, this should trigger a second call. All of a sudden, our steady **ping** stops (! is success, . is timeout), so the test was interrupted to check out the **debug** output.

```
SOHO800#ping
Protocol [ip]:
Target IP address: 192.168.3.1
Repeat count [5]: 1000
Datagram size [100]: 1000
Timeout in seconds [2]:
Extended commands [n]:
Sweep range of sizes [n]:
Type escape sequence to abort.
Sending 1000, 1000-byte ICMP Echos to 192.168.3.1, timeout is 2 seconds:
!!!!!!!!!!!!!!!!!!!!!!!!!!!!!!!!!!!!!!!!!!!!!!!!!!!!!!!!!!!!!!!!!!!!!!!!!!
!!!!!!!!!!!!!!!!!!!!!!!!!!!!!!!!!!!!!!!!!!!!!!!!!!!!!!!!!!!!!!!!!!!!!!!!!!
!!!!!!!!!!!!!!!!!!!!!!!!!!!!!!!!!!!!!!!!!!!!!!!!!!!!!!!!!!!!!!!!!!!!!!!!!!
!!!!!!!!!!!!!!!!!!!!!!!!!!!!!!!!!!!!!!!!!!!!!!!!!!.
Success rate is 99 percent (254/255), round-trip min/avg/max = 140/201/284 ms


00:35:21: BRI0: Attempting to dial 5552004
00:35:22: BRI0: wait for carrier timeout, call id=0x8005
00:35:22: BRI0:2: disconnecting call
00:35:22: BRI0: Attempting to dial 5552005
00:35:22: %LINK-3-UPDOWN: Interface BRI0:2, changed state to up
00:35:22: BR0:2 MLP: Multilink up event pending
00:35:22: BR0:2 MLP: Rome, multilink up
00:35:23: %LINEPROTO-5-UPDOWN: Line protocol on Interface BRI0:2, changed state to up
SOHO800#
```

The **show dialer** command output below shows the overall statistics for all phone numbers at the top, but it is the detail on each B-channel that is the most interesting. B-channel 1 (BRI0:1) shows our original call and identifies this channel as a multilink member. B-channel 2 (BRI0:2) has a little bit different dial reason, Multilink bundle overloaded. This is the second B-channel in our multilink bundle created when an overload condition occurred.

```
SOHO800#show dialer

BRI0 - dialer type = ISDN
```

Dial String	Successes	Failures	Last called	Last status
5552005	1	0	00:00:40	successful
5552004	4	1	00:00:10	failed
5552003	0	0	never	-
5552002	1	0	00:04:37	successful
5552001	0	0	never	-

```
5552000                 1       0     00:05:23        successful
0 incoming call(s) have been screened.
0 incoming call(s) rejected for callback.

BRI0:1 - dialer type = ISDN
Idle timer (120 secs), Fast idle timer (20 secs)
Wait for carrier (30 secs), Re-enable (15 secs)
Dialer state is multilink member
Dial reason: ip (s=172.31.200.4, d=192.168.3.1)
Connected to 5552004 (Rome)

BRI0:2 - dialer type = ISDN
Idle timer (120 secs), Fast idle timer (20 secs)
Wait for carrier (30 secs), Re-enable (15 secs)
Dialer state is multilink member
Dial reason: Multilink bundle overloaded
Connected to 5552004 (Rome)
SOHO800#
```

The **show ppp multilink** command output shows that we have a bundle named Rome, our remote host, made up of two B-channels, BRI0:2 and BRI0:1. This is just what we wanted—two channels for faster round-trip times and higher bandwidth.

```
SOHO800#show ppp multilink

Bundle Rome, 2 members, Master link is Virtual-Access1
Dialer Interface is BRI0
  0 lost fragments, 0 reordered, 0 unassigned, sequence 0x102/0x102 rcvd/sent
  0 discarded, 0 lost received, 1/255 load

Member Links: 2 (max not set, min not set)
BRI0:2
BRI0:1
```

The following is the disconnect sequence for both channels of our PPP multilink bundle.

```
00:37:40: Virtual-Access1: idle timeout
00:37:40: Virtual-Access1: disconnecting call
00:37:40: Rome MLP: Bundle reset
00:37:40: BR0:2 MLP: Multilink down event pending
00:37:40: BR0:2 MLP: Multilink down event pending
00:37:40: BR0:1 MLP: Multilink down event pending
00:37:40: BR0:1 MLP: Multilink down event pending
00:37:40: BR0:2 MLP: Removing link from Rome
00:37:40: BR0:1 MLP: Removing link from Rome
00:37:40: Rome MLP: Removing bundle
00:37:40: %LINK-3-UPDOWN: Interface Virtual-Access1, changed state to down
00:37:41: BRI0:2: disconnecting call
00:37:41: BRI0:1: disconnecting call
00:37:180388626431: %ISDN-6-DISCONNECT: Interface BRI0:2  disconnected from 5552005 Rome,
  call lasted 138 seconds
```

```
00:37:180388626431: %ISDN-6-DISCONNECT: Interface BRI0:1  disconnected from 5552004 Rome,
   call lasted 273 seconds
00:37:41: %LINK-3-UPDOWN: Interface BRI0:2, changed state to down
00:37:41: BRI0:2: disconnecting call
00:37:41: %LINK-3-UPDOWN: Interface BRI0:1, changed state to down
00:37:41: BRI0:1: disconnecting call
00:37:41: %LINEPROTO-5-UPDOWN: Line protocol on Interface BRI0:2, changed state to down
00:37:41: %LINEPROTO-5-UPDOWN: Line protocol on Interface BRI0:1, changed state to down
00:37:41: %LINEPROTO-5-UPDOWN: Line protocol on Interface Virtual-Access1, changed state
   to down
```

Let's try something different. It's time to test out three calls and see how the fast idle timer works. If both B-channels are active and we try a third call, the channel that has been idle the longest should disconnect, and our third call should go through.

First we **ping** Rome and bring up B-channel 1.

```
SOHO800#ping 192.168.3.1

Type escape sequence to abort.
Sending 5, 100-byte ICMP Echos to 192.168.3.1, timeout is 2 seconds:
.!!!!
Success rate is 80 percent (4/5), round-trip min/avg/max = 36/46/72 ms
SOHO800#
00:37:53: %LINK-3-UPDOWN: Interface BRI0:1, changed state to up
00:37:53: %LINK-3-UPDOWN: Interface Virtual-Access1, changed state to up
00:37:54: %LINEPROTO-5-UPDOWN: Line protocol on Interface BRI0:1, changed state to up
00:37:55: %LINEPROTO-5-UPDOWN: Line protocol on Interface Virtual-Access1, changed state
   to up
```

Second, we **ping** NewYork and bring up B-channel 2.

```
SOHO800#ping 192.168.1.1

Type escape sequence to abort.
Sending 5, 100-byte ICMP Echos to 192.168.1.1, timeout is 2 seconds:
.!!!!
Success rate is 80 percent (4/5), round-trip min/avg/max = 32/34/36 ms
SOHO800#
00:38:11: %LINK-3-UPDOWN: Interface BRI0:2, changed state to up
00:38:12: %LINEPROTO-5-UPDOWN: Line protocol on Interface BRI0:2, changed state to up
```

Now for our fast idle timer test. We missed two pings, not one like before. Since it took longer for our **ping** to be successful, we have to look at the debug output to see what happened.

```
SOHO800#ping 192.168.2.1

Type escape sequence to abort.
Sending 5, 100-byte ICMP Echos to 192.168.2.1, timeout is 2 seconds:
..!!!
Success rate is 60 percent (3/5), round-trip min/avg/max = 32/38/48 ms
```

The call tried to go through, but there is no free dialer. So it's time to start fast idle timers on the Virtual Access interface and both BRI interfaces. Look at the difference: the Virtual Access interface only has to be idle for 1 millisecond to be the candidate for shutdown so that we can make the pending call. The individual BRI ports each have a 20-second timer applied. The odds are that the PPP multilink interface will shutdown first. So it does. By disconnecting the Virtual Access interface, it also frees up B-channel 1.

```
SOHO800#
00:38:24: BRI0: No free dialer - starting fast idle timer
00:38:24: Vi1:starting fast idle timer 1 ticks
00:38:24: BR0:1:starting fast idle timer 20000 ticks
00:38:24: BR0:2:starting fast idle timer 20000 ticks
00:38:24: Virtual-Access1: fast idle timeout
00:38:24: Virtual-Access1: disconnecting call
00:38:24: Rome MLP: Bundle reset
00:38:24: BR0:1 MLP: Multilink down event pending
00:38:24: BR0:1 MLP: Multilink down event pending
00:38:24: BR0:1 MLP: Removing link from Rome
00:38:24: Rome MLP: Removing bundle
00:38:24: %LINK-3-UPDOWN: Interface Virtual-Access1, changed state to down
00:38:24: BRI0:1: disconnecting call
00:38:107374182399: %ISDN-6-DISCONNECT: Interface BRI0:1  disconnected from 5552004 Rome,
   call lasted 30 seconds
00:38:24: %LINK-3-UPDOWN: Interface BRI0:1, changed state to down
00:38:24: BRI0:1: disconnecting call
00:38:25: %LINEPROTO-5-UPDOWN: Line protocol on Interface BRI0:1, changed state to down
00:38:25: %LINEPROTO-5-UPDOWN: Line protocol on Interface Virtual-Access1, changed state
   to down
```

Once B-channel 1 is down, our third call is free to use the circuit and attempt a connection to London. We now see the connection to London from the original **ping** above.

```
00:38:26: BRI0: Dialing cause ip (s=172.31.200.4, d=192.168.2.1)
00:38:26: BRI0: Attempting to dial 5552002
00:38:26: %LINK-3-UPDOWN: Interface BRI0:1, changed state to up
00:38:26: dialer Protocol up for BR0:1
00:38:27: %LINEPROTO-5-UPDOWN: Line protocol on Interface BRI0:1, changed state to up
```

Let's verify the connection using the **show dialer** command. The output verifies that we have indeed established communications to London.

```
SOHO800#sho dialer

BRI0 - dialer type = ISDN

Dial String      Successes    Failures    Last called    Last status
5552005                 1           1      00:02:19            failed
5552004                 6           2      00:00:47        successful
5552003                 0           0      never                    -
5552002                 2           0      00:00:14        successful
5552001                 0           0      never                    -
5552000                 2           0      00:00:30        successful
0 incoming call(s) have been screened.
0 incoming call(s) rejected for callback.

BRI0:1 - dialer type = ISDN
Idle timer (120 secs), Fast idle timer (20 secs)
Wait for carrier (30 secs), Re-enable (15 secs)
Dialer state is data link layer up
Dial reason: ip (s=172.31.200.4, d=192.168.2.1)
Time until disconnect 106 secs
Connected to 5552002 (London)

BRI0:2 - dialer type = ISDN
Idle timer (120 secs), Fast idle timer (20 secs)
Wait for carrier (30 secs), Re-enable (15 secs)
Dialer state is data link layer up
Dial reason: ip (s=172.31.200.4, d=192.168.1.1)
Time until disconnect 90 secs, Time until fast disconnect 4294958 secs
Connected to 5552000 (NewYork)
SOHO800#
```

Now that we have looked at our source for the multiple connections from a single source, let's look at the three targets. We will look at each target individually and look at some significant **show** and **debug** commands for each.

New York is our first target. Code Listing 6-4 shows the configuration.

Line 5 defines our authentication database used to connect to SOHO800.

Lines 11 through 20 define our ISDN BRI connection. While we have some PPP commands on lines 13 and 20, we do not have **ppp multilink**. Without this command, we will only use one B-channel for our communications. During the PPP LCP negotiation phase, both sides must agree on a feature to make it active.

Line 23 defines our static default route to the loopback IP address for SOHO800, directing traffic to the exit interface, BRI0/0, and the next hop address, 172.31.200.4.

Line 25 defines our dial control rules—all IP packets are good.

Code Listing 6-4

One-to-many ISDN DDR—NewYork configuration.

```
1    version 11.3
2    !
3    hostname NewYork
4    !
5    username SOHO800 password 0 pass1
6    isdn switch-type basic-ni
7    !
8    interface Loopback0
9     ip address 192.168.1.1 255.255.255.0
10   !
11   interface BRI0/0
12    ip address 172.31.200.1 255.255.255.0
13    encapsulation ppp
14    dialer map ip 172.31.200.4 name SOHO800 5552006
15    dialer map ip 172.31.200.4 name SOHO800 5552007
16    dialer-group 1
17    isdn switch-type basic-ni
18    isdn spid1 21255520000101
19    isdn spid2 21255520010101
20    ppp authentication chap
21   !
22   ip classless
23   ip route 0.0.0.0 0.0.0.0 BRI0/0 172.31.200.4
24   !
25   dialer-list 1 protocol ip permit
26   !
27   !
28   line con 0
29    exec-timeout 0 0
30    length 0
31   line aux 0
32   line vty 0 4
33    password bb
34    login
35   !
36   end
```

The **show dialer** command output shows us that B-channel 1 is used for our connection to London. There is no dial reason shown on BRI0/0:1, indicating that this channel is handling an incoming call.

```
NewYork#show dialer

BRI0/0 - dialer type = ISDN

Dial String      Successes    Failures    Last called    Last status
5552007                  0           0    never                    -
5552006                  0           0    never                    -
0 incoming call(s) have been screened.
0 incoming call(s) rejected for callback.

BRI0/0:1 - dialer type = ISDN
Idle timer (120 secs), Fast idle timer (20 secs)
Wait for carrier (30 secs), Re-enable (15 secs)
Dialer state is data link layer up
```

```
Time until disconnect 10 secs
Connected to 5552006 (SOHO800)

BRI0/0:2 - dialer type = ISDN
Idle timer (120 secs), Fast idle timer (20 secs)
Wait for carrier (30 secs), Re-enable (15 secs)
Dialer state is idle
NewYork#
```

Next we look at the London configuration in Code Listing 6-5. This configuration shows us that London is another target set up without PPP multilink and should only use a single B-channel for communications. See the preceding write-up on NewYork for more details.

Code Listing 6-5
One-to-many DDR—London configuration.

```
1   version 11.3
2   !
3   hostname London
4   !
5   username SOHO800 password 0 pass2
6   isdn switch-type basic-ni
7   !
8   interface Loopback0
9    ip address 192.168.2.1 255.255.255.0
10  !
11  interface BRI0/0
12   ip address 172.31.200.2 255.255.255.0
13   encapsulation ppp
14   dialer map ip 172.31.200.4 name SOHO800 5552006
15   dialer map ip 172.31.200.4 name SOHO800 5552007
16   dialer-group 1
17   isdn switch-type basic-ni
18   isdn spid1 21255520020101
19   isdn spid2 21255520030101
20   ppp authentication chap
21  !
22  ip classless
23  ip route 0.0.0.0 0.0.0.0 BRI0/0 172.31.200.4
24  !
25  dialer-list 1 protocol ip permit
26  !
27  !
28  line con 0
29   exec-timeout 0 0
30   length 0
31  line aux 0
32  line vty 0 4
33   password bb
34   login
35  !
36  end
```

With the new format of the static route used on line 23 in Code Listing 6-5, let's take a look at the **show ip route** command output. The output shows us both the next hop address and the exit interface for our default route.

```
London#show ip route
Codes: C - connected, S - static, I - IGRP, R - RIP, M - mobile, B - BGP
       D - EIGRP, EX - EIGRP external, O - OSPF, IA - OSPF inter area
       N1 - OSPF NSSA external type 1, N2 - OSPF NSSA external type 2
       E1 - OSPF external type 1, E2 - OSPF external type 2, E - EGP
       i - IS-IS, L1 - IS-IS level-1, L2 - IS-IS level-2, * - candidate default
       U - per-user static route, o - ODR

Gateway of last resort is 172.31.200.4 to network 0.0.0.0

     172.31.0.0/24 is subnetted, 1 subnets
C       172.31.200.0 is directly connected, BRI0/0
C    192.168.2.0/24 is directly connected, Loopback0
S*   0.0.0.0/0 [1/0] via 172.31.200.4, BRI0/0
```

Our final target is Rome, and Code Listing 6-6 shows the configuration. The main difference between Rome and the other targets shows up on line 18. This target has **ppp multilink** activated.

Code Listing 6-6
One-to-many ISDN
DDR—Rome configuration.

```
1    hostname Rome
2    !
3    username SOHO800 password 0 pass3
4    isdn switch-type basic-ni1
5    !
6    interface Loopback0
7      ip address 192.168.3.1 255.255.255.0
8    !
9    interface BRI0
10     ip address 172.31.200.3 255.255.255.0
11     encapsulation ppp
12     dialer map ip 172.31.200.4 name SOHO800 5552006
13     dialer map ip 172.31.200.4 name SOHO800 5552007
14     dialer-group 1
15     isdn spid1 21255520040101
16     isdn spid2 21255520050101
17     ppp authentication chap
18     ppp multilink
19     !
20   ip classless
21   ip route 0.0.0.0 0.0.0.0 BRI0 172.31.200.4
22   !
23   dialer-list 1 protocol ip permit
24   !
25   line con 0
26     exec-timeout 0 0
27     length 0
28   line aux 0
```

```
29  line vty 0 4
30   login
31  !
32  end
```

Let's turn on some **debug** statements and watch the results. First we will use the **debug dialer** command to watch the incoming connection process. We see the individual B-channel activate and then the Virtual Access interface activate to indicate that a multilink connection has been negotiated.

```
Rome#debug dialer
Dial on demand events debugging is on
Rome#
00:33:00: %LINK-3-UPDOWN: Interface BRI0:1, changed state to up
00:33:01: %LINK-3-UPDOWN: Interface Virtual-Access1, changed state to up
00:33:01: dialer Protocol up for Vi1
00:33:01: %LINEPROTO-5-UPDOWN: Line protocol on Interface BRI0:1, changed state to up
00:33:01: %LINEPROTO-5-UPDOWN: Line protocol on Interface Virtual-Access1, changed state
    to up
00:33:06: %ISDN-6-CONNECT: Interface BRI0:1 is now connected to 5552006 SOHO800
Rome#
```

The **show dialer** command indicates the BRI0 is up and part of a multilink bundle. There is no dial reason, so this is an incoming call.

```
Rome#show dialer

BRI0 - dialer type = ISDN

Dial String      Successes    Failures    Last called    Last status
5552007             0            0         never              -
5552006             0            0         never              -
0 incoming call(s) have been screened.
0 incoming call(s) rejected for callback.

BRI0:1 - dialer type = ISDN
Idle timer (120 secs), Fast idle timer (20 secs)
Wait for carrier (30 secs), Re-enable (15 secs)
Dialer state is multilink member
Connected to 5552006 (SOHO800)

BRI0:2 - dialer type = ISDN
Idle timer (120 secs), Fast idle timer (20 secs)
Wait for carrier (30 secs), Re-enable (15 secs)
Dialer state is idle
```

The **show ppp multilink** command lets us see our BRI0 interface added to the multilink bundle SOHO800.

```
Rome#show ppp multilink

Bundle SOHO800, 1 member, Master link is Virtual-Access1
Dialer Interface is BRI0
  0 lost fragments, 0 reordered, 0 unassigned, sequence 0x0/0x0 rcvd/sent
  0 discarded, 0 lost received, 1/255 load

Member Link: 1 (max not set, min not set)
BRI0:1
```

Before we activate another channel from SOHO800, we turn on
debug ppp multilink events to observe adding an additional B-channel for the incoming call.

```
Rome#debug ppp multilink events
Multilink events debugging is on
Rome#
```

When BRI0:2 is activated, it is added to our current bundle,
SOHO800.

```
00:35:15: %LINK-3-UPDOWN: Interface BRI0:2, changed state to up
00:35:15: BR0:2 MLP: Multilink up event pending
00:35:15: BR0:2 MLP: SOHO800, multilink up
00:35:16: %LINEPROTO-5-UPDOWN: Line protocol on Interface BRI0:2, changed state to up
00:35:21: %ISDN-6-CONNECT: Interface BRI0:2 is now connected to 5552006 SOHO800
Rome#
```

The **show dialer** command output shows both B-channels up and
running as multilink members connected to SOHO800.

```
Rome#show dialer

BRI0 - dialer type = ISDN

Dial String      Successes    Failures    Last called    Last status
5552007                 0           0     never                    -
5552006                 0           0     never                    -
0 incoming call(s) have been screened.
0 incoming call(s) rejected for callback.

BRI0:1 - dialer type = ISDN
Idle timer (120 secs), Fast idle timer (20 secs)
Wait for carrier (30 secs), Re-enable (15 secs)
Dialer state is multilink member
Connected to 5552006 (SOHO800)

BRI0:2 - dialer type = ISDN
Idle timer (120 secs), Fast idle timer (20 secs)
Wait for carrier (30 secs), Re-enable (15 secs)
Dialer state is multilink member
Connected to 5552006 (SOHO800)
Rome#
```

The **show ppp multilink** command shows us that both channels are members of the SOHO800 bundle.

```
Rome#show ppp multilink

Bundle SOHO800, 2 members, Master link is Virtual-Access1
Dialer Interface is BRI0
   0 lost fragments, 0 reordered, 0 unassigned, sequence 0x102/0x102 rcvd/sent
   0 discarded, 0 lost received, 1/255 load

Member Links: 2 (max not set, min not set)
BRI0:2
BRI0:1
```

When the call is terminated from the other end, we can watch the call termination process with the **debug dialer** and **debug ppp multilink events** active.

```
Rome#
00:37:34: BR0:2 MLP: Multilink down event pending
00:37:34: BR0:2 MLP: Removing link from SOHO800
00:37:34: BR0:1 MLP: Multilink down event pending
00:37:34: BR0:1 MLP: Removing link from SOHO800
00:37:34: SOHO800 MLP: Removing bundle
00:37:34: Virtual-Access1: disconnecting call
00:37:34: %LINK-3-UPDOWN: Interface Virtual-Access1, changed state to down
00:37:34: %ISDN-6-DISCONNECT: Interface BRI0:2  disconnected from 5552006 SOHO800, call
   lasted 139 seconds
00:37:34: %LINK-3-UPDOWN: Interface BRI0:2, changed state to down
00:37:34: BRI0:2: disconnecting call
00:37:34: %ISDN-6-DISCONNECT: Interface BRI0:1  disconnected from 5552006 SOHO800, call
   lasted 273 seconds
00:37:34: %LINK-3-UPDOWN: Interface BRI0:1, changed state to down
00:37:34: BRI0:1: disconnecting call
00:37:35: %LINEPROTO-5-UPDOWN: Line protocol on Interface BRI0:1, changed state to down
00:37:35: %LINEPROTO-5-UPDOWN: Line protocol on Interface BRI0:2, changed state to down
00:37:35: %LINEPROTO-5-UPDOWN: Line protocol on Interface Virtual-Access1, changed state
   to down
```

Basic BRI-to-PRI Connectivity

This example will use a Cisco 1720 BRI interface to connect to the channelized T1/PRI interface on the Cisco 3640. For more information about T1 connections, I recommend reading *T-1 Networking* by William A. Flannagan.

While the following example is similar to the earlier examples, it does highlight the configuration steps necessary to activate an ISDN PRI interface. Figure 6-4 shows the equipment layout.

The following is the configuration for Rome, our BRI device. Code Listing 6-7 shows the configuration. Nothing in Rome's configuration differs from the configuration in our previous example. Oops, I almost forgot—we have a **dialer load-threshold 100 outbound** command on line 17.

Code Listing 6-7
BRI to PRI ISDN
DDR—Rome configuration.

```
1   version 12.0
2   !
3   hostname Rome
4   !
5   username NewYork password 0 cisco
6   ip subnet-zero
7   !
8   isdn switch-type basic-ni
9   !
10  !
11  interface BRI0
12    ip address 172.31.1.2 255.255.255.0
13    no ip directed-broadcast
14    encapsulation ppp
15    load-interval 30
16    dialer map ip 172.31.1.1 name NewYork 5558000
17    dialer load-threshold 100 outbound
18    dialer-group 1
19    isdn switch-type basic-ni
20    isdn spid1 21255520290101
21    isdn spid2 21255520300101
22    ppp authentication chap
23    ppp multilink
24  !
25  interface FastEthernet0
26    ip address 172.31.205.1 255.255.255.0
27    no ip directed-broadcast
28  !
29  ip classless
30  ip route 172.31.200.0 255.255.255.0 BRI0 172.31.1.1
31  no ip http server
32  !
33  dialer-list 1 protocol ip permit
34  !
35  line con 0
36    logging synchronous
37    length 0
38    transport input none
39  line aux 0
40  line vty 0 4
41  !
42  end
```

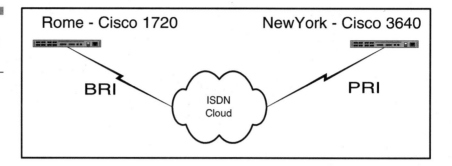

NewYork is where all the new and interesting configuration changes take place. Code Listing 6-8 shows this configuration.

The PRI configuration commands show up in two separate areas below. Lines 10 through 13 are the key to activating PRI communications. Line 10 selects the channelized T1 controller in slot 1, port 0 of our 3640. Line 11 defines the framing type as extended super frame (ESF) for PRI connections. Line 12 defines the way data is transmitted by defining the line encoding as bipolar 8 zero suppression (b8zs). These commands would be typical for a standard T1 connection if we were to set this up as full or multiple fractional T1 serial connections. (Chapter 9 provides an example of channelized T1.) Line 13 is where we change the way we handle communications with the Central Office (CO) switch. The **pri-group** command is entered after the **controller t1 1/0** command, but only after Line 8, **isdn switch-type primary-5ess**, has been entered globally. If the timeslots 1-24 option is omitted, Cisco IOS will generate that information after interrogating the switch. In addition, the second half of our ISDN PRI configuration, interface serial 1/0:23, is automatically generated.

Line 19 is the configuration command generated after the **pri-group** command is entered. You may experience a slight delay while this interface is generated. The balance of the commands on lines 20 through 28 may look familiar; they are exactly the same as in previous examples using BRI interfaces. Even our static route on line 32 looks the same as before, using our generated serial 1/0:23 interface.

Code Listing 6-8

```
1    version 12.0
2    !
3    hostname NewYork
4    !
5    username Rome password 0 cisco
6    ip subnet-zero
7    no ip domain-lookup
8    isdn switch-type primary-5ess
9    !
10   controller T1 1/0
11    framing esf
12    linecode b8zs
13    pri-group timeslots 1-24
14   !
15   interface Ethernet0/0
16    ip address 172.31.200.1 255.255.255.0
17    no ip directed-broadcast
18   !
19   interface Serial1/0:23
20    ip address 172.31.1.1 255.255.255.0
21    no ip directed-broadcast
22    encapsulation ppp
23    dialer map ip 172.31.1.2 name Rome 5552030
24    dialer map ip 172.31.1.2 name Rome 5552029
25    dialer-group 1
26    isdn switch-type primary-5ess
27    ppp authentication chap
28    ppp multilink
29    hold-queue 75 in
30   !
31   ip classless
32   ip route 172.31.205.0 255.255.255.0 Serial1/0:23 172.31.1.2
33   !
34   dialer-list 1 protocol ip permit
35   !
36   line con 0
37    logging synchronous
38    length 0
39    transport input none
40   line 65 70
41   line aux 0
42   line vty 0 4
43   !
44   end
```

Now it's time for some testing. We will use the extended **ping** command to generate a significant amount of data so that we will eventually activate a second B-channel.

```
NewYork#ping
Protocol [ip]:
Target IP address: 172.31.205.1
Repeat count [5]: 1000000
Datagram size [100]:
Timeout in seconds [2]:
```

```
Extended commands [n]:
Sweep range of sizes [n]:
Type escape sequence to abort.
Sending 1000000, 100-byte ICMP Echos to 172.31.205.1, timeout is 2 seconds:
.!!!!!!!!!!!!!!!!!!!!!!!!!!!!!!!!!!!!!!!!!!!!!!!!!!!!!!!!!!!!!!!!!!!!!!!!!!!!!
!!!!!!!!!!!!!!!!!!!!!!!!!!!!!!!!!!!!!!!!!!!!!!!!!!!!!!!!!!!!!!!!!!!!!!!!!!!!!!!
!!!!!!!!!!!!!!!!!!!!!!!!!!!!!!!!!!!!!!!!!!!!!!!!!!!!!
```

We interrupt this **ping** to take a look at events in our target, Rome. If we look at the `txload` and `rxload` values in the **show interface bri 0 1** command output below, we can see if our second channel is ready to be activated.

```
Rome#sho int bri 0 1
BRI0:1 is up, line protocol is up
  Hardware is PQUICC BRI with U interface
  MTU 1500 bytes, BW 64 Kbit, DLY 20000 usec,
     reliability 255/255, txload 51/255, rxload 51/255
  Encapsulation PPP, loopback not set
  Keepalive set (10 sec)
  LCP Open, multilink Open
  Last input 00:00:00, output 00:00:00, output hang never
  Last clearing of "show interface" counters never
  Queueing strategy: fifo
  Output queue 0/40, 0 drops; input queue 0/75, 0 drops
  30 second input rate 13000 bits/sec, 15 packets/sec
  30 second output rate 13000 bits/sec, 15 packets/sec
     14411 packets input, 697286 bytes, 0 no buffer
     Received 0 broadcasts, 0 runts, 0 giants, 0 throttles
     0 input errors, 0 CRC, 0 frame, 0 overrun, 0 ignored, 0 abort
     14402 packets output, 696270 bytes, 0 underruns
     0 output errors, 0 collisions, 0 interface resets
     0 output buffer failures, 0 output buffers swapped out
     55 carrier transitions
```

Several minutes have passed. If we look again at our `txload` value, we see that it is at $99/255$, almost over the limit.

```
Rome#sho int bri 0 1
BRI0:1 is up, line protocol is up
  Hardware is PQUICC BRI with U interface
  MTU 1500 bytes, BW 64 Kbit, DLY 20000 usec,
     reliability 255/255, txload 99/255, rxload 99/255
  Encapsulation PPP, loopback not set
  Keepalive set (10 sec)
  LCP Open, multilink Open
  Last input 00:00:00, output 00:00:00, output hang never
  Last clearing of "show interface" counters never
  Queueing strategy: fifo
  Output queue 0/40, 0 drops; input queue 0/75, 0 drops
  30 second input rate 25000 bits/sec, 31 packets/sec
  30 second output rate 25000 bits/sec, 31 packets/sec
     16285 packets input, 891126 bytes, 0 no buffer
```

```
Received 0 broadcasts, 0 runts, 0 giants, 0 throttles
0 input errors, 0 CRC, 0 frame, 0 overrun, 0 ignored, 0 abort
16276 packets output, 890110 bytes, 0 underruns
0 output errors, 0 collisions, 0 interface resets
0 output buffer failures, 0 output buffers swapped out
55 carrier transitions
Rome#
```

Here we go at last. We hit the limit and activate a second B-channel to be added to our multilink connection.

```
02:47:197568495616: %LINK-3-UPDOWN: Interface BRI0:2, changed state to up
02:47:47: %LINEPROTO-5-UPDOWN: Line protocol on Interface BRI0:2, changed state to up
02:47:52: %ISDN-6-CONNECT: Interface BRI0:1 is now connected to 5558000 NewYork
```

The **show ppp multilink** command identifies our two BRI B-channels as part of the NewYork bundle assigned to interface Virtual Access 1.

```
Rome#show ppp multilink

Virtual-Access1, bundle name is NewYork
  Dialer interface is BRI0
  0 lost fragments, 0 reordered, 0 unassigned, sequence 0x754/0x754 rcvd/sent
  0 discarded, 0 lost received, 67/255 load
  Member links: 2 (max not set, min not set)
    BRI0:1
    BRI0:2
```

The **show dialer** command let us look at the processing sequence for our second B-channel. BRI 0:1 was activated by a call from NewYork. BRI0:2 was brought up due to our multilink bundle being overloaded, and the call was initiated from Rome.

```
Rome#show dialer

BRI0 - dialer type = ISDN

Dial String      Successes    Failures    Last called    Last status
5558000               13           0        00:00:34       successful
0 incoming call(s) have been screened.
0 incoming call(s) rejected for callback.

BRI0:1 - dialer type = ISDN
Idle timer (120 secs), Fast idle timer (20 secs)
Wait for carrier (30 secs), Re-enable (15 secs)
Dialer state is multilink member
Connected to 5558000 (NewYork)

BRI0:2 - dialer type = ISDN
Idle timer (120 secs), Fast idle timer (20 secs)
```

```
Wait for carrier (30 secs), Re-enable (15 secs)
Dialer state is multilink member
Dial reason: Multilink bundle overloaded
Connected to 5558000 (NewYork)
Rome#
```

Looking back to NewYork to see our ISDN PRI information, it seems that our **ping** is still chugging along. Use the standard escape sequence to break out of the **ping** so we can use some **show** commands to verify how the ISDN B-channels are being allocated.

```
!!!!!!!!!!!!!!!!!!!!!!!!!!!!!!!!!!!!!!!!!!!!!!!!!!!!!!!!!!!!!!!!!!!!!
!!!!!!!!!!!!!!!!!!!!!!!!!!!!!!!!!!!!!!!!!!!!!!!!!!!!!!!!!!!!!!!!!!!!!!!
!!!!!!!!!!!!!!!!!!!!!!!!!!!!!!!!!!!!!!!!!!!!!!!!!!!!!!!!!!!!!!!!!!!!!!!
!!!!!!!!!!!!!!!!.
Success rate is 99 percent (5193/5195), round-trip min/avg/max = 20/26/64 ms
NewYork#
```

The following is an excerpt from the **debug ppp negotiation** command showing that each individual B-channel goes through authentication before being added to our multilink bundle.

```
NewYork#
02:52:40: %LINEPROTO-5-UPDOWN: Line protocol on Interface Serial1/0:22, changed state to
   up
02:52:40: %LINEPROTO-5-UPDOWN: Line protocol on Interface Virtual-Access1, changed state
   to up
02:52:45: %ISDN-6-CONNECT: Interface Serial1/0:22 is now connected to 5552030 Rome
02:54:08: %LINK-3-UPDOWN: Interface Serial1/0:21, changed state to up
02:54:08: Se1/0:21 PPP: Treating connection as a callin
02:54:08: Se1/0:21 PPP: Phase is AUTHENTICATING, by both
02:54:08: Se1/0:21 CHAP: O CHALLENGE id 2 len 28 from "NewYork"
02:54:08: Se1/0:21 CHAP: I CHALLENGE id 2 len 25 from "Rome"
02:54:08: Se1/0:21 CHAP: Waiting for peer to authenticate first
02:54:08: Se1/0:21 CHAP: I RESPONSE id 2 len 25 from "Rome"
02:54:08: Se1/0:21 CHAP: O SUCCESS id 2 len 4
02:54:08: Se1/0:21 CHAP: Processing saved Challenge, id 2
02:54:08: Se1/0:21 CHAP: O RESPONSE id 2 len 28 from "NewYork"
02:54:08: Se1/0:21 CHAP: I SUCCESS id 2 len 4
02:54:09: %LINEPROTO-5-UPDOWN: Line protocol on Interface Serial1/0:21, changed state to
   up
02:54:14: %ISDN-6-CONNECT: Interface Serial1/0:21 is now connected to 5552030 Rome
NewYork#
```

The **show ppp multilink** command output shows our two B-channels active on the Rome bundle. In the display below, it shows us that there were 15 reordered fragments during our normal transmission. This is a normal function when PPP multilink operates.

```
NewYork#show ppp multilink

Bundle Rome, 2 members, Master link is Virtual-Access1
Dialer Interface is Serial1/0:23
  0 lost fragments, 15 reordered, 0 unassigned, sequence 0x1364/0x1362 rcvd/sent
  0 discarded, 0 lost received, 47/255 load

Member Links: 2 (max not set, min not set)
Serial1/0:22
Serial1/0:21
```

The **show dialer** command output let us look at all 23 of the B-channels and signaling channel 23. Channel 22 initiated the call to Rome, and channel 21 is the return connection from Rome based on the overload condition.

```
NewYork#show dialer

Serial1/0:0 - dialer type = ISDN
Idle timer (120 secs), Fast idle timer (20 secs)
Wait for carrier (30 secs), Re-enable (15 secs)
Dialer state is idle

    .
    . deleted for clarity
    .

Serial1/0:20 - dialer type = ISDN
Idle timer (120 secs), Fast idle timer (20 secs)
Wait for carrier (30 secs), Re-enable (15 secs)
Dialer state is idle

Serial1/0:21 - dialer type = ISDN
Idle timer (120 secs), Fast idle timer (20 secs)
Wait for carrier (30 secs), Re-enable (15 secs)
Dialer state is multilink member
Connected to 5552030 (Rome)

Serial1/0:22 - dialer type = ISDN
Idle timer (120 secs), Fast idle timer (20 secs)
Wait for carrier (30 secs), Re-enable (15 secs)
Dialer state is multilink member
Dial reason: ip (s=172.31.1.1, d=172.31.205.1)
Connected to 5552030 (Rome)

Serial1/0:23 - dialer type = ISDN

Dial String      Successes    Failures    Last called    Last status
5552029                  0           0    never                    -
5552030                 14           0    00:02:56        successful
0 incoming call(s) have been screened.
0 incoming call(s) rejected for callback.
NewYork#
```

Let's **ping** from Rome to make sure that the connection works both ways.

```
Rome#ping 172.31.200.1

Type escape sequence to abort.
Sending 5, 100-byte ICMP Echos to 172.31.200.1, timeout is 2 seconds:
!!!!!
Success rate is 100 percent (5/5), round-trip min/avg/max = 32/32/32
  ms
```

Looking at B-channel 1 on Rome's BRI interface reveals that LCP and multilink are open and traffic is flowing.

```
Rome#show interface bri 0 1
BRI0:1 is up, line protocol is up
  Hardware is PQUICC BRI with U interface
  MTU 1500 bytes, BW 64 Kbit, DLY 20000 usec,
     reliability 255/255, txload 1/255, rxload 1/255
  Encapsulation PPP, loopback not set
  Keepalive set (10 sec)
  LCP Open, multilink Open
  Last input 00:00:00, output 00:00:00, output hang never
  Last clearing of "show interface" counters never
  Queueing strategy: fifo
  Output queue 0/40, 0 drops; input queue 0/75, 0 drops
  30 second input rate 0 bits/sec, 1 packets/sec
  30 second output rate 0 bits/sec, 0 packets/sec
     18992 packets input, 1056064 bytes, 0 no buffer
     Received 0 broadcasts, 0 runts, 0 giants, 0 throttles
     0 input errors, 0 CRC, 0 frame, 0 overrun, 0 ignored, 0 abort
     18983 packets output, 1055002 bytes, 0 underruns
     0 output errors, 0 collisions, 0 interface resets
     0 output buffer failures, 0 output buffers swapped out
     55 carrier transitions
```

This is the end of the BRI-to-PRI example.

Dialer Profiles

Now that we have covered the basics with interface-to-interface ISDN communications, it is time to extend the scope of Dial-on-Demand Routing (DDR) by adding in dialer profiles. We will change how we connect from a single site to multiple remote sites without using **dialer map** commands. Instead we will create individual dialer profiles for each of our remote sites. With dialer profiles, we have to introduce a new concept, dialer pools. A dialer profile references a dialer pool instead of a specific interface. The individual interfaces can then be assigned to the dialer pool, making the type and number of physical connections completely disconnected from the logical dialer profile. You will learn more details when we get to the NewYork router. Chapter 10 will examine an additional working example.

Figure 6-5 shows the equipment layout for the dialer profile example.

We will examine the three test routers before we implement the dialer profiles in the NewYork Cisco 3640 router.

The first router we will look at is the Cisco 766, SOHO700, with the configuration in Code Listing 6-9. For more information on configuring the Cisco 700 series, check out *Configuring Cisco Routers for ISDN* by Paul Fischer.

At first the configuration looks daunting because of its size; after all, it is 140 lines of information. For this configuration, I have listed all the lines that need to be entered with their meanings.

Line 9 is where we set the switch type.

Lines 10 through 13 are where we define the SPIDs and Local Dial Numbers (LDNs) for our BRI connection. If this router is only going to be used for outgoing calls, then we do not need lines 11 and 13.

Line 36 defines the system name, which then becomes the prompt.

Lines 39 and 40 were set up to enable threshold levels that would trigger an additional B-channel.

Line 58 has to be put in place to enable incoming calls to be processed using CHAP authentication.

Line 62 sets up the local router's CHAP password (encryption key).

Line 69 sets up PPP multilink processing.

Lines 99 through 103 define the operation of our LAN profile, bridging off, IP routing on, and the IP addressing.

Figure 6-5
Dialer profiles equipment layout.

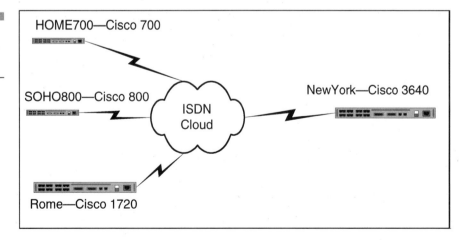

Line 123 defines the user profile for NewYork. If NewYork is going to connect to SOHO700, then the spelling of this profile MUST match the hostname of the device calling.

Lines 127 through 134 and line 140 define the operation of our profile named NewYork. These lines turn off bridging, set the phone numbers to call NewYork, set up our CHAP password (encryption key) for NewYork, turn on IP routing, set the IP addressing, prepare to use PPP encapsulation, and set the default route.

If you take the lines above, put them in a text file, and then apply them to a clean Cisco 7xx router, then the router will be fully functional for a single remote connection. If you have to connect to multiple sites, copy the profile for NewYork, make the appropriate phone number and IP addressing changes, and send the template to the console connection.

Code Listing 6-9

```
1    SOHO700> upload
2    CD
3    SET SCREENLENGTH 20
4    SET COUNTRYGROUP 1
5    SET LAN MODE ANY
6    SET WAN MODE ONLY
7    SET AGE OFF
8    SET MULTIDESTINATION OFF
9    SET SWITCH NI-1
10   SET 1 SPID 21255520310101
11   SET 1 DIRECTORYNUMBER 5552031
12   SET 2 SPID 21255520320101
13   SET 2 DIRECTORYNUMBER 5552032
14   SET AUTODETECTION  OFF
15   SET CONFERENCE 60
16   SET TRANSFER 61
17   SET 1 DELAY 30
18   SET 2 DELAY 30
19   SET BRIDGING ON
20   SET LEARN ON
21   SET PASSTHRU OFF
22   SET SPEED AUTO
23   SET PLAN NORMAL
24   SET 1 AUTO ON
25   SET 2 AUTO ON
26   SET 1 NUMBER
27   SET 2 NUMBER
28   SET 1 BACKUPNUMBER
29   SET 2 BACKUPNUMBER
30   SET 1 RINGBACK
31   SET 2 RINGBACK
32   SET 1 CLIVALIDATENUMBER
33   SET 2 CLIVALIDATENUMBER
34   SET CLICALLBACK OFF
35   SET CLIAUTHENTICATION OFF
36   SET SYSTEMNAME SOHO700
37   LOG CALLS TIME VERBOSE
```

Code Listing 6-9
(continued)

```
38   SET UNICASTFILTER OFF
39   DEMAND 1 THRESHOLD 20
40   DEMAND 2 THRESHOLD 20
41   DEMAND 1 DURATION 1
42   DEMAND 2 DURATION 1
43   DEMAND 1 SOURCE LAN
44   DEMAND 2 SOURCE BOTH
45   TIMEOUT 1 THRESHOLD 0
46   TIMEOUT 2 THRESHOLD 48
47   TIMEOUT 1 DURATION 0
48   TIMEOUT 2 DURATION 0
49   TIMEOUT 1 SOURCE LAN
50   TIMEOUT 2 SOURCE BOTH
51   SET REMOTEACCESS PROTECTED
52   SET LOCALACCESS ON
53   SET LOGOUT 5
54   SET CALLERID OFF
55   SET PPP AUTHENTICATION IN CHAP  PAP
56   SET PPP CHAPREFUSE NONE
57   SET PPP CHAPALLOW MULTIHOST OFF
58   SET PPP AUTHENTICATION OUT CHAP
59   SET PPP AUTHENTICATION ACCEPT EITHER
60   SET PPP TAS CLIENT 0.0.0.0
61   SET PPP TAS CHAPSECRET LOCAL ON
62   SET PPP SECRET CLIENT ENCRYPTED 05080f1c2243
63   SET PPP CALLBACK REQUEST OFF
64   SET PPP CALLBACK REPLY OFF
65   SET PPP NEGOTIATION INTEGRITY 10
66   SET PPP NEGOTIATION COUNT 10
67   SET PPP NEGOTIATION RETRY  3000
68   SET PPP TERMREQ COUNT 2
69   SET PPP MULTILINK ON
70   SET PPP MULTILINK PPPHEADER ON
71   SET COMPRESSION STAC
72   SET PPP BACP ON
73   SET PPP ADDRESS NEGOTIATION LOCAL OFF
74   SET PPP IP NETMASK LOCAL OFF
75   SET IP PAT UDPTIMEOUT 5
76   SET IP PAT TCPTIMEOUT 30
77   SET IP RIP TIME 30
78   SET CALLDURATION 0
79   SET SNMP CONTACT ""
80   SET SNMP LOCATION ""
81   SET SNMP TRAP COLDSTART OFF
82   SET SNMP TRAP WARMSTART OFF
83   SET SNMP TRAP LINKDOWN OFF
84   SET SNMP TRAP LINKUP OFF
85   SET SNMP TRAP AUTHENTICATIONFAIL OFF
86   SET DHCP OFF
87   SET DHCP DOMAIN
88   SET DHCP NETBIOS_SCOPE
89   SET VOICEPRIORITY INCOMING INTERFACE PHONE1 ALWAYS
90   SET VOICEPRIORITY OUTGOING INTERFACE PHONE1 ALWAYS
91   SET CALLWAITING INTERFACE PHONE1 ON
92   SET VOICEPRIORITY INCOMING INTERFACE PHONE2 ALWAYS
93   SET VOICEPRIORITY OUTGOING INTERFACE PHONE2 ALWAYS
94   SET CALLWAITING INTERFACE PHONE2 ON
95   SET CALLTIME VOICE INCOMING OFF
```

Code Listing 6-9
(continued)

```
96   SET CALLTIME VOICE OUTGOING OFF
97   SET CALLTIME DATA INCOMING OFF
98   SET CALLTIME DATA OUTGOING OFF
99   SET USER LAN
100  SET BRIDGING OFF
101  SET IP ROUTING ON
102  SET IP ADDRESS 172.31.215.1
103  SET IP NETMASK 255.255.255.0
104  SET IP FRAMING ETHERNET_II
105  SET IP PROPAGATE ON
106  SET IP COST 1
107  SET IP RIP RECEIVE V1
108  SET IP RIP UPDATE OFF
109  SET IP RIP VERSION 1
110  SET USER Internal
111  SET IP FRAMING ETHERNET_II
112  SET USER Standard
113  SET PROFILE ID 000000000000
114  SET PROFILE POWERUP ACTIVATE
115  SET PROFILE DISCONNECT KEEP
116  SET IP ROUTING ON
117  SET IP ADDRESS 0.0.0.0
118  SET IP NETMASK 0.0.0.0
119  SET IP FRAMING NONE
120  SET IP RIP RECEIVE V1
121  SET IP RIP UPDATE OFF
122  SET IP RIP VERSION 1
123  SET USER NewYork
124  SET PROFILE ID 000000000000
125  SET PROFILE POWERUP ACTIVATE
126  SET PROFILE DISCONNECT KEEP
127  SET BRIDGING OFF
128  SET 1 NUMBER 5558000
129  SET 2 NUMBER 5558000
130  SET PPP SECRET HOST ENCRYPTED 060506324f41
131  SET IP ROUTING ON
132  SET IP ADDRESS 172.31.3.2
133  SET IP NETMASK 255.255.255.0
134  SET IP FRAMING NONE
135  SET IP PROPAGATE ON
136  SET IP COST 1
137  SET IP RIP RECEIVE V1
138  SET IP RIP UPDATE OFF
139  SET IP RIP VERSION 1
140  SET IP ROUTE DEST 0.0.0.0/0 GATEWAY 172.31.3.1 PROPAGATE OFF COST 1
141  CD
142  LOGOUT
143  SOHO700>
```

The standard method for testing is the **ping** command.

```
SOHO700> ping 172.31.200.1
Start sending:01/01/1995 00:20:02  L05  0      5558000  Outgoing Call Initiated
SOHO700> 01/01/1995 00:20:02  L08  1      5558000  Call Connected
SOHO700> 01/01/1995 00:20:02  Connection 2 Add     Link 1 Channel 1
SOHO700>  round trip time is 1950 msec.
```

```
SOHO700> 01/01/1995 00:22:03  Connection 2 Remove  Link 1 Channel 1
SOHO700> 01/01/1995 00:22:03  L12  1               Disconnected Remotely
Cause 16  Normal Disconnect
SOHO700> 01/01/1995 00:22:03  L27  1               Disconnected
```

Now **ping** the other side to verify that the call we received from New-York connects SOHO700 to the rest of the network.

```
SOHO700> 01/01/1995 00:22:40  L11  1               Call Requested
SOHO700> 01/01/1995 00:22:40  L14  1               Accepting Call
SOHO700> 01/01/1995 00:22:41  L08  1               Call Connected
SOHO700> 01/01/1995 00:22:43  Connection 2 Add     Link 1 Channel 1
SOHO700> ping 172.31.200.1
Start sending: round trip time is 50 msec.
SOHO700>
```

Code Listing 6-10 shows the configuration for our Cisco 802 router, SOHO800. While this configuration is almost identical to most of the earlier ISDN BRI examples, there are a few special configuration lines that are important.

Line 19 is especially significant as it will speed up the second B-channel activation process. The normal setting for **load-interval** is 300 seconds. The load on an interface is calculated by taking activity snapshots every five seconds and maintaining a five-minute (300-second) running average. By changing the running average time to 30 seconds, each five-second snapshot takes on a greater importance in the calculation. Additional B-channels will be activated more quickly because the interface reacts more quickly to sudden increases in traffic. The inverse is true as well; when traffic levels drop back down, the interface drops the additional channels more quickly.

■ ■

Code Listing 6-10
Dialer Profiles—
SOHO800 configuration.

```
1    version 12.0
2    !
3    hostname SOHO800
4    !
5    username NewYork password 0 cisco
6    ip subnet-zero
7    !
8    no ip domain-lookup
9    isdn switch-type basic-ni
10   !
11   interface Ethernet0
12     ip address 172.31.210.1 255.255.255.0
13     no ip directed-broadcast
14   !
15   interface BRI0
16     ip address 172.31.2.2 255.255.255.0
```

▪ |

Code Listing 6-10
(continued)

```
17    no ip directed-broadcast
18    encapsulation ppp
19    load-interval 30
20    dialer map ip 172.31.2.1 name NewYork 5558000
21    dialer load-threshold 50 outbound
22    dialer-group 1
23    isdn switch-type basic-ni
24    isdn spid1 21255520270101
25    isdn spid2 21255520280101
26    ppp authentication chap
27    ppp multilink
28    hold-queue 75 in
29    !
30   no ip http server
31   ip classless
32   ip route 172.31.200.0 255.255.255.0 BRI0 172.31.2.1
33   !
34   dialer-list 1 protocol ip permit
35   !
36   line con 0
37    exec-timeout 0 0
38    logging synchronous
39    length 0
40    transport input none
41    stopbits 1
42   line vty 0 4
43    login
44   !
45   end
```

Now for a quick test with a **ping** to NewYork.

```
SOHO800#ping 172.31.200.1

Type escape sequence to abort.
Sending 5, 100-byte ICMP Echos to 172.31.200.1, timeout is 2 seconds:
.!!!!
Success rate is 80 percent (4/5), round-trip min/avg/max = 32/34/36 ms
SOHO800#
```

The **debug dialer** command output follows the activation of BRI0:1, our test connection to NewYork.

```
06:00:06: BRI0: Dialing cause ip (s=172.31.2.2, d=172.31.200.1)
06:00:06: BRI0: Attempting to dial 5558000
06:00:06: %LINK-3-UPDOWN: Interface BRI0:1, changed state to up
06:00:06: %LINK-3-UPDOWN: Interface Virtual-Access1, changed state to up
06:00:06: dialer Protocol up for Vi1
06:00:07: %LINEPROTO-5-UPDOWN: Line protocol on Interface BRI0:1, changed state to up
06:00:07: %LINEPROTO-5-UPDOWN: Line protocol on Interface Virtual-Access1, changed state
     to up
06:00:12: %ISDN-6-CONNECT: Interface BRI0:1 is now connected to 5558000 NewYork
```

It's time for an extended **ping** to see if our second B-channel is activated.

```
SOHO800#ping
Protocol [ip]:
Target IP address: 172.31.200.1
Repeat count [5]: 10000
Datagram size [100]:
Timeout in seconds [2]:
Extended commands [n]:
Sweep range of sizes [n]:
Type escape sequence to abort.
Sending 10000, 100-byte ICMP Echos to 172.31.200.1, timeout is 2 seconds:
!!!!!!!!!!!!!!!!!!!!!!!!!!!!!!!!!!!!!!!!!!!!!!!!!!!!!!!!!!!!!!!!!!!!!!!
.
. Deleted for clarity
.
!!!!!!!!!!!!!!!!!!!!!!!!!!!!!!!!!!!!!!!!!!!!!!!!!!!!!!!!!!!!!!!!!!!!!!!
!!!!!!!!!!!!!!!!!!!!!!!!!!!!!!!!!!!!!!!!!!!!!!!!!!!!!!!!!!!!!!!!!!!
Success rate is 100 percent (10000/10000), round-trip min/avg/max = 20/24/96 ms
SOHO800#
```

Our normal interface state changes show us that the second B-channel does come up. After an appropriate idle time, the Virtual Access interface disconnects the call.

```
06:01:57: BRI0: Attempting to dial 5558000
06:01:58: %LINK-3-UPDOWN: Interface BRI0:2, changed state to up
06:01:59: %LINEPROTO-5-UPDOWN: Line protocol on Interface BRI0:2, changed state to up
06:02:04: %ISDN-6-CONNECT: Interface BRI0:1 is now connected to 5558000 NewYork
SOHO800#
06:07:48: Virtual-Access1: idle timeout
06:07:48: Virtual-Access1: disconnecting call
06:07:48: %LINK-3-UPDOWN: Interface Virtual-Access1, changed state to down
06:07:48: BRI0:1: disconnecting call
06:07:48: BRI0:2: disconnecting call
06:07:206158471168: %ISDN-6-DISCONNECT: Interface BRI0:1  disconnected from 5558000
   NewYork, call lasted 461 seconds
06:07:206158471168: %ISDN-6-DISCONNECT: Interface BRI0:2  disconnected from 5558000
   NewYork, call lasted 350 seconds
06:07:48: %LINK-3-UPDOWN: Interface BRI0:1, changed state to down
06:07:48: BRI0:1: disconnecting call
06:07:48: %LINK-3-UPDOWN: Interface BRI0:2, changed state to down
06:07:48: BRI0:2: disconnecting call
06:07:49: %LINEPROTO-5-UPDOWN: Line protocol on Interface BRI0:1, changed state to down
06:07:49: %LINEPROTO-5-UPDOWN: Line protocol on Interface BRI0:2, changed state to down
06:07:49: %LINEPROTO-5-UPDOWN: Line protocol on Interface Virtual-Access1, changed state
   to down
SOHO800#
```

The last remote we will use is Rome. Code Listing 6-11 shows the configuration for Rome. There are a couple of highlights to point out in this configuration.

Line 5 sets up 16,000 bytes to be used for holding console messages for viewing on a virtual terminal session, after the fact. The default log buffer is 4,096 bytes.

Line 18 again uses the **dialer load-interval 30** command so that there will be a quicker reaction to changes in traffic.

Line 20 sets up the threshold to 75/255 in either direction. In SOHO800 above, we only used output threshold checking.

Code Listing 6-11
Dialer Profiles—Rome
configuration.

```
1    version 12.0
2    !
3    hostname Rome
4    !
5    logging buffered 16000 debugging
6    enable password cisco
7    !
8    username NewYork password 0 cisco
9    memory-size iomem 25
10   ip subnet-zero
11   !
12   isdn switch-type basic-ni
13   !
14   interface BRI0
15     ip address 172.31.1.2 255.255.255.0
16     no ip directed-broadcast
17     encapsulation ppp
18     load-interval 30
19     dialer map ip 172.31.1.1 name NewYork 5558000
20     dialer load-threshold 75 either
21     dialer-group 1
22     isdn switch-type basic-ni
23     isdn spid1 21255520290101
24     isdn spid2 21255520300101
25     ppp authentication chap
26     ppp multilink
27   !
28   interface FastEthernet0
29     ip address 172.31.205.1 255.255.255.0
30     no ip directed-broadcast
31   !
32   ip classless
33   ip route 172.31.200.0 255.255.255.0 BRI0 172.31.1.1
34   no ip http server
35   !
36   dialer-list 1 protocol ip permit
37   !
38   line con 0
39     logging synchronous
40     length 0
41     transport input none
```

Code Listing 6-11
(continued)

```
42   line aux 0
43   line vty 0 4
44    no login
45   !
46   no scheduler allocate
47   end
```

Check out our configuration using a **ping** to New York.

```
Rome#ping 172.31.200.1

Type escape sequence to abort.
Sending 5, 100-byte ICMP Echos to 172.31.200.1, timeout is 2 seconds:
.!!!!
Success rate is 80 percent (4/5), round-trip min/avg/max = 28/28/28 ms
Rome#
```

Yes, it works just fine. We can also watch our `Virtual Access` interface become activated with the **debug dialer** command output.

```
06:11:13: BRI0 DDR: Dialing cause ip (s=172.31.1.2, d=172.31.200.1)
06:11:13: BRI0 DDR: Attempting to dial 5558000
06:11:55834574856: %LINK-3-UPDOWN: Interface BRI0:1, changed state to up
06:11:13: %LINK-3-UPDOWN: Interface Virtual-Access1, changed state to up
06:11:13: Virtual-Access1 DDR: dialer protocol up
06:11:14: %LINEPROTO-5-UPDOWN: Line protocol on Interface BRI0:1, changed state to up
06:11:14: %LINEPROTO-5-UPDOWN: Line protocol on Interface Virtual-Access1, changed state
   to up
06:11:19: %ISDN-6-CONNECT: Interface BRI0:1 is now connected to 5558000 NewYork
```

The **show ppp multilink** command output indicates that there is only one B-channel active.

```
Rome#show ppp multilink

Virtual-Access1, bundle name is NewYork
  Dialer interface is BRI0
  0 lost fragments, 0 reordered, 0 unassigned, sequence 0x0/0x0 rcvd/sent
  0 discarded, 0 lost received, 1/255 load
  Member links: 1 (max not set, min not set)
    BRI0:1
```

An extended **ping** is used to generate enough traffic to verify that our multilink operation successfully activates our second B-channel.

```
Rome#ping
Protocol [ip]:
Target IP address: 172.31.200.1
Repeat count [5]: 10000
Datagram size [100]:
Timeout in seconds [2]:
Extended commands [n]:
Sweep range of sizes [n]:
Type escape sequence to abort.
Sending 10000, 100-byte ICMP Echos to 172.31.200.1, timeout is 2 seconds:
!!!!!!!!!!!!!!!!!!!!!!!!!!!!!!!!!!!!!!!!!!!!!!!!!!!!!!!!!!!!!!!!!!!!!
.
. Deleted for clarity
.
!!!!!!!!!!!!!!!!!!!!!!!!!!!!!!!!!!!!!!!!!!!!!!!!!!!!!!!!!!!!!!!!!!!!!!!!!
!!!!!!!!!!!!!!!!!!!!!!!!!!!!!!!!!!!!!!!!!!!!!!!!!!!!!!!!!!!!!!!!!!!!
Success rate is 100 percent (10000/10000), round-trip min/avg/max = 20/22/76 ms
Rome#
06:12:31: BRI0 DDR: Attempting to dial 5558000
06:12:135300022252: %LINK-3-UPDOWN: Interface BRI0:2, changed state to up
06:12:32: %LINEPROTO-5-UPDOWN: Line protocol on Interface BRI0:2, changed state to up
06:12:37: %ISDN-6-CONNECT: Interface BRI0:2 is now connected to 5558000 NewYork
```

Dialer Profile Sidebar

Before we get to the NewYork configuration, it is appropriate to delve into the dialer profile operation. The key to understanding dialer profiles is to show how the three major components, dialer interfaces, physical interfaces, and dialer pools, work together. In our last example, we set up the S0/0:23 interface with a single specific set of values and left it up to the remote sites to match our configuration. In fact, we added **ppp multilink** even though only one of the remote sites was so configured. A better way would be to set up an individual connection for each remote site, each with its own separate interface. However, this is not practical for large numbers of remote locations.

First, let's discuss dialer pools. A dialer pool is a group of physical interfaces bound together as a set of resources. The physical interfaces are assigned to the dialer pool with the **dialer pool-member # priority nnn** command. The # is the

Dialer Profile Sidebar (continued)

pool number, and the nnn is a priority number used to set each interface's operational sequence, where the higher numbered interface is used first. Look at the listing below to see how physical interfaces are used to build dialer pools.

```
int bri 0
dialer pool-member 1 priority 100
int bri 1
dialer pool-member 1 priority 75
dialer pool-member 2 priority 50
int bri 2
dialer pool-member 1 priority 50
dialer pool-member 2 priority 75
int bri 3
dialer pool-member 2 priority 100
```

QUESTION #1 *In the example above, what interfaces belong in each pool, and in which sequence will they be used?*

Check out the answer at the end of the chapter.

Back to Our Example

Now that we have a dialer pool built, it is time to build our dialer profile and assign the dialer pool to the dialer profile.

```
interface dialer 1
dialer pool 2
```

Using the **interface dialer 1** command, we create the dialer profile, and then the **dialer pool 2** command assigns the physical interface resources in the dialer pool to the profile.

We have successfully separated the logical connection from the physical interfaces.

Now for our NewYork 3640 router with the dialer profiles. Code Listing 6-12 shows this configuration.

Our local authentication database is defined in lines 8 through 10, one entry for each of our three test sites.

Lines 15 through 18 set up our channelized T1 interface for ISDN PRI operation.

Lines 24 through 32 define the physical interface, Serial 1/0:23. Line 25 removes IP processing from the interface, but this is okay, as we will assign the IP addresses in the dialer profile. Lines 27, 30, and 31 set up the interface for PPP processing. Line 28 is the key, assigning the interface as a resource in **dialer pool 5**. Remember, there are 23 B-channels available on an ISDN PRI connection.

Let's build some dialer profiles. Lines 34 through 44 define our first dialer profile. Line 34 creates **interface dialer 1**, our first dialer profile. Line 35 assigns an IP address on a specific IP subnet, 172.31.1.0/24. Lines 37, 43, and 44 set up our PPP operation. Line 38 identifies the remote site's host name, or name used for CHAP (more later in Chapter 10), as Rome. Lines 39 and 40 define the phone numbers to use to connect to the remote site. Line 41 assigns the resources in dialer pool 5 to this dialer profile. Rome can use up to 23 B-channels to connect to New York, but as Rome only has a BRI port, we can only use two B-channels. Line 42 assigns our dialing rules to the profile.

There are two other profiles defined: SOHO800, in lines 46 through 56, and SOHO700, in lines 58 through 68. Please note that each dialer profile uses its own IP subnet, which would not be possible if we did not use dialer profiles.

Lines 71 through 73 define our static routes to our three test sites. Note that these static routes use our dialer profiles as exit interfaces, not Serial 1/0:23.

Line 75 completes the configuration by defining all IP traffic as interesting.

Code Listing 6-12

```
1    version 12.0
2    !
3    hostname NewYork
4    !
5    logging buffered 16000 debugging
6    enable password cisco
7    !
8    username Rome password 0 cisco
9    username SOHO800 password 0 cisco
10   username SOHO700 password 0 cisco
11   ip subnet-zero
12   no ip domain-lookup
13   isdn switch-type primary-5ess
14   !
15   controller T1 1/0
16     framing esf
17     linecode b8zs
18     pri-group timeslots 1-24
19   !
20   interface Ethernet0/0
```

```
21  ip address 172.31.200.1 255.255.255.0
22   no ip directed-broadcast
23   !
24  interface Serial1/0:23
25   no ip address
26   no ip directed-broadcast
27   encapsulation ppp
28   dialer pool-member 5
29   isdn switch-type primary-5ess
30   ppp authentication chap
31   ppp multilink
32  hold-queue 75 in
33   !
34  interface Dialer1
35   ip address 172.31.1.1 255.255.255.0
36   no ip directed-broadcast
37   encapsulation ppp
38  dialer remote-name Rome
39   dialer string 5552029
40   dialer string 5552030
41   dialer pool 5
42   dialer-group 1
43   ppp authentication chap
44   ppp multilink
45   !
46  interface Dialer2
47   ip address 172.31.2.1 255.255.255.0
48   no ip directed-broadcast
49   encapsulation ppp
50   dialer remote-name SOHO800
51   dialer string 5552027
52   dialer string 5552028
53   dialer pool 5
54   dialer-group 1
55   ppp authentication chap
56   ppp multilink
57   !
58  interface Dialer3
59   ip address 172.31.3.1 255.255.255.0
60   no ip directed-broadcast
61   encapsulation ppp
62   dialer remote-name SOHO700
63   dialer string 5552031
64   dialer string 5552032
65   dialer pool 5
66   dialer-group 1
67   ppp authentication chap
68   ppp multilink
69   !
70  ip classless
71  ip route 172.31.205.0 255.255.255.0 Dialer1 172.31.1.2
72  ip route 172.31.210.0 255.255.255.0 Dialer2 172.31.2.2
73  ip route 172.31.215.0 255.255.255.0 Dialer3 172.31.3.2
74   !
75  dialer-list 1 protocol ip permit
76   !
77  line con 0
78   logging synchronous
```

■ |

Code Listing 6-12
(continued)

```
79   length 0
80     transport input none
81   line 65 70
82   line aux 0
83   line vty 0 4
84     no login
85   !
86   end
```

Now for some **debug dialer** command output to watch what happens with our B-channels as our test sites dial in.

First we see a call from SOHO800. In the NewYork configuration, SOHO800 is defined using dialer 2. The B-channel Serial 1/0:22 comes up, is bound to profile Dialer2, and the two components are used to build interface Virtual Access 1. Note that the B-channel Serial 1/0:22 is connected to SOHO800.

```
06:17:08: %LINK-3-UPDOWN: Interface Serial1/0:22, changed state to up
06:17:08: %DIALER-6-BIND: Interface Serial1/0:22 bound to profile Dialer2
06:17:08: %LINK-3-UPDOWN: Interface Virtual-Access1, changed state to up
06:17:09: %LINEPROTO-5-UPDOWN: Line protocol on Interface Serial1/0:22, changed state to
   up
06:17:09: %LINEPROTO-5-UPDOWN: Line protocol on Interface Virtual-Access1, changed state
   to up
06:17:14: %ISDN-6-CONNECT: Interface Serial1/0:22 is now connected to 5552027 SOHO800
```

Next we see the same sequence for SOHO700. The next B-channel, Serial 1/0:21, is used.

```
06:17:23: %LINK-3-UPDOWN: Interface Serial1/0:21, changed state to up
06:17:23: %DIALER-6-BIND: Interface Serial1/0:21 bound to profile Dialer3
06:17:23: %DIALER-6-BIND: Interface Virtual-Access2 bound to profile Dialer3
06:17:23: %LINK-3-UPDOWN: Interface Virtual-Access2, changed state to up
06:17:24: %LINEPROTO-5-UPDOWN: Line protocol on Interface Serial1/0:21, changed state to
   up
06:17:24: %LINEPROTO-5-UPDOWN: Line protocol on Interface Virtual-Access2, changed state
   to up
06:17:29: %ISDN-6-CONNECT: Interface Serial1/0:21 is now connected to 2125552031 SOHO700
```

Last, but not least, we see our incoming connection from Rome. The next B-channel, Serial 1/0:20, gets used. See the pattern? We start using the B-channels starting with 22 and work our way down to 0.

```
06:17:35: %LINK-3-UPDOWN: Interface Serial1/0:20, changed state to up
06:17:35: %DIALER-6-BIND: Interface Serial1/0:20 bound to profile Dialer1
06:17:35: %DIALER-6-BIND: Interface Virtual-Access3 bound to profile Dialer1
06:17:35: %LINK-3-UPDOWN: Interface Virtual-Access3, changed state to up
```

```
06:17:36: %LINEPROTO-5-UPDOWN: Line protocol on Interface Serial1/0:20, changed state to
up
06:17:36: %LINEPROTO-5-UPDOWN: Line protocol on Interface Virtual-Access3, changed state
to up
06:17:41: %ISDN-6-CONNECT: Interface Serial1/0:20 is now connected to 5552029 Rome
```

If we generate enough traffic from Rome, a second B-channel, Serial 1/0:19, is activated. We did not create another `Virtual Access` interface; we just added another B-channel to the existing `Virtual Access` interface.

```
06:18:53: %LINK-3-UPDOWN: Interface Serial1/0:19, changed state to up
06:18:53: %DIALER-6-BIND: Interface Serial1/0:19 bound to profile Dialer1
06:18:54: %LINEPROTO-5-UPDOWN: Line protocol on Interface Serial1/0:19, changed state to
up
06:18:59: %ISDN-6-CONNECT: Interface Serial1/0:19 is now connected to 5552029 Rome
```

We generated enough information from SOHO800 to activate a second B-channel as well.

```
06:18:59: %LINK-3-UPDOWN: Interface Serial1/0:18, changed state to up
06:18:59: %DIALER-6-BIND: Interface Serial1/0:18 bound to profile Dialer2
06:19:00: %LINEPROTO-5-UPDOWN: Line protocol on Interface Serial1/0:18, changed state to
up
06:19:05: %ISDN-6-CONNECT: Interface Serial1/0:18 is now connected to 5552027 SOHO800
```

Now that we have a mix of connections, let's use the **show ppp multilink** command to check out the individual bundles. We can see that our three test sites show up with their corresponding B-channels assigned to our three dialer profiles.

```
NewYork#show ppp multilink

Bundle Rome, 2 members, Master link is Virtual-Access3
Dialer Interface is Dialer1
   0 lost fragments, 4 reordered, 0 unassigned, sequence 0x6AA/0x6AE rcvd/sent
   0 discarded, 0 lost received, 27/255 load

Member Links: 2 (max not set, min not set)
Serial1/0:20
Serial1/0:19

Bundle SOHO700, 1 member, Master link is Virtual-Access2
Dialer Interface is Dialer3
   0 lost fragments, 0 reordered, 0 unassigned, sequence 0x0/0x0 rcvd/sent
   0 discarded, 0 lost received, 1/255 load

Member Link: 1 (max not set, min not set)
Serial1/0:21
```

```
Bundle SOHO800, 2 members, Master link is Virtual-Access1
Dialer Interface is Dialer2
  0 lost fragments, 0 reordered, 0 unassigned, sequence 0x3FA/0x3FC rcvd/sent
  0 discarded, 0 lost received, 15/255 load

Member Links: 2 (max not set, min not set)
Serial1/0:22
Serial1/0:18
```

Now for some more tests after some of our initial calls have timed out and disconnected.

First, telnet to NewYork and change to privileged mode. Isn't that our starting point? Yes, it is, but now we have a telnet session and a console connection active on the same router.

```
NewYork#telnet 172.31.200.1
Trying 172.31.200.1 ... Open

NewYork>en
Password:
NewYork#
```

Test the ability to connect to a test site with a regular **ping**, and then start an extended **ping** to perform some load testing.

```
NewYork#ping 172.31.215.1

Type escape sequence to abort.
Sending 5, 100-byte ICMP Echos to 172.31.215.1, timeout is 2 seconds:
..!!!
Success rate is 60 percent (3/5), round-trip min/avg/max = 36/36/36 ms
NewYork#ping
Protocol [ip]:
Target IP address: 172.31.215.1
Repeat count [5]: 10000
Datagram size [100]:
Timeout in seconds [2]:
Extended commands [n]:
Sweep range of sizes [n]:
Type escape sequence to abort.
Sending 10000, 100-byte ICMP Echos to 172.31.215.1, timeout is 2 seconds:
!!!!!!!!!!!!!!!!!!!!!!!!!!!!!!!!!!!!!!!!!!!!!!!!!!!!!!!!!!!!!!!!!!!!!!!!!!!
!!!!!!!!!!!!!!!!!!!!!!!!!!!!!!!!!!!!!!!!!!!!!!!!!
```

TIP *We interrupt this continuing* ***ping*** *to bring you these commands and* ***debug*** *output from the console? Huh? I thought we were performing a continuous* ***ping.*** *If we use the* <CTRL,SHIFT,6> *x escape sequence in the telnet session, we drop back to the console connection. Wow, a "background" process provides data while we look at console output and issue* ***show*** *commands.*

We use Serial 1/0:21 to connect to SOHO700 and activate our Virtual Access interface.

```
NewYork#
06:20:01: %LINK-3-UPDOWN: Interface Serial1/0:21, changed state to up
06:20:01: %DIALER-6-BIND: Interface Serial1/0:21 bound to profile Dialer3
06:20:04: %DIALER-6-BIND: Interface Virtual-Access2 bound to profile Dialer3
06:20:04: %LINK-3-UPDOWN: Interface Virtual-Access2, changed state to up
06:20:05: %LINEPROTO-5-UPDOWN: Line protocol on Interface Serial1/0:21, changed state to
  up
06:20:05: %LINEPROTO-5-UPDOWN: Line protocol on Interface Virtual-Access2, changed state
  to up
06:20:07: %ISDN-6-CONNECT: Interface Serial1/0:21 is now connected to 5552031 SOHO700
```

Show Dialer Output Start

The **show dialer** command output details our current active connections. We are going to put some comments inline, so there will be a start and end tag in the margin to identify the boundary of the command output.

```
NewYork#show dialer

Serial1/0:0 - dialer type = ISDN
Idle timer (120 secs), Fast idle timer (20 secs)
Wait for carrier (30 secs), Re-enable (15 secs)
Dialer state is idle
.
. Deleted for clarity
.
Serial1/0:17 - dialer type = ISDN
Idle timer (120 secs), Fast idle timer (20 secs)
Wait for carrier (30 secs), Re-enable (15 secs)
Dialer state is idle
```

Existing Incoming Connections

```
Serial1/0:18 - dialer type = ISDN
Idle timer (120 secs), Fast idle timer (20 secs)
Wait for carrier (30 secs), Re-enable (15 secs)
Dialer state is multilink member
Interface bound to profile Dialer2
Current call connected 01:12:37
Connected to 5552027 (SOHO800)

Serial1/0:19 - dialer type = ISDN
Idle timer (120 secs), Fast idle timer (20 secs)
Wait for carrier (30 secs), Re-enable (15 secs)
Dialer state is multilink member
Interface bound to profile Dialer1
Current call connected 01:13:01
Connected to 5552029 (Rome)

Serial1/0:20 - dialer type = ISDN
Idle timer (120 secs), Fast idle timer (20 secs)
Wait for carrier (30 secs), Re-enable (15 secs)
Dialer state is multilink member
Interface bound to profile Dialer1
Current call connected 01:13:02
Connected to 5552029 (Rome)
```

New Outbound Connection to SOHO700

```
Serial1/0:21 - dialer type = ISDN
Idle timer (120 secs), Fast idle timer (20 secs)
Wait for carrier (30 secs), Re-enable (15 secs)
Dialer state is multilink member
Dial reason: ip (s=172.31.3.1, d=172.31.215.1)
Interface bound to profile Dialer3
Current call connected 00:00:47
Connected to 5552031 (SOHO700)
```

Existing Incoming Connection

```
Serial1/0:22 - dialer type = ISDN
Idle timer (120 secs), Fast idle timer (20 secs)
Wait for carrier (30 secs), Re-enable (15 secs)
Dialer state is multilink member
Interface bound to profile Dialer2
Current call connected 01:12:38
Connected to 5552027 (SOHO800)
```

Signaling Channel 24

```
Serial1/0:23 - dialer type = ISDN

Dial String      Successes    Failures    Last called   Last status
0 incoming call(s) have been screened.
0 incoming call(s) rejected for callback.
```

Dialer Profiles

We have added something new here, our dialer profiles. Here is where we have our phone numbers and connection status.

```
Dialer1 - dialer type = DIALER PROFILE
Idle timer (120 secs), Fast idle timer (20 secs)
Wait for carrier (30 secs), Re-enable (15 secs)
Dialer state is data link layer up

Dial String      Successes    Failures    Last called   Last status
5552029              2            0        01:13:03      successful    Default
5552030              0            0        never             -         Default

Dialer2 - dialer type = DIALER PROFILE
Idle timer (120 secs), Fast idle timer (20 secs)
Wait for carrier (30 secs), Re-enable (15 secs)
Dialer state is data link layer up

Dial String      Successes    Failures    Last called   Last status
5552027              2            0        01:12:39      successful    Default
5552028              0            0        never             -         Default

Dialer3 - dialer type = DIALER PROFILE
Idle timer (120 secs), Fast idle timer (20 secs)
Wait for carrier (30 secs), Re-enable (15 secs)
Dialer state is data link layer up

Dial String      Successes    Failures    Last called   Last status
5552031             22            0        00:00:49      successful    Default
5552032              0            0        never             -         Default
```

Show Dialer
Output End

Let's take a look at our bundles again with the **show ppp multilink** command.

```
NewYork#show ppp multilink

Bundle SOHO700, 1 member, Master link is Virtual-Access2
Dialer Interface is Dialer3
   0 lost fragments, 0 reordered, 0 unassigned, sequence 0x0/0x0 rcvd/sent
   0 discarded, 0 lost received, 23/255 load

Member Link: 1 (max not set, min not set)
Serial1/0:21

Bundle Rome, 2 members, Master link is Virtual-Access3
Dialer Interface is Dialer1
   0 lost fragments, 66 reordered, 0 unassigned, sequence 0x2D84/0x2D8A rcvd/sent
   0 discarded, 0 lost received, 85/255 load

Member Links: 2 (max not set, min not set)
Serial1/0:20
Serial1/0:19

Bundle SOHO800, 2 members, Master link is Virtual-Access1
Dialer Interface is Dialer2
   0 lost fragments, 0 reordered, 0 unassigned, sequence 0x25B2/0x25B8 rcvd/sent
   0 discarded, 0 lost received, 75/255 load

Member Links: 2 (max not set, min not set)
Serial1/0:22
Serial1/0:18
```

Two other useful commands are **show isdn active** and **show isdn history**, which can be used to track individual connect times on each B-channel.

```
NewYork#show isdn active
--------------------------------------------------------------------------------
                              ISDN ACTIVE CALLS
--------------------------------------------------------------------------------
History table has a maximum of 100 entries.
History table data is retained for a maximum of 15 Minutes.
--------------------------------------------------------------------------------
Call   Calling or Called   Remote      Seconds Seconds Seconds  Recorded Charges
Type   Phone number        Node Name   Used    Left    Idle     Units/Currency
--------------------------------------------------------------------------------
In  +---Not Available----  SOHO800     303             0
In  +---Not Available----  Rome        277             0
In  +---Not Available----  Rome        198             0
In  +---Not Available----  SOHO800     192             0
Out             5552031    SOHO700     130             0        0
--------------------------------------------------------------------------------
```

```
NewYork#sho isdn history
--------------------------------------------------------------------------
                           ISDN CALL HISTORY
--------------------------------------------------------------------------
History table has a maximum of 100 entries.
History table data is retained for a maximum of 15 Minutes.
--------------------------------------------------------------------------
Call    Calling or Called    Remote      Seconds Seconds Seconds  Recorded Charges
Type    Phone number         Node Name   Used    Left    Idle     Units/Currency
--------------------------------------------------------------------------
In  +---Not Available----    SOHO800     322             0
In              2125552031   SOHO700     120
In  +---Not Available----    Rome        296             0
In  +---Not Available----    Rome        217             0
In  +---Not Available----    SOHO800     211             0
Out             5552031      SOHO700     150             0        0
--------------------------------------------------------------------------
```

We have one last puzzle to solve. We needed static dialer maps to connect to a remote site in all our previous examples. We did not do that this time, so how did we manage to resolve addresses? Let's use the **show dialer map** command and examine the output. With dialer profiles, it appears to have created dynamic dialer maps. Great, one other configuration task we don't have to worry about with dialer profiles.

```
NewYork#show dialer map
Dynamic dialer map ip 172.31.1.2 name Rome () on Dialer1
Dynamic dialer map ip 172.31.3.2 name SOHO700 () on Dialer3
Dynamic dialer map ip 172.31.2.2 name SOHO800 () on Dialer2
NewYork#
```

This is just the start for dialer profiles. In later chapters, we will expand this topic until we building the profile dynamically from our TACACS+ server.

Summary

The primary focus of this chapter dealt with the configuration of ISDN BRI and PRI interfaces.

The dialer profile feature unlocks ISDN's full potential when solving dial-in connectivity challenges.

Questions and Answers

1. *In the example above, what interfaces belong in each pool, and in which sequence will they be used?*

   ```
   Pool 1 uses bri0 first, then bri1, then bri2.
   Pool 2 uses bri3 first, then bri2, then bri1.
   ```

DDR with IP Routing Protocols

In this chapter we will integrate DDR capabilities with IP routing protocols. Up to this point we have been using static routing to define our destination pathway. While this method is fairly easy to maintain in small to medium environments, it does not scale well. Let's take a look at static route redistribution and then at how each of the major routing protocols interact with DDR.

In order for all IP hosts in our routed network to return traffic that originates from our remote sites, all routers must have a return route. We could set up static routes throughout the routed environment, but that would require massive administration and manual intervention to bypass failed circuits. There are many features that simplify the distribution of routes for DDR applications in the IP-routed environment: router redistribution, snapshot routing, OSPF demand circuits, and On-Demand Routing (ODR).

Route Redistribution for Multiple Dial-in Connections

Our first example focuses on the distribution of static routes to the balance of a dynamically routed RIP network. The successful test will be to **ping** the laptop connected to SOHO800's Ethernet port from the loopback interface on Rome. Figure 7-1 shows the equipment layout.

Figure 7-1
Route redistribution for dial-in connections—equipment layout.

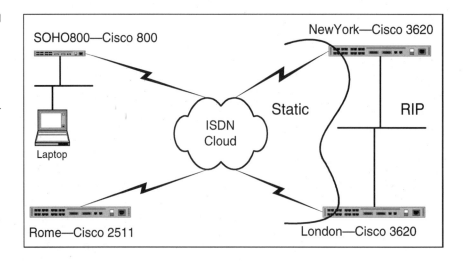

London

The first router we will look at is London. Code Listing 7-1 shows this configuration.

Sticking to the essentials, the lines that matter in this example are lines 28 through 32, which define our RIP routing process. Line 28 starts the RIP configuration mode. Line 29 redistributes all the static routes defined in this router into the RIP process with a default metric of five (5) hops. If you don't put in a default metric, then the redistributed routes will not be sent to this router's neighbors. Each routing protocol uses a different metric to calculate the best pathway; therefore, if you don't use the default metric, the target for redistribution won't understand what to do with the redistributed routes. Line 30 blocks the regular RIP updates from being transmitted over the BRI0 interface. The BRI interface belongs to network 172.31.0.0, which is defined in line 31. The network statements in lines 31 and 32 define the class IP network addresses that will participate in the RIP process.

NOTE *If the IP address on an interface belongs to the class IP addresses defined in the network statements, then the interface will actively transmit routing table updates.*

Line 35 defines the static route to the loopback interface configured in the Rome router.

Code Listing 7-1
Static Route Redistribution—London configuration.

```
1    version 11.3
2    !
3    hostname London
4    !
5    username Rome password 0 cisco
6    isdn switch-type basic-ni
7    !
8    interface Loopback0
9      ip address 192.168.2.1 255.255.255.0
10   !
11   interface BRI0/0
12     ip address 172.31.201.1 255.255.255.0
13     encapsulation ppp
14     dialer idle-timeout 30
15     dialer fast-idle 10
16     dialer map ip 172.31.201.2 name Rome 5552004
17     dialer map ip 172.31.201.2 name Rome 5552005
```

Code Listing 7-1
(continued)

```
18    dialer-group 1
19    isdn switch-type basic-ni
20    isdn spid1 21255520020101
21    isdn spid2 21255520030101
22    ppp authentication chap
23    ppp multilink
24    !
25    interface Ethernet0/0
26     ip address 172.31.100.2 255.255.255.0
27    !
28    router rip
29     redistribute static metric 5
30     passive-interface BRI0/0
31     network 172.31.0.0
32     network 192.168.2.0
33    !
34    ip classless
35    ip route 192.168.3.0 255.255.255.0 BRI0/0 172.31.201.2
36    !
37    dialer-list 1 protocol ip permit
38    !
39    line con 0
40     exec-timeout 0 0
41     length 0
42    line aux 0
43    line vty 0 4
44     password bb
45     login
46    !
47    end
```

The **show ip route** command shows us the directly connected, RIP-derived, and static routes active in this router. Note the static route to Rome, `192.168.3.1`. Also note the route to `192.168.200.0`, which is the remote network on SOHO800. It looks like our static route redistribution from NewYork is working, as the metric showing up in the route as 5 hops (`[120/5]`).

```
London#show ip route

Codes: C - connected, S - static, I - IGRP, R - RIP, M - mobile, B - BGP
       D - EIGRP, EX - EIGRP external, O - OSPF, IA - OSPF inter area
       N1 - OSPF NSSA external type 1, N2 - OSPF NSSA external type 2
       E1 - OSPF external type 1, E2 - OSPF external type 2, E - EGP
       i - IS-IS, L1 - IS-IS level-1, L2 - IS-IS level-2, * - candidate default
       U - per-user static route, o - ODR

Gateway of last resort is not set

     172.31.0.0/24 is subnetted, 3 subnets
C       172.31.201.0 is directly connected, BRI0/0
R       172.31.200.0 [120/1] via 172.31.100.1, 00:00:10, Ethernet0/0
C       172.31.100.0 is directly connected, Ethernet0/0
```

```
R    192.168.200.0/24 [120/5] via 172.31.100.1, 00:00:10, Ethernet0/0
R    192.168.1.0/24 [120/1] via 172.31.100.1, 00:00:10, Ethernet0/0
C    192.168.2.0/24 is directly connected, Loopback0
S    192.168.3.0/24 [1/0] via 172.31.201.2, BRI0/0
```

The **show dialer** command output indicates that there are two active B-channels up and running, and that the connection was initiated by Rome, our peer across the ISDN link. Because this is a PPP multilink connection, interface `Virtual-Access1` is created to handle the multilink bundle.

```
London#show dialer

BRI0/0 - dialer type = ISDN

Dial String       Successes     Failures     Last called   Last status
5552005                  0            0     never                   -
5552004                  0            0     never                   -
0 incoming call(s) have been screened.
0 incoming call(s) rejected for callback.

BRI0/0:1 - dialer type = ISDN
Idle timer (30 secs), Fast idle timer (10 secs)
Wait for carrier (30 secs), Re-enable (15 secs)
Dialer state is multilink member
Connected to 5552004 (Rome)

BRI0/0:2 - dialer type = ISDN
Idle timer (30 secs), Fast idle timer (10 secs)
Wait for carrier (30 secs), Re-enable (15 secs)
Dialer state is multilink member
Connected to 5552004 (Rome)

Virtual-Access1 - dialer type = IN-BAND SYNC NO-PARITY
Rotary group 0, priority 0
Idle timer (30 secs), Fast idle timer (10 secs)
Wait for carrier (30 secs), Re-enable (15 secs)
Dialer state is data link layer up
Connected to 5552004 (Rome)
```

The **show ppp multilink** command shows us our Rome bundle with two channels active and master link `Virtual-Access1`.

```
London#show ppp multilink

Bundle Rome, 2 members, Master link is Virtual-Access1
Dialer Interface is BRI0/0
  0 lost fragments, 0 reordered, 0 unassigned, sequence 0x19E/0x19E rcvd/sent
  0 discarded, 0 lost received, 55/255 load

Member Links: 2 (max not set, min not set)
BRI0/0:2
BRI0/0:1
```

NewYork

NewYork is the other router that is part of our RIP-routed network. Code Listing 7-2 shows this configuration.

Lines 26 through 30 and line 33 define our RIP routing process and the static route to SOHO800. As we saw in the **show ip route** command output in the London section above, the redistribution command on line 27 uses 5 hops as the metric when distributing the route to SOHO800.

■ ■

Code Listing 7-2
Static Route Redistri-bution—NewYork configuration.

```
1    version 11.3
2    !
3    hostname NewYork
4    !
5    username SOHO800 password 0 cisco
6    isdn switch-type basic-ni
7    !
8    interface Loopback0
9     ip address 192.168.1.1 255.255.255.0
10   !
11   interface BRI0/0
12    ip address 172.31.200.1 255.255.255.0
13    encapsulation ppp
14    dialer map ip 172.31.200.2 name SOHO800 5552006
15    dialer map ip 172.31.200.2 name SOHO800 5552007
16    dialer-group 1
17    isdn switch-type basic-ni
18    isdn spid1 21255520000101
19    isdn spid2 21255520010101
20    ppp authentication chap
21    ppp multilink
22   !
23   interface Ethernet0/0
24    ip address 172.31.100.1 255.255.255.0
25   !
26   router rip
27    redistribute static metric 5
28    passive-interface BRI0/0
29    network 172.31.0.0
30    network 192.168.1.0
31   !
32   ip classless
33   ip route 192.168.200.0 255.255.255.0 BRI0/0 172.31.200.2
34   !
35   dialer-list 1 protocol ip permit
36   !
37   line con 0
38    exec-timeout 0 0
39    length 0
40   line aux 0
41   line vty 0 4
42    password bb
43    login
44   !
45   end
```

The **show ip route** command output for NewYork shows our local static route to SOHO800, `172.31.200.0`, and the redistributed route for Rome, `172.31.3.0`, with a metric of 5 hops, indicating that our static route redistribution in London is working.

```
NewYork#show ip route
Codes: C - connected, S - static, I - IGRP, R - RIP, M - mobile, B - BGP
       D - EIGRP, EX - EIGRP external, O - OSPF, IA - OSPF inter area
       N1 - OSPF NSSA external type 1, N2 - OSPF NSSA external type 2
       E1 - OSPF external type 1, E2 - OSPF external type 2, E - EGP
       i - IS-IS, L1 - IS-IS level-1, L2 - IS-IS level-2, * - candidate default
       U - per-user static route, o - ODR

Gateway of last resort is not set

     172.31.0.0/24 is subnetted, 3 subnets
R       172.31.201.0 [120/1] via 172.31.100.2, 00:00:00, Ethernet0/0
C       172.31.200.0 is directly connected, BRI0/0
C       172.31.100.0 is directly connected, Ethernet0/0
S    192.168.200.0/24 [1/0] via 172.31.200.2, BRI0/0
C    192.168.1.0/24 is directly connected, Loopback0
R    192.168.2.0/24 [120/1] via 172.31.100.2, 00:00:00, Ethernet0/0
R    192.168.3.0/24 [120/5] via 172.31.100.2, 00:00:00, Ethernet0/0
```

The **show dialer** command output for NewYork shows our two B-channels up and running, and with a dial reason on `BRI0/0:1`, it identifies NewYork as the originator of the call. With **ppp multilink** active on our B-channels, the `Virtual-Access1` interface is built by IOS to handle the multilink bundle. If you look closely at the information about the destinations and the call status, you will see that even though both B-channels are active, the second B-channel, `BRI0/0:2`, was activated by SOHO800. Check it out later in the SOHO800 section of this example.

```
NewYork#show dialer

BRI0/0 - dialer type = ISDN

Dial String      Successes    Failures    Last called    Last status
5552007              0            0        never              -
5552006              2            0        00:02:22       successful
0 incoming call(s) have been screened.
0 incoming call(s) rejected for callback.

BRI0/0:1 - dialer type = ISDN
Idle timer (120 secs), Fast idle timer (20 secs)
Wait for carrier (30 secs), Re-enable (15 secs)
Dialer state is multilink member
Dial reason: ip (s=172.31.201.2, d=192.168.200.6)
Connected to 5552006 (SOHO800)
```

```
BRI0/0:2 - dialer type = ISDN
Idle timer (120 secs), Fast idle timer (20 secs)
Wait for carrier (30 secs), Re-enable (15 secs)
Dialer state is multilink member
Connected to 5552006 (SOHO800)

Virtual-Access1 - dialer type = IN-BAND SYNC NO-PARITY
Rotary group 0, priority 0
Idle timer (120 secs), Fast idle timer (20 secs)
Wait for carrier (30 secs), Re-enable (15 secs)
Dialer state is data link layer up
Connected to 5552006 (SOHO800)
```

The **show ppp multilink** command verifies that our SOHO800 bundle has both B-channels attached.

```
NewYork#show ppp multilink

Bundle SOHO800, 2 members, Master link is Virtual-Access1
Dialer Interface is BRI0/0
  0 lost fragments, 0 reordered, 0 unassigned, sequence 0x262/0x262 rcvd/sent
  0 discarded, 0 lost received, 1/255 load

Member Links: 2 (max not set, min not set)
BRI0/0:2
BRI0/0:1
```

Rome

Code Listing 7-3 shows the configuration for Rome. This router is the starting point for the end-to-end testing of our DDR and static route interaction. Our DDR configuration is pretty basic, with our default static route on line 26 pointing the way for all unknown traffic to the BRI0 port and the next hop address of 172.31.201.1.

Code Listing 7-3
Static Route Redistribution—Rome configuration.

```
1    version 11.3
2    !
3    hostname Rome
4    !
5    username London password 0 cisco
6    isdn switch-type basic-ni1
7    !
8    interface Loopback0
9     ip address 192.168.3.1 255.255.255.0
10   !
11   interface BRI0
12    ip address 172.31.201.2 255.255.255.0
13    encapsulation ppp
14    dialer idle-timeout 30
15    dialer fast-idle 10
```

```
16   dialer map ip 172.31.201.1 name London 5552002
17    dialer map ip 172.31.201.1 name London 5552003
18    dialer load-threshold 30 outbound
19    dialer-group 1
20    isdn spid1 21255520040101
21    isdn spid2 21255520050101
22    ppp authentication chap
23    ppp multilink
24   !
25   ip classless
26   ip route 0.0.0.0 0.0.0.0 BRI0 172.31.201.1
27   !
28   dialer-list 1 protocol ip permit
29   !
30   line con 0
31    exec-timeout 0 0
32    length 0
33   line aux 0
34   line vty 0 4
35    password cisco
36    login
37   !
38   end
```

The **show ip route** command defines our locally connected interfaces and the default static route to BRI0.

```
Rome#show ip route
Codes: C - connected, S - static, I - IGRP, R - RIP, M - mobile, B - BGP
       D - EIGRP, EX - EIGRP external, O - OSPF, IA - OSPF inter area
       N1 - OSPF NSSA external type 1, N2 - OSPF NSSA external type 2
       E1 - OSPF external type 1, E2 - OSPF external type 2, E - EGP
       i - IS-IS, L1 - IS-IS level-1, L2 - IS-IS level-2, * - candidate default
       U - per-user static route, o - ODR

Gateway of last resort is 172.31.201.1 to network 0.0.0.0

     172.31.0.0/24 is subnetted, 1 subnets
C       172.31.201.0 is directly connected, BRI0
C    192.168.3.0/24 is directly connected, Loopback0
S*   0.0.0.0/0 [1/0] via 172.31.201.1, BRI0
```

Time for a **ping** to test end-to-end connectivity to the attached PC furthest from Rome. The test is successful, but there is a noticeable lag before we achieve success. Two ISDN calls and an ARP between London and NewYork account for the time lag.

```
Rome#ping 192.168.200.6

Type escape sequence to abort.
Sending 5, 100-byte ICMP Echos to 192.168.200.6, timeout is 2 seconds:
....!
Success rate is 100 percent (1/5), round-trip min/avg/max = 100/100/100 ms
```

To check out the ability to activate PPP multilink, we use an extended **ping**. The **show dialer** command identifies the dial reason on BRI0:1 as the first **ping** from our loopback 0 interface, 192.168.3.1, to the target PC, 172.31.200.6. The dial reason for BRI0:2 is Multilink bundle overloaded, indicating we exceeded the load threshold and brought up a second circuit.

```
Rome#show dialer

BRI0 - dialer type = ISDN

Dial String     Successes    Failures     Last called    Last status
5552003              1            0        00:02:04        successful
5552002              4            1        00:02:04            failed
0 incoming call(s) have been screened.
0 incoming call(s) rejected for callback.

BRI0:1 - dialer type = ISDN
Idle timer (30 secs), Fast idle timer (10 secs)
Wait for carrier (30 secs), Re-enable (15 secs)
Dialer state is multilink member
Dial reason: ip (s=192.168.3.1, d=192.168.200.6)
Connected to 5552002 (London)

BRI0:2 - dialer type = ISDN
Idle timer (30 secs), Fast idle timer (10 secs)
Wait for carrier (30 secs), Re-enable (15 secs)
Dialer state is multilink member
Dial reason: Multilink bundle overloaded
Connected to 5552002 (London)
```

The **show ppp multilink** command identifies the two B-channels as active for bundle London.

```
Rome#show ppp multilink

Bundle London, 2 members, Master link is Virtual-Access1
Dialer Interface is BRI0
   0 lost fragments, 0 reordered, 0 unassigned, sequence 0x240/0x23E rcvd/sent
   0 discarded, 0 lost received, 47/255 load

Member Links: 2 (max not set, min not set)
BRI0:2
BRI0:1
```

SOHO800

Code Listing 7-4 shows the SOHO800 router configuration. Like Rome, this is a remote site that uses a static default route to reach all unknown networks (see line 30).

Code Listing 7-4
*Static Route Redistri-
bution—SOHO800
configuration.*

```
1    version 12.0
2    !
3    hostname SOHO800
4    !
5    username NewYork password 0 cisco
6    !
7    ip subnet-zero
8    !
9    isdn switch-type basic-ni
10   !
11   interface Ethernet0
12    ip address 192.168.200.1 255.255.255.0
13    no ip directed-broadcast
14   !
15   interface BRI0
16    ip address 172.31.200.4 255.255.255.0
17    no ip directed-broadcast
18    encapsulation ppp
19    dialer map ip 172.31.200.1 name NewYork 5552000
20    dialer map ip 172.31.200.1 name NewYork 5552001
21    dialer load-threshold 20 either
22    dialer-group 1
23    isdn switch-type basic-ni
24    isdn spid1 21255520060101
25    isdn spid2 21255520070101
26    ppp authentication chap
27    ppp multilink
28   !
29   ip classless
30   ip route 0.0.0.0 0.0.0.0 BRI0 172.31.200.1
31   !
32   dialer-list 1 protocol ip permit
33   !
34   line con 0
35    exec-timeout 0 0
36    logging synchronous
37    length 0
38    transport input none
39    stopbits 1
40   line vty 0 4
41    password cisco
42    login
43   !
44   end
```

The **show ip route** command indicates that our directly connected and static default routes are active.

```
SOHO800#show ip route
Codes: C - connected, S - static, I - IGRP, R - RIP, M - mobile, B - BGP
       D - EIGRP, EX - EIGRP external, O - OSPF, IA - OSPF inter area
       N1 - OSPF NSSA external type 1, N2 - OSPF NSSA external type 2
       E1 - OSPF external type 1, E2 - OSPF external type 2, E - EGP
       i - IS-IS, L1 - IS-IS level-1, L2 - IS-IS level-2, * - candidate default
       U - per-user static route, o - ODR
       T - traffic engineered route

Gateway of last resort is 172.31.200.1 to network 0.0.0.0

     172.31.0.0/24 is subnetted, 1 subnets
C       172.31.200.0 is directly connected, BRI0
C    192.168.200.0/24 is directly connected, Ethernet0
S*   0.0.0.0/0 [1/0] via 172.31.200.1, BRI0
```

Rome initiates the **ping** targeted toward the PC attached on SOHO800's Ethernet interface, and with the traffic generated by the extended **ping**, we activate both B-channels to carry the traffic.

```
00:14:43: %LINK-3-UPDOWN: Interface BRI0:1, changed state to up
00:14:45: %LINK-3-UPDOWN: Interface Virtual-Access1, changed state to up
00:14:45: %LINEPROTO-5-UPDOWN: Line protocol on Interface BRI0:1, changed state to up
00:14:46: %LINEPROTO-5-UPDOWN: Line protocol on Interface Virtual-Access1, changed state
   to up
00:16:06: %LINK-3-UPDOWN: Interface BRI0:2, changed state to up
00:16:08: %LINEPROTO-5-UPDOWN: Line protocol on Interface BRI0:2, changed state to up
```

The **show dialer** command indicates that BRI0:1 received the initial call from NewYork, while SOHO800 opened the second B-channel, BRI0:2, when the multilink connection became overloaded.

```
SOHO800#show dialer

BRI0 - dialer type = ISDN

Dial String      Successes    Failures    Last called    Last status
5552001                  1           0     00:00:33       successful
5552000                  0           1     00:00:03           failed
0 incoming call(s) have been screened.
0 incoming call(s) rejected for callback.

BRI0:1 - dialer type = ISDN
Idle timer (120 secs), Fast idle timer (20 secs)
Wait for carrier (30 secs), Re-enable (15 secs)
Dialer state is multilink member
Connected to 5552000 (NewYork)
```

```
BRI0:2 - dialer type = ISDN
Idle timer (120 secs), Fast idle timer (20 secs)
Wait for carrier (30 secs), Re-enable (15 secs)
Dialer state is multilink member
Dial reason: Multilink bundle overloaded
Connected to 5552000 (NewYork)
```

Let's take a look at the B-channels on the BRI interface. Please note that while LCP and multilink are open on our PPP connection, there are no NCP connections. The NCP information is attached to the `Virtual Access` interface that connects our multilink bundle to the rest of the routed network.

```
SOHO800#sho int bri 0 1 2
BRI0:1 is up, line protocol is up
  Hardware is BRI with U interface and POTS
  MTU 1500 bytes, BW 64 Kbit, DLY 20000 usec,
     reliability 255/255, txload 55/255, rxload 55/255
  Encapsulation PPP, loopback not set, keepalive set (10 sec)
  LCP Open, multilink Open
  Last input 00:00:00, output 00:00:00, output hang never
  Last clearing of "show interface" counters never
  Queueing strategy: fifo
  Output queue 0/40, 0 drops; input queue 0/75, 0 drops
  5 minute input rate 14000 bits/sec, 2 packets/sec
  5 minute output rate 14000 bits/sec, 3 packets/sec
     171 packets input, 128190 bytes, 0 no buffer
     Received 171 broadcasts, 0 runts, 0 giants, 0 throttles
     0 input errors, 0 CRC, 0 frame, 0 overrun, 0 ignored, 0 abort
     170 packets output, 128086 bytes, 0 underruns
     0 output errors, 0 collisions, 0 interface resets
     0 output buffer failures, 0 output buffers swapped out
     4 carrier transitions
BRI0:2 is up, line protocol is up
  Hardware is BRI with U interface and POTS
  MTU 1500 bytes, BW 64 Kbit, DLY 20000 usec,
     reliability 255/255, txload 31/255, rxload 31/255
  Encapsulation PPP, loopback not set, keepalive set (10 sec)
  LCP Open, multilink Open
  Last input 00:00:00, output 00:00:00, output hang never
  Last clearing of "show interface" counters never
  Queueing strategy: fifo
  Output queue 0/40, 0 drops; input queue 0/75, 0 drops
  5 minute input rate 8000 bits/sec, 2 packets/sec
  5 minute output rate 8000 bits/sec, 3 packets/sec
     107 packets input, 71706 bytes, 0 no buffer
     Received 108 broadcasts, 0 runts, 0 giants, 0 throttles
     0 input errors, 0 CRC, 0 frame, 0 overrun, 0 ignored, 0 abort
     108 packets output, 72466 bytes, 0 underruns
     0 output errors, 0 collisions, 0 interface resets
     0 output buffer failures, 0 output buffers swapped out
     2 carrier transitions
```

The **show ppp multilink** command details the NewYork bundle assigned to interface Virtual-Access1.

```
SOHO800#show ppp multilink

Bundle NewYork, 2 members, Master link is Virtual-Access1
Dialer Interface is BRI0
   0 lost fragments, 0 reordered, 0 unassigned, sequence 0x13A/0x13A rcvd/sent
   0 discarded, 0 lost received, 53/255 load

Member Links: 2 (max not set, min not set)
BRI0:2
BRI0:1
```

Snapshot Routing for Distance Vector Protocols

Distance vector protocols—such as IGRP and RIP for IP, RIP and SAP for IPX, and RTMP and ZIP for Appletalk—update their peers with periodic broadcasts. If we let these periodic broadcasts trigger a call in the normal manner, our DDR circuits would always be active. Snapshot routing provides a mechanism for exchanging the broadcasts without keeping the DDR circuit open. Operationally, snapshot routing opens an active time window to exchange routing updates, then goes quiet for a period of anywhere from eight minutes to days. During the quiet time, snapshot routing maintains destination routes that would normally age out of the routing table after missing peer updates.

There are two different modes of snapshot operation. Snapshot routing can exchange updates after regular traffic triggers a call. If this mode of operation is chosen, then the **dialer idle-timeout** value must match the active time period defined in the **snapshot** commands. If snapshot routing is configured to skip updates from being exchanged when normal traffic triggers a call, then the only time routes are exchanged is when the snapshot process itself initiates a call. The suppress-state-change-updates option on the **snapshot client** command sets up this mode of operation. When this second option is used, the sum of the dialer idle timer and the snapshot active window timer is the minimum time that the circuit is active.

> **NOTE** *ISDN circuits and rotary groups have multiple communications channels, but snapshot routing will NOT work with PPP multilink active.*

In our example, SOHO800 and New York use RIP to exchange IP routing information, while the balance of the routers use IGRP to exchange IP routes. Figure 7-2 shows the equipment layout for the snapshot routing example.

London

Code Listing 7-5 shows the London router configuration.

Fairly standard IGRP routing is defined in lines 29 through 31.

Our DDR circuit, BRI0, is defined in lines 11 through 34. Lines 16 and 17 are our **dialer map** commands that have the broadcast option defined. Without the broadcast option, the IGRP broadcast updates will not be sent across the DDR circuit. Line 22 is where London is set up as a snapshot server, with a five-minute active window and accepting route updates only when the snapshot client dials in.

To prevent the IGRP broadcasts from triggering calls, we need to change the set of rules to use an access list. Lines 35 and 36 define the access list that prevents IGRP updates from triggering a call but permits all other IP packets. Line 37 ties the access list into our dialer list to set the call setup and takedown rules.

Figure 7-2
Snapshot routing equipment layout.

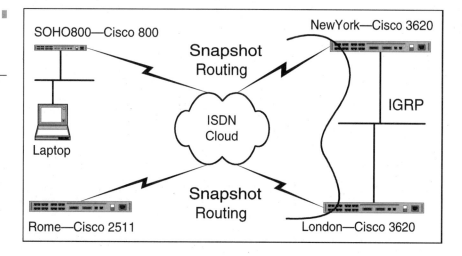

```
1    version 11.3
2    !
3    hostname London
4    !
5    username Rome password 0 cisco
6    isdn switch-type basic-ni
7    !
8    interface Loopback0
9     ip address 192.168.2.1 255.255.255.0
10   !
11   interface BRI0/0
12    ip address 172.31.201.1 255.255.255.0
13    encapsulation ppp
14    dialer idle-timeout 300
15    dialer fast-idle 10
16    dialer map ip 172.31.201.2 name Rome broadcast 5552004
17    dialer map ip 172.31.201.2 name Rome broadcast 5552005
18    dialer-group 1
19    isdn switch-type basic-ni
20    isdn spid1 21255520020101
21    isdn spid2 21255520030101
22    snapshot server 5 dialer
23    ppp authentication chap
24    hold-queue 75 in
25   !
26   interface Ethernet0/0
27    ip address 172.31.100.2 255.255.255.0
28   !
29   router igrp 100
30    network 172.31.0.0
31    network 192.168.2.0
32   !
33   ip classless
34   !
35   access-list 101 deny    igrp any any
36   access-list 101 permit ip any any
37   dialer-list 1 protocol ip list 101
38   !
39   !
40   line con 0
41    exec-timeout 0 0
42    length 0
43   line aux 0
44   line vty 0 4
45    password bb
46    login
47   !
48   end
```

Before snapshot routing is activated for the first time, let's take a look at the IP routing table to see if the route to Rome, 192.168.3.1, is present. No, not yet; snapshot routing has not had a chance to operate.

```
London#show ip route
Codes: C - connected, S - static, I - IGRP, R - RIP, M - mobile, B - BGP
       D - EIGRP, EX - EIGRP external, O - OSPF, IA - OSPF inter area
       N1 - OSPF NSSA external type 1, N2 - OSPF NSSA external type 2
       E1 - OSPF external type 1, E2 - OSPF external type 2, E - EGP
       i - IS-IS, L1 - IS-IS level-1, L2 - IS-IS level-2, * - candidate default
       U - per-user static route, o - ODR

Gateway of last resort is not set

     172.31.0.0/24 is subnetted, 3 subnets
C       172.31.201.0 is directly connected, BRI0/0
I       172.31.200.0 [100/158350] via 172.31.100.1, 00:00:55, Ethernet0/0
C       172.31.100.0 is directly connected, Ethernet0/0
I     192.168.1.0/24 [100/1600] via 172.31.100.1, 00:00:55, Ethernet0/0
C     192.168.2.0/24 is directly connected, Loopback0
```

Next we turn on **debug snapshot** to watch the snapshot process in action.

```
London#debug snapshot
Snapshot support debugging is on
London#
```

The BRI0:1 interface changes to up when the client initiates the snapshot process.

```
00:23:29: %LINK-3-UPDOWN: Interface BRI0/0:1, changed state to up
00:23:30: %LINEPROTO-5-UPDOWN: Line protocol on Interface BRI0/0:1, changed state to up
00:23:35: %ISDN-6-CONNECT: Interface BRI0/0:1 is now connected to 5552004 Rome
```

It's time to check on the status of the snapshot server process with the **show snapshot** command. We see that the interface is up and our active period is five minutes.

```
London#show snapshot
BRI0/0 is up, line protocol is upSnapshot server
  Options: dialer support
  Length of active period:        5 minutes
```

Now for a series of **debug snapshot** command output sequences. Each of the following sequences is the same: snapshot routing moves to the active queue, starts a normal route aging process during the route update exchange, then moves the snapshot process to the post-active or quiet stage.

```
00:24:19: SNAPSHOT: BRIO/0[0]: Move to active queue (Snapshot activity block created)
00:24:19: SNAPSHOT: BRIO/0[0]: moving to active queue
00:24:20: SNAPSHOT: BRIO/0[0]: Starting aging of ip protocol
00:30:16: SNAPSHOT: BRIO/0[0]: moving to server post active queue
```

After the active period, we disconnect the connection to our peer Rome
and move the snapshot process to the creation/deletion queue to terminate the process and move snapshot processing into the quiet time.

```
00:31:29: %ISDN-6-DISCONNECT: Interface BRIO/0:1  disconnected from
5552004 Rome, call lasted 479 seconds
00:31:29: %LINK-3-UPDOWN: Interface BRIO/0:1, changed state to down
00:31:29: %LINEPROTO-5-UPDOWN: Line protocol on Interface BRIO/0:1, changed state to down
00:33:16: SNAPSHOT: BRIO/0[0]: moving to creation/deletion queue
```

The following is a complete snapshot activation sequence. Note the
starting time. When we get to the snapshot client configuration later in
this example, my guess is the quiet time will be configured as 60 minutes.

```
01:29:29: %LINK-3-UPDOWN: Interface BRIO/0:1, changed state to up
01:29:30: %LINEPROTO-5-UPDOWN: Line protocol on Interface BRIO/0:1, changed state to up
01:29:35: %ISDN-6-CONNECT: Interface BRIO/0:1 is now connected to 5552004 Rome
01:30:00: SNAPSHOT: BRIO/0[0]: Move to active queue (Snapshot activity block created)
01:30:00: SNAPSHOT: BRIO/0[0]: moving to active queue
01:30:00: SNAPSHOT: BRIO/0[0]: Starting aging of ip protocol
01:35:16: SNAPSHOT: BRIO/0[0]: moving to server post active queue
01:38:16: SNAPSHOT: BRIO/0[0]: moving to creation/deletion queue
01:40:15: %ISDN-6-DISCONNECT: Interface BRIO/0:1  disconnected from 5552004 Rome, call
  lasted 646 seconds
01:40:15: %LINK-3-UPDOWN: Interface BRIO/0:1, changed state to down
01:40:15: %LINEPROTO-5-UPDOWN: Line protocol on Interface BRIO/0:1, changed state to down
```

One hour later we do it again. (No, I did not baby-sit this to make sure
it worked; I let it run overnight).

```
02:38:43: SNAPSHOT: BRIO/0[0]: Move to active queue (Snapshot activity block created)
02:38:43: SNAPSHOT: BRIO/0[0]: moving to active queue
02:38:43: SNAPSHOT: BRIO/0[0]: Starting aging of ip protocol
02:44:17: SNAPSHOT: BRIO/0[0]: moving to server post active queue
02:47:17: SNAPSHOT: BRIO/0[0]: moving to creation/deletion queue
```

After another hour we activate the process again.

```
03:48:55: SNAPSHOT: BRIO/0[0]: Move to active queue (Snapshot activity block created)
03:48:55: SNAPSHOT: BRIO/0[0]: moving to active queue
03:48:55: SNAPSHOT: BRIO/0[0]: Starting aging of ip protocol
03:54:19: SNAPSHOT: BRIO/0[0]: moving to server post active queue
03:57:19: SNAPSHOT: BRIO/0[0]: moving to creatio9990n/deletion queue
```

NewYork

NewYork is the other router situated in the central location. In this router, we maintain our RIP v1 routes using the snapshot technique with our neighbor, SOHO800. Code Listing 7-6 shows the NewYork router configuration.

Lines 11 through 23 define the ISDN circuit used for DDR, with line 21 setting up this router as a snapshot server.

Lines 15 and 16 define the static dialer address resolution that ties the next hop IP address to a phone number. Snapshot routing REQUIRES the broadcast option on the **dialer map** command in order to exchange routes using IP broadcast packets.

Lines 28 through 32 define the RIP protocol operation. Line 28 starts the RIP configuration process. Line 29 redistributes IGRP 100 routes into the RIP process with a metric of 5 hops. Lines 30 and 31 prevent RIP updates from being sent to the Loopback0 and Ethernet0/0 interfaces. Line 32 ties all interfaces in the 172.31.0.0 network into the RIP process.

Lines 34 through 38 define the IGRP process. Line 34 starts the IGRP configuration process. Line 35 redistributes the RIP-derived routes into the IGRP 100 with a set of metric values: bandwidth equal to 128 Kilobits per second, delay of 20000 milliseconds, reliability factor of 255/255, load factor of 1/255, and maximum transport unit of 1500 bytes.

It is important to prevent RIP updates from triggering a call to SOHO800. Lines 42 and 43 set up the rules used to identify the interesting traffic. Line 42 denies RIP updates, and line 43 permits all other IP packets. Line 44 ties access-list 101 into the dialer-list. Line 17 ties the dialer-list into our BRI0 interface.

Code Listing 7-6

```
1    version 11.3
2    !
3    hostname NewYork
4    !
5    username SOHO800 password 0 cisco
6    isdn switch-type basic-ni
7    !
8    interface Loopback0
9     ip address 192.168.1.1 255.255.255.0
10   !
11   interface BRI0/0
12    ip address 172.31.200.1 255.255.255.0
13    encapsulation ppp
14    dialer idle-timeout 300
15    dialer map ip 172.31.200.2 name SOHO800 broadcast 5552006
16    dialer map ip 172.31.200.2 name SOHO800 broadcast 5552007
```

```
17    dialer-group 1
18    isdn switch-type basic-ni
19    isdn spid1 21255520000101
20    isdn spid2 21255520010101
21    snapshot server 5 dialer
22    ppp authentication chap
23    hold-queue 75 in
24    !
25    interface Ethernet0/0
26     ip address 172.31.100.1 255.255.255.0
27    !
28    router rip
29     redistribute igrp 100 metric 5
30     passive-interface Ethernet0/0
31     passive-interface Loopback0
32     network 172.31.0.0
33    !
34    router igrp 100
35     redistribute rip metric 128 20000 255 1 1500
36     passive-interface BRI0/0
37     network 172.31.0.0
38     network 192.168.1.0
39    !
40    ip classless
41    !
42    access-list 101 deny    udp any any eq rip
43    access-list 101 permit ip any any
44    dialer-list 1 protocol ip list 101
45    !
46    line con 0
47     exec-timeout 0 0
48     length 0
49    line aux 0
50    line vty 0 4
51     password bb
52     login
53    !
54    end
```

Just to make sure that we only have the basic IGRP routes from the core network, we execute the **show ip route** command. The routes to SOHO800, 192.168.200.0/24, and Rome, 192.168.4.0/24, do not appear in the routing table.

```
NewYork#show ip route
Codes: C - connected, S - static, I - IGRP, R - RIP, M - mobile, B - BGP
       D - EIGRP, EX - EIGRP external, O - OSPF, IA - OSPF inter area
       N1 - OSPF NSSA external type 1, N2 - OSPF NSSA external type 2
       E1 - OSPF external type 1, E2 - OSPF external type 2, E - EGP
       i - IS-IS, L1 - IS-IS level-1, L2 - IS-IS level-2, * - candidate default
       U - per-user static route, o - ODR

Gateway of last resort is not set
```

```
        172.31.0.0/24 is subnetted, 3 subnets
I          172.31.201.0 [100/158350] via 172.31.100.2, 00:00:42, Ethernet0/0
C          172.31.200.0 is directly connected, BRI0/0
C          172.31.100.0 is directly connected, Ethernet0/0
C       192.168.1.0/24 is directly connected, Loopback0
I       192.168.2.0/24 [100/1600] via 172.31.100.2, 00:00:42, Ethernet0/0
```

Rome

Rome uses the IGRP routing protocol and is the first **snapshot** routing remote site to be examined. Code Listing 7-7 shows the Rome router configuration.

Lines 11 through 24 define the operation of the BRI0 interface used for DDR. Line 16, **dialer map snapshot 1 name London broadcast 5552002**, defines the command used to activate snapshot dialing from the client side. The 1 after snapshot defines Rome as a specific client to the snapshot server. If there is more than a single snapshot client connected to a server, then each snapshot client that connects to a snapshot server MUST have a unique number. The broadcast option is required so that the first snapshot activation packet will be used to bring up the DDR circuit. Lines 16 and 17 provide the static address resolution to the central site. Make sure to include the broadcast option on these **dialer map** commands to ensure that the RIP broadcast updates make it through to London. Line 23 defines how the Rome snapshot client operates. This client has an active route exchange time of five minutes, a quiet time of 60 seconds, holds routing updates during normal traffic transmission, and activates the DDR circuit when the quiet time expires.

Lines 26 through 29 define the IGRP 100 process.

Lines 33 through 35 set up the interesting traffic rules for the DDR circuit. Lines 33 and 34 deny the IGRP packets and permit all other IP packets. Line 35 ties access list 101 to the dialer rules.

Code Listing 7-7

```
1    version 11.3
2    !
3    hostname Rome
4    !
5    username London password 0 cisco
6    isdn switch-type basic-ni1
7    !
8    interface Loopback0
9     ip address 192.168.3.1 255.255.255.0
10   !
11   interface BRI0
12    ip address 172.31.201.2 255.255.255.0
```

```
13    encapsulation ppp
14    dialer idle-timeout 300
15    dialer fast-idle 10
16    dialer map snapshot 1 name London broadcast 5552002
17    dialer map ip 172.31.201.1 name London broadcast 5552002
18    dialer map ip 172.31.201.1 name London broadcast 5552003
19    dialer load-threshold 30 outbound
20    dialer-group 1
21    isdn spid1 21255520040101
22    isdn spid2 21255520050101
23    snapshot client 5 60 suppress-statechange-update dialer
24    ppp authentication chap
25    !
26   router igrp 100
27    passive-interface Loopback0
28    network 172.31.0.0
29    network 192.168.3.0
30    !
31   ip classless
32   !
33   access-list 101 deny    igrp any any
34   access-list 101 permit ip any any
35   dialer-list 1 protocol ip list 101
36   !
37   line con 0
38    exec-timeout 0 0
39    length 0
40   line aux 0
41   line vty 0 4
42    password cisco
43    login
44   !
45   end
```

Snapshot has not initiated a call, so the only destinations we can reach are on directly connected networks.

```
Rome#show ip route
Codes: C - connected, S - static, I - IGRP, R - RIP, M - mobile, B - BGP
       D - EIGRP, EX - EIGRP external, O - OSPF, IA - OSPF inter area
       N1 - OSPF NSSA external type 1, N2 - OSPF NSSA external type 2
       E1 - OSPF external type 1, E2 - OSPF external type 2, E - EGP
       i - IS-IS, L1 - IS-IS level-1, L2 - IS-IS level-2, * - candidate default
       U - per-user static route, o - ODR

Gateway of last resort is not set

     172.31.0.0/24 is subnetted, 1 subnets
C       172.31.201.0 is directly connected, BRI0
C    192.168.3.0/24 is directly connected, Loopback0
```

After the snapshot process initiates a call to our peer London, the **show dialer** command shows us that the reason for triggering a call to London is snapshot.

```
Rome#show dialer

BRI0 - dialer type = ISDN

Dial String      Successes    Failures     Last called   Last status
5552003                 0           0       never                    -
5552002                 2           6       00:01:12      successful
0 incoming call(s) have been screened.
0 incoming call(s) rejected for callback.

BRI0:1 - dialer type = ISDN
Idle timer (300 secs), Fast idle timer (10 secs)
Wait for carrier (30 secs), Re-enable (15 secs)
Dialer state is data link layer up
Dial reason: snapshot
Time until disconnect 299 secs
Connected to 5552002 (London)

BRI0:2 - dialer type = ISDN
Idle timer (300 secs), Fast idle timer (10 secs)
Wait for carrier (30 secs), Re-enable (15 secs)
Dialer state is idle
```

If snapshot processing dialed our neighbor, then the **show snapshot** command will provide us with details of the current active period. BRI0 is up and active for dialer address 1. Remember, each snapshot client that will attach to a specific snapshot server needs to have a unique number in the **dialer map snapshot** command. Snapshot is working, and IP routing updates have been received on this cycle.

```
Rome#show snapshot
BRI0 is up, line protocol is upSnapshot client
  Options: dialer support, stay asleep on carrier up
  Length of active period:      5 minutes
  Length of quiet period:       60 minutes
  Length of retry period:       8 minutes
   For dialer address 1
    Current state: active, remaining/exchange time: 1/2 minutes
    Connected dialer interface:
      BRI0:1
    Updates received this cycle: ip
```

Let's verify that the IGRP routes have made it to Rome (all roads lead to Rome) using the **show ip route** command.

```
Rome#show ip route
Codes: C - connected, S - static, I - IGRP, R - RIP, M - mobile, B - BGP
       D - EIGRP, EX - EIGRP external, O - OSPF, IA - OSPF inter area
       N1 - OSPF NSSA external type 1, N2 - OSPF NSSA external type 2
       E1 - OSPF external type 1, E2 - OSPF external type 2, E - EGP
       i - IS-IS, L1 - IS-IS level-1, L2 - IS-IS level-2, * - candidate default
       U - per-user static route, o - ODR

Gateway of last resort is not set

     172.31.0.0/16 is variably subnetted, 4 subnets, 2 masks
C       172.31.201.0/24 is directly connected, BRI0
I       172.31.200.0/24 [100/160350] via 172.31.201.1, 00:00:34, BRI0
C       172.31.201.1/32 is directly connected, BRI0
I       172.31.100.0/24 [100/158350] via 172.31.201.1, 00:00:34, BRI0
I    192.168.1.0/24 [100/158850] via 172.31.201.1, 00:00:34, BRI0
I    192.168.2.0/24 [100/158750] via 172.31.201.1, 00:00:34, BRI0
C    192.168.3.0/24 is directly connected, Loopback0
```

Let's take a look at the standard snapshot activation sequence from the client side.

```
03:48:37: SNAPSHOT: BRI0[1]: Move to active queue (Quiet timer expired)
03:48:37: SNAPSHOT: BRI0[1]: moving to active queue
03:48:37: %LINK-3-UPDOWN: Interface BRI0:1, changed state to up
03:48:39: %LINEPROTO-5-UPDOWN: Line protocol on Interface BRI0:1, changed state to up
03:48:43: %ISDN-6-CONNECT: Interface BRI0:1 is now connected to 5552002 London
03:50:05: SNAPSHOT: BRI0[1]: Starting aging of ip protocol
03:54:37: SNAPSHOT: BRI0[1]: moving to client post active->quiet queue
03:57:37: SNAPSHOT: BRI0[1]: moving to quiet queue
03:59:37: %ISDN-6-DISCONNECT: Interface BRI0:1  disconnected from 5552002 London, call
   lasted 659 seconds
03:59:37: %LINK-3-UPDOWN: Interface BRI0:1, changed state to down
03:59:38: %LINEPROTO-5-UPDOWN: Line protocol on Interface BRI0:1, changed state to down
```

Even after the connection is terminated, the **show ip route** command shows us all the routes learned during the active period. Routes are only aged out during the active period, so all routes now present will stay active until the next active period occurs.

```
Rome#show ip route
Codes: C - connected, S - static, I - IGRP, R - RIP, M - mobile, B - BGP
       D - EIGRP, EX - EIGRP external, O - OSPF, IA - OSPF inter area
       N1 - OSPF NSSA external type 1, N2 - OSPF NSSA external type 2
       E1 - OSPF external type 1, E2 - OSPF external type 2, E - EGP
       i - IS-IS, L1 - IS-IS level-1, L2 - IS-IS level-2, * - candidate default
       U - per-user static route, o - ODR

Gateway of last resort is not set

     172.31.0.0/24 is subnetted, 3 subnets
C       172.31.201.0 is directly connected, BRI0
I       172.31.200.0 [100/160350] via 172.31.201.1, 00:16:15, BRI0
```

```
I       172.31.100.0 [100/158350] via 172.31.201.1, 00:16:15, BRI0
I     192.168.200.0/24 [100/178350] via 172.31.201.1, 00:16:15, BRI0
I     192.168.1.0/24 [100/158850] via 172.31.201.1, 00:16:15, BRI0
I     192.168.2.0/24 [100/158750] via 172.31.201.1, 00:16:15, BRI0
C     192.168.3.0/24 is directly connected, Loopback0
Rome#
```

NOTE *If you use the command* **clear ip route ***, *the routing table will be reset, and only directly connected networks will remain. To force the snapshot client to start an active window, use the* **clear snapshot quiet time** *command. The quiet time value is set to one minute so that the process can initialize in a normal manner.*

SOHO800

SOHO800 uses the RIP routing protocol to get the routes to the rest of the network. The Cisco 800 router does not support the IGRP routing protocol; therefore, for our SOHO800 router to participate with DDR snapshot, we have to use RIP. Code Listing 7-8 shows the SOHO800 router configuration.

Lines 15 through 30 define interface BRI0, our DDR circuit. Line 20 defines the snapshot address resolution for our connection to NewYork. Lines 21 and 22 define our address resolution for the regular NewYork connections. All **dialer map** commands must use the broadcast option when being used in a snapshot routing environment.

Lines 32 through 34 define the RIP routing process.

Lines 38 and 39 define access-list 101 as a set of rules that denies any RIP updates but permits all other IP traffic.

Line 40 ties access-list 101 into dialer-list 1 and is used to identify interesting DDR traffic.

Code Listing 7-8

```
1    version 12.0
2    !
3    hostname SOHO800
4    !
5    username NewYork password 0 cisco
6    !
7    ip subnet-zero
8    !
9    isdn switch-type basic-ni
10   !
11   interface Ethernet0
```

■ |

Code Listing 7-8
(continued)

```
12   ip address 192.168.200.1 255.255.255.0
13   no ip directed-broadcast
14  !
15  interface BRI0
16   ip address 172.31.200.2 255.255.255.0
17   no ip directed-broadcast
18   encapsulation ppp
19   dialer idle-timeout 300
20   dialer map snapshot 1 name NewYork broadcast 5552000
21   dialer map ip 172.31.200.1 name NewYork broadcast 5552000
22   dialer map ip 172.31.200.1 name NewYork broadcast 5552001
23   dialer load-threshold 20 outbound
24   dialer-group 1
25   snapshot client 5 60 suppress-statechange-update dialer
26   isdn switch-type basic-ni
27   isdn spid1 21255520060101
28   isdn spid2 21255520070101
29   ppp authentication chap
30   hold-queue 75 in
31  !
32  router rip
33   network 172.31.0.0
34   network 192.168.200.0
35  !
36  ip classless
37  !
38  access-list 101 deny    udp any any eq rip
39  access-list 101 permit ip any any
40  dialer-list 1 protocol ip list 101
41  !
42  line con 0
43   exec-timeout 0 0
44   logging synchronous
45   length 0
46   transport input none
47   stopbits 1
48  line vty 0 4
49   password cisco
50   login
51  !
52  end
```

The **show snapshot** command gives us a picture of the current status of snapshot routing. It will be 34 minutes before we can test—unacceptable.

```
SOHO800#show snapshot
BRI0 is up, line protocol is upSnapshot client
  Options: dialer support, stay asleep on carrier up
  Length of active period:        5 minutes
  Length of quiet period:        60 minutes
  Length of retry period:         8 minutes
   For dialer address 1
    Current state: quiet, remaining: 34 minutes
```

Not being the most patient of people, I want to speed up the process. So I will reset the quiet time to trigger snapshot processing. Within a minute, the B-channel is active and snapshot processing kicks off.

```
SOHO800#clear snap quiet bri 0
SOHO800#
00:02:01: %LINK-3-UPDOWN: Interface BRI0:1, changed state to up
00:02:02: %LINEPROTO-5-UPDOWN: Line protocol on Interface BRI0:1, changed state to up
```

When we look at the **show snapshot** command output, we see that the snapshot process is active and IP routing updates have been exchanged.

```
SOHO800#show snapshot
BRI0 is up, line protocol is upSnapshot client
   Options: dialer support, stay asleep on carrier up
   Length of active period:        5 minutes
   Length of quiet period:         60 minutes
   Length of retry period:         8 minutes
    For dialer address 1
      Current state: active, remaining/exchange time: 4/0 minutes
      Connected dialer interface:
         BRI0:1
      Updates received this cycle: ip
```

The **show ip route** command now has all of the routes in the network. Look at the metrics for the RIP-derived routes. The metric of 5 hops arrived via route redistribution.

```
SOHO800#show ip route
Codes: C - connected, S - static, I - IGRP, R - RIP, M - mobile, B - BGP
       D - EIGRP, EX - EIGRP external, O - OSPF, IA - OSPF inter area
       N1 - OSPF NSSA external type 1, N2 - OSPF NSSA external type 2
       E1 - OSPF external type 1, E2 - OSPF external type 2, E - EGP
       i - IS-IS, L1 - IS-IS level-1, L2 - IS-IS level-2, * - candidate default
       U - per-user static route, o - ODR
       T - traffic engineered route

Gateway of last resort is not set

     172.31.0.0/16 is variably subnetted, 4 subnets, 2 masks
R       172.31.201.0/24 [120/5] via 172.31.200.1, BRI0
C       172.31.200.1/32 is directly connected, BRI0
C       172.31.200.0/24 is directly connected, BRI0
R       172.31.100.0/24 [120/1] via 172.31.200.1, BRI0
C    192.168.200.0/24 is directly connected, Ethernet0
R    192.168.1.0/24 [120/5] via 172.31.200.1, BRI0
R    192.168.2.0/24 [120/5] via 172.31.200.1, BRI0
R    192.168.3.0/24 [120/5] via 172.31.200.1, BRI0
```

Use the **show dialer** command to verify that the snapshot process triggered our DDR connection.

```
SOHO800#show dialer

BRI0 - dialer type = ISDN

Dial String      Successes   Failures    Last called   Last status
5552001                  0          0    never                   -
5552000                  1          0    00:01:39      successful
0 incoming call(s) have been screened.
0 incoming call(s) rejected for callback.

BRI0:1 - dialer type = ISDN
Idle timer (300 secs), Fast idle timer (20 secs)
Wait for carrier (30 secs), Re-enable (15 secs)
Dialer state is data link layer up
Dial reason: snapshot
Time until disconnect 299 secs
Connected to 5552000 (NewYork)

BRI0:2 - dialer type = ISDN
Idle timer (300 secs), Fast idle timer (20 secs)
Wait for carrier (30 secs), Re-enable (15 secs)
Dialer state is idle
```

OSPF Dial-in Connectivity

This example will use the built-in capabilities of the OSPF routing protocol, as implemented by Cisco, to provide DDR services without the need for static routes. NewYork and London make up the core network, Area 0, the backbone. Paris and Rome are remote sights that exist within their own areas. Each remote OSPF area is made up of the remote sight equipment and the wide-area connections to the remote site. Figure 7-3 shows the equipment layout.

London

Code Listing 7-9 shows the configuration for London. The London router is a component in our backbone, Area 0, and is an Area Border Router (ABR) connecting Area 0 and Area 2. In order for OSPF to set up for DDR processing, it is necessary to set up the remote site and its DDR connection as a stubby area. By setting up the sub-areas as totally stubby areas,

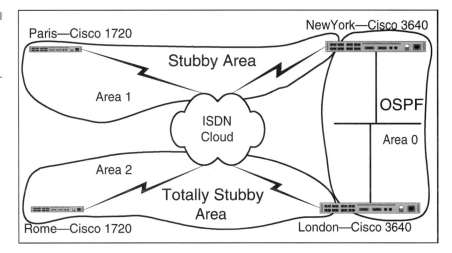

Figure 7-3
OSPF demand circuit
equipment layout.

the backbone ABR pushes a single static default route down to the remote site, and does not send a full routing table.

NOTE *There are two forms of stubby areas. A regular stubby area is where external and inter-area (IA) routes are transmitted to the routers in the stubby area. A totally stubby area is where no additional route except for the static default route is pushed down to the remote site.*

London defines Area 2 as a totally stubby area, and the behavior of a totally stubby area is better for use in a DDR environment. Let's get to the review of the configuration.

Lines 9 through 12 and 26 through 38 define our DDR circuit on an ISDN PRI connection. Line 30 is the key to OSPF DDR operation. By defining the PRI connection as an OSPF demand circuit, the OSPF process eliminates the periodic hellos usually exchanged between OSPF neighbors. It is these hellos that would keep the DDR circuit active.

Lines 40 through 45 define our OSPF routing process. Line 40 starts off our OSPF definition. Lines 41 through 44 assign our interfaces to the appropriate OSPF areas. Line 45 creates our totally stubby area by indicating that no summary Link State Announcements (LSAs) will be advertised to Area 2.

■ |

Code Listing 7-9

```
1    version 12.0
2    !
3    hostname London
4    !
5    username Rome password 0 cisco
6    ip subnet-zero
7    isdn switch-type primary-5ess
8    !
9    controller T1 1/0
10    framing esf
11    linecode b8zs
12    pri-group timeslots 1-24
13   !
14   interface Loopback0
15    ip address 192.168.2.1 255.255.255.0
16    no ip directed-broadcast
17   !
18   interface Loopback2
19    ip address 10.1.1.1 255.0.0.0
20    no ip directed-broadcast
21   !
22   interface Ethernet0/0
23    ip address 172.31.100.2 255.255.255.0
24    no ip directed-broadcast
25   !
26   interface Serial1/0:23
27    ip address 172.31.202.1 255.255.255.0
28    no ip directed-broadcast
29    encapsulation ppp
30    ip ospf demand-circuit
31    dialer idle-timeout 60
32    dialer fast-idle 10
33    dialer map ip 172.31.202.2 name Rome broadcast 5552013
34    dialer map ip 172.31.202.2 name Rome broadcast 5552014
35    dialer-group 1
36    isdn switch-type primary-5ess
37    ppp authentication chap
38    hold-queue 75 in
39   !
40   router ospf 200
41    network 10.0.0.0 0.255.255.255 area 0
42    network 172.31.100.0 0.0.0.255 area 0
43    network 172.31.202.0 0.0.0.255 area 2
44    network 192.168.2.0 0.0.0.255 area 0
45    area 2 stub no-summary
46   !
47   ip classless
48   !
49   dialer-list 1 protocol ip permit
50   !
51   line con 0
52    exec-timeout 0 0
53    length 0
54    transport input none
55   line 65 70
56   line aux 0
57   line vty 0 4
58    password bb
```

■ |

Code Listing 7-9
(continued)

```
59    login
60    !
61    end
```

After both routers in Area 2 have been set up, London initiates a call to Rome and exchanges initial neighbor negotiations. After the initial exchange of information, the DDR circuit terminates and remains closed until regular traffic triggers a call, or until the topology changes on either side of the DDR connection. In the case of a topology change, the peers only need to communicate if the topology change needs to be transmitted. In this example, where Rome is in a totally stubby area, no summary LSAs are transmitted to Rome, so topology changes will not activate the DDR circuit. You'll find more on this topic later in this example. The OSPF (O) route to `192.168.3.1` is derived from Rome during the initial exchange of route information.

```
London#show ip route
Codes: C - connected, S - static, I - IGRP, R - RIP, M - mobile, B - BGP
       D - EIGRP, EX - EIGRP external, O - OSPF, IA - OSPF inter area
       N1 - OSPF NSSA external type 1, N2 - OSPF NSSA external type 2
       E1 - OSPF external type 1, E2 - OSPF external type 2, E - EGP
       i - IS-IS, L1 - IS-IS level-1, L2 - IS-IS level-2, * - candidate default
       U - per-user static route, o - ODR
       T - traffic engineered route

Gateway of last resort is not set

     172.31.0.0/24 is subnetted, 3 subnets
C       172.31.202.0 is directly connected, Serial1/0:23
O IA    172.31.201.0 [110/1572] via 172.31.100.1, 00:16:34, Ethernet0/0
C       172.31.100.0 is directly connected, Ethernet0/0
     192.168.4.0/32 is subnetted, 1 subnets
O IA    192.168.4.1 [110/1573] via 172.31.100.1, 00:04:33, Ethernet0/0
C    10.0.0.0/8 is directly connected, Loopback2
     192.168.1.0/32 is subnetted, 1 subnets
O       192.168.1.1 [110/11] via 172.31.100.1, 00:16:34, Ethernet0/0
C    192.168.2.0/24 is directly connected, Loopback0
     192.168.3.0/32 is subnetted, 1 subnets
O       192.168.3.1 [110/1563] via 172.31.202.2, 00:46:15, Serial1/0:23
```

NewYork

NewYork is the other router in Area 0, the OSPF backbone. Code Listing 7-10 shows the configuration. As in the London example, the DDR circuit is an ISDN PRI interface. Lines 9 through 12 and 22 through 34 define this connection. Line 26, as in London, configures the DDR circuit as an

OSPF demand circuit to eliminate the continuous hellos between OSPF peers.

Lines 36 through 40 define the OSPF process for NewYork. Line 36 starts the configuration process, and lines 37 through 39 tie the interfaces to their respective areas and activate OSPF on the associated interface. Line 40 defines area 1 as a stubby area. A stubby area has a static default route and all summary and external LSAs distributed down from Area 0. Topology changes will activate the DDR interface and update the remote site routing table.

Code Listing 7-10

```
1    version 12.0
2    !
3    hostname NewYork
4    !
5    username Paris password 0 cisco
6    ip subnet-zero
7    isdn switch-type primary-5ess
8    !
9    controller T1 1/0
10     framing esf
11     linecode b8zs
12     pri-group timeslots 1-24
13   !
14   interface Loopback0
15     ip address 192.168.1.1 255.255.255.0
16     no ip directed-broadcast
17   !
18   interface Ethernet0/0
19     ip address 172.31.100.1 255.255.255.0
20     no ip directed-broadcast
21   !
22   interface Serial1/0:23
23     ip address 172.31.201.1 255.255.255.0
24     no ip directed-broadcast
25     encapsulation ppp
26     ip ospf demand-circuit
27     dialer idle-timeout 60
28     dialer fast-idle 10
29     dialer map ip 172.31.201.2 name Rome broadcast 5552009
30     dialer map ip 172.31.201.2 name Rome broadcast 5552010
31     dialer-group 1
32     isdn switch-type primary-5ess
33     ppp authentication chap
34     hold-queue 75 in
35   !
36   router ospf 200
37     network 172.31.100.0 0.0.0.255 area 0
38     network 172.31.201.0 0.0.0.255 area 1
39     network 192.168.1.0 0.0.0.255 area 0
40     area 1 stub
41   !
42   ip classless
43   !
```

```
44   dialer-list 1 protocol ip permit
45   !
46   line con 0
47    exec-timeout 0 0
48    length 0
49    transport input none
50   line 65 70
51   line aux 0
52   line vty 0 4
53    password bb
54    login
55   !
56   end
```

Looking at the **show ip route** command output, we can see the loop-back address route to `192.168.3.1` show up as an Inter Area (`IA`) route. The loopback address in Paris, `192.168.4.1`, shows up as an OSPF (`O`) route.

```
NewYork#show ip route
Codes: C - connected, S - static, I - IGRP, R - RIP, M - mobile, B - BGP
       D - EIGRP, EX - EIGRP external, O - OSPF, IA - OSPF inter area
       N1 - OSPF NSSA external type 1, N2 - OSPF NSSA external type 2
       E1 - OSPF external type 1, E2 - OSPF external type 2, E - EGP
       i - IS-IS, L1 - IS-IS level-1, L2 - IS-IS level-2, * - candidate default
       U - per-user static route, o - ODR
       T - traffic engineered route

Gateway of last resort is not set

     172.31.0.0/16 is variably subnetted, 4 subnets, 2 masks
C       172.31.201.2/32 is directly connected, Serial1/0:23
O IA    172.31.202.0/24 [110/1572] via 172.31.100.2, 00:00:49, Ethernet0/0
C       172.31.201.0/24 is directly connected, Serial1/0:23
C       172.31.100.0/24 is directly connected, Ethernet0/0
     192.168.4.0/32 is subnetted, 1 subnets
O       192.168.4.1 [110/1563] via 172.31.201.2, 00:06:51, Serial1/0:23
     10.0.0.0/32 is subnetted, 1 subnets
O       10.1.1.1 [110/11] via 172.31.100.2, 00:00:49, Ethernet0/0
C    192.168.1.0/24 is directly connected, Loopback0
     192.168.2.0/32 is subnetted, 1 subnets
O       192.168.2.1 [110/11] via 172.31.100.2, 00:00:49, Ethernet0/0
     192.168.3.0/32 is subnetted, 1 subnets
O IA    192.168.3.1 [110/1573] via 172.31.100.2, 00:00:49, Ethernet0/0
```

The **show ip ospf int S1/0:23** command details the definition of the DDR circuit to Paris.

```
NewYork#show ip ospf int s1/0:23
Serial1/0:23 is up, line protocol is up (spoofing)
  Internet Address 172.31.201.1/24, Area 1
  Process ID 200, Router ID 192.168.1.1, Network Type POINT_TO_POINT, Cost: 1562
  Configured as demand circuit.
  Run as demand circuit.
  DoNotAge LSA allowed.
  Transmit Delay is 1 sec, State POINT_TO_POINT,
  Timer intervals configured, Hello 10, Dead 40, Wait 40, Retransmit 5
    Hello due in 00:00:01
  Neighbor Count is 1, Adjacent neighbor count is 1
    Adjacent with neighbor 192.168.4.1  (Hello suppressed)
  Suppress hello for 1 neighbor(s)
```

When the loopback interface in London, 10.1.1.1, is shut down, then the topology changes. If we look at the routing table with the **show ip route** command, we should see that the route to 10.1.1.1 has been removed.

```
NewYork#show ip route
Codes: C - connected, S - static, I - IGRP, R - RIP, M - mobile, B - BGP
       D - EIGRP, EX - EIGRP external, O - OSPF, IA - OSPF inter area
       N1 - OSPF NSSA external type 1, N2 - OSPF NSSA external type 2
       E1 - OSPF external type 1, E2 - OSPF external type 2, E - EGP
       i - IS-IS, L1 - IS-IS level-1, L2 - IS-IS level-2, * - candidate default
       U - per-user static route, o - ODR
       T - traffic engineered route

Gateway of last resort is not set

     172.31.0.0/16 is variably subnetted, 4 subnets, 2 masks
C       172.31.201.2/32 is directly connected, Serial1/0:23
O IA    172.31.202.0/24 [110/1572] via 172.31.100.2, 00:00:16, Ethernet0/0
C       172.31.201.0/24 is directly connected, Serial1/0:23
C       172.31.100.0/24 is directly connected, Ethernet0/0
     192.168.4.0/32 is subnetted, 1 subnets
O       192.168.4.1 [110/1563] via 172.31.201.2, 00:08:25, Serial1/0:23
C    192.168.1.0/24 is directly connected, Loopback0
     192.168.2.0/32 is subnetted, 1 subnets
O       192.168.2.1 [110/11] via 172.31.100.2, 00:00:16, Ethernet0/0
     192.168.3.0/32 is subnetted, 1 subnets
O IA    192.168.3.1 [110/1573] via 172.31.100.2, 00:00:16, Ethernet0/0
```

Serial 1/0:22 is activated when the topology changes, and NewYork brings up the DDR circuit to update the remote peer.

```
01:13:44: %LINK-3-UPDOWN: Interface Serial1/0:22, changed state to up
01:13:46: %LINEPROTO-5-UPDOWN: Line protocol on Interface Serial1/0:22, changed state to
  up
01:13:50: %ISDN-6-CONNECT: Interface Serial1/0:22 is now connected to 5552009 Paris
```

The **show dialer** command shows us that the reason for activating `BRI1/0:22` was a multicast packet to 224.0.0.5, the start of the OSPF topology update sequence.

```
NewYork#show dialer

Serial1/0:0 - dialer type = ISDN
Idle timer (60 secs), Fast idle timer (10 secs)
Wait for carrier (30 secs), Re-enable (15 secs)
Dialer state is idle
.
. Deleted for clarity
.
Serial1/0:21 - dialer type = ISDN
Idle timer (60 secs), Fast idle timer (10 secs)
Wait for carrier (30 secs), Re-enable (15 secs)
Dialer state is idle

Serial1/0:22 - dialer type = ISDN
Idle timer (60 secs), Fast idle timer (10 secs)
Wait for carrier (30 secs), Re-enable (15 secs)
Dialer state is data link layer up
Dial reason: ip (s=172.31.201.1, d=224.0.0.5)
Time until disconnect 6 secs
Connected to 5552009 (Paris)

Serial1/0:23 - dialer type = ISDN

Dial String      Successes    Failures    Last called   Last status
5552010                  4          10     00:09:09      successful
5552009                 11          14     00:00:58      successful
0 incoming call(s) have been screened.
0 incoming call(s) rejected for callback.
```

Rome

Rome is the router in totally stubby Area 2. Code Listing 7-11 shows the configuration.

Lines 15 through 28 define standard DDR over the `BRI0` interface, with line 19 defining this circuit as an OSPF demand circuit.

Lines 30 through 33 define the OSPF process. Note that the definition of the stubby area on line 33 does not have the `no-summary` option as defined in Rome's peer, London.

Code Listing 7-11

```
1    version 12.0
2    !
3    hostname Rome
4    !
5    username London password 0 cisco
6    memory-size iomem 25
7    ip subnet-zero
8    !
9    isdn switch-type basic-ni
10   !
11   interface Loopback0
12    ip address 192.168.3.1 255.255.255.0
13    no ip directed-broadcast
14   !
15   interface BRI0
16    ip address 172.31.202.2 255.255.255.0
17    no ip directed-broadcast
18    encapsulation ppp
19    ip ospf demand-circuit
20    dialer idle-timeout 60
21    dialer fast-idle 10
22    dialer map ip 172.31.202.1 name London broadcast 5554000
23    dialer load-threshold 30 outbound
24    dialer-group 1
25    isdn switch-type basic-ni
26    isdn spid1 21255520130101
27    isdn spid2 21255520140101
28    ppp authentication chap
29   !
30   router ospf 200
31    network 172.31.202.0 0.0.0.255 area 2
32    network 192.168.3.0 0.0.0.255 area 2
33    area 2 stub
34   !
35   ip classless
36   no ip http server
37   !
38   dialer-list 1 protocol ip permit
39   !
40   line con 0
41    exec-timeout 0 0
42    length 0
43    transport input none
44   line aux 0
45   line vty 0 4
46    password cisco
47    login
48   !
49   no scheduler allocate
50   end
```

The **show ip route** command is boring but functional, showing locally connected networks and an Inter Area (IA) static default route pointing to London.

```
Rome#show ip route
Codes: C - connected, S - static, I - IGRP, R - RIP, M - mobile, B - BGP
       D - EIGRP, EX - EIGRP external, O - OSPF, IA - OSPF inter area
       N1 - OSPF NSSA external type 1, N2 - OSPF NSSA external type 2
       E1 - OSPF external type 1, E2 - OSPF external type 2, E - EGP
       i - IS-IS, L1 - IS-IS level-1, L2 - IS-IS level-2, * - candidate default
       U - per-user static route, o - ODR, P - periodic downloaded static route
       T - traffic engineered route

Gateway of last resort is 172.31.202.1 to network 0.0.0.0

     172.31.0.0/24 is subnetted, 1 subnets
C       172.31.202.0 is directly connected, BRI0
C    192.168.3.0/24 is directly connected, Loopback0
O*IA 0.0.0.0/0 [110/1563] via 172.31.202.1, BRI0
```

Let's try a **ping** to the loopback interface in Paris. It looks good, with a fairly quick response time bringing up two ISDN circuits.

```
Rome#ping 192.168.4.1

Type escape sequence to abort.
Sending 5, 100-byte ICMP Echos to 192.168.4.1, timeout is 2 seconds:

..!!!
Success rate is 60 percent (3/5), round-trip min/avg/max = 60/62/64 ms
```

To verify we are following the path, use the **trace** command to check the path to the destination.

```
Rome#trace 192.168.4.1

Type escape sequence to abort.
Tracing the route to 192.168.4.1

  1 172.31.202.1 20 msec 16 msec 16 msec
  2 172.31.100.1 20 msec 16 msec 16 msec
  3 172.31.201.2 36 msec *  32 msec
```

Paris

Code Listing 7-12 shows the configuration of our last router in this OSPF example, Paris.

Lines 16 through 29 define the DDR connection, BRI0, with line 19 defining this as an OSPF demand circuit.

Lines 31 through 34 define our OSPF routing process, tying in our interfaces to the OSPF process and defining Area 2 as a stubby area.

━ ▪ ▫ ▪ ▫ ▪ ▫ ▪ ▫ ▪ ▫ ▪ ▫ ▪ ▫ ▪ ▫ ▪ ▫ ▪ ▫ ▪ ▫ ▪ ▫ ▪ ▫ ▪ ▫ ▪

Code Listing 7-12

```
1    version 12.0
2    !
3    hostname Paris
4    !
5    username NewYork password 0 cisco
6    memory-size iomem 25
7    ip subnet-zero
8    no ip domain-lookup
9    !
10   isdn switch-type basic-ni
11   !
12   interface Loopback0
13    ip address 192.168.4.1 255.255.255.0
14    no ip directed-broadcast
15   !
16   interface BRI0
17    ip address 172.31.201.2 255.255.255.0
18    no ip directed-broadcast
19    encapsulation ppp
20    ip ospf demand-circuit
21    dialer idle-timeout 60
22    dialer fast-idle 10
23    dialer map ip 172.31.201.1 name NewYork broadcast 5553000
24    dialer load-threshold 30 outbound
25    dialer-group 1
26    isdn switch-type basic-ni
27    isdn spid1 21255520090101
28    isdn spid2 21255520100101
29    ppp authentication chap
30   !
31   router ospf 200
32    network 172.31.201.0 0.0.0.255 area 1
33    network 192.168.4.0 0.0.0.255 area 1
34    area 1 stub
35   !
36   ip classless
37   no ip http server
38   !
39   dialer-list 1 protocol ip permit
40   !
41   line con 0
42    exec-timeout 0 0
43    length 0
44    transport input none
45   line aux 0
46   line vty 0 4
47    password cisco
48    login
49   !
50   end
```

The **show ip route** command really points out the difference between a stubby area and a totally stubby area. In addition to the static default route back to the backbone, we can see all the inter-area (IA) summary

LSA routes. At this point in time, the London loopback interface with address 10.1.1.1 is shut down, so there is no route to that destination.

```
Paris#show ip route
Codes: C - connected, S - static, I - IGRP, R - RIP, M - mobile, B - BGP
       D - EIGRP, EX - EIGRP external, O - OSPF, IA - OSPF inter area
       N1 - OSPF NSSA external type 1, N2 - OSPF NSSA external type 2
       E1 - OSPF external type 1, E2 - OSPF external type 2, E - EGP
       i - IS-IS, L1 - IS-IS level-1, L2 - IS-IS level-2, * - candidate default
       U - per-user static route, o - ODR, P - periodic downloaded static route
       T - traffic engineered route

Gateway of last resort is 172.31.201.1 to network 0.0.0.0

     172.31.0.0/24 is subnetted, 3 subnets
O IA    172.31.202.0 [110/3134] via 172.31.201.1, BRI0
C       172.31.201.0 is directly connected, BRI0
O IA    172.31.100.0 [110/1572] via 172.31.201.1, BRI0
C    192.168.4.0/24 is directly connected, Loopback0
     192.168.1.0/32 is subnetted, 1 subnets
O IA    192.168.1.1 [110/1563] via 172.31.201.1, BRI0
     192.168.2.0/32 is subnetted, 1 subnets
O IA    192.168.2.1 [110/1573] via 172.31.201.1, BRI0
     192.168.3.0/32 is subnetted, 1 subnets
O IA    192.168.3.1 [110/3135] via 172.31.201.1, BRI0
O*IA 0.0.0.0/0 [110/1563] via 172.31.201.1, BRI0
```

When the London loopback interface is reactivated, then OSPF running in NewYork activates the DDR circuit and updates the routes maintained by Paris.

```
01:15:27: %LINK-3-UPDOWN: Interface BRI0:1, changed state to up
01:15:28: %LINEPROTO-5-UPDOWN: Line protocol on Interface BRI0:1, changed state to up
01:15:33: %ISDN-6-CONNECT: Interface BRI0:1 is now connected to 5553000 NewYork
```

After the DDR circuit comes up, a second look at the routing table reveals that the route to 10.1.1.1 has been added to the routing table.

```
Paris#show ip route
Codes: C - connected, S - static, I - IGRP, R - RIP, M - mobile, B - BGP
       D - EIGRP, EX - EIGRP external, O - OSPF, IA - OSPF inter area
       N1 - OSPF NSSA external type 1, N2 - OSPF NSSA external type 2
       E1 - OSPF external type 1, E2 - OSPF external type 2, E - EGP
       i - IS-IS, L1 - IS-IS level-1, L2 - IS-IS level-2, * - candidate default
       U - per-user static route, o - ODR, P - periodic downloaded static route
       T - traffic engineered route

Gateway of last resort is 172.31.201.1 to network 0.0.0.0

     172.31.0.0/16 is variably subnetted, 4 subnets, 2 masks
O IA    172.31.202.0/24 [110/3134] via 172.31.201.1, BRI0
C       172.31.201.0/24 is directly connected, BRI0
```

```
C      172.31.201.1/32 is directly connected, BRI0
O IA   172.31.100.0/24 [110/1572] via 172.31.201.1, BRI0
C    192.168.4.0/24 is directly connected, Loopback0
       10.0.0.0/32 is subnetted, 1 subnets
O IA    10.1.1.1 [110/1573] via 172.31.201.1, BRI0
       192.168.1.0/32 is subnetted, 1 subnets
O IA    192.168.1.1 [110/1563] via 172.31.201.1, BRI0
       192.168.2.0/32 is subnetted, 1 subnets
O IA    192.168.2.1 [110/1573] via 172.31.201.1, BRI0
       192.168.3.0/32 is subnetted, 1 subnets
O IA    192.168.3.1 [110/3135] via 172.31.201.1, BRI0
O*IA 0.0.0.0/0 [110/1563] via 172.31.201.1, BRI0
```

Let's make sure we are really following the path through Area 0 by using the **ping** and **trace** commands to reach Rome's loopback address, 192.168.3.1.

```
Paris#ping 192.168.3.1

Type escape sequence to abort.
Sending 5, 100-byte ICMP Echos to 192.168.3.1, timeout is 2 seconds:
.!!!!
Success rate is 80 percent (4/5), round-trip min/avg/max = 60/62/64 ms
Paris#trace 192.168.3.1

Type escape sequence to abort.
Tracing the route to 192.168.3.1

  1 172.31.201.1 20 msec 16 msec 16 msec
  2 172.31.100.2 20 msec 16 msec 16 msec
  3 172.31.202.2 36 msec *   32 msec
```

After the DDR circuit disconnects, we need to make sure that we can **ping** through to Rome at the other end of the network.

```
Paris#ping 192.168.3.1

Type escape sequence to abort.
Sending 5, 100-byte ICMP Echos to 192.168.3.1, timeout is 2 seconds:

...!!
Success rate is 40 percent (2/5), round-trip min/avg/max = 60/62/64 ms

01:17:193273528320: %LINK-3-UPDOWN: Interface BRI0:1, changed state to up
01:17:46: %LINEPROTO-5-UPDOWN: Line protocol on Interface BRI0:1, changed state to up
01:17:50: %LINK-3-UPDOWN: Interface BRI0:2, changed state to up
01:17:51: %LINEPROTO-5-UPDOWN: Line protocol on Interface BRI0:2, changed state to up
01:17:51: %ISDN-6-CONNECT: Interface BRI0:1 is now connected to 5553000 NewYork
01:17:56: %ISDN-6-CONNECT: Interface BRI0:1 is now connected to 5553000 NewYork
```

To make sure we really triggered this connection and not an OSPF update, let's check out the dial reason with the **show dialer** command. Sure enough, the target is the loopback address on Rome.

```
Paris#show dialer

BRI0 - dialer type = ISDN

Dial String      Successes    Failures    Last called    Last status
5553000                  5           0    00:00:17        successful
0 incoming call(s) have been screened.
0 incoming call(s) rejected for callback.

BRI0:1 - dialer type = ISDN
Idle timer (60 secs), Fast idle timer (10 secs)
Wait for carrier (30 secs), Re-enable (15 secs)
Dialer state is data link layer up
Dial reason: ip (s=172.31.201.2, d=192.168.3.1)
Time until disconnect 46 secs
Connected to 5553000 (NewYork)

BRI0:2 - dialer type = ISDN
Idle timer (60 secs), Fast idle timer (10 secs)
Wait for carrier (30 secs), Re-enable (15 secs)
Dialer state is data link layer up
Time until disconnect 48 secs
Connected to 5553000 (NewYork)
```

Following the path to Rome using the **trace** command shows the correct pathway.

```
Paris#trace 192.168.3.1

Type escape sequence to abort.
Tracing the route to 192.168.3.1

  1 172.31.201.1 16 msec 16 msec 16 msec
  2 172.31.100.2 16 msec 16 msec 16 msec
  3 172.31.202.2 36 msec *  32 msec
```

The **show ip ospf int bri 0** command verifies that this interface is set up as a demand circuit with hello processing suppressed.

```
Paris#show ip ospf int bri 0
BRI0 is up, line protocol is up (spoofing)
  Internet Address 172.31.201.2/24, Area 1
  Process ID 200, Router ID 192.168.4.1, Network Type POINT_TO_POINT, Cost: 1562
  Configured as demand circuit.
  Run as demand circuit.
  DoNotAge LSA allowed.
  Transmit Delay is 1 sec, State POINT_TO_POINT,
  Timer intervals configured, Hello 10, Dead 40, Wait 40, Retransmit 5
```

```
Hello due in 00:00:09
Index 1/1, flood queue length 0
Next 0x0(0)/0x0(0)
Last flood scan length is 1, maximum is 1
Last flood scan time is 0 msec, maximum is 0 msec
Neighbor Count is 1, Adjacent neighbor count is 1
   Adjacent with neighbor 192.168.1.1   (Hello suppressed)
Suppress hello for 1 neighbor(s)
```

NOTE *Even if we set up Paris in a stubby area, the default static route forces all traffic to an unknown destination IP address to trigger a call. If this is so, then a totally stubby area provides the same connectivity as a stubby area, but does not require topology updates to function correctly.*

On-Demand Routing with EIGRP

While EIGRP does not have the built-in demand circuit feature that OSPF has, we can use another technique to process routing information from remote sites. The feature we will use is On-Demand Routing (ODR).

When defined on a central site router, CDP extracts the connected routes on the remote site and place these routes in the routing table for the central site. If the ODR routes are redistributed into the EIGRP routing protocol, the remote information will be propagated to all the other routers in the EIGRP network. If you use a distance vector protocol such as IGRP, the ODR routes will not propagate fast enough to allow traffic from the destination to return to the source. The same is true with the standard CDP parameters; shorter is better.

In this example, our goal is to start IP traffic from Rome to any destination within the network and have the ODR routes propagate to New York.

Figure 7-4 shows the equipment layout for the ODR example.

London

Our ODR commands are located in London. Code Listing 7-13 shows the configuration.

There are three sections in the configuration that deal with the ODR routing: defining the ODR process, redistributing ODR into EIGRP, and modifying the CDP parameters.

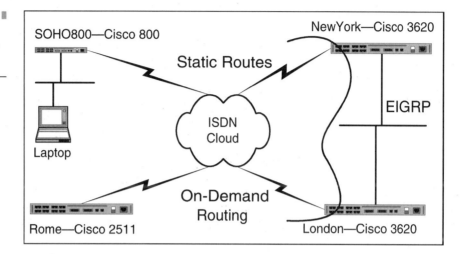

Figure 7-4
On-demand routing
equipment layout.

Lines 26 and 27 define the ODR routing process and include all of the interfaces belonging to network 172.31.0.0.

Lines 29 through 33 define our EIGRP operations. Line 29 activates EIGRP routing for autonomous system 200. Line 30 is the redistribution of routes learned through ODR into our EIGRP process. Line 31 shuts off EIGRP processing on the BRI0 interface. Lines 32 and 33 tie our connected interfaces into the EIGRP process. Lines 38 and 39 change the way CDP operates and are generated by the IOS when ODR is configured on the router. Instead of the 60-second interval between updates, we speed up route convergence by dropping the update timer to five seconds. The time for holding onto IP routes discovered through the CDP process is dropped from 270 seconds to 20 seconds, again for enhanced route convergence.

Code Listing 7-13

```
1    version 11.3
2    hostname London
3    !
4    username Rome password 0 cisco
5    isdn switch-type basic-ni
6    interface Loopback0
7     ip address 192.168.2.1 255.255.255.0
8    !
9    interface BRI0/0
10    ip address 172.31.201.1 255.255.255.0
11    encapsulation ppp
12    dialer idle-timeout 300
13    dialer fast-idle 10
```

Code Listing 7-13
(continued)

```
14   dialer map ip 172.31.201.2 name Rome broadcast 5552004
15   dialer map ip 172.31.201.2 name Rome broadcast 5552005
16   dialer-group 1
17   isdn switch-type basic-ni
18   isdn spid1 21255520020101
19   isdn spid2 21255520030101
20   ppp authentication chap
21   hold-queue 75 in
22   !
23   interface Ethernet0/0
24    ip address 172.31.100.2 255.255.255.0
25   !
26   router odr
27    network 172.31.0.0
28   !
29   router eigrp 300
30    redistribute odr metric 128 20000 255 1 1500
31    passive-interface BRI0/0
32    network 172.31.0.0
33    network 192.168.2.0
34   !
35   ip classless
36   !
37   dialer-list 1 protocol ip permit
38   cdp timer 5
39   cdp holdtime 20
40   !
41   !
42   line con 0
43    exec-timeout 0 0
44    length 0
45   line aux 0
46   line vty 0 4
47    password bb
48    login
49   !
50   end
```

Before Rome dials in, the **show ip route** command has no record of
the remote route to network `192.168.3.0`.

```
London#show ip route
Codes: C - connected, S - static, I - IGRP, R - RIP, M - mobile, B - BGP
       D - EIGRP, EX - EIGRP external, O - OSPF, IA - OSPF inter area
       N1 - OSPF NSSA external type 1, N2 - OSPF NSSA external type 2
       E1 - OSPF external type 1, E2 - OSPF external type 2, E - EGP
       i - IS-IS, L1 - IS-IS level-1, L2 - IS-IS level-2, * - candidate default
       U - per-user static route, o - ODR

Gateway of last resort is not set

     172.31.0.0/16 is variably subnetted, 5 subnets, 3 masks
D       172.31.200.2/32 [90/40537600] via 172.31.100.1, 00:16:35, Ethernet0/0
C       172.31.201.0/24 is directly connected, BRI0/0
D       172.31.200.0/24 [90/40537600] via 172.31.100.1, 00:16:35, Ethernet0/0
```

```
D        172.31.0.0/16 is a summary, 00:16:35, Null0
C        172.31.100.0/24 is directly connected, Ethernet0/0
D EX 192.168.200.0/24 [170/25145600] via 172.31.100.1, 00:16:35, Ethernet0/0
D    192.168.1.0/24 [90/409600] via 172.31.100.1, 00:16:35, Ethernet0/0
C    192.168.2.0/24 is directly connected, Loopback0
```

With **debug ip routing** activated, it is time to test the connection from Rome.

```
London#show debug
IP routing:
  IP routing debugging is on
London#
00:47:43: %LINK-3-UPDOWN: Interface BRI0/0:2, changed state to up
```

After the B-channel comes up, we see that two routes are added to the routing table, the B-channel is connected, and the ODR route added. Based on the time stamp on the output, the discovery and adding of this route happens immediately.

```
00:47:43: RT: add 172.31.201.2/32 via 0.0.0.0, connected metric [0/0]
00:47:43: RT: add 192.168.3.0/24 via 172.31.201.2, odr metric [160/1]
```

The interface finishes the activation process.

```
00:47:43: %LINEPROTO-5-UPDOWN: Line protocol on Interface BRI0/0:2, changed state to up
00:47:49: %ISDN-6-CONNECT: Interface BRI0/0:2 is now connected to 5552004 Rome
```

Now that a connection has been activated, the ODR (o) route appears in the **show ip route** command output.

```
London#show ip route
Codes: C - connected, S - static, I - IGRP, R - RIP, M - mobile, B - BGP
       D - EIGRP, EX - EIGRP external, O - OSPF, IA - OSPF inter area
       N1 - OSPF NSSA external type 1, N2 - OSPF NSSA external type 2
       E1 - OSPF external type 1, E2 - OSPF external type 2, E - EGP
       i - IS-IS, L1 - IS-IS level-1, L2 - IS-IS level-2, * - candidate default
       U - per-user static route, o - ODR

Gateway of last resort is not set

     172.31.0.0/16 is variably subnetted, 6 subnets, 3 masks
C        172.31.201.2/32 is directly connected, BRI0/0
D        172.31.200.2/32 [90/40537600] via 172.31.100.1, 00:22:43, Ethernet0/0
C        172.31.201.0/24 is directly connected, BRI0/0
D        172.31.200.0/24 [90/40537600] via 172.31.100.1, 00:22:43, Ethernet0/0
D        172.31.0.0/16 is a summary, 00:22:43, Null0
C        172.31.100.0/24 is directly connected, Ethernet0/0
```

```
D EX 192.168.200.0/24 [170/25145600] via 172.31.100.1, 00:22:43, Ethernet0/0
D       192.168.1.0/24 [90/409600] via 172.31.100.1, 00:22:43, Ethernet0/0
C       192.168.2.0/24 is directly connected, Loopback0
o       192.168.3.0/24 [160/1] via 172.31.201.2, 00:00:01, BRI0/0
```

After the call is completed, the **debug** output shows the removal of the routes added during circuit activation.

```
00:52:45: %ISDN-6-DISCONNECT: Interface BRI0/0:2  disconnected from 5552004 Rome, call
   lasted 302 seconds
00:52:45: %LINK-3-UPDOWN: Interface BRI0/0:2, changed state to down
00:52:45: RT: del 172.31.201.2/32 via 0.0.0.0, connected metric [0/0]
00:52:45: RT: BRI0/0 peer adjust
00:52:45: RT: delete subnet route to 172.31.201.2/32
00:52:46: %LINEPROTO-5-UPDOWN: Line protocol on Interface BRI0/0:2, changed state to down
00:56:11: RT: flushed route to 192.168.3.0 via 172.31.201.2 (BRI0/0)
00:56:11: RT: no routes to 192.168.3.0
00:57:11: RT: garbage collecting entry for 192.168.3.0
```

NewYork

NewYork is an EIGRP peer and will let us know if the redistribution of the ODR route from London is occurring correctly. Code Listing 7-14 shows the NewYork router configuration. This configuration is similar to the snapshot example found earlier in this chapter. NewYork and SOHO800 use snapshot routing and the RIP routing protocol.

Code Listing 7-14

```
1    version 11.3
2    !
3    hostname NewYork
4    !
5    username SOHO800 password 0 cisco
6    isdn switch-type basic-ni
7    !
8    interface Loopback0
9     ip address 192.168.1.1 255.255.255.0
10   !
11   interface BRI0/0
12    ip address 172.31.200.1 255.255.255.0
13    encapsulation ppp
14    dialer idle-timeout 300
15    dialer map ip 172.31.200.2 name SOHO800 broadcast 5552006
16    dialer map ip 172.31.200.2 name SOHO800 broadcast 5552007
17    dialer-group 1
18    isdn switch-type basic-ni
19    isdn spid1 21255520000101
20    isdn spid2 21255520010101
21    snapshot server 5 dialer
22    ppp authentication chap
```

```
23    hold-queue 75 in
24    !
25    interface Ethernet0/0
26     ip address 172.31.100.1 255.255.255.0
27    !
28    router eigrp 300
29     redistribute rip metric 128 20000 255 1 1500
30     passive-interface BRI0/0
31     network 172.31.0.0
32     network 192.168.1.0
33    !
34    router rip
35     redistribute eigrp 300 metric 6
36     passive-interface Ethernet0/0
37     passive-interface Loopback0
38     network 172.31.0.0
39    !
40    ip classless
41    !
42    access-list 101 deny    udp any any eq rip
43    access-list 101 permit ip any any
44    dialer-list 1 protocol ip list 101
45    !
46    line con 0
47     exec-timeout 0 0
48     length 0
49    line aux 0
50    line vty 0 4
51     password bb
52     login
53    !
54    end
```

Before the Rome dial connection is activated, the **show ip route** command does not show us a route to Rome's loopback interface address, 192.168.3.0.

```
NewYork#show ip route
Codes: C - connected, S - static, I - IGRP, R - RIP, M - mobile, B - BGP
       D - EIGRP, EX - EIGRP external, O - OSPF, IA - OSPF inter area
       N1 - OSPF NSSA external type 1, N2 - OSPF NSSA external type 2
       E1 - OSPF external type 1, E2 - OSPF external type 2, E - EGP
       i - IS-IS, L1 - IS-IS level-1, L2 - IS-IS level-2, * - candidate default
       U - per-user static route, o - ODR

Gateway of last resort is not set

     172.31.0.0/16 is variably subnetted, 4 subnets, 2 masks
D       172.31.201.0/24 [90/40537600] via 172.31.100.2, 00:07:49, Ethernet0/0
C       172.31.200.0/24 is directly connected, BRI0/0
D       172.31.0.0/16 is a summary, 00:15:20, Null0
C       172.31.100.0/24 is directly connected, Ethernet0/0
R     192.168.200.0/24 [120/1] via 172.31.200.2, 00:07:25, BRI0/0
C     192.168.1.0/24 is directly connected, Loopback0
D     192.168.2.0/24 [90/409600] via 172.31.100.2, 00:15:20, Ethernet0/0
```

After an end-to-end connection is established, then the ODR route to Rome, `192.168.3.0`, shows up in NewYork as an external EIGRP (`D EX`) route.

```
NewYork#show ip route
Codes: C - connected, S - static, I - IGRP, R - RIP, M - mobile, B - BGP
       D - EIGRP, EX - EIGRP external, O - OSPF, IA - OSPF inter area
       N1 - OSPF NSSA external type 1, N2 - OSPF NSSA external type 2
       E1 - OSPF external type 1, E2 - OSPF external type 2, E - EGP
       i - IS-IS, L1 - IS-IS level-1, L2 - IS-IS level-2, * - candidate default
       U - per-user static route, o - ODR

Gateway of last resort is not set

     172.31.0.0/16 is variably subnetted, 5 subnets, 3 masks
C       172.31.200.2/32 is directly connected, BRI0/0
D       172.31.201.0/24 [90/40537600] via 172.31.100.2, 00:12:31, Ethernet0/0
C       172.31.200.0/24 is directly connected, BRI0/0
D       172.31.0.0/16 is a summary, 00:20:02, Null0
C       172.31.100.0/24 is directly connected, Ethernet0/0
R    192.168.200.0/24 [120/1] via 172.31.200.2, 00:00:23, BRI0/0
C    192.168.1.0/24 is directly connected, Loopback0
D    192.168.2.0/24 [90/409600] via 172.31.100.2, 00:20:02, Ethernet0/0
D EX 192.168.3.0/24 [170/25145600] via 172.31.100.2, 00:00:48, Ethernet0/0
```

The Rome router is pretty straightforward: a static default route takes us to London, and the rest is fairly straightforward DDR. Code Listing 7-15 shows the Rome router configuration.

Code Listing 7-15

```
1    version 11.3
2    !
3    hostname Rome
4    !
5    username London password 0 cisco
6    no ip domain-lookup
7    isdn switch-type basic-ni1
8    !
9    interface Loopback0
10    ip address 192.168.3.1 255.255.255.0
11    !
12   interface BRI0
13    ip address 172.31.201.2 255.255.255.0
14    encapsulation ppp
15    dialer idle-timeout 300
16    dialer fast-idle 10
17    dialer map ip 172.31.201.1 name London broadcast 5552002
18    dialer map ip 172.31.201.1 name London broadcast 5552003
19    dialer load-threshold 30 outbound
20    dialer-group 1
21    isdn spid1 21255520040101
22    isdn spid2 21255520050101
23    ppp authentication chap
```

Code Listing 7-15
(continued)

```
24  !
25  ip classless
26  ip route 0.0.0.0 0.0.0.0 BRI0 172.31.201.1
27  !
28  access-list 101 deny    igrp any any
29  access-list 101 permit ip any any
30  dialer-list 1 protocol ip list 101
31  cdp timer 5
32  cdp holdtime 20
33  !
34  line con 0
35    exec-timeout 0 0
36    length 0
37  line aux 0
38  line vty 0 4
39    password cisco
40    login
41  !
42  end
```

Time to **ping** the PC's IP address and check out whether or not the EIGRP cloud is distributing the ODR route fast enough to allow return traffic. Sure enough, we have success!

```
Rome#ping 192.168.200.6

Type escape sequence to abort.
Sending 5, 100-byte ICMP Echos to 192.168.200.6, timeout is 2 seconds:

.!!!!

Success rate is 80 percent (4/5), round-trip min/avg/max = 72/79/96 ms
00:53:55: %LINK-3-UPDOWN: Interface BRI0:2, changed state to up
00:53:55: %LINEPROTO-5-UPDOWN: Line protocol on Interface BRI0:2, changed state to upRome#
00:54:01: %ISDN-6-CONNECT: Interface BRI0:2 is now connected to 5552002 London
```

SOHO800

While SOHO800 does not play a direct role in this ODR example. Code Listing 7-16 shows the configuration for completeness.

Code Listing 7-16

```
1  version 12.0
2  !
3  hostname SOHO800
4  !
5  username NewYork password 0 cisco
6  !
7  ip subnet-zero
```

■ ■

Code Listing 7-16
(continued)

```
8    !
9    isdn switch-type basic-ni
10   !
11   interface Ethernet0
12     ip address 192.168.200.1 255.255.255.0
13     no ip directed-broadcast
14   !
15   interface BRI0
16     ip address 172.31.200.2 255.255.255.0
17     no ip directed-broadcast
18     encapsulation ppp
19     dialer idle-timeout 300
20     dialer map snapshot 1 name NewYork broadcast 5552000
21     dialer map ip 172.31.200.1 name NewYork broadcast 5552000
22     dialer map ip 172.31.200.1 name NewYork broadcast 5552001
23     dialer load-threshold 20 outbound
24     dialer-group 1
25     snapshot client 5 60 suppress-statechange-update dialer
26     isdn switch-type basic-ni
27     isdn spid1 21255520060101
28     isdn spid2 21255520070101
29     ppp authentication chap
30     hold-queue 75 in
31   !
32   router rip
33     network 172.31.0.0
34     network 192.168.200.0
35   !
36   ip classless
37   !
38   access-list 101 deny   udp any any eq rip
39   access-list 101 permit ip any any
40   dialer-list 1 protocol ip list 101
41   !
42   line con 0
43     exec-timeout 0 0
44     logging synchronous
45     length 0
46     transport input none
47     stopbits 1
48   line vty 0 4
49     password cisco
50     login
51   !
52   end
```

Just to make sure that Rome's loopback address is showing up in SOHO800, let's look at the **show ip route** command output.

```
SOHO800#show ip route
Codes: C - connected, S - static, I - IGRP, R - RIP, M - mobile, B - BGP
       D - EIGRP, EX - EIGRP external, O - OSPF, IA - OSPF inter area
       N1 - OSPF NSSA external type 1, N2 - OSPF NSSA external type 2
       E1 - OSPF external type 1, E2 - OSPF external type 2, E - EGP
       i - IS-IS, L1 - IS-IS level-1, L2 - IS-IS level-2, * - candidate default
```

```
        U - per-user static route, o - ODR
        T - traffic engineered route

Gateway of last resort is not set

        172.31.0.0/16 is variably subnetted, 4 subnets, 2 masks
R          172.31.201.0/24 [120/6] via 172.31.200.1, BRI0
C          172.31.200.1/32 is directly connected, BRI0
C          172.31.200.0/24 is directly connected, BRI0
R          172.31.100.0/24 [120/1] via 172.31.200.1, BRI0
C       192.168.200.0/24 is directly connected, Ethernet0
R       192.168.1.0/24 [120/6] via 172.31.200.1, BRI0
R       192.168.2.0/24 [120/6] via 172.31.200.1, BRI0
R       192.168.3.0/24 [120/6] via 172.31.200.1, BRI0
SOHO800#
```

Summary

In this chapter we have examined the distribution of static routes used in DDR into regular routing protocols.

While static routes are an acceptable method for managing small-scale DDR environments, snapshot routing for distance vector protocols, OSPF demand circuits, and On-Demand Routing provide dynamic solutions that scale well in larger DDR environments.

The AS5200 High-end Access Server

In this chapter, we will explore the basic Cisco high-end access server, the AS5200. Instead of using external modems with individual DS0 connections (regular phone circuits), the AS5200 uses T1 circuits to make and accept both digital ISDN and analog asynchronous calls.

This chapter combines all that we have learned to explain the configuration of high-end access servers that use T1 or better Central Office (CO) connections to provide simultaneous ISDN and asynchronous connections.

Basics

When a call comes into the AS5200, the call setup contains information that indicates whether the call is setting up an ISDN B-channel data call or a voice grade call. For the ISDN data call, the AS5200 activates a B-channel connection and begins to build the logical connection. When a voice grade call comes in, the AS5200 can be configured to direct the call to a bank of built-in modems. The modems are grouped together using a new command, **interface Group-Async**. With up to 120 modems in an AS5200, and many more in the higher-end access servers like the AS5300 and AS5800, programming each individual interface would be a real pain. The example that follows uses the **interface Group-Async** command to program the modems as a group. How do we break out each incoming call if we only have a single interface definition? Each call creates its own Virtual Access interface.

EXAMPLE

This example ties all of the components of dial-in access together into a single dial-up network. Three remote devices will connect into our AS5200: SOHO700, a Cisco 700; an analog dial-in from a PC with a modem; and London, a Cisco 2522. Figure 8-1 shows the equipment layout.

So now let's go to our configurations. The first is SOHO700, a Cisco 766 that will establish an ISDN BRI connection to the AS5200. The Cisco 766 is a low-cost IP gateway solution that has a different user interface than the standard Cisco IOS. There is a book, ISDN for Cisco Routers by Paul Fischer, that defines the Cisco 700 series and provides many details and configuration tips. The second configuration is London, a Cisco 2522 that will create another ISDN BRI connection to our AS5200. Last is NewYork, the Cisco AS5200, the target of our calls.

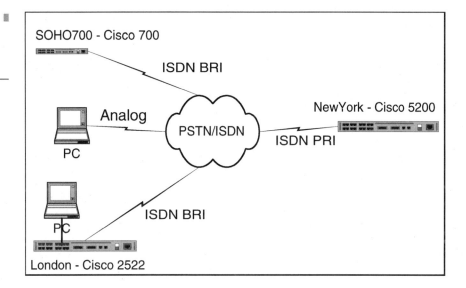

Figure 8-1
AS5200 equipment
layout.

SOHO700

Code Listing 8-1 shows the configuration commands for the SOHO700. The configuration file contains ALL the commands used to configure the router, as opposed to the regular Cisco IOS, where default values do not show up in the configuration file. To see a complete configuration, use the **UPCHUCK**, oops, I mean the **UPLOAD** command. This command will display the complete list of all commands used to program the Cisco 766. Read fast; there is no more in the **UPLOAD** command. Instead of sifting through the complete listing, you can use the following commands to set up the basics for a connection to the central site access server, NewYork. To clean out the configuration on a Cisco 766, use the **SET DEFAULT** command.

The Cisco 766 uses standard and user profiles to segment the configuration process. The three standard profiles are the SYSTEM or root profile, the LAN profile for the ethernet connection, and the INTERNAL profile, which is a work area to dynamically assemble connections. Each of up to 16 USER profiles define the remote connections. Say, does this sound familiar? Go back and review the dialer profile section in Chapter 6.

The SYSTEM profile in lines 1 through 9 are the global configuration commands.

Line 1 sets the system name, which is used as the user name in a CHAP authentication sequence.

Line 2 sets the CO switch type for the ISDN calls.

Line 3 makes sure that no bridging takes place; we only want IP traffic flowing.

Lines 4 and 5 make sure that we can process standard two-way CHAP authentication used with Cisco routers.

Lines 6 through 8 set up the password used in conjunction with SOHO700 for CHAP authentication. Line 6 starts the command that then asks for the password to be entered twice.

Line 9 activates PPP multilink.

Just like all ISDN connections using profiles, the physical connection is where the PPP connection type is negotiated until the user is authenticated and identified.

Lines 10 through 14 define the LAN profile used to set up the Ethernet connection.

Line 10 moves us to the LAN profile. An alternate command that could be used is **CD LAN**, as the LAN profile is created in a default configuration. **CD** always takes you back to the SYSTEM or root profile.

Line 11 turns off bridging.

Line 12 turns on IP routing.

Lines 13 and 14 set up the IP address and network mask.

Lines 15 through 28 define the USER profile for NewYork.

Line 15 must be entered as shown to create the NewYork profile, but CD NewYork can be used to get back to the USER profile for show commands or making changes.

Line 16 turns off bridging.

Lines 17 and 18 identify the telephone numbers used for each of the two ISDN B-channels.

Lines 19 through 21 define the password used for CHAP authentication for the remote user, NewYork.

Lines 22 through 24 are not necessary with the current version of Cisco 766 operating system, but I am superstitious. They always worked before, so I put them in anyway. (Have you seen my rabbit's foot?)

Line 25 turns on IP routing.

Lines 26 and 27 assign the IP address and network mask for the NewYork connection.

Line 28 sets up our default IP route through NewYork to the rest of our IP network.

Code Listing 8-1

```
1    SET SYSTEMNAME SOHO700
2    SET SWITCH 5ESS
3    SET BRIDGING OFF
4    SET PPP AUTHENTICATION IN CHAP
5    SET PPP AUTHENTICATION OUT CHAP
6    SET PPP SECRET CLIENT
7    cisco
8    cisco
9    SET PPP MULTILINK ON
10   SET USER LAN
11   SET BRIDGING OFF
12   SET IP ROUTING ON
13   SET IP ADDRESS 172.31.70.1
14   SET IP NETMASK 255.255.255.0
15   SET USER NewYork
16   SET BRIDGING OFF
17   SET 1 NUMBER 1000
18   SET 2 NUMBER 1000
19   SET PPP SECRET HOST
20   cisco
21   cisco
22   SET PPP SECRET CLIENT
23   cisco
24   cisco
25   SET IP ROUTING ON
26   SET IP ADDRESS 172.31.201.2
27   SET IP NETMASK 255.255.255.0
28   SET IP ROUTE DEST 0.0.0.0/0 GATEWAY 172.31.201.1 PROPAGATE ON COST 1
```

To test the connectivity, let's **ping** the loopback interface in New York. The call is successful, and a second connection is added and mapped to Link 1 Channel 1:

```
SOHO700> ping 172.31.60.1
Start sending:
01/01/1995 17:46:45  L05  0          1000  Outgoing Call Initiated
01/01/1995 17:46:46  L08  1          1000  Call Connected
01/01/1995 17:46:46  Connection 2 Add      Link 1 Channel 1
round trip time is 4250 msec.
```

Let's do it once more to make sure it is working properly:

```
SOHO700> ping 172.31.60.1
Start sending: round trip time is 40 msec.
```

The **show connect** command shows us the current connections:

```
SOHO700> show connect
Connections    01/01/1995 18:05:10
   Start Date & Time  #  Name                #    Ethernet
 1 01/01/1995 00:00:00 #                     #  00 00 00 00 00 00
 2 01/01/1995 00:00:01 # NewYork             #
           Link: 1 Channel:  1 Phone: 1000
```

The **show status** command lets us know the current status of the ISDN circuit:

```
SOHO700> show status
Status     01/01/1995 18:26:22
Line Status
  Line Activated
  Terminal Identifier Assigned
Port Status                              Interface Connection Link
  Ch:  1    64K Call In Progress    1000     DATA         2        1
  Ch:  2      Waiting for Call
```

We need to check out our routing table with the **show ip route all** command. If you leave off the `all` option, it will only show the routes for the current profile:

```
SOHO700> show ip route all
Profile        Type Destination    Bits Gateway         Prop Cost Source Age
------------------------------------------------------------------------------
NewYork        NET  172.31.201.0   24   DIRECT          ON   1    DIRECT 0
LAN            NET  172.31.70.0    24   DIRECT          ON   1    DIRECT 0
NewYork        NET  0.0.0.0        0    172.31.201.1    ON   1    STATIC 0
```

Next we check our IP configuration with the **show ip configuration all** command:

```
SOHO700> show ip config all
Profile      Routing Frame IP Address      Netmask          RIP TX  RX  Prop Cost
---------------------------------------------------------------------------------
LAN          ON      ETH2  172.31.70.1     255.255.255.0    V1  OFF V1  ON   1
Standard     ON      IPCP  0.0.0.0         0.0.0.0          V1  OFF V1  ON   1
NewYork      ON      IPCP  172.31.201.2    255.255.255.0    V1  OFF V1  ON   1

Profile      PAT Multicast Summarization Netbios Spoofing/Left(min)
-----------------------------------------------------------------
LAN          OFF OFF       OFF           OFF     /0
Standard     OFF OFF       OFF           OFF     /0
NewYork      OFF OFF       OFF           OFF     /0
```

After London has connected to NewYork, we should be able to **ping** the loopback interface in London, `172.31.80.1`:

```
SOHO700> ping 172.31.80.1
Start sending: round trip time is 70 msec.
```

We can. Boy, are we good or what?

Later in the London section we will initiate a long `ping` sequence to SOHO700, and once we exceed our thresholds we will activate a second call to increase the bandwidth. The following sequence shows the second link being added:

```
01/01/1995 18:29:37  L05  0          1000  Outgoing Call Initiated
01/01/1995 18:29:37  L08  2          1000  Call Connected
01/01/1995 18:29:37  Connection 2 Add      Link 2 Channel 2
```

Let's use the **show status** command to check out the second call. Sure enough, the second channel has a 64K Call in Progress:

```
SOHO700> show status
Status      01/01/1995 18:30:06
Line Status
  Line Activated
  Terminal Identifier Assigned
Port Status                                Interface Connection Link
  Ch:  1   64K Call In Progress    1000     DATA        2        1
  Ch:  2   64K Call In Progress    1000     DATA        2        2
```

The **show connect** command shows us the second channel bonded to connection 2:

```
SOHO700> show connect
Connections      01/01/1995 18:30:14
   Start Date & Time   #  Name              #      Ethernet
   1 01/01/1995 00:00:00 #                  # 00 00 00 00 00 00
   2 01/01/1995 00:00:01 # NewYork          #
            Link: 1 Channel:  1 Phone: 1000
            Link: 2 Channel:  2 Phone: 1000
```

A command that would be great if added to the regular Cisco IOS is the **disconnect all** command. It is a clean way to terminate an ISDN call:

```
SOHO700> disconnect all
01/01/1995 18:32:33  Connection 2 Remove  Link 1 Channel 1
01/01/1995 18:32:33  Connection 2 Remove  Link 1 Channel 2
01/01/1995 18:32:33  L13  1               Disconnecting Call
01/01/1995 18:32:33  L27  1               Disconnected
01/01/1995 18:32:33  L13  2               Disconnecting Call
01/01/1995 18:32:33  L27  2               Disconnected
```

On to London for more fun.

London

Code Listing 8-2 shows our London configuration. There are some added features defined in this configuration to test out access list and DDR interactions.

Line 7 sets up the `switch-type` globally. Entering this command here also updates each of the individual BRI interfaces, with the same information, automatically (see line 17).

Lines 12 through 20 define the BRI interface as a resource in dialer pool 7, with PPP multilink and CHAP authentication.

Lines 22 through 34 define the dialer profile used for connectivity to NewYork. Line 24 defines a traffic filter for a test later on in this chapter. The balance is a basic dialer profile.

Line 37 is a static route that points all traffic back through the BRI connection to the rest of network 172.31.0.0.

Lines 39 and 40 define `access-list 101`, which defines the traffic filter for transit traffic forwarded to the BRI interface. Only telnet traffic to 172.16.1.1 is allowed through London and out the BRI interface.

Lines 41 and 42 define the access list that defines the interesting traffic used for DDR. Telnet traffic to 172.16.1.1 and any ICMP message will trigger a call on the BRI interface.

Line 43 ties `access-list 102` into `dialer-list 1` to control DDR on the BRI interface.

Code Listing 8-2

```
1    version 12.0
2    !
3    hostname London
4    !
5    username NewYork password 0 cisco
6    ip subnet-zero
7    isdn switch-type basic-5ess
8    !
9    interface Ethernet0
10    ip address 172.31.80.1 255.255.255.0
11    !
12   interface BRI0
13    no ip address
14    no ip directed-broadcast
15    encapsulation ppp
16    dialer pool-member 7
17    isdn switch-type basic-5ess
18    no cdp enable
19    ppp authentication chap
20    ppp multilink
21    !
22   interface Dialer5
```

Code Listing 8-2
(continued)

```
23    ip address 172.31.200.2 255.255.255.0
24    ip access-group 101 out
25    no ip directed-broadcast
26    encapsulation ppp
27    dialer remote-name NewYork
28    dialer string 1000
29    dialer load-threshold 50 outbound
30    dialer pool 7
31    dialer-group 1
32    no cdp enable
33    ppp authentication chap
34    ppp multilink
35    !
36    ip classless
37    ip route 172.31.0.0 255.255.0.0 Dialer5 172.31.200.1
38    !
39    access-list 101 permit tcp any host 172.31.60.1 eq telnet
40    access-list 101 deny   ip any any
41    access-list 102 permit tcp any host 172.31.60.1 eq telnet
42    access-list 102 permit icmp any any
43    dialer-list 1 protocol ip list 102
44    !
45    end
```

In order to track what is going on and get the sequence of DDR events, we need to turn on some debugging:

```
London#debug dialer
Dial on demand events debugging is on
London#show debug
Dial on demand:
  Dial on demand events debugging is on
  Dial on demand packets debugging is on
Generic IP:
  ICMP packet debugging is on
```

Use the **show access-list** command to get a look at the hits on each line in our access lists. List 101 shows matches on both the permit and deny statements. Some traffic went through, but some traffic was denied. List 102 show lots of hits on ICMP, because some continuous **ping**s were used to trigger additional calls and bring up additional B-channels:

```
London#show access-list 101
Extended IP access list 101
    permit tcp any host 172.31.60.1 eq telnet (125 matches)
    deny ip any any (28 matches)
London#show access-list 102
Extended IP access list 102
    permit tcp any host 172.31.60.1 eq telnet (125 matches)
    permit icmp any any (3439 matches)
```

Let's follow the sequence below to identify when access lists kick in during our DDR process. The first test is a **ping** from our workstation with an address of 172.31.60.2. No DDR must mean that access lists are processed before we start the DDR process:

```
20:10:01: ICMP: dst (172.31.60.1) administratively prohibited unreachable sent to
   172.31.80.2
20:10:02: ICMP: dst (172.31.60.1) administratively prohibited unreachable sent to
   172.31.80.2
20:10:03: ICMP: dst (172.31.60.1) administratively prohibited unreachable sent to
   172.31.80.2
20:10:04: ICMP: dst (172.31.60.1) administratively prohibited unreachable sent to
   172.31.80.2
```

Next we start a telnet session from the workstation to the allowed target, 172.31.60.1. The traffic passed the access list applied to the BRI interface and then activated a call:

```
20:10:42: Dialer5 DDR: ip (s=172.31.80.2, d=172.31.60.1), 48 bytes, outgoing int
eresting (list 102)
20:10:42: BRI0 DDR: rotor dialout [priority]
20:10:42: BRI0 DDR: Dialing cause ip (s=172.31.80.2, d=172.31.60.1)
20:10:42: BRI0 DDR: Attempting to dial 1000
20:10:43: %LINK-3-UPDOWN: Interface BRI0:1, changed state to up
20:10:43: %DIALER-6-BIND: Interface BRI0:1 bound to profile Dialer5
20:10:43: %ISDN-6-CONNECT: Interface BRI0:1 is now connected to 1000
20:10:43: %DIALER-6-BIND: Interface Virtual-Access1 bound to profile Dialer5
20:10:43: %LINK-3-UPDOWN: Interface Virtual-Access1, changed state to up
20:10:44: %LINEPROTO-5-UPDOWN: Line protocol on Interface BRI0:1, changed state to up
20:10:44: %LINEPROTO-5-UPDOWN: Line protocol on Interface Virtual-Access1, changed state
   to up
20:10:45: Virtual-Access1 DDR: dialer protocol up
20:10:45: Dialer5 DDR: ip (s=172.31.80.2, d=172.31.60.1), 48 bytes, outgoing interesting
   (list 102)
20:10:49: %ISDN-6-CONNECT: Interface BRI0:1 is now connected to 1000 NewYork
```

Once we stop traffic testing, the idle timer goes to 0, and the call is disconnected. When we get to NewYork, we will see that the remote sites are in control of call duration:

```
20:13:40: Virtual-Access1 DDR: idle timeout
20:13:40: %DIALER-6-UNBIND: Interface Virtual-Access1 unbound from profile Dialer5
20:13:40: Virtual-Access1 DDR: disconnecting call
20:13:40: %LINK-3-UPDOWN: Interface Virtual-Access1, changed state to down
20:13:40: BR0 DDR: has total 2 call(s), dial_out 0, dial_in 0
20:13:40: %DIALER-6-UNBIND: Interface BRI0:1 unbound from profile Dialer5
20:13:40: BRI0:1 DDR: disconnecting call
20:13:40: %ISDN-6-DISCONNECT: Interface BRI0:1  disconnected from 1000 NewYork, call
   lasted 177 seconds
20:13:40: %LINK-3-UPDOWN: Interface BRI0:1, changed state to down
```

```
20:13:40: BRI0:1 DDR: disconnecting call
20:13:41: %LINEPROTO-5-UPDOWN: Line protocol on Interface BRI0:1, changed state to down
20:13:41: %LINEPROTO-5-UPDOWN: Line protocol on Interface Virtual-Access1, changed state
   to down
```

All roads used to lead to Rome, but in this example, all connections lead to New York.

New York

Here is where we get to the core of our example, the AS5200, New York. Code Listing 8-3 shows the configuration.

Lines 7 through 9 make up the local authentication database providing the usernames and passwords for our dial-in clients.

Line 10 defines the switch type for the ISDN PRI connection. When programming T1/E1 controllers, a global switch type must be in place before a channelized T1 circuit can be converted to a PRI circuit.

Lines 12 through 16 configure the T1 controller. Line 13 defines the frame type as Extended Super Frame (ESF). Line 14 is generated by the system and identifies the first controller as the primary source for clocking. Not only is this the clocking source for all the T1/E1 circuits, but this controller also provides the clocking for the Time Division Multiplexing (TDM) bus that ties the three cards together in the AS5200. Line 15 sets the line encoding to Binary 8 Zero Substitution (B8ZS). Line 16 sets up the 24 DS0 channels of the T1 into a PRI connection. When this command is executed, the system creates `interface Serial0:23`. The 0 corresponds to the controller number, and the 23 is the signalling channel as defined by the CO switch.

Lines 22 through 30 define the operation of our PRI connection. In this example, we will build dialer profiles for the individual connections and use the 23 B-channels as resources in dialer pool 1. Line 26 is very important, as it identifies what to do with an incoming voice call. In this case, when an incoming voice call appears, we will route the call across the TDM bus to the built-in modems.

Lines 32 through 39 define an interesting interface, `Group-Async1`. This is a real timesaver when it comes to configuring the operation of incoming asynchronous calls. Group-Async1 is a virtual template used to build `Virtual Access` interfaces for handling individual voice calls. The alternative would be to create individual asynchronous interfaces for each modem. The basic AS5200 configuration would require the creation of 48 individual interfaces with all the options—time-consuming and error-prone. Line 39 defines the modems within the AS5200 that will be used, round robin, to handle incoming voice calls. Line 35 will start up a PPP session if the first packet on the connection is the start of a PPP negotiation. Line 36 will let us dial in and create a terminal exec session if we want to. Dial-in users will get their IP addresses from pool `async-ips` as defined in line 37.

The dialer profiles defined in lines 41 through 64 have two special features that place the control of the calls with the remote sites. Lines 45 and 58 define the idle timeout to be a very high number. This lets the remote sites control the call timing. `Dialer-List 1` on line 71 follows this same theme; all IP traffic is good. This lets the remote sites define interesting traffic and control call duration. Remember to prevent dynamic routing protocols from activating calls by using a **passive-interface** command or by setting up the appropriate outgoing **IP access-group** on the dialer profiles. If we wanted to let all control reside in the remote sites, we could remove the **dialer string** commands from the profiles and make them receive only.

Line 66 sets up our pool of IP addresses to be assigned for our asynchronous PPP connections.

Lines 68 and 69 set up the static routes to our remote sites. This example does not use an IP routing protocol; however, if a routing protocol is used, the static routes must be redistributed into our dynamic protocol for this to work in a larger network.

Lines 73 through 78 set up the 12 modems used in this example.

Lines 85 through 87 set up 16 additional virtual terminal sessions, which is very common with dial-in access servers where the incoming connections are straight `exec` sessions.

Code Listing 8-3

```
1    version 11.2
2    !
3    hostname NewYork
4    !
5    enable password cisco
6    !
7    username London password 0 cisco
8    username bill password 0 cisco
9    username SOHO700 password 0 cisco
10   isdn switch-type primary-5ess
11   !
12   controller T1 0
13    framing esf
14    clock source line primary
15    linecode b8zs
```

Code Listing 8-3
(continued)

```
16    pri-group timeslots 1-24
17    !
18    interface Ethernet0
19     ip address 172.31.60.1 255.255.255.0
20     no ip directed-broadcast
21    !
22    interface Serial0:23
23     no ip address
24     encapsulation ppp
25     no ip mroute-cache
26     isdn incoming-voice modem
27     dialer pool-member 1
28     no fair-queue
29     ppp authentication chap
30     ppp multilink
31    !
32    interface Group-Async1
33     ip unnumbered Loopback0
34     encapsulation ppp
35     autodetect encapsulation ppp
36     async mode interactive
37     peer default ip address pool async-ips
38     ppp authentication chap
39     group-range 1 12
40    !
41    interface Dialer1
42     ip address 172.31.200.1 255.255.255.0
43     encapsulation ppp
44     dialer remote-name London
45     dialer idle-timeout 9999
46     dialer string 2802010
47     dialer pool 1
48     dialer-group 1
49     no fair-queue
50     ppp authentication chap
51     ppp multilink
52     pulse-time 0
53    !
54    interface Dialer5
55     ip address 172.31.201.1 255.255.255.0
56     encapsulation ppp
57     dialer remote-name SOHO700
58     dialer idle-timeout 9999
59     dialer string 2802009
60     dialer pool 1
61     dialer-group 1
62     no fair-queue
63     ppp authentication chap
64     ppp multilink
65    !
66    ip local pool async-ips 192.168.60.2 192.168.60.15
67    ip classless
68    ip route 172.31.70.0 255.255.255.0 Dialer5 172.31.201.2
69    ip route 172.31.80.0 255.255.255.0 Dialer1 172.31.200.2
70    logging buffered 4096 debugging
71    dialer-list 1 protocol ip permit
72    !
73    line 1 12
```

```
74   autoselect during-login
75   autoselect ppp
76   modem InOut
77   modem autoconfigure type microcom_hdms
78   transport input all
79  line 13 24
80   transport input all
81  line aux 0
82  line vty 0 4
83   password cisco
84   login
85  line vty 5 20
86   password cisco
87   login
88  !
89  end
```

Now for some testing. Let's check out which **debug** commands are active using the **show debug** command:

```
NewYork#show debug
Dial on demand:
  Dial on demand events debugging is on
```

Let's watch what happens when SOHO700 dials in: ISDN B-Channel 18 gets the incoming call and gets bound to profile Dialer5, and because ppp multilink is in effect, the AS5200 creates interface Virtual-Access1 to handle multiple incoming B-channels. Everything becomes active when end-to-end connectivity is established:

```
%LINK-3-UPDOWN: Interface Serial0:18, changed state to up
%DIALER-6-BIND: Interface Serial0:18 bound to profile Dialer5
%DIALER-6-BIND: Interface Virtual-Access1 bound to profile Dialer5
%LINK-3-UPDOWN: Interface Virtual-Access1, changed state to up
%LINEPROTO-5-UPDOWN: Line protocol on Interface Serial0:18, changed state to up
%LINEPROTO-5-UPDOWN: Line protocol on Interface Virtual-Access1, changed state to up
dialer Protocol up for Vi1
%ISDN-6-CONNECT: Interface Serial0:18 is now connected to 4102802009 SOHO700
```

Now let's try an incoming asynchronous PPP connection. Before we do that we will turn on **debug modem** and **debug modem csm** (Call Switching Module):

```
NewYork#debug modem ?
  csm    CSM activity
  oob    Modem out of band activity
  trace  Call Trace Upload
  <cr>
```

```
NewYork#debug modem
Modem control/process activation debugging is on
NewYork#debug modem csm
Modem Management Call Switching Module debugging is on
```

Here is the CSM sequence that shows the asynchronous call being directed to the modem located at `slot 1 and port 3`:

```
MODEM_REPORT:dchan_idb=0x21F324, call_id=0x18, ces=0x1
           bchan=0x13, event=0x1, cause=0x0
CSM_MODEM_ALLOCATE: slot 1 and port 3 is allocated.
MODEM_REPORT(0018): DEV_INCALL at slot 1 and port 3
CSM: Fast Ringing On at modem slot 1, port 3
CSM_PROC_IDLE: CSM_EVENT_ISDN_CALL at slot 1, port 3
CSM_PROC_IC1_RING: CSM_EVENT_MODEM_OFFHOOK at slot 1, port 3
CSM: Fast Ringing Off at modem slot 1, port 3
MODEM_REPORT:dchan_idb=0x21F324, call_id=0x18, ces=0x1
           bchan=0x13, event=0x4, cause=0x0
MODEM_REPORT(0018): DEV_CONNECTED at slot 1 and port 3
CSM_PROC_IC2_WAIT_FOR_CARRIER: CSM_EVENT_ISDN_CONNECTED at slot 1, port 3
```

Now for the **debug modem** command output. It shows DSR coming up and making the modem ready, the autoselection of PPP, and the creation of interface `Async4` from our `Group-Async1` definition in the configuration:

```
TTY4: DSR came up
tty4: Modem: IDLE->READY
TTY4: Autoselect started
TTY4: Autoselect sample 7E
TTY4: Autoselect sample 7EFF
TTY4: Autoselect sample 7EFF7D
TTY4: Autoselect sample 7EFF7D23
TTY4 Autoselect cmd: ppp negotiate
TTY4: EXEC creation
%LINK-3-UPDOWN: Interface Async4, changed state to up
%LINEPROTO-5-UPDOWN: Line protocol on Interface Async4, changed state to up
dialer Protocol up for As4
```

Does interface `Async4` look the same as any other interface? Use the **show interface async4** command to check it out. This command really ties the physical components of this connection together. It shows us which modem is used and which B-channel is connected to the remote dial-in client:

```
NewYork#show int async4
Async4 is up, line protocol is up
  modem(slot/port)=1/3, state=CONNECTED
  dsx1(slot/unit/channel)=0/0/19, status=CSM_STATUS_ACTIVE_CALL.
```

```
Hardware is Async Serial
Interface is unnumbered.  Using address of Loopback0 (0.0.0.0)
MTU 1500 bytes, BW 115 Kbit, DLY 100000 usec, rely 255/255, load 1/255
Encapsulation PPP, loopback not set, keepalive not set
DTR is pulsed for 5 seconds on reset
LCP Open
Closed: CDPCP
Open: IPCP
Last input 00:00:00, output 00:00:03, output hang never
Last clearing of "show interface" counters never
Input queue: 2/75/0 (size/max/drops); Total output drops: 0
Queueing strategy: weighted fair
Output queue: 0/1000/64/0 (size/max total/threshold/drops)
    Conversations  0/1/256 (active/max active/max total)
    Reserved Conversations 0/0 (allocated/max allocated)
5 minute input rate 1000 bits/sec, 1 packets/sec
5 minute output rate 0 bits/sec, 0 packets/sec
    29 packets input, 1796 bytes, 0 no buffer
    Received 0 broadcasts, 0 runts, 0 giants, 0 throttles
    1 input errors, 1 CRC, 0 frame, 0 overrun, 0 ignored, 0 abort
    15 packets output, 377 bytes, 0 underruns
    0 output errors, 0 collisions, 0 interface resets
    0 output buffer failures, 0 output buffers swapped out
    0 carrier transitions
```

London is going to call in and generate enough traffic to bring up two B-channels:

```
%LINK-3-UPDOWN: Interface Serial0:20, changed state to up
%DIALER-6-BIND: Interface Serial0:20 bound to profile Dialer1
%DIALER-6-BIND: Interface Virtual-Access2 bound to profile Dialer1
%LINEPROTO-5-UPDOWN: Line protocol on Interface Serial0:20, changed state to up
%LINK-3-UPDOWN: Interface Virtual-Access2, changed state to up
%LINEPROTO-5-UPDOWN: Line protocol on Interface Virtual-Access2, changed state to up
dialer Protocol up for Vi2
%ISDN-6-CONNECT: Interface Serial0:20 is now connected to 4102802010 London
TTY26: EXEC creation
%LINK-3-UPDOWN: Interface Serial0:21, changed state to up
%DIALER-6-BIND: Interface Serial0:21 bound to profile Dialer1
%LINEPROTO-5-UPDOWN: Line protocol on Interface Serial0:21, changed state to up
%ISDN-6-CONNECT: Interface Serial0:21 is now connected to 4102802010 London
```

With several calls active, let's use the **show dialer** command to see what is active. Dialer profiles 1 and 5 are currently active. If we look at the individual B-channels, we can see B-channel 18 connected to SOHO700, and B-channels 20 and 21 connected to London. If we look back at the **show interface async4** command output, we can see that B-channel 19 is used to connect our incoming asynchronous call to the modem at slot 1 and port 3. The **show dialer** command does not track these incoming asynchronous calls:

```
NewYork#show dialer

Dialer1 - dialer type = DIALER PROFILE
Idle timer (9999 secs), Fast idle timer (20 secs)
Wait for carrier (30 secs), Re-enable (15 secs)
Dialer state is data link layer up

Dial String      Successes    Failures    Last called    Last status
2802010                  2           0    01:11:02       successful    Default

Dialer5 - dialer type = DIALER PROFILE
Idle timer (9999 secs), Fast idle timer (20 secs)
Wait for carrier (30 secs), Re-enable (15 secs)
Dialer state is data link layer up

Dial String      Successes    Failures    Last called    Last status
2802009                  2           5    18:55:42       successful    Default

Serial0:0 - dialer type = ISDN
Idle timer (120 secs), Fast idle timer (20 secs)
Wait for carrier (30 secs), Re-enable (15 secs)
Dialer state is shutdown
.
. Output deleted for clarity.
.
Serial0:17 - dialer type = ISDN
Idle timer (120 secs), Fast idle timer (20 secs)
Wait for carrier (30 secs), Re-enable (15 secs)
Dialer state is shutdown

Serial0:18 - dialer type = ISDN
Idle timer (9999 secs), Fast idle timer (20 secs)
Wait for carrier (30 secs), Re-enable (15 secs)
Dialer state is physical layer up
Interface bound to profile Dialer5
Time until disconnect 9998 secs
Connected to 4102802009 (SOHO700)

Serial0:19 - dialer type = ISDN
Idle timer (120 secs), Fast idle timer (20 secs)
Wait for carrier (30 secs), Re-enable (15 secs)
Dialer state is idle

Serial0:20 - dialer type = ISDN
Idle timer (9999 secs), Fast idle timer (20 secs)
Wait for carrier (30 secs), Re-enable (15 secs)
Dialer state is physical layer up
Interface bound to profile Dialer1
Time until disconnect 9998 secs
Connected to 4102802010 (London)

Serial0:21 - dialer type = ISDN
Idle timer (9999 secs), Fast idle timer (20 secs)
Wait for carrier (30 secs), Re-enable (15 secs)
Dialer state is physical layer up
Interface bound to profile Dialer1
Time until disconnect 9998 secs
Connected to 4102802010 (London)
```

```
Serial0:22 - dialer type = ISDN
Idle timer (120 secs), Fast idle timer (20 secs)
Wait for carrier (30 secs), Re-enable (15 secs)
Dialer state is idle

Serial0:23 - dialer type = ISDN

Dial String      Successes   Failures    Last called   Last status
0 incoming call(s) have been screened.
```

Let's take a look at some other **show** commands to check out what is happening on the asynchronous side.

First, let's look at the **show modem** command. There is an asterisk (*) next to modem 1/3 indicating that there is an active call connected to this modem. The third column shows us that the modems are being used in a round-robin fashion. I bet the next asynchronous call uses modem 1/4:

```
NewYork#show modem
                 Inc calls      Out calls    Busied   Failed  No        Succ
      Mdm  Usage  Succ  Fail   Succ  Fail    Out      Dial    Answer    Pct.
      1/0   0%     1     0      0     0       0        0       0         100%
      1/1   0%     1     0      0     0       0        0       0         100%
      1/2   88%    1     0      0     0       0        0       0         100%
   *  1/3   0%     1     0      0     0       0        0       0         100%
      1/4   0%     0     0      0     0       0        0       0         0%
   .
   . Output deleted for clarity
```

Now let's track down the B-channel being used with the **show modem csm 1/3** command. Wow, we get tons of information about the modem at slot 3, port 1. About halfway through the output, look for (s0, u0, c19), slot 0, T1 controller 0, and B-channel 19. We tracked it down. Some other neat information is down at the bottom, where both the called and calling phone numbers are listed:

```
NewYork#show modem csm 1/3
MODEM_INFO: slot 1, port 3, unit 131, modem_mask=0x0008, modem_port_offset=0
tty_hwidb=0x0020B520, modem_tty=0x000E4B7C, mgmt_tty=0x000F201C, modem_pool=0x000C5F60
csm_status(0x00000002): CSM_STATUS_ACTIVE_CALL.
csm_state(0x00000203)=CSM_IC3_CONNECTED, csm_event_proc=0x22090240, current call thru PRI
   line
invalid_event_count=0, wdt_timeout_count=0
wdt_timestamp_started is not activated
wait_for_dialing:False, wait_for_bchan:False
pri_chnl=TDM_PRI_STREAM(s0, u0, c19), modem_chnl=TDM_MODEM_STREAM(s1,c3)
dchan_idb_start_index=0, dchan_idb_index=0, call_id=0x0018, bchan_num=19
csm_event=CSM_EVENT_ISDN_CONNECTED, cause=0x0000
ring_indicator=1, oh_state=0, oh_int_enable=1, modem_reset=1
ring_no_answer=0, ic_failure=0, ic_complete=1
dial_failure=0, oc_failure=0, oc_complete=0
```

```
oc_busy=0, oc_no_dial_tone=0, oc_dial_timeout=0
remote_link_disc=0, busyout=0, modem_reset=0
call_duration_started=19:21:45, call_duration_ended=00:00:00, total_call_duration=00:00:00
The calling party phone number = 4102801001
The called party phone number  = 4102801000
total_free_rbs_timeslot = 0, total_busy_rbs_timeslot = 0, min_free_modem_threshold = 6
```

The next **debug** output sequence shows us the asynchronous call being disconnected:

```
TTY26: Line reset by "Virtual Exec"
TTY26: Modem: READY->READY
%ISDN-6-DISCONNECT: Interface Serial0:19  disconnected from unknown , call lasted 848
   seconds

MODEM_REPORT:dchan_idb=0x21F324, call_id=0x18, ces=0x1
              bchan=0x13, event=0x0, cause=0x0
MODEM_REPORT(0018): DEV_IDLE at slot 1 and port 3
CSM_PROC_IC3_OC6_CONNECTED: CSM_EVENT_ISDN_DISCONNECTED at slot 1, port 3

TTY4: DSR was dropped
tty4: Modem: READY->HANGUP
%LINEPROTO-5-UPDOWN: Line protocol on Interface Async4, changed state to down
TTY4: dropping DTR, hanging up
TTY4: Async Int reset: Dropping DTR
tty4: Modem: HANGUP->IDLE
CSM_PROC_IC4_OC8_DISCONNECTING: CSM_EVENT_MODEM_ONHOOK at slot 1, port 3
CSM_MODEM_DEALLOCATE: slot 1 and port 3 is deallocated
TTY4: cleanup pending. Delaying DTR
%LINK-5-CHANGED: Interface Async4, changed state to reset
TTY4: cleanup pending. Delaying DTR
TTY4: cleanup pending. Delaying DTR
TTY4: cleanup pending. Delaying DTR
Async4: allowing modem_process to continue hangup
TTY4: restoring DTR
TTY4: autoconfigure probe started
%LINK-3-UPDOWN: Interface Async4, changed state to down
```

Summary

In this chapter, we investigated the configuration of the AS5200, and the use of our ISDN PRI connection for both incoming ISDN and asynchronous modem calls. There are many specialized modem debugging commands that can help troubleshoot problems with the built-in modems.

Fixed-facility
WAN Services

We will explore the world of fixed WAN services: standard point-to-point HDLC links, channelized T1, X.25 services, and Frame Relay services.

High-level Data Link Control (HDLC)

HDLC is the default encapsulation for Cisco-to-Cisco serial connections. While HDLC is a standard communications protocol, Cisco uses a modified version to transport multiple protocols.

Normally the HDLC service is used on point-to-point connections with a leased line connected through a service provider. In this mode of operation, the Cisco router is a DTE device connected to a CSU/DSU as the DCE device.

Our example uses a back-to-back cable that requires one end of the cable to be configured as a DCE device and provide the clock signal. Figure 9-1 shows the equipment layout.

NewYork

Code Listing 9-1 shows the configuration for NewYork.

What's going on? There is no **encapsulation hdlc** command on interface Serial 0. Oh, it is not necessary; it is the default. This is a pretty tame example isn't it? We will work with some weighted fair queueing to spice it up. Line 14 configures the Serial0 interface to use the basic FIFO queueing techniques.

Figure 9-1
HDLC equipment
layout.

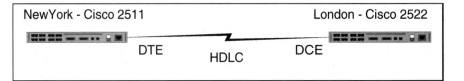

Code Listing 9-1

```
1    version 11.3
2    !
3    hostname NewYork
4    !
5    no ip domain-lookup
6    !
7    interface Ethernet0
8     ip address 172.31.2.1 255.255.255.0
9    !
10   interface Serial0
11    ip address 172.31.100.1 255.255.255.0
12    no ip mroute-cache
13    bandwidth 56
14    no fair-queue
15   !
16   router eigrp 100
17    network 172.31.0.0
18   !
19   ip classless
20   !
21   end
```

The **show ip route** command output will verify that the connection is active:

```
NewYork#show ip route
Codes: C - connected, S - static, I - IGRP, R - RIP, M - mobile, B - BGP
       D - EIGRP, EX - EIGRP external, O - OSPF, IA - OSPF inter area
       N1 - OSPF NSSA external type 1, N2 - OSPF NSSA external type 2
       E1 - OSPF external type 1, E2 - OSPF external type 2, E - EGP
       i - IS-IS, L1 - IS-IS level-1, L2 - IS-IS level-2, * - candidate default
       U - per-user static route, o - ODR

Gateway of last resort is not set

     172.31.0.0/24 is subnetted, 3 subnets
C       172.31.2.0 is directly connected, Ethernet0
D       172.31.1.0 [90/46251776] via 172.31.100.2, 01:00:50, Serial0
C       172.31.100.0 is directly connected, Serial0
```

You can use the **show controller s 0** command to verify the cable type connected to the serial interface:

```
NewYork#show controller s 0
HD unit 0, idb = 0x10E0FC, driver structure at 0x1133A8
buffer size 1524  HD unit 0, V.35 DTE cable
cpb = 0x61, eda = 0x48DC, cda = 0x48F0
.
. Output deleted for clarity
```

The **show interface s 0** command output shows the encapsulation as HDLC, and the queueing strategy as `fifo`:

```
NewYork#show int s 0
Serial0 is up, line protocol is up
  Hardware is HD64570
  Internet address is 172.31.100.1/24
  MTU 1500 bytes, BW 56 Kbit, DLY 20000 usec,
    reliability 255/255, txload 1/255, rxload 1/255
  Encapsulation HDLC, loopback not set, keepalive set (10 sec)
  Last input 00:00:00, output 00:00:02, output hang never
  Last clearing of "show interface" counters never
  Queueing strategy: fifo
  Output queue 0/40, 0 drops; input queue 0/75, 0 drops
  5 minute input rate 0 bits/sec, 0 packets/sec
  5 minute output rate 0 bits/sec, 0 packets/sec
    1596 packets input, 99682 bytes, 0 no buffer
    Received 554 broadcasts, 0 runts, 0 giants, 0 throttles
    0 input errors, 0 CRC, 0 frame, 0 overrun, 0 ignored, 0 abort
    1602 packets output, 99855 bytes, 0 underruns
    0 output errors, 0 collisions, 20 interface resets
    0 output buffer failures, 0 output buffers swapped out
    1 carrier transitions
    DCD=up  DSR=up  DTR=up  RTS=up  CTS=up
```

To look at the settings for weighted fair queueing, use the **show queueing fair** command. The output shows that `Serial1` has an individual conversation packet limit of `64` and that it supports a maximum of `256` conversation queues:

```
NewYork#show queueing fair
Current fair queue configuration:

 Interface        Discard      Dynamic        Reserved
                  threshold    queue count    queue count
 Serial1          64           256            0
```

If we modify the queueing on interface `Serial0`, the **show** commands should indicate the change:

```
NewYork#conf t
Enter configuration commands, one per line.  End with CNTL/Z.

NewYork(config)#int s 0
NewYork(config-if)#fair-queue 128
NewYork(config-if)#^Z
NewYork#
```

An excerpt from the **show running-config** command output does show the weighted fair queueing information:

```
interface Serial0
 ip address 172.31.100.1 255.255.255.0
 no ip mroute-cache
 bandwidth 56
 fair-queue 128 256 0
```

The **show interface** command now reflects the queueing strategy change:

```
NewYork#show int s 0
Serial0 is up, line protocol is up
  Hardware is HD64570
  Internet address is 172.31.100.1/24
  MTU 1500 bytes, BW 56 Kbit, DLY 20000 usec,
     reliability 255/255, txload 1/255, rxload 1/255
  Encapsulation HDLC, loopback not set, keepalive set (10 sec)
  Last input 00:00:02, output 00:00:04, output hang never
  Last clearing of "show interface" counters never
  Input queue: 0/75/0 (size/max/drops); Total output drops: 0
  Queueing strategy: weighted fair
  Output queue: 0/1000/128/0 (size/max total/threshold/drops)
     Conversations  0/1/256 (active/max active/max total)
     Reserved Conversations 0/0 (allocated/max allocated)
  5 minute input rate 0 bits/sec, 0 packets/sec
  5 minute output rate 0 bits/sec, 0 packets/sec
     1667 packets input, 103950 bytes, 0 no buffer
     Received 579 broadcasts, 0 runts, 0 giants, 0 throttles
     0 input errors, 0 CRC, 0 frame, 0 overrun, 0 ignored, 0 abort
     1675 packets output, 104475 bytes, 0 underruns
     0 output errors, 0 collisions, 21 interface resets
     0 output buffer failures, 0 output buffers swapped out
     7 carrier transitions
     DCD=up  DSR=up  DTR=up  RTS=up  CTS=up
```

When we re-issue the **show queueing fair** command, we see the changes we made to interface Serial0:

```
NewYork#show queueing fair
Current fair queue configuration:

    Interface         Discard     Dynamic       Reserved
                      threshold   queue count   queue count
    Serial0           128         256           0
    Serial1           64          256           0
```

London

Code Listing 9-2 shows the configuration for London.

Again, this is really basic stuff. There is nothing to spice it up except for the **clock rate** command on line 13 because we are using a back-to-back cable, with this end acting as the DCE device.

Code Listing 9-2

```
1    version 11.3
2    !
3    hostname London
4    !
5    interface Ethernet0
6     ip address 172.31.1.1 255.255.255.0
7    !
8    interface Serial0
9     ip address 172.31.100.2 255.255.255.0
10    no ip mroute-cache
11    bandwidth 56
12    no fair-queue
13    clockrate 56000
14   !
15   router eigrp 100
16    network 172.31.0.0
17   !
18   end
```

NOTE *Please be careful when putting in the* **bandwidth** *command. Clockrate is in bits per second, and bandwidth is in kilobits per second. Some routing protocols use the bandwidth to calculate the best pathway through the network.* **Bandwidth 56000** *looks like a 59 megabit-per-second circuit to those protocols.*

Let's use the **show controller s 0** command to check out the cable connected to the interface and verify that the clock rate has been set:

```
London#show controller s 0
HD unit 0, idb = 0x11D030, driver structure at 0x1222D8
buffer size 1524  HD unit 0, V.35 DCE cable, clockrate 56000
cpb = 0x62, eda = 0x40DC, cda = 0x40F0
.
. Output deleted for Clarity
```

Channelized T1

This is a short section that highlights the capabilities of the channelized T1 connection. We will use a simple back-to-back crossover cable to connect London and NewYork via channelized T1. Figure 9-2 shows the equipment layout.

London

Code Listing 9-3 shows the configuration for London.

Lines 5 through 10 define our T1 configuration and the association between the channels and the serial interfaces used for the fractional T1 connections. Lines 9 and 10 allocate DS0 channels to each of two channel groups. When the **channel-group** command is entered, the system generates the associated serial port; channel-group 1 creates Serial0:1.

The serial interfaces get their IP addresses and the appropriate bandwidth commands in lines 15 through 21.

Code Listing 9-3

```
1    version 11.2
2    !
3    hostname London
4    !
5    controller T1 0
6      framing esf
7      clock source internal
8      linecode b8zs
9      channel-group 1 timeslots 1-14
10     channel-group 2 timeslots 15-24
11   !
12   interface Ethernet0
13     ip address 172.31.2.1 255.255.255.0
14   !
15   interface Serial0:1
16     ip address 172.31.101.2 255.255.255.0
17   bandwidth 896
18   !
```

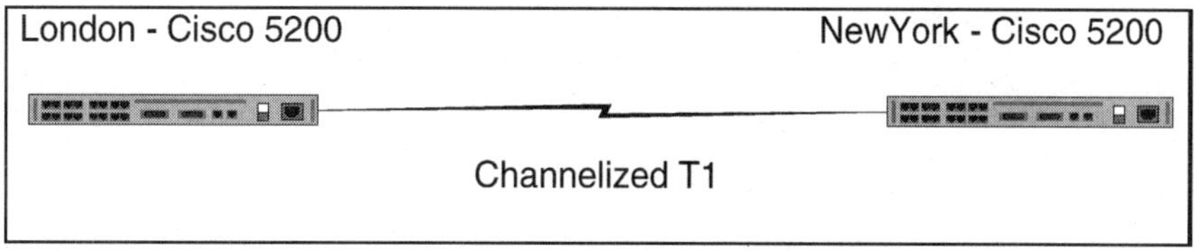

Figure 9-2
Channelized T1
equipment layout.

London - Cisco 5200   NewYork - Cisco 5200

Channelized T1

```
19   interface Serial0:2
20     ip address 172.31.102.2 255.255.255.0
21     bandwidth 640
22   !
23   router eigrp 100
24     network 172.31.0.0
25   !
26   end
```

The **show ip route** command output shows us the two active pathways between the routers. EIGRP has calculated that Serial0:1 has the best pathway:

```
London#show ip route
Codes: C - connected, S - static, I - IGRP, R - RIP, M - mobile, B - BGP
       D - EIGRP, EX - EIGRP external, O - OSPF, IA - OSPF inter area
       N1 - OSPF NSSA external type 1, N2 - OSPF NSSA external type 2
       E1 - OSPF external type 1, E2 - OSPF external type 2, E - EGP
       i - IS-IS, L1 - IS-IS level-1, L2 - IS-IS level-2, * - candidate default
       U - per-user static route, o - ODR

Gateway of last resort is not set

     172.31.0.0/24 is subnetted, 4 subnets
C       172.31.2.0 is directly connected, Ethernet0
D       172.31.1.0 [90/3394560] via 172.31.101.1, 00:01:42, Serial0:1
C       172.31.102.0 is directly connected, Serial0:2
C       172.31.101.0 is directly connected, Serial0:1
```

The **show interface** command output for our generated serial ports identifies the associated DS0s from the T1:

```
London#sho int s 0:1
Serial0:1 is up, line protocol is up
  Hardware is DSX1
  Internet address is 172.31.101.2/24
  MTU 1500 bytes, BW 896 Kbit, DLY 20000 usec, rely 255/255, load 1/255
  Encapsulation HDLC, loopback not set, keepalive set (10 sec)
.
. Output Deleted for clarity
.
  Timeslot(s) Used:1-14, Transmitter delay is 0 flags

London#sho int s 0:2
Serial0:2 is up, line protocol is up
  Hardware is DSX1
  Internet address is 172.31.102.2/24
  MTU 1500 bytes, BW 640 Kbit, DLY 20000 usec, rely 255/255, load 1/255
  Encapsulation HDLC, loopback not set, keepalive set (10 sec)
.
. Output deleted for clarity
.
  Timeslot(s) Used:15-24, Transmitter delay is 0 flags
```

NewYork

Code Listing 9-4 shows the configuration of NewYork . If you think it looks the same as London, you are absolutely correct.

Code Listing 9-4

```
1   version 11.1
2   !
3   hostname NewYork
4   !
5   controller T1 0
6    framing esf
7    linecode b8zs
8    channel-group 1 timeslots 1-14
9    channel-group 2 timeslots 15-24
10  !
11  interface Ethernet0
12   ip address 172.31.1.1 255.255.255.0
13  !
14  interface Serial0:1
15   ip address 172.31.101.1 255.255.255.0
16   bandwidth 896
17  !
18  interface Serial0:2
19   ip address 172.31.102.1 255.255.255.0
20   bandwidth 640
21  !
22  router eigrp 100
23   network 172.31.0.0
24  !
25  end
```

Use the **show ip route** command to verify connectivity over the fractional T1 connections:

```
NewYork#show ip route
Codes: C - connected, S - static, I - IGRP, R - RIP, M - mobile, B - BGP
       D - EIGRP, EX - EIGRP external, O - OSPF, IA - OSPF inter area
       E1 - OSPF external type 1, E2 - OSPF external type 2, E - EGP
       i - IS-IS, L1 - IS-IS level-1, L2 - IS-IS level-2, * - candidate default
       U - per-user static route

Gateway of last resort is not set

     172.31.0.0/24 is subnetted, 4 subnets
D       172.31.2.0 [90/3394560] via 172.31.101.2, 00:00:05, Serial0:1
C       172.31.1.0 is directly connected, Ethernet0
C       172.31.102.0 is directly connected, Serial0:2
C       172.31.101.0 is directly connected, Serial0:1
```

Test connectivity to the other side with a **ping** command:

```
NewYork#ping 172.31.2.1

Type escape sequence to abort.
Sending 5, 100-byte ICMP Echoes to 172.31.2.1, timeout is 2 seconds:
!!!!!
Success rate is 100 percent (5/5), round-trip min/avg/max = 8/8/8 ms
```

Use the **trace** command to make sure we are following the correct pathway to reach the destination:

```
NewYork#trace 172.31.2.1
Type escape sequence to abort.
Tracing the route to 172.31.2.1

  1 172.31.101.2 4 msec *  8 msec

NewYork#trace 172.31.102.2
Type escape sequence to abort.
Tracing the route to 172.31.102.2

  1 172.31.102.2 8 msec *  8 msec


Transmitter delay is 0 flags
```

Shut down the Serial0:1 interface and verify that Serial0:2 is operational using the **show ip route** command:

```
NewYork#conf t
Enter configuration commands, one per line.  End with CNTL/Z.
NewYork(config)#int s 0:1
NewYork(config-if)#shut
NewYork(config-if)#
%LINEPROTO-5-UPDOWN: Line protocol on Interface Serial0:1, changed state to down
%LINK-5-CHANGED: Interface Serial0:1, changed state to administratively down
NewYork(config-if)#^Z

NewYork#show ip route
Codes: C - connected, S - static, I - IGRP, R - RIP, M - mobile, B - BGP
       D - EIGRP, EX - EIGRP external, O - OSPF, IA - OSPF inter area
       E1 - OSPF external type 1, E2 - OSPF external type 2, E - EGP
       i - IS-IS, L1 - IS-IS level-1, L2 - IS-IS level-2, * - candidate default
       U - per-user static route

Gateway of last resort is not set

     172.31.0.0/24 is subnetted, 3 subnets
D       172.31.2.0 [90/4537600] via 172.31.102.2, 00:00:32, Serial0:2
C       172.31.1.0 is directly connected, Ethernet0
C       172.31.102.0 is directly connected, Serial0:2
```

X.25 Packet Services

This section describes the configurations needed to set up X.25 on Cisco routers. First we need to talk a little about the technology (very little). Refer to authors and standards listed in the appendixes for a more in-depth view of X.25.

X.25 is a network-layer transportation protocol that provides an end-to-end connection-oriented protocol for reliable transportation of data. In addition to providing end-to-end reliability, LAPB is the data-link layer for X.25 and is also connection-oriented. Remember, this protocol was developed in a hostile data communications environment where 4,800 bits per second was considered high speed.

The key to routing X.25 traffic across the service provider's cloud is the ability to route X.25 packets across a public network environment. To do this, each end point must have a unique global address, referred to as an X.121 address. Figure 9-3 shows the format of the address. It looks like a standard hierarchical network address scheme: DNIC is the network number, and NTN is the node ID. All we need to do is recognize these addresses and route the traffic through the X.25 network.

Now that we know the network addressing scheme, we can start our example. Figure 9-4 shows the equipment layout.

Figure 9-3
X.121 address format.

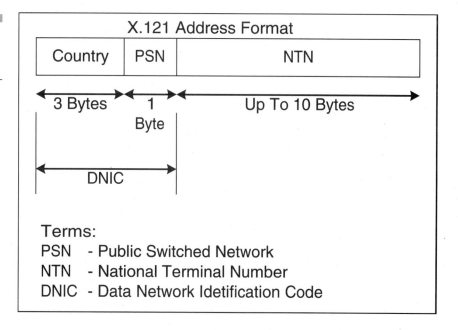

X.121 Address Format

Country	PSN	NTN
3 Bytes	1 Byte	Up To 10 Bytes

DNIC

Terms:
PSN - Public Switched Network
NTN - National Terminal Number
DNIC - Data Network Idetification Code

Now let's look at the configurations that make X.25 operate in the Cisco environment.

X25 Switch

Code Listing 9-5 shows the first configuration, for our Cisco router acting as an X.25 switch.

Line 5 is where we activate X25 routing capabilities; without this command we cannot forward X.25 packets through the router.

Lines 7 through 23 define the serial ports that act as DCE connections to the DTE devices outside the X.25 cloud. Let's use Serial0 to define connection options as we would do as a service provider.

Line 8 removes IP on this interface because no IP processing is required to provide basic X.25 processing.

Line 9 sets up the serial interface as an X.25 DCE connection to the outside world.

Lines 10 through 13 set up the basic transmission policies for this connection. The default window size is two packets. Transmission will stop until a positive acknowledgment is received. The default packet size is 128 bytes, which is effective in low-speed noisy communications environments but not necessary with today's cleaner transmission media. Lines 10 and 11 modify the window size to the maximum modulo 8 window size of 7 for both input and output traffic. Lines 12 and 13 change the input and output packet sizes to 1024 bytes. In order to work, the DTE devices on the outside of the X.25 network must be programmed to match these parameters exactly.

Figure 9-4
X.25 equipment layout.

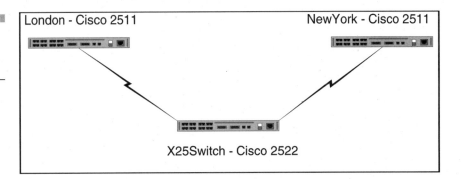

London - Cisco 2511

NewYork - Cisco 2511

X25Switch - Cisco 2522

Lines 25 and 26 define the routing of the X.25 traffic. Each line routes specific global X.121 addresses to a destination. In this example, we will route the traffic to local interfaces. There is no X.25 routing protocol, so all X.25 routes must be statically defined.

Code Listing 9-5

```
1    version 11.3
2    !
3    hostname X25Switch
4    !
5    x25 routing
6    !
7    interface Serial0
8     no ip address
9     encapsulation x25 dce
10    x25 win 7
11    x25 wout 7
12    x25 ips 1024
13    x25 ops 1024
14    clockrate 56000
15    !
16   interface Serial1
17    no ip address
18    encapsulation x25 dce
19    x25 win 7
20    x25 wout 7
21    x25 ips 1024
22    x25 ops 1024
23    clockrate 56000
24    !
25   x25 route 311010100101 interface Serial0
26   x25 route 311010100102 interface Serial1
27   !
28   end
```

To see all of the routes defined in the switch, use the **show x25 route** command:

```
X25Switch#show x25 route
  #  Match                   Substitute        Route to
  1  dest 311010100101                         Serial0
  2  dest 311010100102                         Serial1
```

The many different **show** commands that you can use to view the X.25 parameters and processing are shown below. Our example uses many of these commands.

```
X25Switch#show x25 ?
  context    Show X.25 or CMNS state for one or all interfaces
  interface  Show X.25 or CMNS VCs on one interface
```

```
map           Show x25 map table
route         Show x25 routing table
services      Show X.25 services information (default)
vc            Show specific X.25/CMNS virtual circuit(s)
xot           Show XOT (X.25-Over-TCP) VCs
<cr>
pad           X25 pad connection status
remote-red    X25 REMOTE-RED table
```

Let's take a look at the X.25 global parameters with the **show x25** command:

```
X25Switch#show x25
X.25 software, Version 3.0.0.
  2 configurations supporting 2 active contexts
  VCs allocated, freed and in use: 19 - 15 = 4
  VCs active and idle: 2, 2
XOT software, Version 2.0.0.
  configured, not in use
```

Because there are so many areas that we need to examine in the **show interface s 0** command, this command's output is shown in Code Listing 9-6 so these highlights can be easily identified.

Line 5 identifies the interface as an X.25 device.

Lines 6 through 12 show us the configured parameters operating at the network layer. This is a DCE device with no address, operating with modulo 8 windowing. Virtual circuits (VCs) timeout immediately, cisco encapsulation is used, window sizes are set to 7 on input and output, and the packet sizes are set to 1024 bytes. Timer values, virtual circuit types, and statistics are also shown.

Lines 13 through 17 show us the configured parameters operating at the data-link layer. LAPB is the protocol in use, and this is a DCE connection. Operating parameters and statistics complete this section.

The balance of the command is identical to that for other serial interfaces.

Code Listing 9-6

```
1   X25Switch#show int s 0
2   Serial0 is up, line protocol is up
3     Hardware is HD64570
4     MTU 1500 bytes, BW 1544 Kbit, DLY 20000 usec, reliability 255/
      255, txload 1/255, rxload 1/255
5     Encapsulation X25, loopback not set
6     X.25 DCE, address <none>, state R1, modulo 8, timer 0
7   Defaults: idle VC timeout 0
8           cisco encapsulation
9           input/output window sizes 7/7, packet sizes 1024/1024
```

Code Listing 9-6
(continued)

```
10          Timers: T10 60, T11 180, T12 60, T13 60
11          Channels: Incoming-only none, Two-way 1-1024, Outgoing-only
            none
12          RESTARTs 4/0 CALLs 0+0/0+0/0+0 DIAGs 0/0
13     LAPB DCE, state CONNECT, modulo 8, k 7, N1 12056, N2 20
14          T1 3000, T2 0, interface outage (partial T3) 0, T4 0
15          VS 5, VR 0, tx NR 0, Remote VR 5, Retransmissions 0
16          Queues: U/S frames 0, I frames 0, unack. 0, reTx 0
17          IFRAMEs 213/223 RNRs 0/0 REJs 0/0 SABM/Es 4/0 FRMRs 0/0
            DISCs 0/0
18     Last input never, output 00:00:16, output hang never
19     Last clearing of "show interface" counters never
20     Queueing strategy: fifo
21     Output queue 0/40, 0 drops; input queue 0/75, 0 drops
22     5 minute input rate 0 bits/sec, 0 packets/sec
23     5 minute output rate 0 bits/sec, 0 packets/sec
24          371 packets input, 10994 bytes, 0 no buffer
25          Received 0 broadcasts, 0 runts, 0 giants, 0 throttles
26          0 input errors, 0 CRC, 0 frame, 0 overrun, 0 ignored, 0
            abort
27          436 packets output, 10879 bytes, 0 underruns
28          0 output errors, 0 collisions, 68 interface resets
29          0 output buffer failures, 0 output buffers swapped out
30          7 carrier transitions
31          DCD=up  DSR=up  DTR=up  RTS=up  CTS=up
```

Now on to the routers that are DTE devices outside the PSN network.

London

First we start with the London configuration shown in Code Listing 9-7.

Lines 8 through 16 set up our `serial0` interface for X.25 processing. Line 9 assigns our IP address. Line 10 sets up the encapsulation as X.25 with DTE (default) functionality. Line 11 sets up this interface with a specific X.121 address, 311010100101. Lines 12 through 15 define the window sizes and packet sizes to match up with the switch parameters. Line 16 provides address resolution so that traffic destined to our peer across the X.25 network will use the appropriate X.121 device address. The broadcast option permits broadcast and multicast packets to be forwarded.

Code Listing 9-7

```
1     version 11.3
2     !
3     hostname London
4     !
5     interface Ethernet0
```

Code Listing 9-7
(continued)

```
 6    ip address 172.31.1.1 255.255.255.0
 7   !
 8   interface Serial0
 9    ip address 172.31.100.1 255.255.255.0
10    encapsulation x25
11    x25 address 311010100101
12    x25 win 7
13    x25 wout 7
14    x25 ips 1024
15    x25 ops 1024
16    x25 map ip 172.31.100.2 311010100102 broadcast
17   !
18   router eigrp 100
19    network 172.31.0.0
20   !
21   end
```

The **show x25** command output defines our global X.25 operational parameters:

```
London#show x25
X.25 software, Version 3.0.0.
  1 configurations supporting 1 active contexts
  VCs allocated, freed and in use: 12 - 10 = 2
  VCs active and idle: 1, 1
XOT software, Version 2.0.0.
  not configured
```

The **show x25 map** command shows us the address resolution that maps our next hop IP address to the global X.121 address, with broadcast traffic enabled:

```
London#show x25 map
Serial0: X.121 311010100102 <-> ip 172.31.100.2
  permanent, packetsize 1024 1024, broadcast, 1 VC: 1
  drops: hold-queue full: 12, output queues full: 0
```

The **show interface s 0** command provides information about our X.25 DTE connection at the network and data-link layers. This is a great place to verify the assigned X.121 address, a common place for typing errors that can create problems that are simple but tough to detect.

```
London#show int s 0
Serial0 is up, line protocol is up
  Hardware is HD64570
  Internet address is 172.31.100.1/24
  MTU 1500 bytes, BW 1544 Kbit, DLY 20000 usec, reliability 255/255, txload 1/255, rxload
  1/255
```

```
Encapsulation X25, loopback not set
X.25 DTE, address 311010100101, state R1, modulo 8, timer 0
    Defaults: idle VC timeout 0
      cisco encapsulation
      input/output window sizes 7/7, packet sizes 1024/1024
    Timers: T20 180, T21 200, T22 180, T23 180
    Channels: Incoming-only none, Two-way 1-1024, Outgoing-only none
    RESTARTs 1/0 CALLs 0+0/0+0/0+0 DIAGs 0/0
LAPB DTE, state CONNECT, modulo 8, k 7, N1 12056, N2 20
    T1 3000, T2 0, interface outage (partial T3) 0, T4 0
    VS 4, VR 1, tx NR 1, Remote VR 4, Retransmissions 0
    Queues: U/S frames 0, I frames 0, unack. 0, reTx 0
    IFRAMEs 235/224 RNRs 0/0 REJs 0/0 SABM/Es 0/4 FRMRs 0/0 DISCs 0/0
Last input 00:00:02, output 00:00:02, output hang never
Last clearing of "show interface" counters never
Queueing strategy: fifo
Output queue 0/40, 12 drops; input queue 0/75, 0 drops
5 minute input rate 0 bits/sec, 0 packets/sec
5 minute output rate 0 bits/sec, 0 packets/sec
    459 packets input, 11818 bytes, 0 no buffer
    Received 0 broadcasts, 0 runts, 0 giants, 0 throttles
    0 input errors, 0 CRC, 0 frame, 0 overrun, 0 ignored, 0 abort
    408 packets output, 12496 bytes, 0 underruns
    0 output errors, 0 collisions, 23 interface resets
    0 output buffer failures, 0 output buffers swapped out
    22 carrier transitions
    DCD=up  DSR=up  DTR=up  RTS=up  CTS=up
```

The **show ip route** command shows us the EIGRP route to our peer across the X.25 network; our X.25 connection is working:

```
London#show ip route
Codes: C - connected, S - static, I - IGRP, R - RIP, M - mobile, B - BGP
       D - EIGRP, EX - EIGRP external, O - OSPF, IA - OSPF inter area
       N1 - OSPF NSSA external type 1, N2 - OSPF NSSA external type 2
       E1 - OSPF external type 1, E2 - OSPF external type 2, E - EGP
       i - IS-IS, L1 - IS-IS level-1, L2 - IS-IS level-2, * - candidate default
       U - per-user static route, o - ODR

Gateway of last resort is not set

     172.31.0.0/24 is subnetted, 3 subnets
D       172.31.2.0 [90/2195456] via 172.31.100.2, 01:35:21, Serial0
C       172.31.1.0 is directly connected, Ethernet0
C       172.31.100.0 is directly connected, Serial0
```

NewYork

Now let's look at the New York configuration, shown in Code Listing 9-8. If it looks almost identical to the London configuration, that is because it is. Only the addresses have been changed to protect the innocent.

```
1    version 11.2
2    !
3    hostname NewYork
4    !
5    interface Ethernet0
6     ip address 172.31.2.1 255.255.255.0
7    !
8    interface Serial0
9     ip address 172.31.100.2 255.255.255.0
10    encapsulation x25
11    x25 address 311010100102
12    x25 win 7
13    x25 wout 7
14    x25 ips 1024
15    x25 ops 1024
16    x25 map ip 172.31.100.1 311010100101 broadcast
17   !
18   router eigrp 100
19    network 172.31.0.0
20   !
21   end
```

The **show x25 map** command shows our address resolution for the next hop address to reach our peer:

```
NewYork#show x25 map
Serial0: X.121 311010100101 <--> ip 172.31.100.1
   PERMANENT, BROADCAST, PACKETSIZE 1024 1024, 1 VC: 1024*
```

The **show x25 vc** command details the defined SVCs. There is lots of great information here for debugging:

```
NewYork#show x25 vc
SVC 1024,  State: D1,  Interface: Serial0
 Started 01:40:05, last input 00:00:50, output 00:00:30
 Connects 311010100101 <-->
    ip 172.31.100.1
 cisco cud pid, no Tx data PID
 Window size input: 7, output: 7
 Packet size input: 1024, output: 1024
 PS: 0  PR: 7  ACK: 7  Remote PR: 7  RCNT: 0  RNR: FALSE
 Retransmits: 0  Timer (secs): 0  Reassembly (bytes): 0
 Held Fragments/Packets: 0/0
 Bytes 8256/8224 Packets 128/127 Resets 0/0 RNRs 0/0 REJs 0/0 INTs 0/0
```

This is a very basic X.25 configuration, but it is typical of edge devices connected to a Public Service Network.

LAB This is a basic exercise used to acquaint the reader with basic X.25 connectivity. Set up a back-to-back connection with one side acting as the DTE side and one side as the DCE side. Then try some **debug** *commands.*

Frame Relay Services

Frame Relay service is a shared service. For a cross-country T1 circuit to be financially viable, a 50% or higher utilization on a 7-by-24 basis would be required. With Frame Relay service, you can purchase a Committed Information Rate (CIR), in bits per second, that matches your general needs and only pay the cost of a T1 circuit from each location to their local Central Office. The CIR can be different for each connection and is usually slower than the speed of the connection. If the circuits are not busy, it may be possible to send data faster than the CIR, up to the maximum speed of the circuit. A T1 Frame Relay connection may have a CIR of 256 kilobits per second. That CIR speed is what your service provider uses to design the Frame Relay network. The ideal would be to provide service at the CIR level for all users. If no one else is using the Frame Relay network, it would make sense that you could successfully transmit data at full T1 speeds.

The method used for addressing in a Frame Relay network is the Data Link Connection Identifier (DLCI), which is often referred to as a "DELSIE" (rhymes with Elsie). This number, between 16 and 1018, is used by the local Frame Relay switch to start the incoming frame down the pathway to the destination. The primary method for transmitting traffic across the Frame Relay cloud is a Permanent Virtual Circuit (PVC). I like the term PVC, as it reminds me of a plastic pipe. Think of a Frame Relay switch as the device that forwards your frame to the appropriate *pipe* to reach the destination. You don't really care how many turns are in the pipe, only that the pipe delivers your frame to the proper destination. When making a bank deposit at the bank drive-in window, you place your deposit (data) into the carrier (frame), you place the carrier (frame) into the box (switch), and the carrier (frame) travels down the tube (PVC) to reach the teller inside the bank. You put it in one side, and it comes out on the other.

There is one special DLCI, called the Local Management Interface (LMI), that is used by the router and the switch to exchange information about the status of each PVC. This is your local feedback from the switch concerning the status of your PVCs used to reach your destinations.

The nature of the actual data transmission is a secret known only to the Frame Relay service provider and could take on many forms. Because there is no frame-by-frame acknowledgment, there needs to be a special mechanism to provide feedback when congestion that can affect traffic on your PVC occurs inside the Frame Relay network. These mechanisms are Forward Explicit Congestion Notification (FECN) and Backward Explicit Congestion Notification (BECN). If a router transmitting information across the Frame Relay cloud gets BECNs, then the router can be configured to slow down to the CIR.

EXAMPLES

Figure 9-5 shows the equipment layout that will be used for our three Frame Relay examples. We will treat NewYork as our central site. (I know I should have used Rome, as all roads lead to it.)

Multipoint Frame Relay with Static Mapping

This example is the standard method for providing Frame Relay services. It requires a static address resolution between the next hop IP address and the DLCI.

In this example, we define the connectivity using a fully meshed network, where each edge router connected to the Frame Relay switch has a static map for each neighbor across the network. Appendix F shows the configuration and the **show** commands used to verify the switch operation.

Rome

Rome is our first edge router. Code Listing 9-9 shows its configuration.

Lines 8 through 15 define Frame Relay connectivity. Line 10 sets the encapsulation to Frame Relay, and lines 13 through 15 provide static address resolution for the next hop addresses. Note the `broadcast` option; without this option, broadcasts and multicasts would not be transmitted to our neighbors.

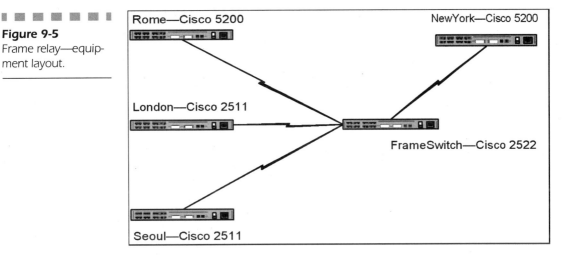

Figure 9-5
Frame relay—equipment layout.

Code Listing 9-9

```
1    version 11.2
2    !
3    hostname Rome
4    !
5    interface Loopback0
6     ip address 172.30.2.1 255.255.255.0
7    !
8    interface Serial0
9     ip address 172.30.100.101 255.255.255.0
10    encapsulation frame-relay
11    bandwidth 115
12    no fair-queue
13    frame-relay map ip 172.30.100.100 100 broadcast
14    frame-relay map ip 172.30.100.102 102 broadcast
15    frame-relay map ip 172.30.100.103 103 broadcast
16    !
17   router eigrp 100
18    network 172.30.0.0
19    !
20   end
```

The **show frame map** command shows that the next hop to DLCI mapping is statically defined, broadcast capable, and active:

```
Rome#show frame map
Serial0 (up): ip 172.30.100.100 dlci 100(0x64,0x1840), static,
              broadcast,
              CISCO, status defined, active
Serial0 (up): ip 172.30.100.102 dlci 102(0x66,0x1860), static,
              broadcast,
              CISCO, status defined, active
```

```
Serial0 (up): ip 172.30.100.103 dlci 103(0x67,0x1870), static,
               broadcast,
               CISCO, status defined, active
```

The **show ip route** command verifies that EIGRP routes are being learned across the Frame Relay connection:

```
Rome#show ip route
Codes: C - connected, S - static, I - IGRP, R - RIP, M - mobile, B - BGP
       D - EIGRP, EX - EIGRP external, O - OSPF, IA - OSPF inter area
       N1 - OSPF NSSA external type 1, N2 - OSPF NSSA external type 2
       E1 - OSPF external type 1, E2 - OSPF external type 2, E - EGP
       i - IS-IS, L1 - IS-IS level-1, L2 - IS-IS level-2, * - candidate default
       U - per-user static route, o - ODR

Gateway of last resort is not set

     172.30.0.0/24 is subnetted, 5 subnets
C       172.30.2.0 is directly connected, Loopback0
D       172.30.3.0 [90/22900736] via 172.30.100.102, 00:15:57, Serial0
D       172.30.1.0 [90/22900736] via 172.30.100.100, 00:16:20, Serial0
D       172.30.4.0 [90/22900736] via 172.30.100.103, 00:01:49, Serial0
C       172.30.100.0 is directly connected, Serial0
```

Next we try a series of pings to verify true connectivity. If the round-trip times seem to vary wildly, check out the configuration in Appendix F to determine possible causes.

```
Rome#ping 172.30.1.1

Type escape sequence to abort.
Sending 5, 100-byte ICMP Echos to 172.30.1.1, timeout is 2 seconds:
!!!!!
Success rate is 100 percent (5/5), round-trip min/avg/max = 8/8/8 ms

Rome#ping 172.30.3.1

Type escape sequence to abort.
Sending 5, 100-byte ICMP Echos to 172.30.3.1, timeout is 2 seconds:
!!!!!
Success rate is 100 percent (5/5), round-trip min/avg/max = 20/21/24 ms

Rome#ping 172.30.2.1

Type escape sequence to abort.
Sending 5, 100-byte ICMP Echos to 172.30.2.1, timeout is 2 seconds:
!!!!!
Success rate is 100 percent (5/5), round-trip min/avg/max = 4/4/4 ms
Rome#ping 172.30.4.1

Type escape sequence to abort.
Sending 5, 100-byte ICMP Echos to 172.30.4.1, timeout is 2 seconds:
!!!!!
Success rate is 100 percent (5/5), round-trip min/avg/max = 24/24/24 ms
```

London

Code Listing 9-10 shows the London configuration. It's no different than Rome's.

Code Listing 9-10

```
1    version 11.3
2    !
3    hostname London
4    !
5    interface Loopback0
6     ip address 172.30.3.1 255.255.255.0
7    !
8    interface Serial0
9     ip address 172.30.100.102 255.255.255.0
10    encapsulation frame-relay
11    bandwidth 115
12    no fair-queue
13    frame-relay map ip 172.30.100.100 100 broadcast
14    frame-relay map ip 172.30.100.101 101 broadcast
15    frame-relay map ip 172.30.100.103 103 broadcast
16   !
17   router eigrp 100
18    network 172.30.0.0
19   !
20   end
```

The **show frame pvc** command displays PVC status and statistics. There are three different PVC status values: ACTIVE, INACTIVE, and DELETED. ACTIVE is good, full end-to-end connectivity. INACTIVE means the local switch knows about the connection, but the end-to-end circuit is not complete. DELETED means you have defined a PVC in your router configuration, and the switch has no idea what the router is talking about.

```
London#show fr pvc

PVC Statistics for interface Serial0 (Frame Relay DTE)

DLCI = 100, DLCI USAGE = LOCAL, PVC STATUS = ACTIVE, INTERFACE = Serial0

  input pkts 67          output pkts 60          in bytes 5072
  out bytes 4240         dropped pkts 0          in FECN pkts 0
  in BECN pkts 0         out FECN pkts 0         out BECN pkts 0
  in DE pkts 0           out DE pkts 0
  out bcast pkts 30         out bcast bytes 1852
  pvc create time 00:26:39, last time pvc status changed 00:26:40

DLCI = 101, DLCI USAGE = LOCAL, PVC STATUS = ACTIVE, INTERFACE = Serial0
```

```
input pkts 37          output pkts 43          in bytes 2556
out bytes 2952         dropped pkts 0          in FECN pkts 0
in BECN pkts 0         out FECN pkts 0         out BECN pkts 0
in DE pkts 0           out DE pkts 0
out bcast pkts 24       out bcast bytes 1536
pvc create time 00:26:40, last time pvc status changed 00:21:10

DLCI = 103, DLCI USAGE = LOCAL, PVC STATUS = ACTIVE, INTERFACE = Serial0

input pkts 43          output pkts 44          in bytes 2676
out bytes 2664         dropped pkts 0          in FECN pkts 0
in BECN pkts 0         out FECN pkts 0         out BECN pkts 0
in DE pkts 0           out DE pkts 0
out bcast pkts 30       out bcast bytes 1852
pvc create time 00:26:40, last time pvc status changed 00:26:40
```

Seoul

Code Listing 9-11 shows the configuration for our next router, Seoul. There is no significant change from Rome or London's configuration.

Code Listing 9-11

```
1    version 11.3
2    !
3    hostname Seoul
4    !
5    interface Loopback0
6     ip address 172.30.4.1 255.255.255.0
7    !
8    interface Ethernet0
9     ip address 192.168.200.100 255.255.255.0
10   !
11   interface Serial0
12    ip address 172.30.100.103 255.255.255.0
13    encapsulation frame-relay
14    bandwidth 115
15    no fair-queue
16    frame-relay map ip 172.30.100.100 100 broadcast
17    frame-relay map ip 172.30.100.101 101 broadcast
18    frame-relay map ip 172.30.100.102 102 broadcast
19   !
20   router eigrp 100
21    network 172.30.0.0
22   !
23   end
```

The **show frame lmi** command gets statistics about the LMI connection to the local switch. It shows us any errors, the number of status inquiries, and the number of status messages received.

```
Seoul#show frame lmi

LMI Statistics for interface Serial0 (Frame Relay DTE) LMI TYPE = CISCO
  Invalid Unnumbered info 0  Invalid Prot Disc 0
  Invalid dummy Call Ref 0   Invalid Msg Type 0
  Invalid Status Message 0   Invalid Lock Shift 0
  Invalid Information ID 0    Invalid Report IE Len 0
  Invalid Report Request 0   Invalid Keep IE Len 0
  Num Status Enq. Sent 362   Num Status msgs Rcvd 363
  Num Update Status Rcvd 0    Num Status Timeouts 0
```

NewYork

This is the NewYork router in our static example. Code Listing 9-12 shows the configuration, which is just like the other routers' configurations in the example. Don't worry; it gets a lot more interesting in the next two examples.

Code Listing 9-12

```
1   version 11.1
2   !
3   hostname NewYork
4   !
5   interface Loopback0
6    ip address 172.30.1.1 255.255.255.0
7   !
8   interface Serial0
9    ip address 172.30.100.100 255.255.255.0
10   encapsulation frame-relay
11   bandwidth 115
12   no fair-queue
13   frame-relay map ip 172.30.100.101 101 broadcast
14   frame-relay map ip 172.30.100.102 102 broadcast
15   frame-relay map ip 172.30.100.103 103 broadcast
16   !
17  router eigrp 100
18   network 172.30.0.0
19   !
20  end
```

The **show interface serial0** command also has information about our Frame Relay connection to the switch. The most important during troubleshooting is the LMI section.

```
NewYork#show int s 0
Serial0 is up, line protocol is up
  Hardware is HD64570
  Internet address is 172.30.100.100/24
  MTU 1500 bytes, BW 115 Kbit, DLY 20000 usec, rely 255/255, load 1/255
  Encapsulation FRAME-RELAY, loopback not set, keepalive set (10 sec)
```

```
LMI enq sent  309, LMI stat recvd 309, LMI upd recvd 0, DTE LMI up
LMI enq recvd 0, LMI stat sent  0, LMI upd sent  0
LMI DLCI 1023  LMI type is CISCO  frame relay DTE
Broadcast queue 0/64, broadcasts sent/dropped 64/0, interface broadcasts 50
Last input 00:00:04, output 00:00:04, output hang never
Last clearing of "show interface" counters never
Queueing strategy: fifo
Output queue 0/40, 0 drops; input queue 0/75, 0 drops
5 minute input rate 0 bits/sec, 0 packets/sec
5 minute output rate 0 bits/sec, 0 packets/sec
   411 packets input, 11913 bytes, 0 no buffer
   Received 309 broadcasts, 0 runts, 0 giants
   0 input errors, 0 CRC, 0 frame, 0 overrun, 0 ignored, 0 abort
   408 packets output, 10289 bytes, 0 underruns
   0 output errors, 0 collisions, 23 interface resets
   0 output buffer failures, 0 output buffers swapped out
   0 carrier transitions
   DCD=up  DSR=up  DTR=up  RTS=up  CTS=up
```

Multipoint Frame Relay with Inverse ARP

This is the same layout as in the previous example, but it uses the Inverse ARP feature instead of static maps and adds fixed CIR traffic shaping.

Rome

We start again with Rome. Code Listing 9-13 shows our configuration.

Two major changes have taken place: first, there are no more static Frame Relay maps, and second, commands have been added to provide some traffic shaping.

Line 13 activates traffic shaping as a feature, and the **frame-relay class FIXEDCIR** command on line 14 directs us to global **map-class** commands on lines 19 and 20, where we define the traffic-shaping parameters.

Line 19 creates a Frame Relay **map-class** and names it FIXEDCIR, and line 20 sets a static maximum transmission rate of 65000 bits per second. Even if the traffic traveling out of this serial port is capable of transmitting data at a faster speed, the router will throttle the traffic flow back in order not to exceed the CIR.

Code Listing 9-13

```
1    version 11.2
2    !
3    hostname Rome
4    !
5    interface Loopback0
6     ip address 172.30.2.1 255.255.255.0
7    !
8    interface Serial0
9     ip address 172.30.100.101 255.255.255.0
10    encapsulation frame-relay
11    bandwidth 115
12    no fair-queue
13    frame-relay traffic-shaping
14    frame-relay class FIXEDCIR
15    !
16   router eigrp 100
17    network 172.30.0.0
18    !
19   map-class frame-relay FIXEDCIR
20     frame-relay cir 65000
21    !
22   end
```

Our **show frame map** command seems to be the same, but it built the maps dynamically when the Frame Relay PVC became active:

```
Rome#show frame map
Serial0 (up): ip 172.30.100.100 dlci 100(0x64,0x1840), dynamic,
              broadcast,, status defined, active
Serial0 (up): ip 172.30.100.102 dlci 102(0x66,0x1860), dynamic,
              broadcast,, status defined, active
Serial0 (up): ip 172.30.100.103 dlci 103(0x67,0x1870), dynamic,
              broadcast,, status defined, active
```

NOTE *If your Frame Relay service provider changes the configuration on the switch, you may need to bounce the serial interface using the* shutdown/no-shutdown *sequence to trigger an inverse ARP and dynamically rebuild the maps.*

The **show frame pvc** command looks the same as before:

```
Rome#show frame pvc

PVC Statistics for interface Serial0 (Frame Relay DTE)

DLCI = 100, DLCI USAGE = LOCAL, PVC STATUS = ACTIVE, INTERFACE = Serial0
```

```
    input pkts 51          output pkts 51          in bytes 3188
    out bytes 3258         dropped pkts 1          in FECN pkts 0
    in BECN pkts 0         out FECN pkts 0         out BECN pkts 0
    in DE pkts 0           out DE pkts 0
    out bcast pkts 44         out bcast bytes 2782
    pvc create time 00:39:53, last time pvc status changed 00:39:43

DLCI = 102, DLCI USAGE = LOCAL, PVC STATUS = ACTIVE, INTERFACE = Serial0

    input pkts 48          output pkts 53          in bytes 3022
    out bytes 3410         dropped pkts 0          in FECN pkts 0
    in BECN pkts 0         out FECN pkts 0         out BECN pkts 0
    in DE pkts 0           out DE pkts 0
    out bcast pkts 43         out bcast bytes 2718
    pvc create time 00:39:05, last time pvc status changed 00:39:05

DLCI = 103, DLCI USAGE = LOCAL, PVC STATUS = ACTIVE, INTERFACE = Serial0

    input pkts 58          output pkts 60          in bytes 4062
    out bytes 4262         dropped pkts 0          in FECN pkts 0
    in BECN pkts 0         out FECN pkts 0         out BECN pkts 0
    in DE pkts 0           out DE pkts 0
    out bcast pkts 43         out bcast bytes 2718
    pvc create time 00:39:06, last time pvc status changed 00:39:06
```

Now it's time for some **ping** tests to make sure we have full connectivity. What's up with London, 172.30.3.1? In our previous example, the round-trip times were much faster. There must be some traffic shaping going on, because the minimum and maximum times are very different.

```
Rome#ping 172.30.1.1

Type escape sequence to abort.
Sending 5, 100-byte ICMP Echos to 172.30.1.1, timeout is 2 seconds:
!!!!!
Success rate is 100 percent (5/5), round-trip min/avg/max = 8/8/8 ms

Rome#ping 172.30.2.1

Type escape sequence to abort.
Sending 5, 100-byte ICMP Echos to 172.30.2.1, timeout is 2 seconds:
!!!!!
Success rate is 100 percent (5/5), round-trip min/avg/max = 4/4/4 ms

Rome#ping 172.30.3.1

Type escape sequence to abort.
Sending 5, 100-byte ICMP Echos to 172.30.3.1, timeout is 2 seconds:
!!!!!
Success rate is 100 percent (5/5), round-trip min/avg/max = 20/63/124 ms
Rome#ping 172.30.4.1

Type escape sequence to abort.
Sending 5, 100-byte ICMP Echos to 172.30.4.1, timeout is 2 seconds:
!!!!!
Success rate is 100 percent (5/5), round-trip min/avg/max = 24/25/28 ms
```

London

Code Listing 9-14 shows the London configuration, which looks very similar to Rome's.

The difference is in the **map-class** commands on lines 20 through 22. Line 20 is the same, but we have changed the speed on line 21 to 9600 bits per second. Line 22 wasn't used in Rome. Why do we need it now? Check out the IOS version numbers on line 1: IOS 11.3 for London, IOS 11.2 for Rome.

Code Listing 9-14

```
1    version 11.3
2    !
3    hostname London
4    !
5    interface Loopback0
6      ip address 172.30.3.1 255.255.255.0
7    !
8    interface Serial0
9      ip address 172.30.100.102 255.255.255.0
10     encapsulation frame-relay
11     no ip mroute-cache
12     bandwidth 115
13     no fair-queue
14     frame-relay traffic-shaping
15     frame-relay class FIXEDCIR
16   !
17   router eigrp 100
18     network 172.30.0.0
19   !
20   map-class frame-relay FIXEDCIR
21     frame-relay cir 9600
22     no frame-relay adaptive-shaping
23   !
24   end
```

Just to make sure that our traffic shaping is causing the difference, let's run an experiment. First, deactivate traffic shaping on London's Frame Relay connection:

```
London#conf t
Enter configuration commands, one per line.  End with CNTL/Z.
London(config)#int s 0
London(config-if)#no frame traffic-shap
London(config-if)#^Z
```

Next, **ping** NewYork. The round-trip times look fairly steady to me:

```
London#ping 172.31.1.1

Type escape sequence to abort.
Sending 5, 100-byte ICMP Echos to 172.30.1.1, timeout is 2 seconds:
!!!!!
Success rate is 100 percent (5/5), round-trip min/avg/max = 20/22/24 ms
```

Now reactivate traffic shaping for London's Frame Relay connection:

```
London#conf t
Enter configuration commands, one per line.  End with CNTL/Z.
London(config)#int s 0
London(config-if)# frame-relay traffic-shaping
London(config-if)# frame-relay class FIXEDCIR
London(config-if)#^Z
```

Try that **ping** to NewYork again. Wow, it really works with only five 100-byte **ping** messages. Is this cool or what?

```
London#ping 172.30.1.1

Type escape sequence to abort.
Sending 5, 100-byte ICMP Echos to 172.30.1.1, timeout is 2 seconds:
!!!!!
Success rate is 100 percent (5/5), round-trip min/avg/max = 20/64/128 ms
```

Seoul

The next router we will deal with is the Seoul frame-connected router.

In the Seoul configuration shown in Code Listing 9-15, we are traffic shaping, but only for broadcasts (not for regular traffic). Line 16 sets up a broadcast/multicast limiter. We are allowed to have 40 elements in the broadcast/multicast queue and transmit no more than 24000 bits per second and 7 packets per second out of that queue.

Code Listing 9-15

```
1    version 11.3
2    !
3    hostname Seoul
4    !
5    interface Loopback0
6     ip address 172.30.4.1 255.255.255.0
7    !
```

```
8    interface Ethernet0
9      ip address 192.168.200.100 255.255.255.0
10   !
11   interface Serial0
12     ip address 172.30.100.103 255.255.255.0
13     encapsulation frame-relay
14     bandwidth 115
15     no fair-queue
16     frame-relay broadcast-queue 40 24000 7
17   !
18   router eigrp 100
19     network 172.30.0.0
20   !
21   end
```

NewYork

Code Listing 9-16 shows the New York configuration, which is really a plain vanilla configuration with no traffic shaping at all.

It does make sense in this multipoint environment to let all traffic shaping take place at the remote sites where we have direct control over the individual circuits. At the central site, NewYork, we have a single interface that has no specific reference in the configuration to the remote sites. We will get more control over remote connections in the next example.

```
1    version 11.1
2    !
3    hostname NewYork
4    !
5    interface Loopback0
6      ip address 172.30.1.1 255.255.255.0
7    !
8    interface Serial0
9      ip address 172.30.100.100 255.255.255.0
10     encapsulation frame-relay
11     bandwidth 115
12     no fair-queue
13   !
14   router eigrp 100
15     network 172.30.0.0
16   !
17   end
```

Let's use the **show frame map** command to verify that our PVCs are up and running. Everything looks good to me:

```
NewYork#show frame map
Serial0 (up): ip 172.30.100.101 dlci 101(0x65,0x1850), dynamic,
              broadcast,, status defined, active
Serial0 (up): ip 172.30.100.102 dlci 102(0x66,0x1860), dynamic,
              broadcast,, status defined, active
Serial0 (up): ip 172.30.100.103 dlci 103(0x67,0x1870), dynamic,
              broadcast,, status defined, active
```

Ping 'em all to make sure we are really talking to the remote sites. London is still the slowpoke in the bunch with that 9,600 bits-per-second CIR.

```
NewYork#ping 172.30.2.1

Type escape sequence to abort.
Sending 5, 100-byte ICMP Echoes to 172.30.2.1, timeout is 2 seconds:
!!!!!
Success rate is 100 percent (5/5), round-trip min/avg/max = 8/8/8 ms

NewYork#ping 172.30.2.1

Type escape sequence to abort.
Sending 5, 100-byte ICMP Echoes to 172.30.2.1, timeout is 2 seconds:
!!!!!
Success rate is 100 percent (5/5), round-trip min/avg/max = 8/8/8 ms

NewYork#ping 172.30.3.1

Type escape sequence to abort.
Sending 5, 100-byte ICMP Echoes to 172.30.3.1, timeout is 2 seconds:
!!!!!
Success rate is 100 percent (5/5), round-trip min/avg/max = 24/64/124 ms

NewYork#ping 172.30.4.1

Type escape sequence to abort.
Sending 5, 100-byte ICMP Echoes to 172.30.4.1, timeout is 2 seconds:
!!!!!
Success rate is 100 percent (5/5), round-trip min/avg/max = 20/24/28 ms
```

Point-to-Point Frame Relay Using Subinterfaces

This is an example of the paradigm shift to using the Frame Relay network to simulate a leased-line environment. The Non-Broadcast Multi-Access (NBMA) network used in our two previous examples works fine, but some protocols that use split-horizon features do not play well in an NBMA environment.

We will also add in a traffic-shaping technique based on BECNs, and Frame Relay data compression.

Rome

Code Listing 9-17 shows the Rome configuration.

Whoa, pardner! I thought this example was going to use subinterfaces. Lines 8 through 12 set up Frame Relay, but it looks like inverse ARP to me. Well, it is a remote site, and yes, there is only one connection back to NewYork. Okay, let's check it out and see if it works.

Code Listing 9-17

```
1    version 11.2
2    !
3    hostname Rome
4    !
5    interface Loopback0
6     ip address 172.30.2.1 255.255.255.0
7    !
8    interface Serial0
9     ip address 172.30.101.2 255.255.255.0
10    encapsulation frame-relay
11    bandwidth 115
12    no fair-queue
13   !
14   router eigrp 100
15    network 172.30.0.0
16   !
17   end
```

The **show frame map** command output looks good:

```
Rome#show fr map
Serial0 (up): ip 172.30.101.1 dlci 100(0x64,0x1840), dynamic,
              broadcast,, status defined, active
```

We can **ping** NewYork:

```
Rome#ping 172.30.1.1

Type escape sequence to abort.
Sending 5, 100-byte ICMP Echos to 172.30.1.1, timeout is 2 seconds:
!!!!!
Success rate is 100 percent (5/5), round-trip min/avg/max = 8/8/8 ms
```

The **show frame pvc 100** command output lists our PVC as ACTIVE, so it seems to be working just fine:

```
Rome#show frame pvc 100

PVC Statistics for interface Serial0 (Frame Relay DTE)

DLCI = 100, DLCI USAGE = LOCAL, PVC STATUS = ACTIVE, INTERFACE = Serial0

    input pkts 87              output pkts 21            in bytes 7262
    out bytes 1674            dropped pkts 0            in FECN pkts 0
    in BECN pkts 0            out FECN pkts 0          out BECN pkts 0
    in DE pkts 0             out DE pkts 0
    out bcast pkts 6         out bcast bytes 350
    pvc create time 00:26:33, last time pvc status changed 00:05:34
```

London

Code Listing 9-18 shows the configuration for London. This is more like it—subinterfaces at last.

Frame Relay looks different in this configuration. Lines 8 through 14 set up the Serial0 interface with the encapsulation for Frame Relay, and also apply the map-class ADAPTIVE to the interface. However, there is no mapping for the next hop, and no IP addressing. I guess we can consider these to be globally significant for all subinterfaces.

With adaptive traffic shaping, the router will reduce traffic flow on any PVC that indicates that BECN flags are being received by the router. I leave you to come up with a test for this.

Lines 16 through 19 define the operation of our subinterface. Line 16 identifies the subinterface and determines its mode of operation as point-to-point. Line 17 identifies the incoming DLCI of 100 as the traffic to be processed by this subinterface. Just for fun, we added some payload compression for this connection to NewYork in line 19.

Code Listing 9-18

```
1    version 11.3
2    !
3    hostname London
4    !
5    interface Loopback0
6      ip address 172.30.3.1 255.255.255.0
7    !
8    interface Serial0
9      no ip address
10     encapsulation frame-relay
11     bandwidth 115
```

Code Listing 9-18
(continued)

```
12    no fair-queue
13    frame-relay traffic-shaping
14    frame-relay class ADAPTIVE
15   !
16   interface Serial0.1 point-to-point
17    ip address 172.30.102.2 255.255.255.0
18    frame-relay interface-dlci 100
19    frame-relay payload-compression packet-by-packet
20   !
21   router eigrp 100
22    network 172.30.0.0
23   !
24   map-class frame-relay ADAPTIVE
25    frame-relay adaptive-shaping becn
26   !
27   end
```

The **show frame map** command output has changed significantly from previous examples. Serial 0.1 uses DLCI 100 as a point-to-point connection, just like a leased line. There is no need to map DLCIs to network addresses.

```
London#show frame map
Serial0.1 (up): point-to-point dlci, dlci 100(0x64,0x1840), broadcast status defined, active
```

The **show frame pvc** command output lists more than the one PVC we expected to see. DLCI 100 is active on interface Serial0.1, but DLCIs 101 and 103 are also active. If we look closer at 101 and 103, we see that they are assigned to Serial0 and are UNUSED. The switch knows about them, they are complete end-to-end, but we have no static maps on Serial0 that make use of these PVCs. It's DLCI cleanup time for our Frame Relay service provider.

```
London#show frame pvc

PVC Statistics for interface Serial0 (Frame Relay DTE)

DLCI = 100, DLCI USAGE = LOCAL, PVC STATUS = ACTIVE, INTERFACE = Serial0.1

    input pkts 304          output pkts 309          in bytes 29243
    out bytes 28680         dropped pkts 0           in FECN pkts 0
    in BECN pkts 0          out FECN pkts 0          out BECN pkts 0
    in DE pkts 0            out DE pkts 0
    out bcast pkts 127       out bcast bytes 10272
    pvc create time 00:09:15, last time pvc status changed 00:06:16

DLCI = 101, DLCI USAGE = UNUSED, PVC STATUS = ACTIVE, INTERFACE = Serial0

    input pkts 18           output pkts 0            in bytes 540
```

```
out bytes 0              dropped pkts 0          in FECN pkts 0
in BECN pkts 0           out FECN pkts 0         out BECN pkts 0
in DE pkts 0             out DE pkts 0
out bcast pkts 0         out bcast bytes 0          Num Pkts Switched 0

pvc create time 04:25:58, last time pvc status changed 00:06:16

DLCI = 103, DLCI USAGE = UNUSED, PVC STATUS = ACTIVE, INTERFACE = Serial0

input pkts 0             output pkts 0           in bytes 0
out bytes 0              dropped pkts 0          in FECN pkts 0
in BECN pkts 0           out FECN pkts 0         out BECN pkts 0
in DE pkts 0             out DE pkts 0
out bcast pkts 0         out bcast bytes 0          Num Pkts Switched 0

pvc create time 04:27:48, last time pvc status changed 00:06:17
```

The **show frame lmi** command output shows everything in order:

```
London#show frame lmi

LMI Statistics for interface Serial0 (Frame Relay DTE) LMI TYPE = ANSI
    Invalid Unnumbered info 0Invalid Prot Disc 0
    Invalid dummy Call Ref 0Invalid Msg Type 0
    Invalid Status Message 0Invalid Lock Shift 0
    Invalid Information ID 0Invalid Report IE Len 0
    Invalid Report Request 0Invalid Keep IE Len 0
    Num Status Enq. Sent 105Num Status msgs Rcvd 106
    Num Update Status Rcvd 0Num Status Timeouts 0
```

When we **ping** all the other routers, we can reach them all, proving that we are working correctly. Remember that when we **ping** Rome and Seoul, we go through NewYork—no more full mesh.

```
London#ping
Protocol [ip]:
London#ping 172.30.1.1

Type escape sequence to abort.
Sending 5, 100-byte ICMP Echos to 172.30.1.1, timeout is 2 seconds:
!!!!!
Success rate is 100 percent (5/5), round-trip min/avg/max = 16/19/20 ms

London#ping 172.30.2.1

Type escape sequence to abort.
Sending 5, 100-byte ICMP Echos to 172.30.2.1, timeout is 2 seconds:
!!!!!
Success rate is 100 percent (5/5), round-trip min/avg/max = 24/25/28 ms

London#ping 172.30.3.1

Type escape sequence to abort.
Sending 5, 100-byte ICMP Echos to 172.30.3.1, timeout is 2 seconds:
```

```
!!!!!
Success rate is 100 percent (5/5), round-trip min/avg/max = 1/3/4 ms
London#ping 172.30.4.1

Type escape sequence to abort.
Sending 5, 100-byte ICMP Echos to 172.30.4.1, timeout is 2 seconds:
!!!!!
Success rate is 100 percent (5/5), round-trip min/avg/max = 36/38/40 ms
London#
```

Seoul

Code Listing 9-19 shows the configuration for Seoul.

The only change from London is the removal of the traffic-shaping commands, and payload compression.

Code Listing 9-19

```
1    version 11.3
2    !
3    hostname Seoul
4    !
5    interface Loopback0
6     ip address 172.30.4.1 255.255.255.0
7    !
8    interface Ethernet0
9     ip address 192.168.200.100 255.255.255.0
10   !
11   interface Serial0
12    no ip address
13    encapsulation frame-relay
14    bandwidth 115
15    no fair-queue
16   !
17   interface Serial0.1 point-to-point
18    ip address 172.30.103.2 255.255.255.0
19    no arp frame-relay
20    frame-relay interface-dlci 100
21   !
22   router eigrp 100
23    network 172.30.0.0
24   !
25   end
```

Let's take a quick look at the debug options for this version of the IOS. Quite a few of these options are for debugging Frame Relay SVC processing, which is now being offered by several service providers.

```
Seoul#debug frame ?
  detailed    Detailed Debug: Only for Lab use
  dlsw        Frame Relay dlsw
  events      Important Frame Relay packet events
  foresight   Frame Relay router ForeSight support
  hpr         Frame Relay APPN HPR
  ip          Frame Relay Internet Protocol
  l3cc        Frame Relay Layer 3 Call Control
  l3ie        Frame Relay IE parsing/construction
  lapf        Frame Relay SVC Layer 2
  llc2        Frame Relay llc2
  lmi         LMI packet exchanges with service provider
  nli         Network Layer interface
  packet      Frame Relay packets
  rsrb        Frame Relay rsrb
  verbose     Frame Relay
```

Here is a sample of the **debug frame lmi** command output:

```
Seoul#debug frame lmi
Frame Relay LMI debugging is on
Displaying all Frame Relay LMI data
Seoul#
05:42:08: Serial0: FR ARP input
05:42:08: datagramstart = 0x61A970, datagramsize = 30
05:42:08: FR encap = 0x18510300
05:42:08: 80 00 00 00 08 06 00 0F 08 00 02 04 00 08 00 00
05:42:08: AC 1E 65 02 18 71 00 00 00 00
05:42:08:
05:42:13: Serial0(out): StEnq, myseq 108, yourseen 104, DTE up
05:42:13: datagramstart = 0x6318E8, datagramsize = 13
05:42:13: FR encap = 0xFCF10309
05:42:13: 00 75 01 01 01 03 02 6C 68
05:42:13:
05:42:13: Serial0(in): Status, myseq 108
05:42:13: RT IE 1, length 1, type 1
05:42:13: KA IE 3, length 2, yourseq 105, myseq 108
05:42:23: Serial0(out): StEnq, myseq 109, yourseen 105, DTE up
05:42:23: datagramstart = 0x6318E8, datagramsize = 13
05:42:23: FR encap = 0xFCF10309
05:42:23: 00 75 01 01 01 03 02 6D 69
```

NewYork

Now for our central site, NewYork. Code Listing 9-20 shows the configuration, which has a great deal more on subinterfaces.

Lines 8 through 13 set up Frame Relay on the primary interface, Serial0. There is a command on line 13 that defines our LMI processing as ANSI. The default is the Cisco LMI type. The newer versions of the IOS will pick up this information from the switch, so the command is not required. I'm from the old school and like to configure it anyway.

Lines 15 through 17 define our subinterface connection to Rome.

Lines 19 through 22 define our subinterface connection to London. Remember, we have payload compression in place in London, so we must match it here.

Lines 24 through 26 define our subinterface connection to Seoul.

■ |

Code Listing 9-20

```
1    version 11.2
2    !
3    hostname NewYork
4    !
5    interface Loopback0
6     ip address 172.30.1.1 255.255.255.0
7    !
8    interface Serial0
9     no ip address
10    encapsulation frame-relay
11    bandwidth 115
12    no fair-queue
13    frame-relay lmi-type ansi
14    !
15   interface Serial0.1 point-to-point
16    ip address 172.30.101.1 255.255.255.0
17    frame-relay interface-dlci 101
18    !
19   interface Serial0.2 point-to-point
20    ip address 172.30.102.1 255.255.255.0
21    frame-relay interface-dlci 102
22    frame-relay payload-compression packet-by-packet
23    !
24   interface Serial0.3 point-to-point
25    ip address 172.30.103.1 255.255.255.0
26    frame-relay interface-dlci 103
27    !
28   router eigrp 100
29    network 172.30.0.0
30    !
31   end
```

Let's check out the subinterface mapping with the **show frame map** command. All three subinterfaces are mapped point-to-point, even the one to Rome (Serial0.1), where Rome used inverse ARP to dynamically build a map with no sub-interfaces:

```
NewYork#show fr map
Serial0.3 (up): point-to-point dlci, dlci 103(0x67,0x1870), broadcast
          status defined, active
Serial0.1 (up): point-to-point dlci, dlci 101(0x65,0x1850), broadcast
          status defined, active
Serial0.2 (up): point-to-point dlci, dlci 102(0x66,0x1860), broadcast
          status defined, active
```

The **show frame pvc** command indicates that all our PVCs are mapped to subinterfaces, are used locally, and are active:

```
NewYork#show frame pvc

PVC Statistics for interface Serial0 (Frame Relay DTE)

DLCI = 101, DLCI USAGE = LOCAL, PVC STATUS = ACTIVE, INTERFACE = Serial0.1

  input pkts 73           output pkts 346         in bytes 5538
  out bytes 28068         dropped pkts 0          in FECN pkts 0
  in BECN pkts 0          out FECN pkts 0         out BECN pkts 0
  in DE pkts 0            out DE pkts 0
  out bcast pkts 302      out bcast bytes 24168
  pvc create time 00:33:32, last time pvc status changed 00:21:53

DLCI = 102, DLCI USAGE = LOCAL, PVC STATUS = ACTIVE, INTERFACE = Serial0.2

  input pkts 953          output pkts 497         in bytes 68644
  out bytes 45043         dropped pkts 0          in FECN pkts 0
  in BECN pkts 0          out FECN pkts 0         out BECN pkts 0
  in DE pkts 0            out DE pkts 0
  out bcast pkts 297      out bcast bytes 24243
  pvc create time 00:33:33, last time pvc status changed 00:10:24

DLCI = 103, DLCI USAGE = LOCAL, PVC STATUS = ACTIVE, INTERFACE = Serial0.3

  input pkts 678          output pkts 352         in bytes 45785
  out bytes 28420         dropped pkts 0          in FECN pkts 0
  in BECN pkts 0          out FECN pkts 0         out BECN pkts 0
  in DE pkts 0            out DE pkts 0
  out bcast pkts 304      out bcast bytes 24296
  pvc create time 00:33:33, last time pvc status changed 00:23:15
```

Let's **ping** the remote sites to make sure we can communicate properly. Notice how the round-trip times for London (172.30.3.1) are slightly faster than those to Seoul (172.31.4.1). It looks like our payload compression is paying off as far as round-trip times, even with 100-byte packets:

```
NewYork#ping 172.31.2.1

Type escape sequence to abort.
Sending 5, 100-byte ICMP Echos to 172.30.2.1, timeout is 2 seconds:
!!!!!
Success rate is 100 percent (5/5), round-trip min/avg/max = 8/8/8 ms

NewYork#ping 172.30.3.1

Type escape sequence to abort.
Sending 5, 100-byte ICMP Echos to 172.30.3.1, timeout is 2 seconds:
!!!!!
Success rate is 100 percent (5/5), round-trip min/avg/max = 16/17/20 ms

NewYork#ping 172.30.4.1
```

```
Type escape sequence to abort.
Sending 5, 100-byte ICMP Echos to 172.30.4.1, timeout is 2 seconds:
!!!!!
Success rate is 100 percent (5/5), round-trip min/avg/max = 20/20/24 ms
```

Finally, the **show ip route** command lets us know that our routing protocol was able to use multicast packets to establish full connectivity, even though we did not have to configure broadcast handling anywhere:

```
NewYork#show ip route
Codes: C - connected, S - static, I - IGRP, R - RIP, M - mobile, B - BGP
       D - EIGRP, EX - EIGRP external, O - OSPF, IA - OSPF inter area
       N1 - OSPF NSSA external type 1, N2 - OSPF NSSA external type 2
       E1 - OSPF external type 1, E2 - OSPF external type 2, E - EGP
       i - IS-IS, L1 - IS-IS level-1, L2 - IS-IS level-2, * - candidate default
       U - per-user static route, o - ODR

Gateway of last resort is not set

     172.30.0.0/24 is subnetted, 7 subnets
D       172.30.2.0 [90/22900736] via 172.30.101.2, 00:12:54, Serial0.1
D       172.30.3.0 [90/22900736] via 172.30.102.2, 00:12:53, Serial0.2
C       172.30.1.0 is directly connected, Loopback0
D       172.30.4.0 [90/22900736] via 172.30.103.2, 00:12:53, Serial0.3
C       172.30.102.0 is directly connected, Serial0.2
C       172.30.103.0 is directly connected, Serial0.3
C       172.30.101.0 is directly connected, Serial0.1
```

Summary

In this chapter, we covered basic wide area network (WAN) connectivity, point-to-point HDLC and channelized T1 connections, and the use of external services with X.25 and Frame Relay.

This is one of the most challenging areas of networking, as the network administrator has to turn control of the network components over to the service vendor. If both parties speak the same language, troubleshooting WAN problems is much easier.

Backing Up Fixed WAN Connections

This chapter examines the options available for backing up fixed WAN connections. The three options for providing dial backup service are: backup interfaces, floating static routes, and the new Dialer Watch feature.

As networks grew beyond the bounds of a single location, WAN connectivity became an increasingly more important component of our network environment. As companies came to rely on WAN connectivity being in place, there was an increased need for backup pathways for the primary link.

Backup Interface Command

Cisco always had dial backup capabilities. With a primary leased line and a backup Switched 56 circuit, Cisco required two physical connections for each remote site, and two interfaces at the central site—a costly way to do business but very functional. With the latest dialer profile techniques, the **backup interface** method has become more flexible and economical. The example later in this chapter highlights this method.

Floating Static Routes

AS OSPF and EIGRP became more popular, a new technique for providing dial backup became useful. When a normal static IP route is defined, it carries more weight (referred to as Administrative Distance) and is preferred over the dynamic routing protocols. Administrative Distances are either zero or one for static routes, and 20 to 200 for dynamic routing protocols. The lower the number, the more trusted the route. When configuring a static route, place an additional parameter at the end of the command for Administrative Distance. It must be a number, between zero and 255, that is higher than the highest Administrative Distance used by the active dynamic routing protocols. This technique floats the static route above the dynamic route and provides a backup direction if the dynamic protocol drops the primary route.

```
ip route 172.31.0.0 255.255.0.0 BRI0 172.31.200.1 180
```

Dial backup should be timely, and with RIP and IGRP, a dynamic route is dropped from the routing table only after the holddown timer expires—after at least three minutes!

Dialer Watch

A fairly new technique isDialer Watch. A list of routes is defined and assigned to a dial interface. If the routes in the list disappear from the routing table, the dial interface makes a call to provide a backup connection. This feature only works for the IGRP and EIGRP routing protocols.

Making It Work

This example shows us two of the techniques used to provide Frame Relay or leased-line dial backup using an ISDN BRI connection. London is our remote site with two Frame Relay PVCs, one each to Tokyo and NewYork. The two different techniques used for dial backup from London are the **backup interface** command and the **dialer watch** command. Dialer profiles provide the framework that makes these techniques scalable and flexible.

Figure 10-1 shows the equipment layout for our dial backup example.

Now it's time to look at the configurations that make this work. We will start off with London, where all the action is located, followed by our two central sites, NewYork and Tokyo.

London

London is the remote site initiating the dial backup. Code Listing 10-1 shows its configuration.

Primary connectivity to NewYork and Tokyo is established through a Frame Relay connection defined in lines 18 through 30. This connection uses the subinterface model to isolate each remote connection to a specific subinterface. Lines 18 through 20 define our primary interface as a Frame Relay connection.

Figure 10-1
Dial backup—
equipment layout.

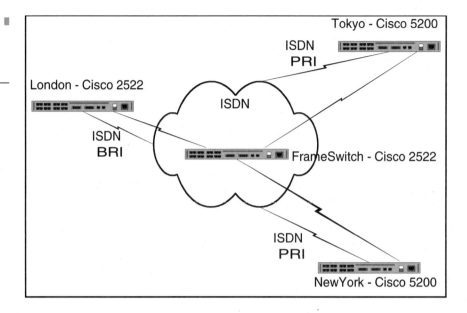

Lines 22 through 24 define our subinterface connection to NewYork. Note that there are no backup configuration commands on the interface itself. This will be backed up using the Dialer Watch feature.

Lines 26 through 30 define our subinterface connection to Tokyo. Lines 27 and 28 contain the legacy backup interface commands. Line 27 defines the delay times: 3 seconds after the primary link is down, start the dial backup process; 10 seconds after the primary link is active, drop the backup link. Line 28 places the Dialer2 interface in standby mode until it is needed for backup purposes. By assigning the dialer profile, Dialer2, as the backup interface, we free up the physical interface BRI0 for other purposes.

Lines 32 through 37 configure the BRI0 interface as a resource in dialer pool 5. Please note that this interface has not been configured with PPP multilink.

Lines 39 through 47 define the first dialer profile, Dialer1. This is our backup connection to NewYork. Line 45 is the new command **dialer watch-group 2**, which will trigger a dial call if the routes defined in the associated **dialer watch-list** are removed from the routing table. Line 46 assigns the rules in dialer-list 1 to track interesting traffic. Line 64 indicates that access-list 101 should be used to determine interesting traffic. Lines 61 and 62 define the interesting traffic as all IP traffic except for EIGRP routing information. If we didn't block EIGRP as interesting traffic, the `Dialer1` connection would be activated constantly by neighbor multicasts.

Lines 49 through 56 define the dialer profile, `Dialer2`. This is the backup interface for the connection to Tokyo. There are no special commands needed on this interface because when it is configured as the backup interface in line 28, `Dialer2` goes into standby mode.

Code Listing 10-1

```
1    version 12.0
2    !
3    hostname London
4    !
5    enable password cisco
6    !
7    username NewYork password 0 cisco
8    username Tokyo password 0 cisco
9
10   isdn switch-type basic-5ess
11   !
12   interface Loopback0
13    ip address 172.31.50.1 255.255.255.0
14   !
15   interface Ethernet0
16    ip address 192.168.200.196 255.255.255.0
17   !
18   interface Serial9
19    no ip address
20    encapsulation frame-relay
21   !
22   interface Serial9.1 point-to-point
23    ip address 172.31.100.2 255.255.255.0
24    frame-relay interface-dlci 100
25   !
26   interface Serial9.2 point-to-point
27    backup delay 3 10
28    backup interface Dialer2
29    ip address 172.31.101.2 255.255.255.0
30    frame-relay interface-dlci 101
31   !
32   interface BRI0
33    no ip address
34    encapsulation ppp
35    dialer pool-member 5
36    isdn switch-type basic-5ess
37    ppp authentication chap
38   !
39   interface Dialer1
40    ip address 172.31.200.2 255.255.255.0
41    encapsulation ppp
42    dialer remote-name NewYork
43    dialer string 1000
44    dialer pool 5
45    dialer watch-group 2
46    dialer-group 1
47    ppp authentication chap
```

```
48  !
49  interface Dialer2
50   ip address 172.31.201.2 255.255.255.0
51   encapsulation ppp
52   dialer remote-name Tokyo
53   dialer string 2000
54   dialer pool 5
55   dialer-group 2
56   ppp authentication chap
57  !
58  router eigrp 100
59   network 172.31.0.0
60  !
61  access-list 101 deny    eigrp any any
62  access-list 101 permit ip any any
63  dialer watch-list 2 ip 172.31.60.0 255.255.255.0
64  dialer-list 1 protocol ip list 101
65  dialer-list 2 protocol ip permit
66  !
67  end
```

Now it's time for some **show** commands and dial backup testing.

The **show ip route** command indicates that the remote sites are connected using their subinterfaces:

```
London#show ip route
Codes: C - connected, S - static, I - IGRP, R - RIP, M - mobile, B - BGP
       D - EIGRP, EX - EIGRP external, O - OSPF, IA - OSPF inter area
       N1 - OSPF NSSA external type 1, N2 - OSPF NSSA external type 2
       E1 - OSPF external type 1, E2 - OSPF external type 2, E - EGP
       i - IS-IS, L1 - IS-IS level-1, L2 - IS-IS level-2, * - candidate default
       U - per-user static route, o - ODR


Gateway of last resort is not set

     172.31.0.0/24 is subnetted, 6 subnets
C       172.31.200.0 is directly connected, Dialer1
C       172.31.50.0 is directly connected, Loopback0
D       172.31.60.0 [90/22900736] via 172.31.100.1, 00:01:47, Serial9.1
C       172.31.101.0 is directly connected, Serial9.2
C       172.31.100.0 is directly connected, Serial9.1
D       172.31.70.0 [90/22900736] via 172.31.101.1, 00:01:45, Serial9.2
C    192.168.200.0/24 is directly connected, Ethernet0
```

Now the Frame Relay switch is modified to take down the PVC between London and Tokyo. Serial9.2 changes state to down, but not Serial9, because Serial9 is still active and communicating to the frame switch. Sub-interfaces mapped to a single DLCI tie the status of the subinterface to the status of the DLCI. If the DLCI goes down, the sub-interface goes down. When Serial9.2 goes down, the backup interface, `Dialer2`, becomes active, and the first hello from EIGRP triggers a call to Tokyo. It looks like five seconds went by after the interface went down before the backup interface became active. That goes along with our three-second activation delay.

```
03:31:41: %FR-5-DLCICHANGE: Interface Serial9 - DLCI 101 state changed to DELETED
03:31:41: %LINEPROTO-5-UPDOWN: Line protocol on Interface Serial9.2,changed state to down
03:31:46: BRI0 DDR: rotor dialout [priority]
03:31:46: BRI0 DDR: Dialing cause ip (s=172.31.201.2, d=224.0.0.10)
03:31:46: BRI0 DDR: Attempting to dial 2000
03:31:46: %LINK-3-UPDOWN: Interface BRI0:1, changed state to up
03:31:46: %DIALER-6-BIND: Interface BRI0:1 bound to profile Dialer2
03:31:46: BRI0:1 DDR: dialer protocol up
03:31:47: %LINK-3-UPDOWN: Interface Dialer2, changed state to up
03:31:47: %LINEPROTO-5-UPDOWN: Line protocol on Interface BRI0:1, changed state to up
03:31:52: %ISDN-6-CONNECT: Interface BRI0:1 is now connected to 2000 Tokyo
```

Let's see what happens when we shut down the PVC that uses DLCI 100. As soon as interface `Serial9.1` changes state to down, the dialer watch feature kicks in when the primary link to 172.31.60.0/24 is no longer active. It looks like two seconds pass between detection and when the backup connection to NewYork becomes active. This works great with EIGRP.

```
03:32:41: %FR-5-DLCICHANGE: Interface Serial9 - DLCI 100 state changed to DELETED
03:32:41: %LINEPROTO-5-UPDOWN: Line protocol on Interface Serial9.1, changed state to down
03:32:41: DDR: Dialer Watch: watch-group = 2
03:32:41: DDR:    network 172.31.60.0/255.255.255.0 DOWN,
03:32:41: DDR:    primary DOWN
03:32:41: DDR: Dialer Watch: Dial Reason: Primary of group 2 DOWN
03:32:41: DDR: Dialer Watch: watch-group = 2,
03:32:41: BRI0 DDR: rotor dialout [priority]
03:32:41: DDR:    dialing secondary by dialer string 1000 on Dialer1
03:32:41: BRI0 DDR: Attempting to dial 1000
03:32:41: DDR: Dialer Watch: Dial Reason: Primary of group 2 DOWN
03:32:41: DDR: Dialer Watch: watch-group = 2,
03:32:42: %LINK-3-UPDOWN: Interface BRI0:2, changed state to up
03:32:42: BR0:2 DDR: Dialer Watch: resetting call in progress
03:32:42: %DIALER-6-BIND: Interface BRI0:2 bound to profile Dialer1
03:32:42: %ISDN-6-CONNECT: Interface BRI0:2 is now connected to 1000
03:32:42: BRI0:2 DDR: dialer protocol up
03:32:43: %LINEPROTO-5-UPDOWN: Line protocol on Interface BRI0:2, changed state to up
03:32:48: %ISDN-6-CONNECT: Interface BRI0:2 is now connected to 1000 NewYork
```

Let's see if the **show ip route** command displays all the proper pathways to NewYork and Tokyo. Everything looks good:

```
London#show ip route
Codes: C - connected, S - static, I - IGRP, R - RIP, M - mobile, B - BGP
       D - EIGRP, EX - EIGRP external, O - OSPF, IA - OSPF inter area
       N1 - OSPF NSSA external type 1, N2 - OSPF NSSA external type 2
       E1 - OSPF external type 1, E2 - OSPF external type 2, E - EGP
       i - IS-IS, L1 - IS-IS level-1, L2 - IS-IS level-2, * - candidate default
       U - per-user static route, o - ODR

Gateway of last resort is not set

     172.31.0.0/16 is variably subnetted, 7 subnets, 2 masks
C       172.31.200.1/32 is directly connected, Dialer1
C       172.31.201.0/24 is directly connected, Dialer2
C       172.31.201.1/32 is directly connected, Dialer2
C       172.31.200.0/24 is directly connected, Dialer1
C       172.31.50.0/24 is directly connected, Loopback0
D       172.31.60.0/24 [90/46354176] via 172.31.200.1, 00:01:17, Dialer1
D       172.31.70.0/24 [90/46354176] via 172.31.201.1, 00:01:16, Dialer2
C    192.168.200.0/24 is directly connected, Ethernet0
```

Backups are successful, but let's reconnect the PVCs to see if the routes get back to normal:

```
03:35:21: %FR-5-DLCICHANGE: Interface Serial9 - DLCI 100 state changed to ACTIVE
03:35:21: %LINEPROTO-5-UPDOWN: Line protocol on Interface Serial9.1, changed state to up
03:36:21: %FR-5-DLCICHANGE: Interface Serial9 - DLCI 101 state changed to ACTIVE
03:36:21: %LINEPROTO-5-UPDOWN: Line protocol on Interface Serial9.2, changed state to up
```

Primary links are back up. Let's check out the routing table with the **show ip route** command to make sure the routes are back:

```
London#show ip route
Codes: C - connected, S - static, I - IGRP, R - RIP, M - mobile, B - BGP
       D - EIGRP, EX - EIGRP external, O - OSPF, IA - OSPF inter area
       N1 - OSPF NSSA external type 1, N2 - OSPF NSSA external type 2
       E1 - OSPF external type 1, E2 - OSPF external type 2, E - EGP
       i - IS-IS, L1 - IS-IS level-1, L2 - IS-IS level-2, * - candidate default
       U - per-user static route, o - ODR

Gateway of last resort is not set

     172.31.0.0/24 is subnetted, 6 subnets
C       172.31.200.0 is directly connected, Dialer1
C       172.31.50.0 is directly connected, Loopback0
D       172.31.60.0 [90/22900736] via 172.31.100.1, 00:01:34, Serial9.1
C       172.31.101.0 is directly connected, Serial9.2
C       172.31.100.0 is directly connected, Serial9.1
D       172.31.70.0 [90/22900736] via 172.31.101.1, 00:01:32, Serial9.2
C    192.168.200.0/24 is directly connected, Ethernet0
London#
```

Tokyo

Code Listing 10-2 shows the configuration for Tokyo.

Lines 20 through 29 set up our Frame Relay connection with the sub-interface and our dial backup commands. When configuring the backup interface feature, it only makes sense that both sides have to be configured the same. Notice the times; an additional second or two on one side may be in order to make sure that both sides don't call at the same time and get a busy signal.

We are using the ISDN PRI connection as the target for dial backup. With multiple remote sites, replication of the Dialer1 dialer profile, lines 40 through 48, would be all that you would need to create a central site to handle multiple remote sites.

Code Listing 10-2

```
1    version 12.0
2    !
3    hostname Tokyo
4    !
5    enable password cisco
6    !
7    username London password 0 cisco
8    ip subnet-zero
9    isdn switch-type primary-5ess
10   !
11   controller T1 0
12     framing esf
13     clock source line primary
14     linecode b8zs
15     pri-group timeslots 1-24
16   !
17   interface Loopback0
18     ip address 172.31.70.1 255.255.255.0
19   !
20   interface Serial0
21     no ip address
22     encapsulation frame-relay
23     no fair-queue
24   !
25   interface Serial0.1 point-to-point
26     backup delay 4 11
27     backup interface Dialer1
28     ip address 172.31.101.1 255.255.255.0
29     frame-relay interface-dlci 102
30   !
31   interface Serial0:23
32     no ip address
33     encapsulation ppp
34     dialer pool-member 1
35     isdn switch-type primary-5ess
36     no fair-queue
```

■ ▪

Chapter 10

Code Listing 10-2
(continued)

```
37    ppp authentication chap
38    ppp multilink
39    !
40   interface Dialer1
41    ip address 172.31.201.1 255.255.255.0
42    encapsulation ppp
43    dialer remote-name London
44    dialer idle-timeout 9999
45    dialer pool 1
46    dialer-group 1
47    no fair-queue
48    ppp authentication chap
49    !
50   router eigrp 100
51    network 172.31.0.0
52    !
53   end
```

The **show ip route** command displays a routing table where all routes go through London:

```
Tokyo#show ip route
Codes: C - connected, S - static, I - IGRP, R - RIP, M - mobile, B - BGP
       D - EIGRP, EX - EIGRP external, O - OSPF, IA - OSPF inter area
       N1 - OSPF NSSA external type 1, N2 - OSPF NSSA external type 2
       E1 - OSPF external type 1, E2 - OSPF external type 2, E - EGP
       i - IS-IS, L1 - IS-IS level-1, L2 - IS-IS level-2, * - candidate default
       U - per-user static route, o - ODR

Gateway of last resort is not set

     172.31.0.0/16 is variably subnetted, 7 subnets, 2 masks
D       172.31.200.1/32 [90/46738176] via 172.31.101.2, 00:01:48, Serial0.1
D       172.31.200.0/24 [90/46738176] via 172.31.101.2, 00:02:25, Serial0.1
D       172.31.50.0/24 [90/2297856] via 172.31.101.2, 00:02:25, Serial0.1
D       172.31.60.0/24 [90/23412736] via 172.31.101.2, 00:01:03, Serial0.1
C       172.31.101.0/24 is directly connected, Serial0.1
D       172.31.100.0/24 [90/23284736] via 172.31.101.2, 00:01:07,Serial0.1
C       172.31.70.0/24 is directly connected, Loopback0
```

Let's use an extended **ping** to check out the time it takes to switch over when we break the PVC between Tokyo and London. The number of dots indicates that the switchover takes about 22 seconds:

```
Tokyo#ping
Protocol [ip]:
Target IP address: 172.31.50.1
Repeat count [5]: 1000
Datagram size [100]: 1000
Timeout in seconds [2]:
Extended commands [n]:
Sweep range of sizes [n]:
```

```
Type escape sequence to abort.
Sending 1000, 1000-byte ICMP Echos to 172.31.50.1, timeout is 2 seconds:
!!!!!!!!!!!!!!!!!!!!!!!!!!!!!!!!!!!!!!!!!!!!!!!!!!!!!!!!!!!!!!!!!!!!!!!!!!!
!!!!!!!!!!!!!!!!!!!!!!!!!!!!!!!!!!!!!!!!!!!!!!!!!!!!!!!!!!!!!!!!!!!!!!!!!!!
!!!!!!!!!!!!!!!!!!!!.........!!!!!!!!!!!!!!!!!!!!!!!!!!!!!!!!!!!!!!!!!!!!!!
!!!!!!!!!!!!!!!!!!!!!!!!!!!!!!!!!!!!!!!!!!!!!!!!!!!!!!!!!!!!!!!!!!!!!!!!!!!
!!!!!!!!!!!!!!!!!!!!!!!!!!!!!!!!!!!!!!!!!!!!!!!!!!!!!!!!!!!!!!!!!!!!!!!!!!!
!!!!!!!!!!!!!!!!!!!!!!!!!!!!!!!!!!!!!!!!!!!!!!!!!!!!!!!!!!!!!!!!!!!!!!!!!!!
!!!!!!!!!!.
Success rate is 97 percent (419/431), round-trip min/avg/max = 156/224/408 ms
```

Let's check out our routes again to make sure we are using the backup connection:

```
Tokyo#show ip route
Codes: C - connected, S - static, I - IGRP, R - RIP, M - mobile, B - BGP
       D - EIGRP, EX - EIGRP external, O - OSPF, IA - OSPF inter area
       N1 - OSPF NSSA external type 1, N2 - OSPF NSSA external type 2
       E1 - OSPF external type 1, E2 - OSPF external type 2, E - EGP
       i - IS-IS, L1 - IS-IS level-1, L2 - IS-IS level-2, * - candidate default
       U - per-user static route, o - ODR

Gateway of last resort is not set

     172.31.0.0/16 is variably subnetted, 7 subnets, 2 masks
C       172.31.201.2/32 is directly connected, Dialer1
D       172.31.200.1/32 [90/46738176] via 172.31.201.2, 00:00:31, Dialer1
C       172.31.201.0/24 is directly connected, Dialer1
D       172.31.200.0/24 [90/46738176] via 172.31.201.2, 00:01:21, Dialer1
D       172.31.50.0/24 [90/46354176] via 172.31.201.2, 00:01:21, Dialer1
D       172.31.60.0/24 [90/46866176] via 172.31.201.2, 00:00:27, Dialer1
C       172.31.70.0/24 is directly connected, Loopback0
```

When the Frame Relay circuit changes state to up, the backup interface disconnects and goes back to standby mode.

```
1d06h: %FR-5-DLCICHANGE: Interface Serial0 - DLCI 102 state changed to ACTIVE
1d06h: %LINEPROTO-5-UPDOWN: Line protocol on Interface Serial0.1, changed state to up
1d06h: Se0:23 DDR: has total 23 call(s), dial_out 0, dial_in 0
1d06h: %DIALER-6-UNBIND: Interface Serial0:18 unbound from profile Dialer1
1d06h: Serial0:18 DDR: disconnecting call
1d06h: %ISDN-6-DISCONNECT: Interface Serial0:18  disconnected from 4102802001 London, call
   lasted 272 seconds
1d06h: %LINK-3-UPDOWN: Interface Serial0:18, changed state to down
1d06h: Serial0:18 DDR: disconnecting call
1d06h: %LINEPROTO-5-UPDOWN: Line protocol on Interface Serial0:18, changed state to down
1d06h: %LINK-5-CHANGED: Interface Dialer1, changed state to standby mode
```

NewYork

NewYork is the last stop on the dial backup trip. Code Listing 10-3 shows the configuration.

This configuration is identical to the configuration for Tokyo, except that the Dialer Watch feature at the remote site does not require any additional configuration at the central site.

Note that I left a bug in this configuration. With the quality test mentioned in the beginning of the book, this is an easy way to get a certificate and a buck. Careful, the bug is not obvious.

Code Listing 10-3

```
1    version 11.2
2    !
3    hostname NewYork
4    !
5    enable password cisco
6    !
7    username London password 0 cisco
8    isdn switch-type primary-5ess
9    !
10   controller T1 0
11     framing esf
12     clock source line primary
13     linecode b8zs
14     pri-group timeslots 1-24
15   !
16   interface Loopback0
17     ip address 172.31.60.1 255.255.255.0
18   !
19   interface Serial0
20     no ip address
21     encapsulation frame-relay
22     no fair-queue
23   !
24   interface Serial0.1 point-to-point
25     ip address 172.31.100.1 255.255.255.0
26     frame-relay interface-dlci 102
27   !
28   interface Serial0:23
29     no ip address
30     encapsulation ppp
31     dialer pool-member 1
32     no fair-queue
33     ppp authentication chap
34     ppp multilink
35   !
36   interface Dialer1
37     ip address 172.31.200.1 255.255.255.0
38     encapsulation ppp
39     dialer remote-name London
40     dialer idle-timeout 9999
41     dialer pool 1
```

Code Listing 10-3
(continued)

```
42    dialer-group 1
43    no fair-queue
44    ppp authentication chap
45    !
46  router eigrp 100
47    network 172.31.0.0
48    !
49  end
```

Check out the routes to make sure we are using the frame circuit:

```
NewYork#show ip route
Codes: C - connected, S - static, I - IGRP, R - RIP, M - mobile, B - BGP
       D - EIGRP, EX - EIGRP external, O - OSPF, IA - OSPF inter area
       N1 - OSPF NSSA external type 1, N2 - OSPF NSSA external type 2
       E1 - OSPF external type 1, E2 - OSPF external type 2, E - EGP
       i - IS-IS, L1 - IS-IS level-1, L2 - IS-IS level-2, * - candidate default
       U - per-user static route, o - ODR

Gateway of last resort is not set

     172.31.0.0/16 is variably subnetted, 7 subnets, 2 masks
C       172.31.200.0/24 is directly connected, Dialer1
D       172.31.50.0/24 [90/2297856] via 172.31.100.2, 00:01:09, Serial0.1
C       172.31.60.0/24 is directly connected, Loopback0
D       172.31.101.0/24 [90/23284736] via 172.31.100.2, 00:01:09, Serial0.1
C       172.31.100.0/24 is directly connected, Serial0.1
D       172.31.70.0/24 [90/23412736] via 172.31.100.2, 00:01:09, Serial0.1
```

Start up an extended **ping** to London and count the dots. Seven dots indicate 14 seconds for the switchover:

```
NewYork#ping
Protocol [ip]:
Target IP address: 172.31.50.1
Repeat count [5]: 1000
Datagram size [100]: 1000
Timeout in seconds [2]:
Extended commands [n]:
Sweep range of sizes [n]:
Type escape sequence to abort.
Sending 1000, 1000-byte ICMP Echos to 172.31.50.1, timeout is 2 seconds:
!!!!!!!!!!!!!!!!!!!!!!!!!!!!!!!!!!!!!!!!!!!!!!!!!!!!......!!!!!!!!!!!!
!!!!!!!!!!!!!!!!!!!!!!!!!!!!!!!!!!!!!!!!!!!!!!!!!!!!!!!!!!!!!!!!!!!!!!!!
!!!!!!!!!!!!!!!!!!!!!!!!!!!!!!!!!!!!!!!!!!!!!!!!!!!!!!!!!!!!!!!!
Success rate is 96 percent (199/206), round-trip min/avg/max = 156/234/332 ms
```

Now let's look at the messages that report the frame circuit failure and activation of the backup BRI circuit:

```
%DIALER-6-BIND: Interface Serial0:18 bound to profile Dialer1
%LINK-3-UPDOWN: Interface Serial0:18, changed state to up
dialer Protocol up for Se0:18
%LINEPROTO-5-UPDOWN: Line protocol on Interface Serial0:18, changed state to up
%ISDN-6-CONNECT: Interface Serial0:18 is now connected to 4102802001 London
%FR-5-DLCICHANGE: Interface Serial0 - DLCI 102 state changed to INACTIVE
%LINEPROTO-5-UPDOWN: Line protocol on Interface Serial0.1, changed state to down
```

The routes check out okay:

```
NewYork#show ip route
Codes: C - connected, S - static, I - IGRP, R - RIP, M - mobile, B - BGP
       D - EIGRP, EX - EIGRP external, O - OSPF, IA - OSPF inter area
       N1 - OSPF NSSA external type 1, N2 - OSPF NSSA external type 2
       E1 - OSPF external type 1, E2 - OSPF external type 2, E - EGP
       i - IS-IS, L1 - IS-IS level-1, L2 - IS-IS level-2, * - candidate default
       U - per-user static route, o - ODR

Gateway of last resort is not set

     172.31.0.0/16 is variably subnetted, 7 subnets, 2 masks
C       172.31.200.2/32 is directly connected, Dialer1
D       172.31.201.0/24 [90/46738176] via 172.31.200.2, 00:01:04, Dialer1
D       172.31.201.1/32 [90/46738176] via 172.31.200.2, 00:01:04, Dialer1
C       172.31.200.0/24 is directly connected, Dialer1
D       172.31.50.0/24 [90/46354176] via 172.31.200.2, 00:00:58, Dialer1
C       172.31.60.0/24 is directly connected, Loopback0
D       172.31.70.0/24 [90/46866176] via 172.31.200.2, 00:01:04, Dialer1
```

Start another extended **ping** to see if there is any disruption when we switch back to the primary link:

```
NewYork#ping
Protocol [ip]:
Target IP address: 172.31.50.1
Repeat count [5]: 1000
Datagram size [100]: 1000
Timeout in seconds [2]:
Extended commands [n]:
Sweep range of sizes [n]:
Type escape sequence to abort.
Sending 1000, 1000-byte ICMP Echos to 172.31.50.1, timeout is 2 seconds:
!!!!!!!!!!!!!!!!!!!!!!!!!!!!!!!!!!!!!!!!!!!!!!!!!!!!!!!!!!!!!!!!!!!!!!!!!!
!!!!!!!!!!!!!!!!!!!!!!!!!!!!!!!!!!!!!!!!!!!!!!!!!!!!!!!!!!!!!!!!!!!!!!!!!!
!!!!!!!!!!!!!!!!!!!!!!!!!!!!!!!!!!!!!!!!!!!!!!!!!!!!!!!!!!!!!!!!!!!!!!!!!!
!!!!!!!!!!!!!!!!!!!!!!!!!!!!!!!!!!!!!!!!.
```

Now let's make sure we did indeed switch back to our primary link:

```
NewYork#show ip route
Codes: C - connected, S - static, I - IGRP, R - RIP, M - mobile, B - BGP
       D - EIGRP, EX - EIGRP external, O - OSPF, IA - OSPF inter area
       N1 - OSPF NSSA external type 1, N2 - OSPF NSSA external type 2
       E1 - OSPF external type 1, E2 - OSPF external type 2, E - EGP
       i - IS-IS, L1 - IS-IS level-1, L2 - IS-IS level-2, * - candidate default
       U - per-user static route, o - ODR

Gateway of last resort is not set

     172.31.0.0/16 is variably subnetted, 7 subnets, 2 masks
C       172.31.200.0/24 is directly connected, Dialer1
D       172.31.50.0/24 [90/2297856] via 172.31.100.2, 00:01:06, Serial0.1
C       172.31.60.0/24 is directly connected, Loopback0
D       172.31.101.0/24 [90/23284736] via 172.31.100.2, 00:01:06, Serial0.1
C       172.31.100.0/24 is directly connected, Serial0.1
D       172.31.70.0/24 [90/23412736] via 172.31.100.2, 00:01:06, Serial0.1
```

LAB Challenge

Set up two routers using back-to-back cables for the serial link, and set up dial backup using two modems connected to the Auxiliary ports. Use floating static routes to trigger the backup call.

Summary

In this chapter, we covered dial backup and used Frame Relay connections as the primary link. The backup process works equally well for regular leased-line connections.

Remember not to mix techniques on a single backup connection; the routers may get confused.

11

Advanced Security with TACACS+ and RADIUS

In this chapter, we will take the example we used in Chapter 8 and increase security by using the Authentication, Authorization, Accounting (AAA) security technique. To support this new style of security, we will use a CiscoSecure for NT and the TACACS+ protocol.

First, let's define the three main topics by asking some questions: Who are you? What will we allow you to do? Who were you, what did you do, and how long did you do it?

Authentication provides a means to identify those users known to us and permit them to access devices and services. Think of the bouncer behind the red ropes—if you are on the list, you are in; if not, you are out.

Authorization makes sure that when you type in a command or attempt to connect to a remote device, you have been placed on the list of users permitted to perform those functions.

Accounting keeps track of users rejected while trying to get access, the time a user spends connected to specific devices, and even which commands are executed while on an active connection. This is very useful when problems occur, as a quick review of the command log can show which commands could have caused the problem.

TACACS+

TACACS+ uses TCP to transport requests from the network access server (NAS) to the UNIX or NT server. There are two modes of operation: Single Connection and As Needed. Single Connection mode establishes a single session between the NAS and the CiscoSecure server and maintains that connection while both sides of the conversation are active. As Needed requests establish a TCP connection, process requests, and then terminate the TCP session. On a busy NAS, this can cause a bottleneck for authenticating incoming requests.

All traffic between the NAS and the server is encrypted.

Appendix C lists the TACACS+ RFCs and reference sites.

RADIUS

RADIUS uses UDP to transport requests from the NAS to the server. UDP transport has less overhead than TACACS+ and is more popular with vendors other than Cisco.

Passwords that travel between the NAS and the server are encrypted. Appendix C lists the Radius RFCs and reference sites.

CiscoSecure ACS v2.1 for NT

It's time for a short tutorial on CiscoSecure. Install the software from the distribution CD. During the installation you will be asked to identify the server IP address and name, and at least one router/access server. When finished, you should have an ACS Admin icon on your NT Server or NT Workstation desktop. Start it up and you should see an opening screen that has a section on the left-hand side that looks like Figure 11-1.

A short paragraph on each of the items on the menu would be in order. Because the features and capabilities change version by version, we will only configure some of the most basic features.

We need to set up users for each authentication object. These objects could be a remote router or a dial-in user. Each user must belong to a group, where most of the authorization takes place.

There is a set of default groups created at startup that we will use for this example: Group01 for user-level operations, Group10 for limited-privilege operations, and Group15 for full-privilege operations.

The network configuration is where we define our access servers and AAA servers. The basic information is set up during the installation phase.

The System Configuration section lets the administrator check the status of the background daemons and start or restart the CiscoSecure daemons. There is a section in which to view and modify the fields used for the various accounting logs.

While you would expect the interface configuration section to deal with the routers, it actually defines the features and capabilities displayed and processed by each section of CiscoSecure ACS.

Administration Control manages user access to CiscoSecure ACS administration. By default, the local system is allowed to connect and administer CiscoSecure.

External User Database control lets us define external databases, such as Windows NT or CRYPTOcard Token Card server, for password validation.

Reports and Activity lets us view the canned reports. Appendix G contains some samples of these reports, which are generated from Excel

Figure 11-1
CiscoSecure—
administration
selection.

spreadsheets. You will also find a directory structure definition for the log files with the examples.

Online Documentation completes the menu.

Click on Network Configuration to display the initial setup of the components defined during installation. Figure 11-2 shows a sample network configuration. The access server defined during installation is NewYork; I added SOHO800 afterwards. The name of the system on which CiscoSecure is installed is bbdell.

Taking a closer look at the router/access server configuration in Figure 11-3, we see the Key used to validate incoming connections from NewYork. When we configure NewYork, we must use the key <ciscosecure>. The single connection box has been checked. If NewYork is configured properly, then a connection will be made once and maintained. Without a single connection, there would be a delay as each request establishes a TCP connection. The last piece of information we need in order to configure the router/access server is the protocol to be used to process AAA requests. Our choice is TACACS+.

While there are three different groups defined, we will take a look at Group10. Figure 11-4 shows us how to select the group from the list.

Figure 11-2
CiscoSecure—network configuration.

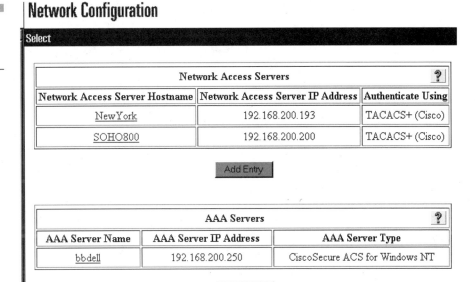

Network Configuration

Select

Network Access Servers		
Network Access Server Hostname	Network Access Server IP Address	Authenticate Using
NewYork	192.168.200.193	TACACS+ (Cisco)
SOHO800	192.168.200.200	TACACS+ (Cisco)

Add Entry

AAA Servers		
AAA Server Name	AAA Server IP Address	AAA Server Type
bbdell	192.168.200.250	CiscoSecure ACS for Windows NT

Add Entry

Distribution Table			
Character String	AAA Servers	Strip	Account
(Default)	bbdell	No	Local

Click on the Edit Settings button to view and change the current settings.

The first section we need to set up for Group10 is the PPP section, shown in Figure 11-5. In this example, we will limit the processing to CHAP authentication. Look at all the options. The time-of-day access for this group has not been activated, as it has been set up for individual user-level control.

NOTE *In this version of CiscoSecure, the references to access-lists will only work if the access-list has been configured on the router/access server. Future releases will allow access-lists to be defined and downloaded from CiscoSecure to the router.*

Figure 11-3
CiscoSecure—access
server configuration.

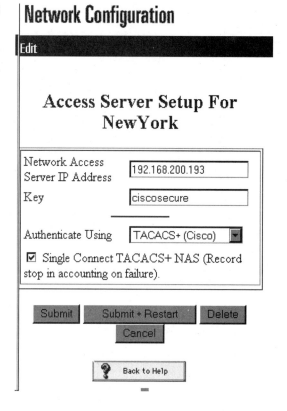

The next part of the TACACS+ configuration deals with command-line and dial-in access, as shown in Figure 11-6. We have limited executive-level access to level 10. For this level setting to work, we must define the commands available at level 10 in the router/access server.

NOTE *In order for group changes and additions to take effect, the daemons must be restarted to reflect the new information. An alternate method would be to go to the Control Panel under Service and restart all the daemons manually.*

Figure 11-7 shows the user selection page. To update or delete users, you must first identify and select them. Either type in the user name and click on Add/Edit, or click on Find for a complete list, or click on a letter

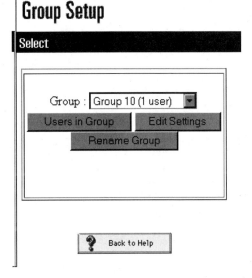

for a list of users whose names start with that letter. To add a new user, simply type in the user name and click on Add/Edit.

The first part of the MidLevel user configuration asks for some descriptive information and the passwords to be used for authentication. Figure 11-8 shows the basic configuration.

Continuing with user setup in Figure 11-9, we see the end of the password setup. For additional security, we can have separate passwords for PPP authentication and login authentication. In this example, we will use only one password for all authentication.

This is where we also assign the user to a group, Group10.

Figure 11-10 shows the last user setup page we will use in our example. Here we assign the maximum executive level that this user will be allowed to access. When the user changes to the enable mode on the router, a separate password, defined here, is used.

When all additions and changes are complete, click on Submit to update the user information. While all the other sections require a restart, the user portion of the database is accessed for each request. It must be this way because users can be authenticated by external databases that can constantly change.

The last item we will review is the System Configuration element, shown in Figure 11-11. If you are having trouble establishing the initial connectivity from the router/access server, check here to make sure that everything is up and running.

Figure 11-5
CiscoSecure—group
TACAS+ PPP settings.

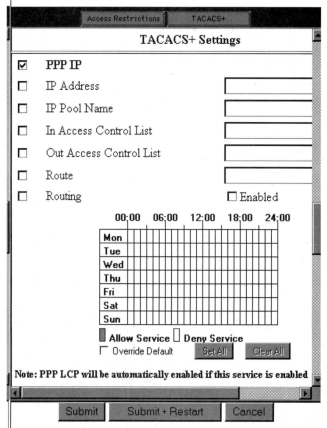

AAA Operating Commands

There are three main commands used to configure AAA operations: **aaa authentication**, **aaa authorization**, and **aaa accounting**.

Authentication

The first type of processing is **aaa authentication**. There are two options for this command: setting the default operation, and defining a

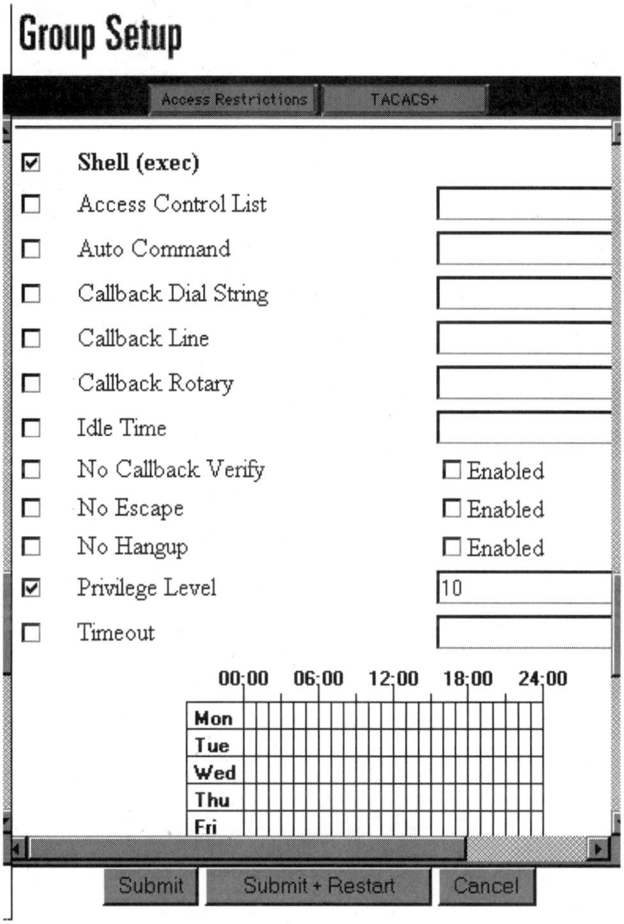

■ ■ ■ ■ ■ ■ ■
Figure 11-6
CiscoSecure—group
shell configuration.

Group Setup

| Access Restrictions | TACACS+ |

☑ **Shell (exec)**

☐ Access Control List

☐ Auto Command

☐ Callback Dial String

☐ Callback Line

☐ Callback Rotary

☐ Idle Time

☐ No Callback Verify   ☐ Enabled

☐ No Escape   ☐ Enabled

☐ No Hangup   ☐ Enabled

☑ Privilege Level   `10`

☐ Timeout

```
           00;00   06;00   12;00   18;00   24;00
   Mon
   Tue
   Wed
   Thu
   Fri
```

| Submit | Submit + Restart | Cancel |

named operation. When a default authentication command is entered, any authentication object not specifically defined will use the default definition. Table 11-1 lists the objects and methods for these commands. Table 11-2 defines the operational methods used for all three of the AAA commands.

The formats for both a default and a named command are as follows:

```
aaa authentication Object default method1 method2 method3 method4

aaa authentication Object BACKDOOR method1 method2 method3 method4
```

By using up to four methods on each command, we can define the sequence of operation for authentication lookup techniques. If the first method is unavailable, then we move on to the second method, and so on.

Figure 11-7
CiscoSecure—user
selection.

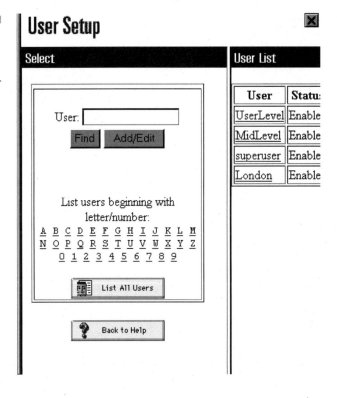

TABLE 11-1	Authentication Object	Methods
AAA authentication command parameters	login	enable
		line
		local
		none
		tacacs+
		radius
	enable	enable
		line
		none
		tacacs+
		radius
	arap	guest
		auth-guest
		line
		local
		tacacs+

TABLE 11-1
(continued)

Authentication Object	Methods
ppp	if-needed
	krb5
	local
	none
	tacacs+
	radius
nasi	enable
	line
	local
	none
	tacacs+

TABLE 11-2

AAA methods

Method	Description
enable	Uses the enable password
line	Uses the password defined on the line
local	Uses the local username/password database
none	Does not do an authentication or authorization check
tacacs+	Uses the TACACS+ server
radius	Uses the RADIUS server
if-needed	PPP only—authenticates if not authenticated already
krb5	PPP only—uses Kerberos 5
if-authenticated	Authorizes operation if user is already authenticated
krb5-instance	Uses the instance defined by the kerberos instance map command
guest	AppleTalk only—allows guest logins without passwords
auth-gues	AppleTalk only—allows guest logins only if the user has already logged in to exec

Figure 11-8
CiscoSecure—user
information and pass-
word setup, part 1.

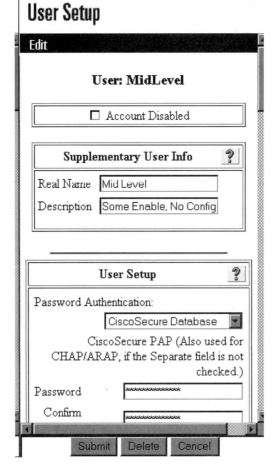

Authorization

The second type of processing is **aaa authorization**. This operation authorizes logged-in users to perform a variety of operations.

The format of the command is as follows:

```
aaa authorization Object method1 method2 method3 method4
```

Table 11-3 defines the operation methods for our authorization objects.

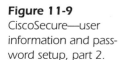

Figure 11-9
CiscoSecure—user
information and pass-
word setup, part 2.

User Setup

checked.)

Password

Confirm
Password

☐ Separate (CHAP/ARAP)

Password

Confirm
Password

When using a Token Card server for
authentication, supplying a separate CHAP
password for a token card user allows
CHAP authentication. This is especially
useful when token caching is enabled.

Group to which the user is assigned:

Group 10

Static
IP
address

Callback string

| Submit | Delete | Cancel |

Accounting

The third type of processing is **aaa accounting**. This feature provides
the means to track logins, exec sessions, command execution, system
operations, and so on.

The format of the command is as follows:

```
aaa accounting Object method format
```

Table 11-4 lists the accounting objects to be tracked, the recording
methods, and the reporting formats. Table 11-5 lists a description for
each recording method.

Figure 11-10
CiscoSecure—user
TACAS+ setup.

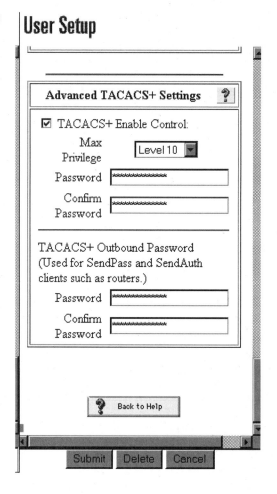

User Setup

Advanced TACACS+ Settings

☑ TACACS+ Enable Control:

Max Privilege   [Level 10 ▼]

Password   ████████████

Confirm Password   ████████████

TACACS+ Outbound Password
(Used for SendPass and SendAuth
clients such as routers.)

Password   ████████████

Confirm Password   ████████████

Back to Help

Submit   Delete   Cancel

EXAMPLE   Back we go to the Cisco AS5200 used in Chapter 8. Instead of using a local database made up of user names and passwords, however, we add the CiscoSecure NT application to the mix. We stick to the basics in this book for Authentication, Authorization, and Accounting. Figure 11-12 shows the equipment layout for the AAA example.

We will authenticate and track two different device types: a network device making a DDR connection, and an individual dial-in user who may need to examine and modify router configurations.

Figure 11-11
CiscoSecure—system control.

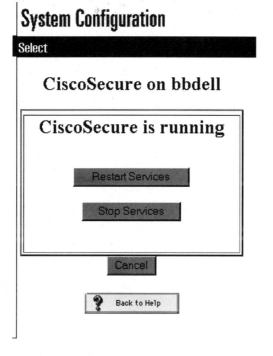

Figure 11-12
AAA equipment layout.

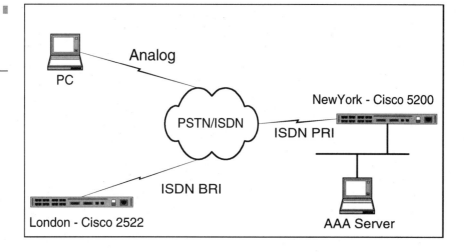

TABLE 11-3
AAA authorization command parameters

Authorization Object	Methods
network (ppp, slip, etc.)	if-authenticated local none radius tacacs+ krb5-instance
exec (start CLI)	if-authenticated local none radius tacacs+ krb5-instance
command *level (0 through 15)*	if-authenticated local none radius tacacs+ krb5-instance

TABLE 11-4
AAA accounting objects

Accounting Option	Recording Method	Reporting Format
command *level (0 through 15)*	start-stop stop-only wait-start	tacacs+ radius
connection (outbound connections such as telnet, rlogin)	start-stop stop-only wait-start	tacacs+ radius
exec	start-stop stop-only wait-start	tacacs+ radius
network (SLIP and PPP)	start-stop stop-only wait-start	tacacs+ radius
system (system-level events such as reload)	start-stop stop-only wait-start	tacacs+ radius

TABLE 11-5

AAA recording method description

Recording Method	Description
start-stop	Records start and stop times for actions and sessions
stop-only	Records stop times only
wait-start	Executes a command only after a command is logged

London

The first device to look at is London, a router with an ISDN connection to NewYork. Code Listing 11-1 shows this configuration.

Unless we have a local TACACS+ server, we still need to use a local username and password database. Line 5 defines the local database.

Lines 12 through 19 define the BRI0 interface as a member of dialer pool 7.

Lines 21 through 32 define the Dialer5 interface, the dialer profile for the NewYork connection. Remember that the access list will only act on through-traffic, but if we test from the router command line, we bypass the **ip access-group 101 out** command.

Code Listing 11-1

```
1    version 12.0
2    !
3    hostname London
4    !
5    username NewYork password 0 cisco
6    !
7    isdn switch-type basic-5ess
8    !
9    interface Ethernet0
10     ip address 172.31.80.1 255.255.255.0
11   !
12   interface BRI0
13     no ip address
14     encapsulation ppp
15     dialer pool-member 7
16     isdn switch-type basic-5ess
17     no cdp enable
18     ppp authentication chap
19     ppp multilink
20   !
21   interface Dialer5
22     ip address 172.31.200.2 255.255.255.0
23     ip access-group 101 out
24     encapsulation ppp
25     dialer remote-name NewYork
26     dialer string 1000
```

```
27   dialer load-threshold 50 outbound
28   dialer pool 7
29   dialer-group 1
30   no cdp enable
31   ppp authentication chap
32   ppp multilink
33   !
34   ip route 172.31.0.0 255.255.0.0 Dialer5 172.31.200.1
35   ip route 192.168.200.0 255.255.255.0 Dialer5 172.31.200.1
36   !
37   access-list 101 permit tcp any host 192.168.200.193 eq telnet
38   access-list 101 deny   ip any any
39   access-list 102 permit tcp any host 172.31.60.1 eq telnet
40   access-list 102 permit icmp any any
41   dialer-list 1 protocol ip list 102
42   !
43   end
```

Now for some testing. Let's **ping** the NewYork Ethernet0 address to see if it works! It does, but the initial connection takes longer, as the AAA authentication requires a server lookup for validating PPP using CHAP:

```
London#ping 192.168.200.193

Type escape sequence to abort.
Sending 5, 100-byte ICMP Echos to 192.168.200.193, timeout is 2 seconds:
...!!
Success rate is 40 percent (2/5), round-trip min/avg/max = 36/56/76 ms
London#
2d14h: %LINK-3-UPDOWN: Interface BRI0:1, changed state to up
2d14h: %DIALER-6-BIND: Interface BRI0:1 bound to profile Dialer5
2d14h: %DIALER-6-BIND: Interface Virtual-Access1 bound to profile Dialer5
2d14h: %LINK-3-UPDOWN: Interface Virtual-Access1, changed state to up
2d14h: %LINEPROTO-5-UPDOWN: Line protocol on Interface BRI0:1, changed state to up
2d14h: %LINEPROTO-5-UPDOWN: Line protocol on Interface Virtual-Access1, changed state to
  up
2d14h: %ISDN-6-CONNECT: Interface BRI0:1 is now connected to 1000 NewYork
```

After 120 seconds of inactivity, the circuit terminates:

```
2d14h: %DIALER-6-UNBIND: Interface Virtual-Access1 unbound from profile Dialer5
2d14h: %LINK-3-UPDOWN: Interface Virtual-Access1, changed state to down
2d14h: %DIALER-6-UNBIND: Interface BRI0:1 unbound from profile Dialer5
2d14h: %ISDN-6-DISCONNECT: Interface BRI0:1  disconnected from 1000 NewYork, call lasted
  125 seconds
2d14h: %LINK-3-UPDOWN: Interface BRI0:1, changed state to down
2d14h: %LINEPROTO-5-UPDOWN: Line protocol on Interface BRI0:1, changed state to down
2d14h: %LINEPROTO-5-UPDOWN: Line protocol on Interface Virtual-Access1, changed state to
  down
```

New York

Now for the central router in this example, New York. Code Listing 11-2 shows this configuration.

Boy, do we start this one with a bang! All the **aaa** commands appear at the beginning of the configuration.

On line 5 the **aaa new-model** command must be entered so that the other **aaa** commands can be entered and processed. When this command is entered, all authentication must be performed within the AAA umbrella.

Line 6 sets up the default operational mode for all undefined login processes. The authentication source is TACACS+.

Line 7 sets up a specific named login process named BACKDOOR. This authentication process must be specified in order to be used and requires the `enable` password for authentication.

For all logged-in users, authentication for the **enable** command will use TACACS+. Line 8 shows this command.

Line 9 defines TACACS+ as the operational method for authenticating incoming PPP connections.

Line 10 will check all attempts to start an `exec` session with the TACACS+ method to verify that the user is permitted to start the session.

Any attempt to execute a level 15 command such as **show running-configuration** will be authorized using the TACACS+ method.

Lines 12 through 14 log all exec sessions, level 15 commands, command-line network operations, and system-level commands using the TACACS+ reporting method. Remember to look in Appendix G for sample reports.

Line 16 is a secret password for level 10 commands.

Line 17 is the standard enable password for level 15 commands. This is the password used for the enable method used in line 7.

Lines 19 through 21 are the local database commands used before AAA was added to the configuration.

Line 83 sets up the pool of local addresses to be assigned to the asynchronous dial-in connections.

Line 85 is the static route on which to send all traffic destined for network 172.31.80.0/24 to the `Dialer1` interface.

Line 88 configures the connection to the TACACS+ server. This connection will establish and maintain a single TCP connection to speed up the TACACS+ operation. The key, `<ciscosecure>`, provides a common encryption key for hiding the contents of the AAA packets as they travel between the NAS and the server.

Lines 92 through 97 are really important for companies that have a need for different levels of privilege commands.

Line 92 sets the privilege level for the configure command to 15, the highest level.

Lines 93 through 95 are the result of entering a single command in the configure mode, **privilege exec level 10 debug ip icmp**. In order for help or ? to operate properly, lines 94 and 95 are generated. After logging in as a level 10 user, if you type in **debug ip ?**, there will be a limited response that includes only those options available for level 10—the icmp option. A console capture later on in this chapter details this operation.

Lines 98 and 99 work the same as above: Only **privilege exec 10 clear line** is entered, generating line 99.

Lines 101 through 106 define the operation of our console port. Line 102 specifically defines the method to be used for logging into the console as BACKDOOR. Recall that line 7 defines BACKDOOR as a login process that uses the enable password that is defined in line 17 as enable15.

Lines 113 through 115 define the operation of the aux port and virtual terminal sessions 0 through 20, vty 0 4 and vty 5 20. You will notice that there is no login authentication method specifically defined. With no method defined, use TACACS+, the default login authentication method shown in line 6.

Throughout NewYork we define CHAP as our dial-in authentication method for PPP connections. Our default is set up on line 9 as TACACS+.

Code Listing 11-2

```
1    version 11.2
2    !
3    hostname NewYork
4    !
5    aaa new-model
6    aaa authentication login default tacacs+
7    aaa authentication login BACKDOOR enable
8    aaa authentication enable default tacacs+
9    aaa authentication ppp default tacacs+
10   aaa authorization exec tacacs+
11   aaa authorization commands 15 tacacs+
12   aaa accounting exec start-stop radius
13   aaa accounting commands 15 start-stop radius
14   aaa accounting network start-stop radius
15   aaa accounting system wait-start radius
16   enable secret level 10 5 $1$P4SR$vzOBEQni9vB8pxpweuFXD1
17   enable password cisco15
18   !
19   username London password 0 cisco
20   username bill password 0 cisco
```

Code Listing 11-2
(continued)

```
21   username SOHO700 password 0 cisco
22   isdn switch-type primary-5ess
23   !
24   controller T1 0
25    framing esf
26    clock source line primary
27    linecode b8zs
28    pri-group timeslots 1-24
29   !
30   interface Loopback0
31    ip address 172.16.1.1 255.255.255.0
32   !
33   interface Loopback1
34    ip address 172.16.2.1 255.255.255.0
35   !
36   interface Ethernet0
37    ip address 192.168.200.193 255.255.255.0
38   !
39   interface Serial0:23
40    no ip address
41    encapsulation ppp
42    no ip mroute-cache
43    isdn incoming-voice modem
44    dialer pool-member 1
45    no fair-queue
46    ppp authentication chap
47    ppp multilink
48   !
49   interface Group-Async1
50    ip unnumbered Loopback0
51    encapsulation ppp
52    autodetect encapsulation ppp
53    async mode interactive
54    peer default ip address pool async-ips
55    ppp authentication chap
56    group-range 1 12
57   !
58   interface Dialer1
59   ip address 172.31.200.1 255.255.255.0
60    encapsulation ppp
61    dialer remote-name London
62    dialer idle-timeout 9999
63    dialer string 2802010
64   dialer pool 1
65    dialer-group 1
66    no fair-queue
67    ppp authentication chap
68    ppp multilink
69    pulse-time 0
70   !
71   interface Dialer5
72    ip address 172.31.201.1 255.255.255.0
73    encapsulation ppp
74    dialer remote-name SOHO700
75    dialer idle-timeout 9999
76    dialer string 2802009
77    dialer pool 1
78    dialer-group 1
```

■ ■

Code Listing 11-2
(continued)

```
79   no fair-queue
80    ppp authentication chap
81    ppp multilink
82   !
83   ip local pool async-ips 192.168.60.2 192.168.60.15
84   ip classless
85   ip route 172.31.70.0 255.255.255.0 Dialer5 172.31.201.2
86   ip route 172.31.80.0 255.255.255.0 Dialer1 172.31.200.2
87   !
88   tacacs-server host 192.168.200.250 single-connection key
     ciscosecure
89   !
90   dialer-list 1 protocol ip permit
91   !
92   privilege exec level 15 configure
93   privilege exec level 10 debug ip icmp
94   privilege exec level 10 debug ip
95   privilege exec level 10 debug
96   privilege exec level 10 clear line
97   privilege exec level 10 clear
98   !
99   line con 0
100    login authentication BACKDOOR
101    exec-timeout 0 0
102    logging synchronous
103    length 0
104    transport input none
105  line 1 12
106    autoselect during-login
107    autoselect ppp
108    modem InOut
109    modem autoconfigure type microcom_hdms
110    transport input all
111  line 13 24
112    transport input all
113  line aux 0
114  line vty 0 4
115  line vty 5 20
116  !
117  end
```

Now for some testing. The first test is a DDR connection from London, our Cisco 2522.

The initial call comes in and B-channel 18 is activated:

```
%LINK-3-UPDOWN: Interface Serial0:18, changed state to up
```

After LCP is active on this new connection, we start CHAP authentication by creating a user on the router and storing the known parameters:

```
AAA/AUTHEN: create_user (0x2A36F4) user='London' ruser=''
  port='Serial0:18' rem_addr='4102802010' authen_type=CHAP
  service=PPP priv=1
```

We then assemble the information we will use to authenticate the CHAP request as TACACS+ and assemble the packet:

```
AAA/AUTHEN/START (897856351): port='Serial0:18' list='' action=LOGIN service=PPP
AAA/AUTHEN/START (897856351): using "default" list
AAA/AUTHEN/START (897856351): Method=TACACS+
```

Now send the authentication packet to the TACACS+ server defined in the server list:

```
TAC+: send AUTHEN/START packet ver=193 id=897856351
TAC+: Using default tacacs server list.
TAC+: 192.168.200.250 (897856351) AUTHEN/START/LOGIN/CHAP queued
```

We haven't used the connection for a while, so we close down the old session and open a fresh one:

```
TAC+: Closing TCP/IP 0x235358 connection to 192.168.200.250/49
TAC+: Opening TCP/IP to 192.168.200.250/49 timeout=5

TAC+: Opened TCP/IP handle 0x2AA4C0 to 192.168.200.250/49
```

The TACACS+ server responds back with the status of the request. We passed authentication!

```
TAC+: (897856351) AUTHEN/START/LOGIN/CHAP processed
TAC+: ver=193 id=897856351 received AUTHEN status = PASS
AAA/AUTHEN (897856351): status = PASS
```

We use dialer profile `Dialer1` and bind `Serial0:18` to continue building an active connection:

```
%DIALER-6-BIND: Interface Serial0:18 bound to profile Dialer1
```

Hello, what have we here? We are authenticating again! Before we can process the activation of the `Dialer1` dialer profile, we must go back to the well and attempt to re-authenticate using a new user tag, (`0x29FC84`):

```
AAA/AUTHEN: create_user (0x29FC84) user='London' ruser='' port='Serial0:18'
   rem_addr='4102802010' authen_type=CHAP service=PPP priv=1
AAA/AUTHEN/START (3777983887): port='Serial0:18' list='' action=SENDAUTH service=PPP
AAA/AUTHEN/START (3777983887): using "default" list
AAA/AUTHEN/START (3777983887): Method=TACACS+
```

```
TAC+: send AUTHEN/START packet ver=193 id=3777983887
TAC+: Using default tacacs server list.
TAC+: 192.168.200.250 (3777983887) AUTHEN/START/SENDAUTH/CHAP queued
TAC+: (3777983887) AUTHEN/START/SENDAUTH/CHAP processed
TAC+: ver=193 id=3777983887 received AUTHEN status = PASS
AAA/AUTHEN (3777983887): status = PASS
```

Man, is this router smart or what? It realizes that this was a duplicate request and frees up the second user request:

```
AAA/AUTHEN: free_user (0x29FC84) user='London' ruser=''
    port='Serial0:18' rem_addr='4102802010' authen_type=CHAP
    service=PPP priv=1
```

One last step before we are finished. When we build this PPP multi-link bundle, we can't use the `Dialer1` interface to establish the connection. Instead, create a `Virtual Access` interface. Look at the following output, which indicates multilink PPP, source='AAA dup mlp':

```
AAA/AUTHEN: dup_user (0x2A048C) user='London' ruser=''
    port='Serial0:18' rem_addr='4102802010' authen_type=CHAP
    service=PPP priv=1 source='AAA dup mlp'
```

Now we can complete the processing to activate the connection to London:

```
%DIALER-6-BIND: Interface Virtual-Access1 bound to profile Dialer1
%LINK-3-UPDOWN: Interface Virtual-Access1, changed state to up
%LINEPROTO-5-UPDOWN: Line protocol on Interface Serial0:18, changed state to up
%LINEPROTO-5-UPDOWN: Line protocol on Interface Virtual-Access1, changed state to up
%ISDN-6-CONNECT: Interface Serial0:18 is now connected to 4102802010 London
```

As the London call is disconnected, we unbind the logical connections and free up the authentications objects used to create the connection:

```
%DIALER-6-UNBIND: Interface Virtual-Access1 unbound from profile Dialer1
%LINK-3-UPDOWN: Interface Virtual-Access1, changed state to down
AAA/AUTHEN: free_user (0x2A048C) user='London' ruser='' port='Serial0:18'
   rem_addr='4102802010' authen_type=CHAP service=PPP priv=1
%ISDN-6-DISCONNECT: Interface Serial0:18  disconnected from 4102802010 London, call lasted
   126 seconds
%LINK-3-UPDOWN: Interface Serial0:18, changed state to down
%DIALER-6-UNBIND: Interface Serial0:18 unbound from profile Dialer1
NewYork#
AAA/AUTHEN: free_user (0x2A36F4) user='London' ruser='' port='Serial0:18'
   rem_addr='4102802010' authen_type=CHAP service=PPP priv=1
%LINEPROTO-5-UPDOWN: Line protocol on Interface Serial0:18, changed state to down
%LINEPROTO-5-UPDOWN: Line protocol on Interface Virtual-Access1, changed state to down
```

There will be three dial-in samples: UserLevel with only user privileges, midlevel with limited privileges, and superuser with full privileges. After we examine the TACACS+ debug output, we will show the actual terminal operations.

Now for the dial-in connections. Don't worry, we will not go into much detail on each connection. We have provided the output for you and highlighted only changes from our last example.

Incoming! Prepare for contingencies; we might get a plain terminal connection, so set up for that possibility. See line 53 in Code Listing 11-2, where we set up for interactive mode on our Group-Async1 interface.

```
AAA/AUTHEN: create_user (0x1DC09C) user='' ruser='' port='tty4' rem_addr='4102801001/
    4102801000' authen_type=ASCII service=LOGIN priv=1
AAA/AUTHEN/START (842890453): port='tty4' list='' action=LOGIN service=LOGIN
AAA/AUTHEN/START (842890453): using "default" list
AAA/AUTHEN/START (842890453): Method=TACACS+
TAC+: send AUTHEN/START packet ver=192 id=842890453
TAC+: Using default tacacs server list.
TAC+: 192.168.200.250 (842890453) AUTHEN/START/LOGIN/ASCII queued
TAC+: (842890453) AUTHEN/START/LOGIN/ASCII processed
TAC+: ver=192 id=842890453 received AUTHEN status = GETUSER
AAA/AUTHEN (842890453): status = GETUSER
```

Shucks, all that work for nothing. A PPP packet came in instead, and PPP was automatically selected, so shut down the asynchronous connection process:

```
AAA/AUTHEN/ABORT: (842890453) because Autoselected.
TAC+: send abort reason=Autoselected
TAC+: 192.168.200.250 (842890453) AUTHEN/CONT queued
TAC+: (842890453) AUTHEN/CONT processed
AAA/AUTHEN: free_user (0x1DC09C) user='' ruser='' port='tty4'
    rem_addr='4102801001/4102801000' authen_type=ASCII service=LOGIN priv=1
```

The physical connection, Async4, gets activated:

```
%LINK-3-UPDOWN: Interface Async4, changed state to up
```

Now we do our CHAP authentication. if it's successful, the interface will be up and running.

```
AAA/AUTHEN: create_user (0x1DBFF8) user='UserLevel' ruser='' port='Async4'
    rem_addr='4102801001/4102801000' authen_type=CHAP service=PPP priv=1
AAA/AUTHEN/START (1152166029): port='Async4' list='' action=LOGIN service=PPP
AAA/AUTHEN/START (1152166029): using "default" list
AAA/AUTHEN/START (1152166029): Method=TACACS+
TAC+: send AUTHEN/START packet ver=193 id=1152166029
TAC+: Using default tacacs server list.
TAC+: 192.168.200.250 (1152166029) AUTHEN/START/LOGIN/CHAP queued
```

```
TAC+: (1152166029) AUTHEN/START/LOGIN/CHAP processed
TAC+: ver=193 id=1152166029 received AUTHEN status = PASS
AAA/AUTHEN (1152166029): status = PASS
%LINEPROTO-5-UPDOWN: Line protocol on Interface Async4, changed state to up
```

CHAP authentication is finished. Now the user has to log in to the router, so we create a blank user for TACACS+ to complete.

First, TACACS+ asks for the user name:

```
AAA/AUTHEN: create_user (0x2AA86C) user='' ruser='' port='tty26' rem_addr='192.168.60.2'
  authen_type=ASCII service=LOGIN priv=1
AAA/AUTHEN/START (3809369991): port='tty26' list='' action=LOGIN service=LOGIN
AAA/AUTHEN/START (3809369991): using "default" list
AAA/AUTHEN/START (3809369991): Method=TACACS+
TAC+: send AUTHEN/START packet ver=192 id=3809369991
TAC+: Using default tacacs server list.
TAC+: 192.168.200.250 (3809369991) AUTHEN/START/LOGIN/ASCII queued
TAC+: (3809369991) AUTHEN/START/LOGIN/ASCII processed
TAC+: ver=192 id=3809369991 received AUTHEN status = GETUSER
AAA/AUTHEN (3809369991): status = GETUSER
AAA/AUTHEN/CONT (3809369991): continue_login (user='(undef)')
AAA/AUTHEN (3809369991): status = GETUSER
AAA/AUTHEN (3809369991): Method=TACACS+
TAC+: send AUTHEN/CONT packet id=3809369991
TAC+: 192.168.200.250 (3809369991) AUTHEN/CONT queued
TAC+: (3809369991) AUTHEN/CONT processed
```

The user name has been entered and sent to TACACS+, which then asks for the password:

```
TAC+: ver=192 id=3809369991 received AUTHEN status = GETPASS
AAA/AUTHEN (3809369991): status = GETPASS
```

User name UserLevel is in place, so retrieve the password and process the request. We get a PASS—we are authenticated, and the PPP connection is up:

```
AAA/AUTHEN/CONT (3809369991): continue_login (user='UserLevel')
AAA/AUTHEN (3809369991): status = GETPASS
AAA/AUTHEN (3809369991): Method=TACACS+
TAC+: send AUTHEN/CONT packet id=3809369991
TAC+: 192.168.200.250 (3809369991) AUTHEN/CONT queued
TAC+: (3809369991) AUTHEN/CONT processed
TAC+: ver=192 id=3809369991 received AUTHEN status = PASS
AAA/AUTHEN (3809369991): status = PASS
```

We are not finished yet. Line 11 in Code Listing 11-2 says we must get an authorization from the TACACS+ server to start an exec session, so when we telnet into the router, we must get authorized:

```
TAC+: Opened 192.168.200.250 index=1
TAC+: 192.168.200.250 (2018451800) AUTHOR/START queued
TAC+: (2018451800) AUTHOR/START processed
TAC+: (2018451800): received author response status = PASS_ADD
```

We made it into the router with our remote dial-in connection, but now we are getting a little bolder and want to get into the privileged mode by entering the **enable** command. TACACS+ gets queried and asks us for the password (we know the user name):

```
AAA/AUTHEN: dup_user (0x2A04D0) user='UserLevel' ruser='' port='tty26'
  rem_addr='192.168.60.2' authen_type=ASCII service=ENABLE priv=15 source='AAA dup
  enable'
AAA/AUTHEN/START (1630671400): port='tty26' list='default' action=LOGIN service=ENABLE
AAA/AUTHEN/START (1630671400): found list default
AAA/AUTHEN/START (1630671400): Method=TACACS+
TAC+: send AUTHEN/START packet ver=192 id=1630671400
TAC+: Opened 192.168.200.250 index=1
TAC+: 192.168.200.250 (1630671400) AUTHEN/START/LOGIN/ASCII queued
TAC+: (1630671400) AUTHEN/START/LOGIN/ASCII processed
TAC+: ver=192 id=1630671400 received AUTHEN status = GETPASS
AAA/AUTHEN (1630671400): status = GETPASS
```

We will check the password associated with UserLevel. Unfortunately UserLevel is limited to privilege level 1, the user mode, and fails authentication:

```
AAA/AUTHEN/CONT (1630671400): continue_login (user='UserLevel')
AAA/AUTHEN (1630671400): status = GETPASS
AAA/AUTHEN (1630671400): Method=TACACS+
TAC+: send AUTHEN/CONT packet id=1630671400
TAC+: 192.168.200.250 (1630671400) AUTHEN/CONT queued
TAC+: (1630671400) AUTHEN/CONT processed
TAC+: ver=192 id=1630671400 received AUTHEN status = FAIL
AAA/AUTHEN (1630671400): status = FAIL
AAA/AUTHEN: free_user (0x2A04D0) user='UserLevel' ruser=''
  port='tty26' rem_addr='192.168.60.2' authen_type=ASCII
  service=ENABLE priv=15
```

Let's try that again with a different dial-in user, midlevel. Oops, check the password—it must be incorrect, because we had a failure to communicate:

```
AAA/AUTHEN: create_user (0x2AE0EC) user='' ruser='' port='tty26' rem_addr='192.168.60.2'
    authen_type=ASCII service=LOGIN priv=1
AAA/AUTHEN/START (2964792910): port='tty26' list='default' action=LOGIN service=LOGIN
AAA/AUTHEN/START (2964792910): found list default
AAA/AUTHEN/START (2964792910): Method=TACACS+
TAC+: send AUTHEN/START packet ver=192 id=2964792910
TAC+: Using default tacacs server list.
TAC+: 192.168.200.250 (2964792910) AUTHEN/START/LOGIN/ASCII queued
TAC+: (2964792910) AUTHEN/START/LOGIN/ASCII processed
TAC+: ver=192 id=2964792910 received AUTHEN status = GETUSER
AAA/AUTHEN (2964792910): status = GETUSER
AAA/AUTHEN/CONT (2964792910): continue_login (user='(undef)')
AAA/AUTHEN (2964792910): status = GETUSER
AAA/AUTHEN (2964792910): Method=TACACS+
TAC+: send AUTHEN/CONT packet id=2964792910
TAC+: 192.168.200.250 (2964792910) AUTHEN/CONT queued
TAC+: (2964792910) AUTHEN/CONT processed
TAC+: ver=192 id=2964792910 received AUTHEN status = GETPASS
AAA/AUTHEN (2964792910): status = GETPASS
AAA/AUTHEN/CONT (2964792910): continue_login (user='midlevel')
AAA/AUTHEN (2964792910): status = GETPASS
AAA/AUTHEN (2964792910): Method=TACACS+
TAC+: send AUTHEN/CONT packet id=2964792910
TAC+: 192.168.200.250 (2964792910) AUTHEN/CONT queued
TAC+: (2964792910) AUTHEN/CONT processed
TAC+: ver=192 id=2964792910 received AUTHEN status = FAIL
AAA/AUTHEN (2964792910): status = FAIL
AAA/AUTHEN: free_user (0x2AE0EC) user='midlevel' ruser='' port='tty26'
    rem_addr='192.168.60.2' authen_type=ASCII service=LOGIN priv=1
```

Let's try that again, being a little more careful with our typing:

```
AAA/AUTHEN: create_user (0x2AE6EC) user='' ruser='' port='tty26' rem_addr='192.168.60.2'
    authen_type=ASCII service=LOGIN priv=1
AAA/AUTHEN/START (3871805537): port='tty26' list='default' action=LOGIN service=LOGIN
AAA/AUTHEN/START (3871805537): found list default
AAA/AUTHEN/START (3871805537): Method=TACACS+
TAC+: send AUTHEN/START packet ver=192 id=3871805537
TAC+: Using default tacacs server list.
TAC+: 192.168.200.250 (3871805537) AUTHEN/START/LOGIN/ASCII queued
TAC+: (3871805537) AUTHEN/START/LOGIN/ASCII processed
TAC+: ver=192 id=3871805537 received AUTHEN status = GETUSER
AAA/AUTHEN (3871805537): status = GETUSER
NewYork#
AAA/AUTHEN/CONT (3871805537): continue_login (user='(undef)')
AAA/AUTHEN (3871805537): status = GETUSER
AAA/AUTHEN (3871805537): Method=TACACS+
TAC+: send AUTHEN/CONT packet id=3871805537
TAC+: 192.168.200.250 (3871805537) AUTHEN/CONT queued
TAC+: (3871805537) AUTHEN/CONT processed
TAC+: ver=192 id=3871805537 received AUTHEN status = GETPASS
AAA/AUTHEN (3871805537): status = GETPASS
AAA/AUTHEN/CONT (3871805537): continue_login (user='midlevel')
AAA/AUTHEN (3871805537): status = GETPASS
AAA/AUTHEN (3871805537): Method=TACACS+
TAC+: send AUTHEN/CONT packet id=3871805537
TAC+: 192.168.200.250 (3871805537) AUTHEN/CONT queued
```

```
TAC+: (3871805537) AUTHEN/CONT processed
TAC+: ver=192 id=3871805537 received AUTHEN status = PASS
AAA/AUTHEN (3871805537): status = PASS
TAC+: Opened 192.168.200.250 index=1
TAC+: 192.168.200.250 (1988629917) AUTHOR/START queued
TAC+: (1988629917) AUTHOR/START processed
TAC+: (1988629917): received author response status = PASS_ADD
```

Last one—the sequence for superuser:

```
AAA/AUTHEN: create_user (0x2AA8B0) user='' ruser='' port='tty26' rem_addr='192.168.60.2'
   authen_type=ASCII service=LOGIN priv=1
AAA/AUTHEN/START (2517904094): port='tty26' list='default' action=LOGIN service=LOGIN
AAA/AUTHEN/START (2517904094): found list default
AAA/AUTHEN/START (2517904094): Method=TACACS+
TAC+: send AUTHEN/START packet ver=192 id=2517904094
TAC+: Using default tacacs server list.
TAC+: 192.168.200.250 (2517904094) AUTHEN/START/LOGIN/ASCII queued
TAC+: (2517904094) AUTHEN/START/LOGIN/ASCII processed
TAC+: ver=192 id=2517904094 received AUTHEN status = GETUSER
AAA/AUTHEN (2517904094): status = GETUSER
AAA/AUTHEN/CONT (2517904094): continue_login (user='(undef)')
AAA/AUTHEN (2517904094): status = GETUSER
AAA/AUTHEN (2517904094): Method=TACACS+
TAC+: send AUTHEN/CONT packet id=2517904094
TAC+: 192.168.200.250 (2517904094) AUTHEN/CONT queued
TAC+: (2517904094) AUTHEN/CONT processed
TAC+: ver=192 id=2517904094 received AUTHEN status = GETPASS
AAA/AUTHEN (2517904094): status = GETPASS
AAA/AUTHEN/CONT (2517904094): continue_login (user='superuser')
AAA/AUTHEN (2517904094): status = GETPASS
AAA/AUTHEN (2517904094): Method=TACACS+
TAC+: send AUTHEN/CONT packet id=2517904094
TAC+: 192.168.200.250 (2517904094) AUTHEN/CONT queued
TAC+: (2517904094) AUTHEN/CONT processed
TAC+: ver=192 id=2517904094 received AUTHEN status = PASS
AAA/AUTHEN (2517904094): status = PASS
TAC+: Opened 192.168.200.250 index=1
TAC+: 192.168.200.250 (1070043337) AUTHOR/START queued
TAC+: (1070043337) AUTHOR/START processed
TAC+: (1070043337): received author response status = PASS_ADD
AAA/AUTHEN: free_user (0x2AE6EC) user='midlevel' ruser='' port='tty26'
   rem_addr='192.168.60.2' authen_type=ASCII service=LOGIN priv=1
NewYork#
```

Exec-Level Testing

We've seen what the router does in the background. Now it's time to take a look at what happens from the dial-in side.

When we open up a new telnet session, we log in with our user name and password:

```
User Access Verification

Username: UserLevel
Password:
```

We can execute user-level commands such as **who** with no problems. Look Ma, I can see myself (tty4):

```
NewYork>who
      Line       User       Host(s)                      Idle Location
    0 con 0    superuser idle                           2d14h
    4 tty 4    UserLevel Async interface              00:00:00
  * 26 vty 0   UserLevel idle                         00:00:00 192.168.60.2
    Vi2        London     Virtual PPP (Bundle) 00:00:03
    Se0:22     London     Sync PPP                   00:00:03
```

When we enter **enable**, we get asked for a password. Even if we know a good password, we are not set up for privileged operations as User-Level, and so get rejected:

```
NewYork>enable
Password:
% Error in authentication.
```

Let's switch to a different user, midlevel. Recall that when we set up our TACACS+ database for midlevel, we limited the commands we could process to privilege level 10.

```
NewYork>login

User Access Verification

Username: midlevel
Password:
```

Hold on—we went directly to the privilege level (NewYork#), did not pass go, did not collect our $200 dollars. Show me the privilege level. It's level 10, just like we defined. When a special privilege level is set up in TACACS+ (see Figure 11-6) with limited commands, a user set to that level is automatically logged in at that level:

```
NewYork#show privilege
Current privilege level is 10
```

If we have logged in at level 10, then we should have limited access to the privileged commands. Let's try **debug**. Lines 93 through 95 set up debugging for ICMP packets but nothing else. When we enter **debug ?**, there are only three options shown; one of them is ip.

NOTE *Although I have not found any documentation that defines the privilege level of* exec *commands, it is obvious in the debug output that there is a differentiation internally in the Cisco IOS. To the best of my knowledge there are four default levels: 0—ready for login, 1—user level, 12—limited-privilege level, 15—full-privilege level.*

```
NewYork#debug ?
  ip     IP information
  ncia   Native Client Interface Architecture (NCIA) events
  tdm    TDM connection information
```

Continuing with **debug ip ?**, we see that there is only one option authorized for level 10 users, icmp:

```
NewYork#debug ip ?
  icmp  ICMP transactions
```

Does it really accept the command? Yes, it does:

```
NewYork#debug ip icmp
ICMP packet debugging is on
```

We can try some other **debug** commands, but it doesn't look like they will be successful:

```
NewYork#debug ip routing
                 ^
% Invalid input detected at '^' marker.

NewYork#debug dialer
              ^
% Invalid input detected at '^' marker.
```

The other command authorized for level 10 is the **clear line** command. Let's verify that this also works. It does:

```
NewYork#clear ?
  line  Reset a terminal line
  ncia  Native Client Interface Architecture (NCIA)

NewYork#clear line ?
  <0-46>   Line number
  aux      Auxiliary line
  console  Primary terminal line
  tty      Terminal controller
  vty      Virtual terminal

NewYork#clear line aux 0
[confirm]
  [OK]
```

Now let's drop back to the user level using the **disable** command and log back in as superuser:

```
NewYork#disable
NewYork>show privilege
Current privilege level is 1
NewYork>login

User Access Verification

Username: superuser
Password:
```

Right in at level 15, let's go for the jugular up front, and enter **debug ?**. Yes indeedy, folks, it's all there:

```
NewYork#show privilege
Current privilege level is 15
NewYork#debug ?
  aaa                AAA Authentication, Authorization and Accounting
  access-expression  Boolean access expression
  all                Enable all debugging
  arp                IP ARP and HP Probe transactions
.
. Output deleted for clarity
.
  v120               V120 information
  vpdn               VPDN information
  vtemplate          Virtual Template information
  x25                X.25 information
```

Summary

This was a fun chapter. We set up an external server to provide Authentication, Authorization, and Accounting (remember Appendix G) for our network. By maintaining the information in a central location, users can log into the network at any access point and have consistent secure operations.

12

Protocol
Translation

This chapter deals with a somewhat arcane function, the translation of terminal sessions between X.25, LAT, and TCP/IP. There are two methods for providing these translations: two-step and one-step. The two-step method is a manual process for end-to-end connectivity, and the one-step method provides an automatic translation path from end to end.

As we delve into the world of protocol translation, it is important to realize that the examples in this chapter are fairly basic but representative of the technique to use when connecting legacy network terminals into newer servers, and vice versa.

The two-step protocol translation is not covered in any detail because it is inherent in the Cisco routers and access servers to string together two single-step connections to create an end-to-end terminal session. Use the X.25 **pad** command to establish an X.25 terminal connection from A to B. Then, at the command prompt, use the **telnet** command to establish a TCP/IP connection from B to C. The end result is what looks like a terminal session from A to C. However, the two-step protocol translation between X.25 and TCP/IP takes place in device B. There are no configuration commands required to make this happen as there would be in a one-step protocol translation.

Figure 12-1 shows the equipment layout for the one-step protocol translation example.

London and Paris are connected through an X.25 switch and a shared Ethernet segment, and NewYork and Paris are connected over an HDLC point-to-point link.

Each of the configurations are listed below with **debug** output, show output, and the actual tests following each router's configuration.

Figure 12-1
Protocol translation—
equipment layout.

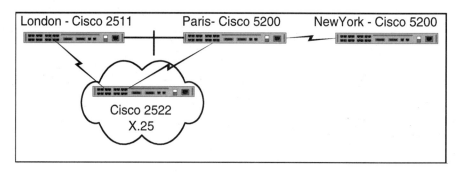

X.25 Switch

Code Listing 12-1 shows the configuration for the X25 switch. Please refer to the X.25 section in Chapter 9 for more details.

The only line that is significant is line 30. An extra route has been added, defining the route to reach X.121 address 311010100103. This is the target address for one of our one-step protocol translations.

Code Listing 12-1

```
1   version 12.0
2   !
3   hostname X25Switch
4   !
5   enable password cisco
6   !
7   ip subnet-zero
8   x25 routing
9   !
10  interface Ethernet0
11   ip address 192.168.200.196 255.255.255.0
12  !
13  interface Serial0
14   no ip address
15   encapsulation x25 dce
16   clockrate 64000
17  !
18  interface Serial1
19   no ip address
20   encapsulation x25 dce
21   clockrate 64000
22  !
23  x25 route 311010100101 interface Serial0
24  x25 route 311010100102 interface Serial1
25  x25 route 311010100103 interface Serial1
26  !
27  end
```

To verify the X.25 routes, use the **show x25 route** command:

```
X25Switch#show x25 route
    #  Match                    Substitute        Route to
    1  dest 311010100101                          Serial0
    2  dest 311010100102                          Serial1
    3  dest 311010100103                          Serial1
X25Switch#
```

London

London has a fairly straightforward configuration, as shown in Code Listing 12-2. This device is being used for terminal services.

Note that line 7 sets up a local DNS resolution for communicating to NewYork by name. Lines 30 and 31 set up names for X.25 connections to targets across the X.25 cloud.

▪ ▪

Code Listing 12-2

```
1    version 12.0
2    !
3    hostname London
4    !
5    enable password cisco
6    !
7    ip host TCPNewYork 172.31.160.1
8    !
9    interface Loopback0
10    ip address 172.31.110.1 255.255.255.0
11    !
12   interface Ethernet0
13    ip address 172.31.100.1 255.255.255.0
14    !
15   interface Serial1
16    ip address 172.31.150.1 255.255.255.0
17    no ip directed-broadcast
18    encapsulation x25
19    no ip mroute-cache
20    x25 address 311010100101
21    x25 win 7
22    x25 wout 7
23    x25 ips 1024
24    x25 ops 1024
25    x25 map ip 172.31.150.2 311010100102 broadcast
26    !
27   router eigrp 100
28    network 172.31.0.0
29    !
30   x25 host X25Paris 311010100102
31   x25 host X25NewYork 311010100103
32    !
33   end
```

Use the **pad** command to connect to NewYork, and then use the escape sequence to return to London:

```
London#pad X25NewYork
Trying 311010100103...Open

User Access Verification

Password:
NewYork>
```

Use the **pad** command to connect to Paris, and then use the escape sequence to return to London:

```
London#pad X25Paris

Trying 311010100102...Open

User Access Verification

Password:
Paris>
<ctrl+shft+6> x .............escape sequence
```

The **who** command shows us incoming connections and suspended outgoing connections from the console port. Someone out there has connected to London:

```
London#who
      Line      User      Host(s)                Idle Location
*   0 con 0               X25NewYork         00:00:49
                          X25Paris           00:00:30
     18 vty 0             idle               00:02:13 172.31.100.2
     19 vty 1             idle               00:01:21 311010100102
```

The **where** command identifies active remote terminal sessions:

```
London#where
Conn Host               Address        Byte  Idle Conn Name
    1 X25NewYork                           0     0 X25NewYork
*   2 X25Paris                             0     0 X25Paris
```

NewYork

NewYork is another router being used for its terminal services. Code Listing 12-3 shows its configuration.

Code Listing 12-3

```
1    version 12.0
2    !
3    hostname NewYork
4    !
5    enable password cisco
6    !
7    ip subnet-zero
8    no ip domain-lookup
9    !
```

```
10  interface Loopback0
11  ip address 172.31.130.1 255.255.255.0
12  !
13  interface Ethernet0
14   ip address 172.31.50.1 255.255.255.0
15  !
16  interface Serial0
17   ip address 172.31.160.1 255.255.255.0
18   lat enabled
19  !
20  router eigrp 100
21   passive-interface Ethernet0
22   network 172.31.0.0
23  !
24  end
```

In NewYork, we will use the ability to operate with DEC's Local Area Transport (LAT) protocol. Use the **show lat advertised** command to check out which LAT services are being advertised:

```
NewYork#show lat adv
Service Name            Rating      Rotary   Flags
LAT-LONDON              4(Dynamic)  None
```

Let's use the **lat** command to connect a terminal session to London using the advertised service LAT-LONDON:

```
NewYork#lat LAT-LONDON
Trying LAT-LONDON...Open
Trying 172.31.110.1 ... Open


User Access Verification

Password:
London>
```

While we are connected to London, let's use the **show tcp** command to take a look at the active TCP connections, then escape back to NewYork:

```
London>show tcp
Stand-alone TCP connection from host 172.31.100.2
Connection state is TIMEWAIT, I/O status: 1, unread input bytes: 1
Local host: 172.31.110.1, Local port: 23
Foreign host: 172.31.100.2, Foreign port: 64539

Enqueued packets for retransmit: 0, input: 0  mis-ordered: 0 (0 bytes)

Event Timers (current time is 0x6A6CEC):
```

```
Timer           Starts     Wakeups         Next
Retrans           14          0            0x0
TimeWait           2          0            0x6AE2A0
AckHold           21          8            0x0
SendWnd            0          0            0x0
KeepAlive          0          0            0x0
GiveUp             0          0            0x0
PmtuAger           0          0            0x0
DeadWait           0          0            0x0

iss: 3640343016   snduna: 3640343134   sndnxt: 3640343134     sndwnd: 4012
irs: 3280867432   rcvnxt: 3280867494   rcvwnd:        4068  delrcvwnd: 60
```

SRTT: 408 ms, RTTO: 2346 ms, RTV: 765 ms, KRTT: 0 ms minRTT: 8 ms, maxRTT: 300 ms, ACK
   hold: 200 ms
Flags: passive open, higher precedence, retransmission timeout closed

Datagrams (max data segment is 1460 bytes):
Rcvd: 35 (out of order: 0), with data: 24, total data bytes: 60
Sent: 30 (retransmit: 0), with data: 19, total data bytes: 116

tty18, virtual tty from host 172.31.100.2
Connection state is ESTAB, I/O status: 1, unread input bytes: 0
Local host: 172.31.110.1, Local port: 23
Foreign host: 172.31.100.2, Foreign port: 65051

Enqueued packets for retransmit: 0, input: 0 mis-ordered: 0 (0 bytes)

```
Event Timers (current time is 0x6A7A6C):
Timer           Starts     Wakeups         Next
Retrans           16          0            0x6A82CD
TimeWait           0          0            0x0
AckHold           18          4            0x0
SendWnd            0          0            0x0
KeepAlive          0          0            0x0
GiveUp             0          0            0x0
PmtuAger           0          0            0x0
DeadWait           0          0            0x0

iss: 3672525474   snduna: 3672527569   sndnxt: 3672527569     sndwnd: 3685
irs: 3313049400   rcvnxt: 3313049456   rcvwnd:        4073  delrcvwnd: 55
```

SRTT: 372 ms, RTTO: 1821 ms, RTV: 538 ms, KRTT: 0 ms minRTT: 4 ms, maxRTT: 300 ms, ACK
   hold: 200 ms
Flags: passive open, higher precedence, retransmission timeout

Datagrams (max data segment is 1460 bytes):
Rcvd: 37 (out of order: 0), with data: 22, total data bytes: 55
Sent: 26 (retransmit: 0), with data: 21, total data bytes: 2094
London>
<ctrl+shft+6> x ....escape sequence

Now we **telnet** to London, log in, and then escape back to NewYork:

```
NewYork#telnet 172.31.120.2
Trying 172.31.120.2 ... Open


User Access Verification

Password:
London>
<ctrl+shft+6> x .............escape sequence
```

Let's use the **who** and **where** commands to check out incoming and outgoing terminal sessions:

```
NewYork#who
     Line      User      Host(s)                 Idle Location
*    0 con 0             LAT-LONDON         00:01:27
                         172.31.120.2       00:00:02
    26 vty 0             idle               00:04:02 172.31.160.2
NewYork#where
Conn Host                Address           Byte  Idle Conn Name
     1 LAT-LONDON                             0     1 LAT-LONDON
*    2 172.31.120.2      172.31.120.2         0     0 172.31.120.2

NewYork#
```

Paris

Now for Paris, where all the translations take place. Code Listing 12-4 shows the configuration for Paris.

There are two special areas in this configuration: one where we set up advertising for LAT services, and one where we define the translation processes.

Lines 35 and 36 define the LAT service name and service advertising.

Lines 38 through 40 define the one-step protocol translations.

Line 38 translates an incoming X.25 PAD request to a TCP telnet connection to 172.31.160.1, NewYork. This matches our testing from London, where a pad connection to X.121 address 311010100103 resulted in a console connection to NewYork. Without the `printer` option, X.25-to-TCP translations are really two separate protocol sessions mapped together. With the `printer` option in place, a single end-to-end session is built.

Line 39 translates an incoming TCP telnet connection to IP address 172.31.120.2 to an X.25 PAD connection to 311010100101. How does the router respond to a connection request for IP address 172.31.120.2? This IP address is on the same subnet as our Loopback 0 interface, so the router knows how to reach the network and respond to ARP requests using proxy ARP.

Line 40 is the last translation. An incoming request for a LAT connection to LAT-LONDON is translated into a TCP telnet request for 172.31.110.1, London. No `printer` option is required; LAT-to-TCP translations always build an end-to-end session.

Code Listing 12-4

```
1    version 12.0
2    !
3    hostname Paris
4    !
5    enable password cisco
6    !
7    ip host TCPNewYork 172.31.160.1
8    !
9    interface Loopback0
10    ip address 172.31.120.1 255.255.255.0
11   !
12   interface Ethernet0
13    ip address 172.31.100.2 255.255.255.0
14   !
15   interface Serial0
16    ip address 172.31.160.2 255.255.255.0
17    lat enabled
18    no fair-queue
19    clockrate 64000
20   !
21   interface Serial1
22    ip address 172.31.150.2 255.255.255.0
23    encapsulation x25
24    no ip mroute-cache
25    x25 address 311010100102
26    x25 win 7
27    x25 wout 7
28    x25 ips 1024
29    x25 ops 1024
30    x25 map ip 172.31.150.1 311010100101 broadcast
31   !
32   router eigrp 100
33    network 172.31.0.0
34   !
35   lat node-name LAT-LONDON
36   lat service-responder
37   !
38   translate x25 311010100103 printer tcp 172.31.160.1 quiet
39   translate tcp 172.31.120.2 printer x25 311010100101 quiet
40   translate lat LAT-LONDON tcp 172.31.110.1
41   !
42   end
```

The **who** and **where** commands show us no active local connections, so the incoming requests and outgoing requests do not use local terminal services:

```
Paris#who
    Line      User      Host(s)                    Idle Location
*  0 con 0              idle              00:00:00

Paris#where
% No connections open
```

Now we turn on **debug translate** and watch a translation request come in for X.25 address 311010100103:

```
Paris#debug translate
Protocol Translation debugging is on
Paris#
01:48:09: PAD: translate call to 311010100103
01:48:09:    Call User Data (4): 0x01000000 (pad)
01:48:09: padtcp26: fork started
01:48:09: PADTCP26: Telnet received WILL ECHO (1)
01:48:09: PADTCP26: Telnet received DO TTY-TYPE (24)
01:48:09: PADTCP26: Telnet received DONT TTY-LOCATION (23)
01:48:09: PADTCP26: Telnet received DONT TTY-SPEED (32)
```

The **show translate** command shows us the translations configured on Paris, and the current statistics for active translations:

```
Paris#show translate

Translate From: X25 311010100103
               printer
       To:   TCP 172.31.160.1 Port 23
       Quiet
       1/0 users active, 1 peak, 3 total, 0 failures

Translate From: TCP 172.31.120.2 Port 23 Printer
       To:   X25 311010100101
       Quiet
       0/0 users active, 1 peak, 1 total, 0 failures

Translate From: LAT LAT-LONDON
       To:   TCP 172.31.110.1 Port 23
       0/0 users active, 1 peak, 1 total, 0 failures
```

Now let's look at the **debug translate** output for an incoming LAT request for LAT-LONDON into a telnet:

```
Paris#debug translate

Protocol Translation debugging is on

01:49:30: LAT: Host delay = 4 tics
01:49:30: LAT: Got new inbound host connection
01:49:30: LAT27: created new inbound session
01:49:30: lattcp27: fork 66 started
```

Sure enough, when we look at our translations with the **show translate** command, we see that there is an active session for LAT-LONDON:

```
Paris#show translate

Translate From: X25 311010100103
               printer
       To:     TCP 172.31.160.1 Port 23
       Quiet
       1/0 users active, 1 peak, 3 total, 0 failures

Translate From: TCP 172.31.120.2 Port 23 Printer
       To:     X25 311010100101
       Quiet
       0/0 users active, 1 peak, 1 total, 0 failures

Translate From: LAT LAT-LONDON
       To:     TCP 172.31.110.1 Port 23
       1/0 users active, 1 peak, 3 total, 0 failures
```

Now for our last translation, an incoming TCP connection translated to an X.25 connection:

```
01:51:10: tcppad28: fork started
01:51:10: tcppad28: Sending WILL ECHO
```

Check it out with the **show translate** command. We now have one active session for each of our translations:

```
Paris#show translate

Translate From: X25 311010100103
               printer
       To:     TCP 172.31.160.1 Port 23
       Quiet
```

```
        1/0 users active, 1 peak, 3 total, 0 failures

Translate From: TCP 172.31.120.2 Port 23 Printer
           To:    X25 311010100101
           Quiet
           1/0 users active, 1 peak, 2 total, 0 failures

Translate From: LAT LAT-LONDON
           To:   TCP 172.31.110.1 Port 23
           1/0 users active, 1 peak, 3 total, 0 failures
```

The **who** command shows the termination of our translation sessions:

```
Paris#who
     Line      User       Host(s)                 Idle Location
*   0 con 0               idle                  00:00:00
   26 vty 0               TCPNewYork            00:04:11 311010100101
   27 vty 1               172.31.110.1          00:02:03 NEWYORK
   28 vty 2               311010100101          00:01:11 TCPNewYork
   29 vty 3               idle                  00:00:24 311010100101
```

Summary

In this chapter, we explored the protocol translation process for terminal services. Two-step protocol translation requires manual connections to be established through an intermediate device. Instead of manually entering this information every time a mismatched protocol connection is established, automate the connection using a one-step protocol translation. Remember, one-step protocol translation requires two commands, one in each direction.

Network
Address
Translation

In this chapter, we will look at the process that delayed the implementation of IPv6, Network Address Translation (NAT). NAT permits the use of private class addresses 10.0.0.0, 172.16.0.0 through 172.31.0.0, and 192.168.0.0 through 192.168.255.0 inside the local network but communicates outside our local network over the internet with a global address.

There are four terms used in NAT that we must understand before we look into the configuration of the Cisco routers:

- inside: A device is inside if it is physically connected to a network defined by applying the **ip nat inside** command to an interface on the NAT translation device.

- outside: A device is outside if it is physically connected to a network defined by applying the **ip nat outside** command to an interface on the NAT translation device.

- local: A local address is used between inside and outside devices to communicate in the NAT *Inside* space.

- global: A global address is used between inside and outside devices to communicate in the NAT *Outside* space.

EXAMPLE

Figure 13-1 shows the NAT equipment layout example and indicates the logical location of each of the four terms defined above. For those of you who have taken Cisco's CMTD or BCRAN courses, this may look familiar, as it is the dreaded overlapping IP address slide come to life. A room full of instructors and Cisco folks spent two hours going over this example before they agreed it was correct. The DNS component threw us I think. (Yes, I was there.)

A quick note on our network layout: The NAT router is connected on one side to the *Inside* network, and connected through a neutral network to the *Outside* network. This is a normal situation when using NAT to connect two overlapping networks.

In this example, we have two companies that have merged together, and both companies' networks are using the same private address space, network 10.0.0.0. The company on the *Outside* has services that need to be used by the *Inside* company. The target server we wish to reach is Rome, defined on our DNS server as address 10.2.2.2. Address 10.2.2.2 is the IP address on the loopback0 interface defined in the OUTSIDE2 router. The problem is that the workstation connected to the Ethernet0 interface also has the same IP address, 10.2.2.2.

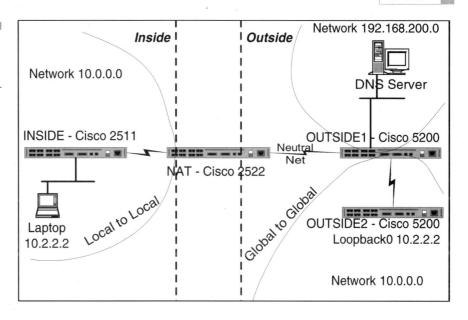

Figure 13-1
NAT terminology and
equipment layout.

INSIDE

This fairly simple configuration, shown in Code Listing 13-1, is for our INSIDE router.

Lines 5 and 6 are probably the most important, as they set up the router, INSIDE, to use a DNS server located on the *Outside*. Please forgive the billburton.net, but I have a DNS server set up for my local lab, and it was just easier to use it. The workstation with IP address 10.2.2.2 is connected to the Ethernet0 interface.

Code Listing 13-1

```
1    version 11.3
2    !
3    hostname INSIDE
4    !
5    ip domain-name billburton.net
6    ip name-server 192.168.200.6
7    !
8    interface Ethernet0
9      ip address 10.2.2.1 255.255.255.0
10   !
11   interface Serial0
12     ip address 10.1.1.1 255.255.255.0
13   !
14   router rip
15     network 10.0.0.0
16   !
17   end
```

The **show ip route** command will show us if there is a route to the *Outside* network. There sure is:

```
INSIDE#show ip route
Codes: C - connected, S - static, I - IGRP, R - RIP, M - mobile, B - BGP
       D - EIGRP, EX - EIGRP external, O - OSPF, IA - OSPF inter area
       N1 - OSPF NSSA external type 1, N2 - OSPF NSSA external type 2
       E1 - OSPF external type 1, E2 - OSPF external type 2, E - EGP
       i - IS-IS, L1 - IS-IS level-1, L2 - IS-IS level-2, * - candidate default
       U - per-user static route, o - ODR

Gateway of last resort is 10.1.1.2 to network 0.0.0.0

     10.0.0.0/24 is subnetted, 2 subnets
C       10.1.1.0 is directly connected, Serial0
C       10.2.2.0 is directly connected, Ethernet0
R*   0.0.0.0/0 [120/4] via 10.1.1.2, 00:00:12, Serial0
```

If we **ping** Rome, we will be able to reach our target. The **debug nat translation** command output later in this chapter will show how this operates.

```
INSIDE#ping Rome
Translating "Rome"...domain server (192.168.200.6) [OK]
Translating "Rome"...domain server (192.168.200.6) [OK]

Type escape sequence to abort.
Sending 5, 100-byte ICMP Echos to 192.168.3.2, timeout is 2 seconds:
!!!!!
Success rate is 100 percent (5/5), round-trip min/avg/max = 32/39/64 ms
```

OUTSIDE1

OUTSIDE1 is the router connected to the NAT router by the neutral network. Code Listing 13-2 shows the configuration. This router has quite a few interesting components.

Lines 5 and 6 set up our DNS configuration.

Lines 8 and 9 are the connection to the network where the DNS server is located.

Lines 11 through 14 set up our connection to the router OUTSIDE2.

Lines 16 and 17 set up Serial1, our connection through the neutral network to our address translation router, NAT.

Lines 19 through 21 set up the RIP routing protocol to feed routing updates to our server network, including the DNS server. In order for the DNS server to reach all of our networks, we have to redistribute IGRP into RIP.

Lines 23 to 27 set up the IGRP routing protocol used in the balance of the *Outside* network. We redistribute the static route defined in line 29 into IGRP so traffic can return to the *Inside* network.

Line 29 is a static route through the neutral network to 192.168.2.0/24, the network being used by NAT to represent the *Inside* network to the *Outside* network.

Code Listing 13-2

```
1    version 11.2
2    !
3    hostname OUTSIDE1
4    !
5    ip domain-name billburton.net
6    ip name-server 192.168.200.6
7    !
8    interface Ethernet0
9     ip address 192.168.200.193 255.255.255.0
10   !
11   interface Serial0
12    ip address 10.1.1.1 255.255.255.0
13    no fair-queue
14    clockrate 2000000
15   !
16   interface Serial1
17    ip address 172.16.1.1 255.255.255.0
18   !
19   router rip
20    redistribute igrp 100 metric 3
21    network 192.168.200.0
22   !
23   router igrp 100
24    redistribute static
25    network 10.0.0.0
26    network 192.168.200.0
27    default-metric 56 200000 255 1 1500
28   !
29   ip route 192.168.2.0 255.255.255.0 Serial1 172.16.1.2
30   !
31   end
```

The **show ip route** command verifies that we have valid routes to all the networks:

```
OUTSIDE1#show ip route
Codes: C - connected, S - static, I - IGRP, R - RIP, M - mobile, B - BGP
       D - EIGRP, EX - EIGRP external, O - OSPF, IA - OSPF inter area
       N1 - OSPF NSSA external type 1, N2 - OSPF NSSA external type 2
       E1 - OSPF external type 1, E2 - OSPF external type 2, E - EGP
       i - IS-IS, L1 - IS-IS level-1, L2 - IS-IS level-2, * - candidate default
       U - per-user static route, o - ODR

Gateway of last resort is not set
```

```
       10.0.0.0/24 is subnetted, 2 subnets
I         10.2.2.0 [100/8976] via 10.1.1.2, 00:00:32, Serial0
C         10.1.1.0 is directly connected, Serial0
S      192.168.2.0/24 [1/0] via 172.16.1.2, Serial1
C      192.168.200.0/24 is directly connected, Ethernet0
       172.16.0.0/24 is subnetted, 1 subnets
C         172.16.1.0 is directly connected, Serial1
```

OUTSIDE2

OUTSIDE2 is at the far end of the *Outside* network. Code Listing 13-3 shows its configuration.

Lines 5 through 7 define a `loopback` interface with the address defined on our DNS server for the host named Rome.

██

Code Listing 13-3

```
1    version 12.0
2    !
3    hostname OUTSIDE2
4    !
5    interface Loopback0
6      Description - This is the Rome IP Address
7      ip address 10.2.2.2 255.255.255.0
8    !
9    interface Serial0
10     ip address 10.1.1.2 255.255.255.0
11     no fair-queue
12   !
13   router igrp 100
14     network 10.0.0.0
15   !
16   end
```

The **show ip route** command shows that we have the routes needed to reach all the devices in the balance of our network:

```
OUTSIDE2#show ip route
Codes: C - connected, S - static, I - IGRP, R - RIP, M - mobile, B - BGP
       D - EIGRP, EX - EIGRP external, O - OSPF, IA - OSPF inter area
       N1 - OSPF NSSA external type 1, N2 - OSPF NSSA external type 2
       E1 - OSPF external type 1, E2 - OSPF external type 2, E - EGP
       i - IS-IS, L1 - IS-IS level-1, L2 - IS-IS level-2, * - candidate default
       U - per-user static route, o - ODR

Gateway of last resort is not set

I    192.168.200.0/24 [100/8576] via 10.1.1.1, 00:00:14, Serial0
     10.0.0.0/24 is subnetted, 2 subnets
C       10.1.1.0 is directly connected, Serial0
C       10.2.2.0 is directly connected, Loopback0
I    192.168.2.0/24 [100/380571] via 10.1.1.1, 00:00:14, Serial0
```

NAT

Now for the main event, the NAT router. Code Listing 13-4 shows the configuration.

Lines 5 through 9 define the Serial0 interface. This interface is our connection to the *Inside* network. Later in the configuration, and also in the debug output when there is a reference to inside translations, this interface is the reference point.

Lines 11 through 14 define the Serial1 interface. This interface connects the NAT router across the neutral network to the *Outside* network. Later in the configuration, and also in the debug output when there is a reference to outside translations, this interface is the reference point.

Lines 16 through 19 define the RIP routing process. We redistribute the static route defined in line 26 so that the *Inside* network forwards all unknown addresses, such as the address of the DNS server, to the NAT router.

Line 21 defines Net192-2, a pool of addresses that address translation will use to represent *Inside* network addresses to the *Outside* network.

Line 22 defines Net192-3, a pool of addresses that address translation will use to represent *Outside* network addresses to the *Inside* network.

Line 23 is the *Inside* translation command. When an IP packet comes into the router on the inside interface (Serial0), check the source address of the packet against access-list 1. If the source address is permitted, assign an IP address from the pool Net192-2.

Line 24 is the *Outside* translation command. When an IP packet comes into the router on the outside interface (Serial1), check the source address of the packet against access-list 1. If the source address is permitted, assign an IP address from the pool Net192-3.

NOTE *The translation process also looks into service requests, such as DNS lookups, to check for IP addresses that need to be translated.*

Line 26 is the default route that directs all packets with an unknown destination to be transmitted out interface Serial1.

Line 28 is the access-list used to identify IP addresses that will be translated. Any IP address that is part of class A IP address 10.0.0.0 will be translated.

■ |

Code Listing 13-4

```
1    version 12.0
2    !
3    hostname NAT
4    !
5    interface Serial0
6     ip address 10.1.1.2 255.255.255.0
7     ip nat inside
8     no fair-queue
9     clockrate 2000000
10   !
11   interface Serial1
12    ip address 172.16.1.2 255.255.255.0
13    ip nat outside
14    clockrate 2000000
15   !
16   router rip
17    redistribute static
18    network 10.0.0.0
19    default-metric 4
20   !
21   ip nat pool Net192-2 192.168.2.2 192.168.2.253 netmask
     255.255.255.0
22   ip nat pool Net192-3 192.168.3.2 192.168.3.253 netmask
     255.255.255.0
23   ip nat inside source list 1 pool Net192-2
24   ip nat outside source list 1 pool Net192-3
25   !
26   ip route 0.0.0.0 0.0.0.0 Serial1 172.16.1.1
27   !
28   access-list 1 permit 10.0.0.0 0.255.255.255
29   !
30   end
```

The **show ip route** command shows us where IP traffic will be directed:

```
NAT#show ip route
Codes: C - connected, S - static, I - IGRP, R - RIP, M - mobile, B - BGP
       D - EIGRP, EX - EIGRP external, O - OSPF, IA - OSPF inter area
       N1 - OSPF NSSA external type 1, N2 - OSPF NSSA external type 2
       E1 - OSPF external type 1, E2 - OSPF external type 2, E - EGP
       i - IS-IS, L1 - IS-IS level-1, L2 - IS-IS level-2, * - candidate default
       U - per-user static route, o - ODR

Gateway of last resort is 172.16.1.1 to network 0.0.0.0

     172.16.0.0/24 is subnetted, 1 subnets
C       172.16.1.0 is directly connected, Serial1
     10.0.0.0/24 is subnetted, 1 subnets
C       10.1.1.0 is directly connected, Serial0
R 192.168.2.0/24 [100/380571] via 10.1.1.1, 00:00:14, Serial0
S*  0.0.0.0/0 [1/0] via 172.16.1.1, Serial1
```

There are two different options for the **show ip nat** command, `translations` and `statistics`:

```
NAT#show ip nat ?
  statistics    Translation statistics
  translations  Translation entries
```

NOTE *Inside addresses are physically located on the Inside network, and outside addresses are physically located on the Outside network. Local addresses are used to communicate on the Inside network. Global addresses are used to communicate on the Outside network.*

Let's look at the output of the **show ip nat translations** command. The first two lines map inside address translations, and the next two lines map outside address translations. The last two lines define end-to-end translation pathways. Look at the `debug` output later in this chapter to track these translations in progress.

```
NAT#show ip nat trans
Pro Inside global    Inside local    Outside local    Outside global
--- 192.168.2.2      10.2.2.2        ---              ---
--- 192.168.2.3      10.1.1.1        ---              ---
--- ---              ---             192.168.3.3      10.1.1.2
--- ---              ---             192.168.3.2      10.2.2.2
--- 192.168.2.2      10.2.2.2        192.168.3.2      10.2.2.2
--- 192.168.2.3      10.1.1.1        192.168.3.2      10.2.2.2
```

Because these are dynamic address translations, the **clear ip nat translation** * command can clear out all dynamic translations:

```
NAT#clear ip nat trans *
NAT#show ip nat trans
NAT#
```

We will start testing by turning on the **debug ip nat** command:

```
NAT#debug ip nat
IP NAT debugging is on
```

Now it is time to go through the first of four **pings** from the workstation on the *Inside* network.

The first packet that the workstation sends out is a DNS request. As the packet hits the `inside` interface, the local address of `10.2.2.2` gets translated to the first address from pool `Net192-2`, `192.168.2.2`, a global address:

```
18:34:49: NAT: s=10.2.2.2->192.168.2.2, d=192.168.200.6 [63232]
```

When the DNS response hits the `outside` interface, the router recognizes the DNS response, looks inside the data portion of the packet, and checks if the address matches `access-list 1`. If so, the router creates a translation table entry and modifies the IP address in the data to match the locally assigned address. The global IP address for Rome on the *Outside*, 10.2.2.2, is changed to 192.168.3.2, a local address on the *Inside*:

```
18:34:49: NAT: DNS resource record 10.2.2.2 -> 192.168.3.2
```

When the returning packet hits the `inside` interface, we translate the global address for the workstation, 192.168.2.2, back into the local address, 10.2.2.2:

```
18:34:49: NAT: s=192.168.200.6, d=192.168.2.2->10.2.2.2 [20021]
```

Now for the first **ping**. The workstation sends a packet from the local inside address, 10.2.2.2, to the local outside address, 192.168.3.2. As the packet passes through the `inside` interface, the source address is translated from the inside local address to the inside global address:

```
18:34:49: NAT: s=10.2.2.2->192.168.2.2, d=192.168.3.2 [63488]
```

As the packet passes through the `outside` interface, the outside local address is translated to the outside global address:

```
18:34:49: NAT: s=192.168.2.2, d=192.168.3.2->10.2.2.2 [63488]
```

Now for the **ping** response. When the packet hits the `outside` interface, the outside global address is translated to the outside local address. The `NAT*` at the beginning of the line indicates that this packet has been fast-switched, speeding up the processing of the packet through the router:

```
18:34:49: NAT*: s=10.2.2.2->192.168.3.2, d=192.168.2.2 [63488]
```

When this first **ping** response hits the `inside` interface, the inside global address is translated to the inside local address:

```
18:34:49: NAT*: s=192.168.3.2, d=192.168.2.2->10.2.2.2 [63488]
```

The last three pings follow:

```
18:34:50: NAT: s=10.2.2.2->192.168.2.2, d=192.168.3.2 [63744]
18:34:50: NAT: s=192.168.2.2, d=192.168.3.2->10.2.2.2 [63744]
18:34:50: NAT*: s=10.2.2.2->192.168.3.2, d=192.168.2.2 [63744]
18:34:50: NAT*: s=192.168.3.2, d=192.168.2.2->10.2.2.2 [63744]

18:34:51: NAT: s=10.2.2.2->192.168.2.2, d=192.168.3.2 [64000]
18:34:51: NAT: s=192.168.2.2, d=192.168.3.2->10.2.2.2 [64000]
18:34:51: NAT*: s=10.2.2.2->192.168.3.2, d=192.168.2.2 [64000]
18:34:51: NAT*: s=192.168.3.2, d=192.168.2.2->10.2.2.2 [64000]

18:34:52: NAT: s=10.2.2.2->192.168.2.2, d=192.168.3.2 [64256]
18:34:52: NAT: s=192.168.2.2, d=192.168.3.2->10.2.2.2 [64256]
18:34:52: NAT*: s=10.2.2.2->192.168.3.2, d=192.168.2.2 [64256]
18:34:52: NAT*: s=192.168.3.2, d=192.168.2.2->10.2.2.2 [64256]
```

The **show ip nat translation** command shows us the individual translations and the end-to-end mapping. On the *Inside* network, the workstation sends a packet to Rome with a source address of 10.2.2.2 and a destination address of 192.168.3.2. When *Outside* device Rome sends a response back to the workstation, it sends a packet with a source address of 10.2.2.2 and a destination address of 192.168.2.2. Remember, local addresses work on the *Inside*, and global addresses work on the *Outside*.

```
NAT#show ip nat trans
Pro Inside global    Inside local    Outside local    Outside global
--- 192.168.2.2      10.2.2.2        ---              ---
--- ---              ---             192.168.3.2      10.2.2.2
--- 192.168.2.2      10.2.2.2        192.168.3.2      10.2.2.2
```

Instead of using the regular **debug ip nat** command, the detail option provides a different look at the translation process:

```
NAT#debug ip nat detail
IP NAT detailed debugging is on
NAT#clear ip nat trans *
NAT#
```

The **debug** output looks very different. The first three lines represent the DNS lookup process. The first line indicates a UDP packet that hits the inside interface (NAT: i udp), and shows us the source and destination address and port number. The second line indicates a UDP packet that hits the outside interface (NAT: o: udp), and again shows us the source and destination address and port number:

```
18:37:51: NAT: i: udp (10.2.2.2, 1032) -> (192.168.200.6, 53) [64768]
18:37:51: NAT: o: udp (192.168.200.6, 53) -> (192.168.2.2, 1032) [22837]
```

Now for the four **pings**. The information we get from the `detail` debug option provides us with more information about the packet that triggers a translation event. The second line of output that follows has special meaning. With the first DNS request, we created two individual translation maps, one for *Inside*, and one for *Outside*. However, when we first transmit data end-to-end, the two individual translation entries are tied together and tracked as a translation conversation. Once a conversation is identified, fast switching of packets can occur. With UDP traffic, each packet becomes a conversation, so only returning traffic is fast-switched.

```
18:37:51: NAT: i: icmp (10.2.2.2, 512) -> (192.168.3.2, 512) [65024]
18:37:51: NAT: setting up outside mapping 192.168.3.2->10.2.2.2
18:37:51: NAT*: o: icmp (10.2.2.2, 512) -> (192.168.2.2, 512) [65024]

18:37:52: NAT: i: icmp (10.2.2.2, 512) -> (192.168.3.2, 512) [65280]
18:37:52: NAT*: o: icmp (10.2.2.2, 512) -> (192.168.2.2, 512) [65280]

18:37:53: NAT: i: icmp (10.2.2.2, 512) -> (192.168.3.2, 512) [1]
18:37:53: NAT*: o: icmp (10.2.2.2, 512) -> (192.168.2.2, 512) [1]

18:37:54: NAT: i: icmp (10.2.2.2, 512) -> (192.168.3.2, 512) [257]
18:37:54: NAT*: o: icmp (10.2.2.2, 512) -> (192.168.2.2, 512) [257]
```

Let's clear everything out, turn on regular and detailed debugging, and see what we get:

```
NAT#clear ip nat trans *
NAT#debug ip nat
IP NAT debugging is on
```

With both regular and detailed debugging activated, we get a complete picture of each packet's processing. Detailed information comes first, showing the trigger that starts the translation process, followed by the regular debugging that shows the addresses being translated. The DNS request comes first:

```
18:38:50: NAT: i: udp (10.2.2.2, 1033) -> (192.168.200.6, 53) [513]
18:38:50: NAT: s=10.2.2.2->192.168.2.2, d=192.168.200.6 [513]
18:38:50: NAT: o: udp (192.168.200.6, 53) -> (192.168.2.2, 1033) [23093]
18:38:50: NAT: DNS resource record 10.2.2.2 -> 192.168.3.2
18:38:50: NAT: s=192.168.200.6, d=192.168.2.2->10.2.2.2 [23093]
```

The four `pings` come next:

```
18:38:50: NAT: i: icmp (10.2.2.2, 512) -> (192.168.3.2, 512) [769]
18:38:50: NAT: setting up outside mapping 192.168.3.2->10.2.2.2
18:38:50: NAT: s=10.2.2.2->192.168.2.2, d=192.168.3.2 [769]
18:38:50: NAT: s=192.168.2.2, d=192.168.3.2->10.2.2.2 [769]
18:38:50: NAT*: o: icmp (10.2.2.2, 512) -> (192.168.2.2, 512) [769]
18:38:50: NAT*: s=10.2.2.2->192.168.3.2, d=192.168.2.2 [769]
18:38:50: NAT*: s=192.168.3.2, d=192.168.2.2->10.2.2.2 [769]

18:38:51: NAT: i: icmp (10.2.2.2, 512) -> (192.168.3.2, 512) [1025]
18:38:51: NAT: s=10.2.2.2->192.168.2.2, d=192.168.3.2 [1025]
18:38:51: NAT: s=192.168.2.2, d=192.168.3.2->10.2.2.2 [1025]
18:38:51: NAT*: o: icmp (10.2.2.2, 512) -> (192.168.2.2, 512) [1025]
18:38:51: NAT*: s=10.2.2.2->192.168.3.2, d=192.168.2.2 [1025]
18:38:51: NAT*: s=192.168.3.2, d=192.168.2.2->10.2.2.2 [1025]

18:38:52: NAT: i: icmp (10.2.2.2, 512) -> (192.168.3.2, 512) [1281]
18:38:52: NAT: s=10.2.2.2->192.168.2.2, d=192.168.3.2 [1281]
18:38:52: NAT: s=192.168.2.2, d=192.168.3.2->10.2.2.2 [1281]
18:38:52: NAT*: o: icmp (10.2.2.2, 512) -> (192.168.2.2, 512) [1281]
18:38:52: NAT*: s=10.2.2.2->192.168.3.2, d=192.168.2.2 [1281]
18:38:52: NAT*: s=192.168.3.2, d=192.168.2.2->10.2.2.2 [1281]

18:38:53: NAT: i: icmp (10.2.2.2, 512) -> (192.168.3.2, 512) [1537]
18:38:53: NAT: s=10.2.2.2->192.168.2.2, d=192.168.3.2 [1537]
18:38:53: NAT: s=192.168.2.2, d=192.168.3.2->10.2.2.2 [1537]
18:38:53: NAT*: o: icmp (10.2.2.2, 512) -> (192.168.2.2, 512) [1537]
18:38:53: NAT*: s=10.2.2.2->192.168.3.2, d=192.168.2.2 [1537]
18:38:53: NAT*: s=192.168.3.2, d=192.168.2.2->10.2.2.2 [1537]
```

Here is a test ping from a different source, the router INSIDE. The DNS processing takes place twice (there must have been a timeout on the first request), then come the five **pings**:

```
18:39:25: NAT: i: udp (10.1.1.1, 7768) -> (192.168.200.6, 53) [0]
18:39:25: NAT: s=10.1.1.1->192.168.2.3, d=192.168.200.6 [0]
18:39:25: NAT: o: udp (192.168.200.6, 53) -> (192.168.2.3, 7768) [23605]
18:39:25: NAT: DNS resource record 10.2.2.2 -> 192.168.3.2
18:39:25: NAT: s=192.168.200.6, d=192.168.2.3->10.1.1.1 [23605]
18:39:25: NAT: i: udp (10.1.1.1, 1106) -> (192.168.200.6, 53) [0]
18:39:25: NAT: s=10.1.1.1->192.168.2.3, d=192.168.200.6 [0]
18:39:25: NAT: o: udp (192.168.200.6, 53) -> (192.168.2.3, 1106) [23861]
18:39:25: NAT: DNS resource record 10.2.2.2 -> 192.168.3.2
18:39:25: NAT: s=192.168.200.6, d=192.168.2.3->10.1.1.1 [23861]

18:39:25: NAT: i: icmp (10.1.1.1, 2367) -> (192.168.3.2, 2367) [50]
18:39:25: NAT: setting up outside mapping 192.168.3.2->10.2.2.2
18:39:25: NAT: s=10.1.1.1->192.168.2.3, d=192.168.3.2 [50]
18:39:25: NAT: s=192.168.2.3, d=192.168.3.2->10.2.2.2 [50]
18:39:25: NAT*: o: icmp (10.2.2.2, 2367) -> (192.168.2.3, 2367) [50]
18:39:25: NAT*: s=10.2.2.2->192.168.3.2, d=192.168.2.3 [50]
18:39:25: NAT*: s=192.168.3.2, d=192.168.2.3->10.1.1.1 [50]

18:39:25: NAT: i: icmp (10.1.1.1, 2368) -> (192.168.3.2, 2368) [51]
```

```
18:39:25: NAT: s=10.1.1.1->192.168.2.3, d=192.168.3.2 [51]
18:39:25: NAT: s=192.168.2.3, d=192.168.3.2->10.2.2.2 [51]
18:39:25: NAT*: o: icmp (10.2.2.2, 2368) -> (192.168.2.3, 2368) [51]
18:39:25: NAT*: s=10.2.2.2->192.168.3.2, d=192.168.2.3 [51]
18:39:25: NAT*: s=192.168.3.2, d=192.168.2.3->10.1.1.1 [51]

18:39:25: NAT: i: icmp (10.1.1.1, 2369) -> (192.168.3.2, 2369) [52]
18:39:25: NAT: s=10.1.1.1->192.168.2.3, d=192.168.3.2 [52]
18:39:25: NAT: s=192.168.2.3, d=192.168.3.2->10.2.2.2 [52]
18:39:25: NAT*: o: icmp (10.2.2.2, 2369) -> (192.168.2.3, 2369) [52]
18:39:25: NAT*: s=10.2.2.2->192.168.3.2, d=192.168.2.3 [52]
18:39:25: NAT*: s=192.168.3.2, d=192.168.2.3->10.1.1.1 [52]

18:39:25: NAT: i: icmp (10.1.1.1, 2370) -> (192.168.3.2, 2370) [53]
18:39:25: NAT: s=10.1.1.1->192.168.2.3, d=192.168.3.2 [53]
18:39:25: NAT: s=192.168.2.3, d=192.168.3.2->10.2.2.2 [53]
18:39:25: NAT*: o: icmp (10.2.2.2, 2370) -> (192.168.2.3, 2370) [53]
18:39:25: NAT*: s=10.2.2.2->192.168.3.2, d=192.168.2.3 [53]
18:39:25: NAT*: s=192.168.3.2, d=192.168.2.3->10.1.1.1 [53]

18:39:25: NAT: i: icmp (10.1.1.1, 2371) -> (192.168.3.2, 2371) [54]
18:39:25: NAT: s=10.1.1.1->192.168.2.3, d=192.168.3.2 [54]
18:39:25: NAT: s=192.168.2.3, d=192.168.3.2->10.2.2.2 [54]
18:39:25: NAT*: o: icmp (10.2.2.2, 2371) -> (192.168.2.3, 2371) [54]
18:39:26: NAT*: s=10.2.2.2->192.168.3.2, d=192.168.2.3 [54]
NAT#18:39:26: NAT*: s=192.168.3.2, d=192.168.2.3->10.1.1.1 [54]
```

The **show ip nat translations** command shows us the individual inside and outside mappings and the two end-to-end mappings:

```
NAT#show ip nat translations
Pro Inside global      Inside local      Outside local      Outside global
--- 192.168.2.2        10.2.2.2          ---                ---
--- 192.168.2.3        10.1.1.1          ---                ---
--- ---                ---               192.168.3.2        10.2.2.2
--- 192.168.2.2        10.2.2.2          192.168.3.2        10.2.2.2
--- 192.168.2.3        10.1.1.1          192.168.3.2        10.2.2.2
```

The **show ip nat statistics** command provides more details on the operation of the NAT feature. This is great stuff: the number of active translations, which interfaces are inside and outside, global statistics, and pool statistics:

```
NAT#show ip nat statistics
Total active translations: 5 (0 static, 5 dynamic; 0 extended)
Outside interfaces:
  Serial1
Inside interfaces:
  Serial0
Hits: 274  Misses: 16
Expired translations: 0
Dynamic mappings:
-- Inside Source
```

```
access-list 1 pool Net192-2 refcount 2
 pool Net192-2: netmask 255.255.255.0
   start 192.168.2.2 end 192.168.2.253
   type generic, total addresses 252, allocated 2 (0%), misses 0
-- Outside Source
access-list 1 pool Net192-3 refcount 3
 pool Net192-3: netmask 255.255.255.0
   start 192.168.3.2 end 192.168.3.253
   type generic, total addresses 252, allocated 1 (0%), misses 0
```

Summary

Network Address Translation is not just for Internet connections; it has many other uses, such as that shown in the merged company example in this chapter. A client I worked with went on an acquisition spree and set up this exact scenario five times in a two-month period.

This was great—one of those tasks you always meant to get around to but never did. For those readers who have taken or will take either BCRAN or CMTD, when you get to "the slide," you can say, "Yes, it really works!"

Troubleshooting

This chapter provides a concentrated look at troubleshooting techniques and tips. The command guidelines are listed in the sequence that I use for troubleshooting problems, but each reader has their own troubleshooting technique.

We will review the troubleshooting process from the bottom up, starting with the physical layer.

If you have a troubleshooting technique that you are familiar with, it is much better to stick with your method. Always use that method consistently, and document the steps as they are performed, to make sure you didn't miss anything. Documentation can be your friend.

Physical Layer

Starting from the bottom up makes sense to me because the number of times I have found problems with cabling or power is too high for me to count. (I only have ten fingers and ten toes.)

Asynchronous Connections

Verify modem connectivity by checking the connection to the phone system. Make sure the RJ11 is plugged into the correct port on the modem, as many modems require the telco connection to be in a specific port.

If you are installing more than one asynchronous connection, get an inexpensive phone with both pulse and DTMF capabilities and carry it with you to test the wire and the destination phone number.

Using the **show controller** command, verify that the TIA/EIA232 cable plugged into the modem is not connected to the router interface upside down.

ISDN BRI Connections

Cisco routers have either an S/T or U interface. With an S/T interface, an NT1 must be used to convert the local loop (two-wire) to the S/T interface (two-pair). The NT1 has LED indicators, which are documented by the manufacturer. You can use the LED indicators to check both the S/T connection and the U connection. The Cisco 7XX models may have both the

S/T and U interfaces, so make sure that an external NT1 is used for the S/T port and a direct telco connection is used for the U port.

Synchronous Connections

Use the **show controller** command to make sure the correct cable is plugged into the serial interface on the router. If you connect the cable to a DTE device such as an IBM cluster controller or an IBM front-end processor, the router becomes a DCE device and must supply the clocking with the **clock rate** command. A symptom of missing clocking is the interface bouncing up and down.

Many Cisco routers have built-in CSUs that must be programmed to match the circuit setup used by your service provider. The **framing** and **linecode** commands program the T1/E1/T3/E3 controller on Cisco routers.

Data-link Layer

Next let's look at the data-link layer, where we establish and monitor connectivity between two devices. In the remote access arena, the data-link layer may require communications with the service provider to make sure that both sides are on the same page.

HDLC Connections

HDLC is the standard method for direct links between Cisco routers. The prime method for verifying connectivity at the data-link layer is the transmission and reception of keepalive messages every ten seconds. You can have keepalives disabled by Cisco IOS when you change encapsulation methods on serial interfaces.

PPP Connections

PPP is established at the physical interface where all LCP options are negotiated. PPP encapsulation, authentication method, compression, and multilink are examples of options that are negotiated at the LCP layer. To watch the LCP negotiation process, use the **debug ppp negotiation** command to verify that all options required have been negotiations.

Authentication occurs at the data-link layer based on the process negotiated by the two end stations. For more detailed troubleshooting information than is shown using the **debug ppp negotiation** command, use the **debug ppp authentication** command.

ISDN BRI Connections

A single command is used to verify ISDN BRI operation: **show isdn status**. This command verifies that the switch type is set on the interface and that the data-link layer (layer 2) is active. If SPIDs are required on this interface, the status of the SPIDs will be shown after the status of the data-link layer. At the data-link layer, TEIs should be assigned between 64 and 126, and the phrase MULTIPLE_FRAME_ESTABLISHED should appear on the same line as the TEI assignment.

NOTE MULTIPLE_FRAME_ESTABLISHED *does not insure that ISDN calls can be made, only that layer 2 on the D-channel is available and communications can take place with the switch at layer 3. B-channels may not be available if the SPIDs are not valid.*

If SPIDs are required but not programmed on the Cisco router, there are no indications of failure using the **show isdn status** command. Most installations require SPIDs, so make sure you check with your service provider.

To check for connectivity, use the **debug isdn q921** command. If the ISDN connection is working properly, you should see packets transmitted and received every ten seconds (keepalives). If no packets show up at all, then the switch type is probably not set. If only transmitted packets show up, go back and check physical connectivity; the router is working, but the service provider ISDN switch is not responding.

ISDN PRI Connections

The **show isdn status** command verifies LAPD data-link layer connectivity. There are no SPIDs on a PRI connection, and the TEI for Cisco PRI connections is always zero.

X.25 Connections

The **show interface** command checks out the LAPB data-link layer for X.25 connections. The one parameter to check is the DTE or DCE mode of operation. Cisco routers connected to an X.25 service provider should be set to DTE.

Frame Relay Connections

The **show interface** command can verify data-link layer connectivity to the Fame Relay service provider. The interface should be set up as a DTE device, and the LMI type must match the LMI type in the Frame Relay switch. Watch out for the new automatic LMI detection feature with IOS version 12.0; the router and switch may pick an LMI type that does not meet your requirements.

For detailed information on the LMI connection, use the **show frame lmi** command.

Network Layer

Three protocols have network layer components: X.25, ISDN, and PPP (this is a stretch).

X.25 Connections

The **show interface** command details information on X.25 connectivity. The items to check out are X.121 address, window sizes, and packet sizes. The most common error is configuring the X.121 address incorrectly.

ISDN Connections

While the **show isdn status** command gives us basic information about the status of the ISDN layer 3, it will not help us troubleshoot ISDN calls.

The **debug isdn q931** command provides detailed information about each call attempt. There are three common call failures recorded that help with troubleshooting. User busy is self-explanatory; it means there are no B-channels available on the called destination, or the calling number is not on the approved list of the destination. No channel available indicates that the switch has no circuits that it can use to connect the call to the destination. This can be caused by excessive **clear interface bri** commands during testing. Intercept, or invalid number format occurs when the number used to call your destination is blocked by the ISDN switch or does not conform to standard telephone numbering formats.

PPP Connections

While PPP does not really have a network-layer component, I moved the discussion of Network Control Protocols (NCPs) to the this section because the negotiation phase deals with network-layer components such as addressing. The **debug ppp negotiation** command provides details on the successful NCP negotiations.

Dial-on-Demand Routing (DDR)

There is a whole section devoted to DDR because there are many complex interactions when you attempt to complete an on-demand call.

Figure 14-1 is the jump-off point for the discussion. A packet enters the router or is generated by a command from the command-line interface. If there is a route to the destination address, then the packet continues toward the destination; if there is no route, the packet is sent to the bit bucket.

Figure 14-2 continues the process by checking an access-list for transit traffic and determining whether the traffic is permitted to be sent to the dialer interface.

Figure 14-1
DDR—does the route exist?

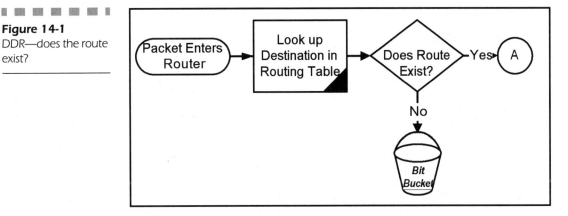

Figure 14-2
DDR—access-list and dialer list check.

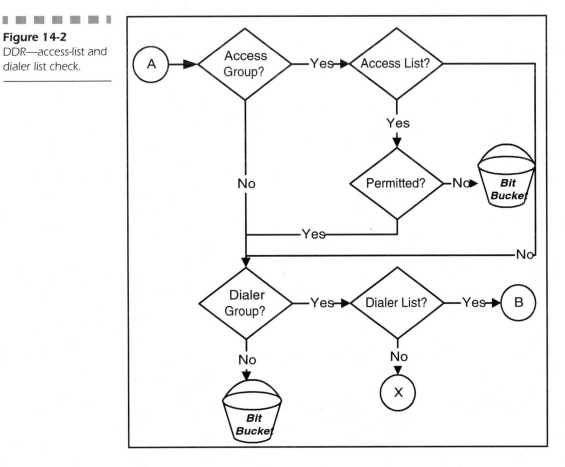

NOTE *Only traffic transiting the routers will go through the access-list process. Output access-lists do not apply to traffic initiated from the router.*

If the transit traffic is not permitted by an output access-list, then the process is finished and the traffic is sent to the bit bucket. If there is no access-group or access-list, then the packet goes on to the interesting traffic section.

Next, traffic headed to the interface goes through the interesting traffic test. If there is no dialer-group applied to the interface, the packet goes to the bit bucket. If there are no rules defined by a dialer-list, then the packet is sent on to check the interface status. If there is a dialer-list, the packet is passed on to the interesting traffic test.

Figure 14-3 shows how we check for interesting traffic.

If there is no dialer list and the interface is not up, the packet goes into the bit bucket. If the interface is up, the packet gets sent out.

Figure 14-3
DDR—interesting
traffic check.

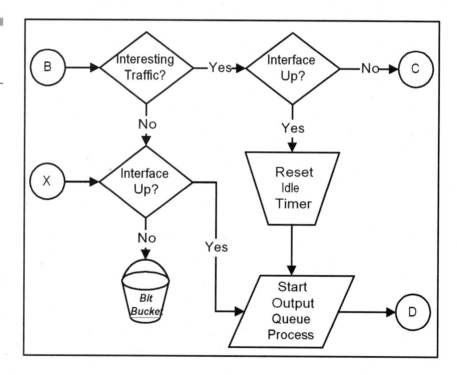

If there is a dialer-list, the packet is not interesting, and the interface is not up, then the packet goes to the bit bucket. If the interface is up, the packet gets sent out.

If the packet is interesting and the interface is up, the idle timer gets reset to keep the interface up and running, and the packet gets sent out.

If the packet is interesting and the interface is not up, the packet gets sent on to the address resolution process.

Figure 14-4 shows how we make one of the final decisions about the disposition of the packet in question: Do we have a phone number to call or not?

If there is a dialer profile, is there a dial string? If not, the packet goes to the bit bucket; otherwise it goes to the call process.

If there is no dialer profile, check the **dialer map** commands on the interface for the next hop address. If the next hop address is not found in the **dialer map** commands, then the packet hits the bit bucket.

With the next hop address resolved, we are ready to start the dial process.

In Figure 14-5, the dialer string is found, and it is time to make a call. If there is a circuit available, we will attempt the call. If there is no circuit available, we will start a fast idle timer on all busy circuits that we

Figure 14-4
DDR—address resolu-
tion.

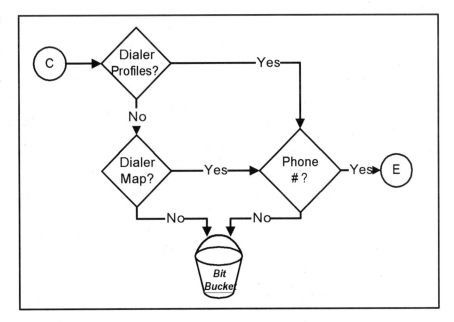

could use for this call. When one of the circuits has been idle for the entire fast idle time period, the current call is terminated, and the circuit is freed up for the waiting packet. If a circuit has already been idle for the entire fast idle time period, the circuit is immediately freed up for the waiting packet. The call is initiated from where the circuit is free.

Figure 14-6 shows how the call is initiated. After the call is placed, the circuit is checked to see if it is active. If the circuit does not activate before the wait-for-carrier timer expires, the packet is sent to the bit bucket. If the circuit is active after the call is placed, we check to see if the dialer hold queue is empty. If the queue is empty, the packet goes into the regular output queue. If the dialer hold queue is not empty, the packet gets added to the end of the dialer hold queue, and we continue processing.

Figure 14-7 shows the last step for a packet being processed through the normal queue, checking for broadcast capabilities. If the packet is not a broadcast, then it is transmitted. If the packet is a broadcast or multicast, and broadcasts or multicasts are permitted, the packet is transmitted; if not, it's off to the bit bucket.

Figure 14-5
DDR—ready to dial.

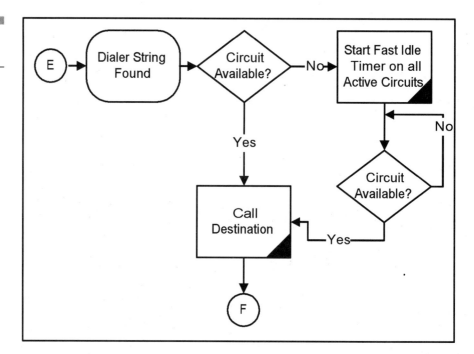

■ ▨ ▨ ▨ ▨ ▨ ▮
Figure 14-6
DDR—circuit activa-
tion.

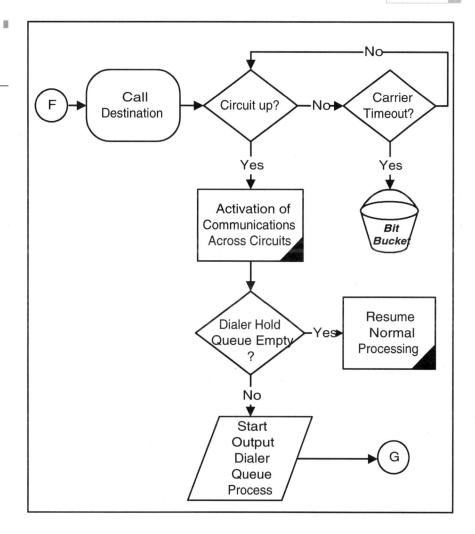

In Figure 14-8, we follow the packets that have been placed in the dialer hold queue while the circuit is down. The dialer hold queue processes packet by packet, checking for broadcasts until the hold queue is empty. Once the hold queue is empty, we resume normal output queue processing.

Figure 14-7
DDR—broadcast
check.

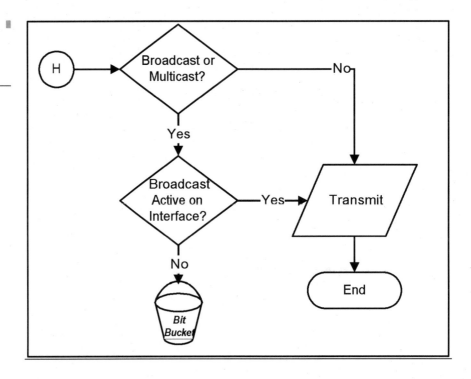

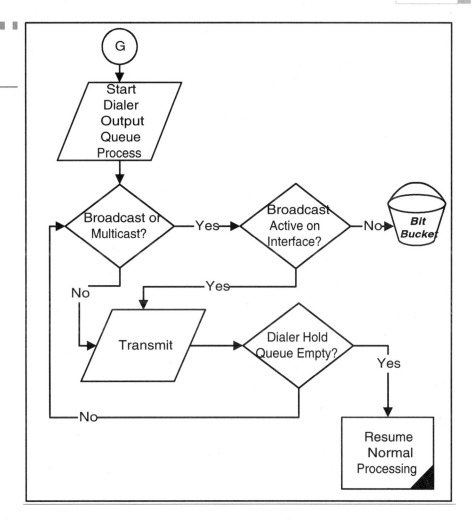

Figure 14-8
DDR—dialer hold
queue processing.

Summary

In this chapter, we reviewed some troubleshooting techniques for remote access circuits. Remember to follow a standard troubleshooting process and document the steps taken to solve the problem.

We also followed packet flow through the DDR process. While the DDR process is complex, following the flow chart will allow you to break down the DDR process into easy-to-debug sections.

APPENDIX A

EIA/TIA-232 PHYSICAL SPECIFICATIONS

This section covers three cabling specifications: the standard TIA/EIA-232 specification shown in Figure A-1, the null modem specifications for DB-25 connectors shown in Figure A-2, and the RJ45 cable specifications used for Cisco routers shown in Figure A-3.

If you will be connecting many RS232 connections (I'm old fashioned), your best tool is a breakout box.

Remember, voltage levels on RS232 are usually ±3 volts and ±15 volts, with ±12 volts as the normal value.

Null modem cables are used to connect DTE devices to DTE devices.

Keep a set of DB25 and DB9 connectors on hand to go with your Cisco rolled cable. If one doesn't work, switch to another one. A special connector is required for the Cisco 766 if you do not have handy the console cable that came with the router.

Figure A-1
TIA/EIA-232
specification.

TIA/EIA-232 Specification		DB-25 Pins	DTE	DCE
Data Transfer	TxD (Transmit Data)	2	→	
	RxD (Recieve Data)	3	←	
Ground	GRD (Ground)	7	←→	
Hardware Flow Control	RTS (Request To Send)	4	→	
	CTS (Clear To Send)	5	←	
Modem Control	DTR (Data Terminal Ready)	20	→	
	CD (Carrier Detect)	8	←	
	DSR (Data Set Ready)	6	←	

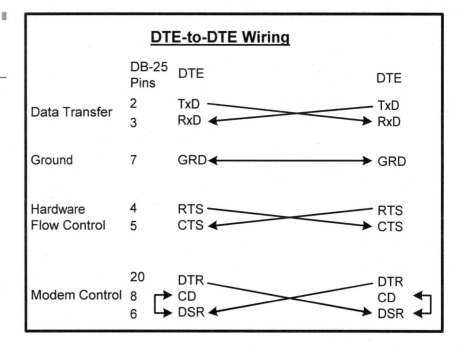

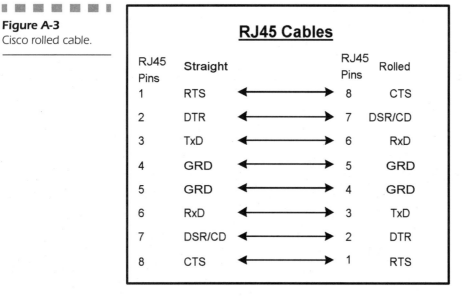

APPENDIX B

AT MODEM COMMANDS

Table B-1 is a sample list of modems, and the basic **AT** commands that can be used in the router chat-script command for modem initialization. In Table B-1 there are special arrows, —> and <—, that point to the command used to program a feature. For example, Lock DTE Speed for the AT&T Paradyne Dataport is programmed by the **AT** command **\N7**.

TABLE B-1 AT modem commands

Settings for All Modems					Error Correction and Compression Settings					
Modem	FD	AA	CD	DTR	RTS/ CTS Flow	Lock DTE Speed	Best Error	Best Compr.	No Error	No Compr.
AT&T Paradyne Dataport	&F	S0=1	&C1	&D2	\Q3	—>	\N7	%C1	\N0	%C0
Codex 3260	&F	S0=1	&C1	&D2	*FL3	*SC1	*SM3	*DC1	*SM1	*DC0
Digicom Scout Plus	&F	S0=1	&C1	&D2	*F3	*S1	*E9	<—	*E0	<—
Digicom SoftModem	&F	S0=1	&C1	&D2	&K3	—>	\N5	%C1	\N0	%C0
Global Village	&F	S0=1	&C1	&D2	\Q3	\J0	\N7	%C1	\N0	%C0
Hayes Accura	&F	S0=1	&C1	&D2	&K3	&Q6	&Q5	&Q9	&Q6	<—
Hayes Accura	&F	S0=1	&C1	&D2	&K3	&Q6	&Q5	&Q9	&Q6	<—
Intel External	&F	S0=1	&C1	&D2	\Q3	\J0	\N6	%C1	\N0	%C0
Microcom QX4232	&F	S0=1	&C1	&D2	\Q3	\J0	\N6	%C1	\N0	%C0
Motorola UDS FastTalk II	&F	S0=1	&C1	&D2	\Q3	\J0	\N6	%C1	\N0	%C0
Multitech MT1432	&F	S0=1	&C1	&D2	&E4	$BA0	&E1	&E15	&E0	&E14
Multitech MT932	&F	S0=1	&C1	&D2	&E4	$BA0	&E1	&E15	&E0	&E14
Practical Peripherals	&F	S0=1	&C1	&D2	&K3	—>	&Q5	&Q9	&Q6	<—
Supra V.32bis/28.8	&F	S0=1	&C1	&D2	&K3	—>	\N3	%C1	\N0	%C0
Telebit 2500(ECM)	&F	S0=1	&C1	&D2	S58=2 S68=2	S51=6	S95=2	S98=1 S96=1	S95=0	S98=0 S96=0

TABLE B-1 AT modem commands (continued)

Settings for All Modems					Error Correction and Compression Settings					
Modem	FD	AA	CD	DTR	RTS/ CTS Flow	Lock DTE Speed	Best Error	Best Compr.	No Error	No Compr.
Telebit T1600	&F1	S0=1	&C1	&D2	S58=2 S68=2	S51=6	S180=2 S181=1	S190=1	S180=0 S181=1	S190=0
Telebit T3000	&F1	S0=1	&C1	&D2	S58=2 S68=2	S51=6	S180=2 S181=1	S190=1	S180=0 S181=1	S190=0
Telebit Trailblazer	&F	S0=1	&C1							
Telebit WB	&F1	S0=1	&C1	&D2	S58=2 S68=2	S51=6	S180=2 S181=1	S190=1	S180=0 S181=1	S190=0
Teleport Gold	&F	S0=1	&C1	&D2	\Q3	\J0	\N7	%C1	\N0	%C0
USR Courier	&F	S0=1	&C1	&D2	&H1& R2	&B1	&M4	&K1	&M0	&K0
USR Courier	&F	S0=1	&C1	&D2	&H1& R2	&B1	&M4	&K1	&M0	&K0
Viva 14.4/9642e	&F	S0=1	&C1	&D2	&K3	—>	\N3	%M3	\N0	%M0
Zoom 14.4	&F	S0=1	&C1	&D2	&K3	—>	\N3	%C1*H3	\N0	%C0
ZyXel U-1496E	&F	S0=1	&C1	&D2	&H3	&B1	&K4	<—	&K0	<—

APPENDIX C

PPP

2125 The PPP Bandwidth Allocation Protocol (BAP) / The PPP Bandwidth Allocation Control Protocol (BACP). C. Richards, K. Smith. March 1997. (Format: TXT = 49213 bytes) (Status: PROPOSED STANDARD)

2097 The PPP NetBIOS Frames Control Protocol (NBFCP). G. Pall. January 1997. (Format: TXT = 27104 bytes) (Status: PROPOSED STANDARD)

2043 The PPP SNA Control Protocol (SNACP). A. Fuqua. October 1996. (Format: TXT = 13719 bytes) (Status: PROPOSED STANDARD)

2023 IP Version 6 over PPP. D. Haskin, E. Allen. October 1996. (Format: TXT = 20275 bytes) (Status: PROPOSED STANDARD)

1994 PPP Challenge Handshake Authentication Protocol (CHAP). W. Simpson. August 1996. (Format: TXT = 24094 bytes) (Obsoletes RFC1334) (Status: DRAFT STANDARD)

1990 The PPP Multilink Protocol (MP). K. Sklower, B. Lloyd, G. McGregor, D. Carr & T. Coradetti. August 1996. (Format: TXT = 53271 bytes) (Obsoletes RFC1717) (Status: DRAFT STANDARD)

1989 PPP Link Quality Monitoring. W. Simpson. August 1996. (Format: TXT = 29289 bytes) (Obsoletes RFC1333) (Status: DRAFT STANDARD)

1978 PPP Predictor Compression Protocol. D. Rand. August 1996. (Format: TXT = 17424 bytes) (Status: INFORMATIONAL)

1977 PPP BSD Compression Protocol. V. Schryver. August 1996. (Format: TXT = 50747 bytes) (Status: INFORMATIONAL)

1976 PPP for Data Compression in Data Circuit-Terminating Equipment (DCE). K. Schneider & S. Venters. August 1996. (Format: TXT = 19781 bytes) (Status: INFORMATIONAL)

1975 PPP Magnalink Variable Resource Compression. D. Schremp, J. Black, J. Weiss. August 1996. (Format: TXT = 8655 bytes) (Status: INFORMATIONAL)

1974 PPP Stac LZS Compression Protocol. R. Friend & W. Simpson. August 1996. (Format: TXT = 45267 bytes) (Status: INFORMATIONAL)

1973 PPP in Frame Relay. W. Simpson. June 1996. (Format: TXT = 14780 bytes) (Status: PROPOSED STANDARD)

1969 The PPP DES Encryption Protocol (DESE). K. Sklower & G. Meyer. June 1996. (Format: TXT = 20383 bytes) (Status: INFORMATIONAL)

1968 The PPP Encryption Control Protocol (ECP). G. Meyer. June 1996. (Format: TXT = 20781 bytes) (Status: PROPOSED STANDARD)

1967 PPP LZS-DCP Compression Protocol (LZS-DCP). K. Schneider & R. Friend. August 1996. (Format: TXT = 40039 bytes) (Status: INFORMATIONAL)

1963 PPP Serial Data Transport Protocol (SDTP). K. Schneider & S. Venters. August 1996. (Format: TXT = 38185 bytes) (Status: INFORMATIONAL)

1962 The PPP Compression Control Protocol (CCP). D. Rand. June 1996. (Format: TXT = 18005 bytes) (Updated by RFC2153) (Status: PROPOSED STANDARD)

1877 PPP Internet Protocol Control Protocol Extensions for Name Server Addresses. S. Cobb. December 1995. (Format: TXT = 10591 bytes) (Status: INFORMATIONAL)

1841 PPP Network Control Protocol for LAN Extension. J. Chapman, D. Coli, A. Harvey, B. Jensen & K. Rowett. September 1995. (Format: TXT = 146206 bytes) (Status: INFORMATIONAL)

1764 The PPP XNS IDP Control Protocol (XNSCP). S. Senum. March 1995. (Format: TXT = 9525 bytes) (Status: PROPOSED STANDARD)

1763 The PPP Banyan Vines Control Protocol (BVCP). S. Senum. March 1995. (Format: TXT = 17817 bytes) (Status: PROPOSED STANDARD)

1762 The PPP DECnet Phase IV Control Protocol (DNCP). S. Senum. March 1995. (Format: TXT = 12709 bytes) (Obsoletes RFC1376) (Status: DRAFT STANDARD)

1717 The PPP Multilink Protocol (MP). K. Sklower, B. Lloyd, G. McGregor & D. Carr. November 1994. (Format: TXT = 46264 bytes) (Obsoleted by RFC1990) (Status: PROPOSED STANDARD)

1663 PPP Reliable Transmission. D. Rand. July 1994. (Format: TXT = 17281 bytes) (Status: PROPOSED STANDARD)

1662 PPP in HDLC-like Framing. W. Simpson, Editor. July 1994. (Format: TXT = 48058 bytes) (Obsoletes RFC1549) (Also STD0051) (Status: STANDARD)

1661 The Point-to-Point Protocol (PPP). W. Simpson, Editor. July 1994. (Format: TXT = 103026 bytes) (Obsoletes RFC1548) (Updated by RFC2153) (Also STD0051) (Status: STANDARD)

1638 PPP Bridging Control Protocol (BCP). F. Baker & R. Bowen. June 1994. (Format: TXT = 58477 bytes) (Obsoletes RFC1220) (Status: PROPOSED STANDARD)

1618 PPP over ISDN. W. Simpson. May 1994. (Format: TXT = 14896 bytes) (Status: PROPOSED STANDARD)

1598 PPP in X.25. W. Simpson. March 1994. (Format: TXT = 13835 bytes) (Status: PROPOSED STANDARD)

1598 PPP in X.25. W. Simpson. March 1994. (Format: TXT = 13835 bytes) (Status: PROPOSED STANDARD)

1552 The PPP Internetworking Packet Exchange Control Protocol (IPXCP). W. Simpson. December 1993. (Format: TXT = 29173 bytes) (Status: PROPOSED STANDARD)

1549 PPP in HDLC Framing. W. Simpson. December 1993. (Format: TXT = 36352 bytes) (Obsoleted by RFC1662, STD0051) (Status: DRAFT STANDARD)

1548 The Point-to-Point Protocol (PPP). W. Simpson. December 1993. (Format: TXT = 111638 bytes) (Obsoletes RFC1331) (Obsoleted by RFC1661) (Updated by RFC1570) (Status: DRAFT STANDARD)

1378 The PPP AppleTalk Control Protocol (ATCP). B. Parker. November 1992. (Format: TXT = 28496 bytes) (Status: PROPOSED STANDARD)

1377 The PPP OSI Network Layer Control Protocol (OSINLCP). D. Katz. November 1992. (Format: TXT = 22109 bytes) (Status: PROPOSED STANDARD)

1376 The PPP DECnet Phase IV Control Protocol (DNCP). S. Senum. November 1992. (Format: TXT = 12448 bytes) (Obsoleted by RFC1762) (Status: PROPOSED STANDARD)

1334 PPP Authentication Protocols. B. Lloyd, W. Simpson. October 1992. (Format: TXT = 33248 bytes) (Obsoleted by RFC1994) (Status: PROPOSED STANDARD)

1333 PPP Link Quality Monitoring. W. Simpson. May 1992. (Format: TXT = 29965 bytes) (Obsoleted by RFC1989) (Status: PROPOSED STANDARD)

1332 The PPP Internet Protocol Control Protocol (IPCP). G. McGregor. May 1992. (Format: TXT = 17613 bytes) (Obsoletes 1172) (Status: PROPOSED STANDARD)

1331 The Point-to-Point Protocol (PPP) for the Transmission of Multi-protocol Datagrams over Point-to-Point Links. W. Simpson. May 1992. (Format: TXT = 129892 bytes) (Obsoletes RFC1171, RFC1172) (Obsoleted by RFC1548) (Status: PROPOSED STANDARD)

1172 Point-to-Point Protocol (PPP) Initial Configuration Options. D. Perkins, R. Hobby. Jul-01-1990. (Format: TXT = 76132 bytes) (Obsoleted by RFC1331) (Status: PROPOSED STANDARD)

Frame Relay

1586 Guidelines for Running OSPF Over Frame Relay Networks. O. deSouza & M. Rodrigues. March 1994. (Format: TXT = 14968 bytes) (Status: INFORMATIONAL)

1490 Multiprotocol Interconnect over Frame Relay. T. Bradley, C. Brown, & A. Malis. July 1993. (Format: TXT = 75206 bytes) (Obsoletes RFC1294) (Status: DRAFT STANDARD)

Books

Cisco IOS Wide Area Networking Solutions, ISBN 157870054X

Frame Relay Internet Working, ISBN 0782125190

X.25 and Related Protocols, IEEE Computer Society, ISBN 0818659769

The Basics Book of X.25 Packet Switching, Motorola Codex, ASIN 020156369X

Inside X.25: A Manager's Guide, ASIN 0070553270

APPENDIX D

ISDN SPID GUIDELINES

The following are examples of SPID formats, grouped by service provider. This information may not be fully up to date, but it is the most current I could find.

Ameritech: 5ESS-Custom: 01 "seven digits" 0
example: phone # 555-555-1234 SPID: 01-555-1234-0

5ESS-NI1 (5E8 ver software): 01 "seven digits" 011
example: phone # 555-555-1234 SPID: 01-555-1234-011

5ESS-NI1 (5E9 ver software): "ten digits" 0111
example: phone # 555-555-1234 SPID: 555-555-1234-0111

DMS100-NI: "ten digits" 0111
example: phone # 555-555-1234 SPID: 555-555-1234-0111

DMS100-Custom: "ten digits" ?? (?? = 0, 1, 01, or 11)
example: phone # 555-555-1234 SPID: 555-555-1234-0
example: phone # 555-555-1234 SPID: 555-555-1234-1
example: phone # 555-555-1234 SPID: 555-555-1234-01
example: phone # 555-555-1234 SPID: 555-555-1234-11

Siemens EWSD-NI1: "ten digits" 0111
example: phone # 555-555-1234 SPID: 555-555-1234-0111

Bell Atlantic: 5ESS-NI1: 01 "seven digits" 000
example: phone # 555-555-1234 SPID: 01-555-1234-000

DMS100-NI1: "ten digits" 100
example: phone # 555-555-1234 SPID: 555-555-1234-100

Custom ISDN: 01 "seven digits" 0
example: phone # 555-555-1234 SPID: 01-555-1234-0

Bell Canada: DMS100-NI1: "seven digits" 00
example: phone # 555-555-1234 SPID: 555-1234-00

BellSouth: 5ESS NI-1: "ten digits" 0100
example: phone # 555-555-1234 SPID: 555-555-1234-0100

DMS100: "ten digits" with last two digits repeated
example: phone # 555-555-1234 SPID: 555-555-123434

DMS100: "ten digits" with last digit repeated
example: phone # 555-555-1234 SPID: 555-555-12344

DMS100 NI1: "ten digits" 0100
example: phone # 555-555-1234 SPID: 555-555-1234-0100

NI1: "ten digits" ??? (??? = 0, 00, or 000)
example: phone # 555-555-1234 SPID: 555-555-1234-0
example: phone # 555-555-1234 SPID: 555-555-1234-00
example: phone # 555-555-1234 SPID: 555-555-1234-000

GTE: (North Carolina) DMS100 NI1: "ten digits" ???? (???? = 0100 or 0000)
example: phone # 555-555-1234 SPID: 555-555-1234-0100
example: phone # 555-555-1234 SPID: 555-555-1234-0000

(Oregon) NI-1 AT&T: 01 "seven digits" 000
example: phone # 555-555-1234 SPID: 01-555-1234-000

(Oregon) AT&ampT Custom: 01 "seven digits" 0
example: phone # 555-555-1234 SPID: 01-555-1234-0

Bell Atlantic   5ESS-NI1: "ten digits" 0000
(Nynex):   example: phone # 555-555-1234 SPID: 555-555-1234-0000

DMS100 NI-1: "ten digits" 0001
example: phone # 555-555-1234 SPID: 555-555-1234-0001

Pac Bell: DMS100: "ten digits" ???? (???? = 1, 10, 100, 1000, 2, 20, 200, or 2000)
example: phone # 555-555-1234 SPID: 555-555-1234-1
example: phone # 555-555-1234 SPID: 555-555-1234-10

example: phone # 555-555-1234 SPID: 555-555-1234-100
example: phone # 555-555-1234 SPID: 555-555-1234-1000
example :phone # 555-555-1234 SPID: 555-555-1234-2
example: phone # 555-555-1234 SPID: 555-555-1234-20
example: phone # 555-555-1234 SPID: 555-555-1234-200
example: phone # 555-555-1234 SPID: 555-555-1234-2000

DMS100: "ten digits" 1 (for both DNs)
example: phone # 555-555-1234 SPID: 555-555-1234-1

DMS100: "ten digits" ???? (???? = 1, 01, 0100, 2, 02, or 0200)
example: phone # 555-555-1234 SPID: 555-555-1234-1
example: phone # 555-555-1234 SPID: 555-555-1234-01
example: phone # 555-555-1234 SPID: 555-555-1234-0100
example: phone # 555-555-1234 SPID: 555-555-1234-2
example: phone # 555-555-1234 SPID: 555-555-1234-02
example: phone # 555-555-1234 SPID: 555-555-1234-0200

5ESS-Custom: 01 "seven digits" 0
example: phone # 555-555-1234 SPID: 01-555-1234-0

5ESS-NI1: 01 "seven digits" 000
example: phone # 555-555-1234 SPID: 01-555-1234-000

Southern New England Telephone:

5ESS-NI1: 01 "seven digits" 000
example: phone # 555-555-1234 SPID: 01-555-1234-000

SouthWestern Bell:

DMS100: "ten digits" 01
example: phone # 555-555-1234 SPID: 555-555-1234-01

Siemens-NI1: "ten digits" 0100
example: phone # 555-555-1234 SPID: 555-555-1234-0100

5ESS-NI1: 01 "seven digits" 000
example: phone # 555-555-1234 SPID: 01-555-1234-000

NOTE   *You may need to add two zeros to the SPID defined by SouthWestern Bell if the original SPID doesn't work.*

US West: 5ESS-NI1: 01 "seven digits" 000
example: phone #555-555-1234 SPID: 01-555-1234-000

5ESS-Custom: 01 "seven digits" 0
example: phone # 555-555-1234 SPID: 01-555-1234-0

5ESS NI1: "seven digits" 1111
example: phone # 555-555-1234 SPID: 555-1234-1111

APPENDIX E

ISDN Q921 DEBUGGING

First we take a look at the output from the **debug isdn q921** command used to solve problems with the ISDN signaling channel at the data link layer:

```
NewYork#debug isdn q921
ISDN Q921 packets debugging is on
NewYork#
00:06:01: ISDN BR0/0: TX ->  IDREQ  ri = 86    ai = 127
00:06:03: ISDN BR0/0: TX ->  IDREQ  ri = 1463  ai = 127
00:06:05: ISDN BR0/0: TX ->  IDREQ  ri = 24872 ai = 127
00:06:07: ISDN BR0/0: TX ->  IDREQ  ri = 29609 ai = 127
```

Once the physical connection is active, the router sends out an ID request (IDREQ) with an action indicator of 127, or broadcast (ai = 127). Each IDREQ sent by the router is assigned a new reference number (ri), picked at random, until an IDASSN message is received with the terminal endpoint identifier (tei) in the action indicator field (ai = 64).

```
00:06:07: ISDN BR0/0: RX <-  IDASSN  ri = 29609  ai = 64
```

Now that we have the tei for B-channel 1, we can send the SPID and make the channel active:

```
00:06:07: ISDN BR0/0: TX ->  SABMEp sapi = 0  tei = 64
00:06:07: ISDN BR0/0: RX <-  UAf sapi = 0  tei = 64
00:06:07: %ISDN-6-LAYER2UP: Layer 2 for Interface BR0/0, TEI 64 changed to up
```

The next line is our SPID being sent to the switch. If we decode the hex into ASCII, the last 20 hex digits are 21255520000101. The following messages complete the initialization of B channel 1:

```
00:06:07: ISDN BR0/0: TX ->  INFOc sapi = 0  tei = 64  ns = 0  nr = 0  i =
   0x08007B3A0E3231323535353230303030313031
00:06:07: ISDN BR0/0: RX <-  RRr sapi = 0  tei = 64  nr = 1
00:06:07: ISDN BR0/0: RX <-  INFOc sapi = 0  tei = 64  ns = 0  nr = 1  i =
   0x08007B3B02F081
00:06:07: ISDN BR0/0: TX ->  RRr sapi = 0  tei = 64  nr = 1
```

We follow the same sequence for B-channel 2:

```
00:06:07: ISDN BR0/0: TX ->  IDREQ  ri = 44602  ai = 127
00:06:07: ISDN BR0/0: RX <-  IDASSN ri = 44602  ai = 65
00:06:07: ISDN BR0/0: TX ->  SABMEp sapi = 0  tei = 65
00:06:07: ISDN BR0/0: RX <-  UAf sapi = 0  tei = 65
00:06:07: %ISDN-6-LAYER2UP: Layer 2 for Interface BR0/0, TEI 65 changed to up
00:06:07: ISDN BR0/0: TX ->  INFOc sapi = 0  tei = 65  ns = 0  nr = 0  i =
    0x08007B3A0E3231323535353230303130313031
00:06:07: ISDN BR0/0: RX <-  RRr sapi = 0  tei = 65  nr = 1
00:06:07: ISDN BR0/0: RX <-  INFOc sapi = 0  tei = 65  ns = 0  nr = 1  i =
    0x08007B3B02F082
00:06:07: ISDN BR0/0: TX ->  RRr sapi = 0  tei = 65  nr = 1
```

The next four messages occur every ten seconds; can you say keep-alive? There is a pair of RRp (Receiver Ready poll) and RRf (Receiver Ready final) packets exchanged for each B-channel to verify that the switch is active, can talk to the end points, and can process information:

```
00:06:17: ISDN BR0/0: RX <-  RRp sapi = 0  tei = 64 nr = 1
00:06:17: ISDN BR0/0: TX ->  RRf sapi = 0  tei = 64  nr = 1
00:06:17: ISDN BR0/0: RX <-  RRp sapi = 0  tei = 65 nr = 1
00:06:17: ISDN BR0/0: TX ->  RRf sapi = 0  tei = 65  nr = 1
```

Table E-1 lists detailed definitions of all the fields that are produced by the **debug isdn q921** command.

	Fields	Definitions
TABLE E-1 Debug ISDN Q921—definitions	**TX**	Indicates that this frame is being transmitted from the ISDN interface on the local router (user side)
	RX	Indicates that this frame is being received by the ISDN interface on the local router from the peer (network side)
	IDREQ	Indicates the Identity Request message type sent from the local router to the network (assignment source point [ASP]) during the automatic terminal endpoint identifier (TEI) assignment procedure. This message is sent in a UI command frame. The service access point identifier (SAPI) value for this message type is always 63 (indicating that it is a Layer 2 management procedure), but it is not displayed. The TEI value for this message type is 127 (indicating that it is a broadcast operation).

TABLE E-1 (continued)	Fields	Definitions
	ri = 31815	Indicates the reference number used to differentiate between user devices requesting TEI assignment. This value is a randomly generated number between 0 and 65535. The same `ri` value sent in the IDREQ message should be returned in the corresponding IDASSN message. Note that a reference number of 0 indicates that the message is sent from the network-side management layer entity and a reference number has not been generated.
	ai = 127	Indicates the action indicator used to request that the ASP assign any TEI value. It is always 127 for the broadcast TEI. Note that in some message types, such as IDREM, a specific TEI value is indicated.
	IDREM	Indicates the Identity Remove message type sent from the ASP to the user-side layer management entity during the TEI removal procedure. This message is sent in a UI command frame. The message includes a reference number that is always 0, because it is not responding to a request from the local router. The ASP sends the Identity Remove message twice to avoid message loss.
	IDASSN	Indicates the Identity Assigned message type sent from the ISDN service provider on the network to the local router during the automatic TEI assignment procedure. This message is sent in a UI command frame. The SAPI value for this message type is always 63 (indicating that it is a Layer 2 management procedure). The TEI value for this message type is 127 (indicating that it is a broadcast operation).
	ai = 64	Indicates the TEI value automatically assigned by the ASP. This TEI value is used by data-link layer entities on the local router in subsequent communications with the network. The valid values are in the range 64 to 126.
	SABME	Indicates the set asynchronous balanced mode extended (SABME) command. This command places the recipient into `modulo 128` multiple-frame acknowledged operation. This command also indicates that all exception conditions have been cleared. The SABME command is sent once a second for N200 times (typically three times) until its acceptance is confirmed with a UA response. For a list and brief description of other commands and responses that can be exchanged between the data-link layer entities on the local router and the network, see *ITU-T Recommendation Q.921*.

Fields	Definitions
TABLE E-1 (continued)	
sapi = 0	Identifies the service access point at which the data-link layer entity provides services to Layer 3 or to the management layer. A SAPI with the value zero indicates it is a call control procedure. Note that Layer 2 management procedures such as TEI assignment, TEI removal, and TEI checking, which are tracked with the **debug isdn q921** command, do not display the corresponding SAPI value; it is implicit. If the SAPI value were displayed, it would be 63.
tei = 64	Indicates the TEI value automatically assigned by the ASP. This TEI value will be used by data-link layer entities on the local router in subsequent communication with the network. The valid values are in the range 64 to 126.
IDCKRQ	Indicates the Identity Check Request message type sent from the ISDN service provider on the network to the local router during the TEI check procedure. This message is sent in a UI command frame. The ri field is always 0. The ai field for this message contains either a specific TEI value for the local router to check or 127, which indicates that the local router should check all TEI values. For a list and brief description of other message types that can be exchanged between the local router and the ISDN service provider on the network, see Table E-3 and Table E-4 for codes and values.
IDCKRP	Indicates the Identity Check Response message type sent from the local router to the ISDN service provider on the network during the TEI check procedure. This message is sent in a UI command frame in response to the IDCKRQ message. The ri field is a randomly generated number between 0 and 65535. The ai field for this message contains the specific TEI value that has been checked.
UAf	Confirms that the network side has accepted the SABME command previously sent by the local router. The final bit is set to 1.
INFOc	Indicates that this is an information command. It is used to transfer sequentially numbered frames containing information fields that are provided by Layer 3. The information is transferred across a data-link connection.
INFORMATION **pd = 8 callref = (null)**	Indicates the information fields provided by Layer 3. The information is sent one frame at a time. If multiple frames need to be sent, several information commands are sent. The pd value is the protocol discriminator. The value 8 indicates it is call control information. The call reference number is always null for SPID information.

Fields	Definitions
SPID information i = 0x3431353930333833 36363031	Indicates the service profile identifier (SPID). The local router sends this information to the ISDN switch to indicate the services to which it subscribes. SPIDs are assigned by the service provider and are usually ten-digit telephone numbers followed by optional numbers. Currently only the DMS-100 switch supports SPIDs, one for each B channel. If SPID information is sent to a switch type other than DMS-100, an error may be displayed in the debug information.
ns = 0	Indicates the send sequence number of transmitted I frames (information frames)
nr = 0	Indicates the expected send sequence number of the next received I frame. At time of transmission, this value should be equal to the value of ns. The value of nr is used to determine whether frames need to be retransmitted for recovery.
RRr	Indicates the Receive Ready response for unacknowledged information transfer. The RRr is a response to an INFOc.
RRp	Indicates the Receive Ready command with the poll bit set. The data-link layer entity on the user side uses the poll bit in the frame to solicit a response from the peer on the network side.
RRf	Indicates the Receive Ready response with the final bit set. The data-link layer entity on the network side uses the final bit in the frame to indicate a response to the poll.
sapi	Indicates the service access point identifier. The SAPI is the point at which data-link services are provided to a network layer or management entity. Currently, this field can have the value 0 (for call control procedure) or 63 (for Layer 2 management procedures).
tei	Indicates the terminal endpoint identifier (TEI) that has been assigned automatically by the assignment source point (ASP). (The ASP is also called the layer management entity on the network side.) The valid range is 64 to 126. The value 127 indicates a broadcast.

TABLE E-1
(continued)

ISDN Q931 Debugging

The next area to investigate is the output of the **debug isdn q931** command.

First, let's turn on this debugging feature.

```
NewYork#debug isdn q931
ISDN Q931 packets debugging is on
```

First, a SETUP message is sent to the switch. The key here is the phone number, 5552003:

```
00:08:36: ISDN BR0/0: TX ->  SETUP pd = 8  callref = 0x01
00:08:36:            Bearer Capability i = 0x8890
00:08:36:            Channel ID i = 0x83
00:08:36:            Keypad Facility i = '5552003'
```

The router receives a call proceeding (CALL_PROC) message from the switch telling us the phone call has been passed to the destination:

```
00:08:36: ISDN BR0/0: RX <-  CALL_PROC pd = 8  callref = 0x81
00:08:36:            Channel ID i = 0x89
```

Next the router gets a connect (CONNECT) message indicating that the called party has gone off-hook (answered the call):

```
00:08:36: ISDN BR0/0: RX <-  CONNECT pd = 8  callref = 0x81
00:08:36:            Channel ID i = 0x89
```

The BRI 0/0 interface changes state to up, and the router sends a connection acknowledgment (CONNECT_ACK) back to the switch so that data transmission can start. Our interface comes up, and our PPP connection is established:

```
00:08:36: %LINK-3-UPDOWN: Interface BRI0/0:1, changed state to up
00:08:36: ISDN BR0/0: TX ->  CONNECT_ACK pd = 8  callref = 0x01
00:08:37: %LINEPROTO-5-UPDOWN: Line protocol on Interface BRI0/0:1, changed state to up
00:08:42: %ISDN-6-CONNECT: Interface BRI0/0:1 is now connected to 5552003 London
```

Table E-2 lists detailed definitions of all the fields that are produced by the **debug isdn q931** command.

TABLE E-2 Debug ISDN Q931—definitions	Fields	Definitions
	TX ->	Indicates that this message is being transmitted from the local router (user side) to the network side of the ISDN interface
	RX <-	Indicates that this message is being received by the user side of the ISDN interface from the network side
	SETUP	Indicates that the SETUP message type has been sent to initiate call establishment between peer network layers. This message can be sent from either the local router or the network.
	pd	Indicates the protocol discriminator. The protocol discriminator distinguishes messages for call control over the user-network ISDN interface from other ITU-T-defined messages, including other Q.931 messages. The protocol discriminator is 8 for call control messages such as SETUP. For the ISDN switch type `basic-1tr6`, the protocol discriminator is 65.
	callref	Indicates the call reference number in hexadecimal format. The value of this field indicates the number of calls made from either the router (outgoing calls) or the network (incoming calls). Note that the originator of the SETUP message sets the high-order bit of the call reference number to 0. The destination of the connection sets the high-order bit to 1 in subsequent call control messages, such as the CONNECT message. For example, `callref = 0x04` in the request becomes `callref = 0x84` in the response.
	Bearer Capability	Indicates the requested bearer service to be provided by the network. Refer to Table E-5 for detailed information about bearer capability values.
	i =	Indicates the information element identifier. The value depends on the field with which it is associated. Refer to the ITU-T Q.931 specification for details about the possible values associated with each field for which this identifier is relevant.
	Channel ID	Indicates the channel identifier. The value 83 indicates any channel, 89 indicates B-channel 1, and 8A indicates B-channel 2. For more information about the Channel Identifier, refer to *ITU-T Recommendation Q.931*.
	Called Party Number	Identifies the called party. This field is only present in outgoing SETUP messages. Note that it can be replaced by the Keypad facility field. This field uses the IA5 character set.

TABLE E-2
(continued)

Fields	Definitions
Calling Party Number	Identifies the origin of the call. This field is present only in incoming SETUP messages. This field uses the IA5 character set.
CALL_PROC	Indicates the CALL PROCEEDING message. The requested call setup has begun and no more call setup information will be accepted.
CONNECT	Indicates that the called user has accepted the call
CONNECT_ACK	Indicates that the calling user acknowledges the called user's acceptance of the call
DISCONNECT	Indicates either that the user side has requested the network to clear an end-to-end connection or that the network has cleared the end-to-end connection
Cause	Indicates the cause of the disconnect. Refer to Table E-3 and Table E-4 for detailed information about DISCONNECT cause codes and RELEASE cause codes.
Looking Shift to Codeset 6	Indicates that the next information elements will be interpreted according to information element identifiers assigned in codeset 6. Codeset 6 means that the information elements are specific to the local network.
Codeset 6 IE 0x1 i = 0x82, '10'	Indicates charging information. This information is specific to the NTT switch type and may not be sent by other switch types.
RELEASE	Indicates that the sending equipment will release the channel and call reference. The recipient of this message should prepare to release the call reference and channel.
RELEASE_COMP	Indicates that the sending equipment has received a RELEASE message and has now released the call reference and channel

The specific fields listed in Table E-3 tie into the template that shows up in the **debug isdn** command output as:

```
i=0xy1y2z1z2a1a2
```

Field	Value—Description
TABLE E-3 ISDN— DISCONNECT and RELEASE cause codes	

Field	Value—Description
0x	Indicates that the following values are hexadecimal digits 0 through F
y1	8—ITU-T standard coding
y2	0—User 1—Private network serving local user 2—Public network serving local user 3—Transit network 4—Public network serving remote user 5—Private network serving remote user 7—International network A—Network beyond internetworking point
z1	(See values in Table E-4)—Class of cause value
z2	(See values in Table E-4)—Value of cause value
a1	8—Optional diagnostic field value (when present)
a2	0—Unknown 1—Permanent 2—Transient

Table E-4 defines the values for z1, class of cause value, and z2, value of cause value, as defined in Table E-3.

TABLE E-4
ISDN—
DISCONNECT and
RELEASE cause
values

z1 (hex)	Z2 (hex)	Cause # (decimal)	Cause Description
0	1	1	Unallocated or assigned number
0	2	2	No route to specified transit network
0	3	3	No route to destination
0	6	6	Channel unacceptable
0	7	7	Call awarded and being delivered in an established channel
1	0	16	Normal call clearing
1	1	17	User busy

TABLE E-4
(continued)

z1 (hex)	Z2 (hex)	Cause # (decimal)	Cause Description
1	2	18	No user responding
1	3	19	No answer from user (has been alerted)
1	5	21	Call rejected
1	6	22	Number changed
1	A	26	Non-selected user clearing
1	B	27	Designation out of order
1	C	28	Invalid number format
1	D	29	Facility rejected
1	E	30	Response to Status Inquiry
1	F	31	Normal, reason unspecified
2	2	34	No channel/circuit available
2	6	38	Network out of order
2	9	41	Temporary failure
2	A	42	Switching equipment congestion
2	B	43	Access information discarded
2	C	44	Requested channel/circuit not available
2	F	47	Resources unavailable
3	1	49	QOS unavailable
3	2	50	Requested facility not subscribed
3	8	57	Bearer capability not authorized
3	A	58	Bearer capability not presently available
3	F	63	Service or option not available
4	1	65	Bearer capability not implemented
4	2	66	Channel type not implemented
4	5	69	Requested facility not implemented
4	6	70	Only restricted digital information bearer capability is available
4	F	79	Service or option not implemented
5	1	81	Invalid call reference value
5	2	82	Identified channel does not exist

	z1 (hex)	Z2 (hex)	Cause # (decimal)	Cause Description
TABLE E-4 (continued)	5	3	83	A suspended call exists, but not this call
	5	4	84	Call identity in use
	5	5	85	No call suspended
	5	6	86	Call having the correct call identity has been cleared
	5	8	88	Incompatible destination
	5	B	91	Invalid transit network selection
	5	F	95	Invalid message
	6	0	96	Mandatory information element is missing
	6	1	97	Message type non-existent or not implemented
	6	2	98	Message not compatible with call state (or97)
	6	3	99	Information element nonexistent or not implemented
	6	4	100	Invalid information element contents
	6	5	101	Message not compatible with call state
	6	6	102	Recovery on timer expired
	6	F	111	Protocol error
	7	F	127	Internetworking

Table E-5 lists the ISDN bearer capabilities used in the output of the **debug isdn** commands. Examples of the output are be as follows:

```
0x8890 for 64Kbps
0x218f for 56Kbps
```

	Field	Description
TABLE E-5 ISDN—bearer capabilities	0x	Values that follow are hexadecimal digits
	88	ITU-T coding standard with unrestricted digital information
	90	Circuit mode, 64 Kbps
	21	Layer 1, V.110/X.30
	8F	Synchronous, no in-band negotiation, 56 Kbps

APPENDIX F

THE FRAME RELAY SWITCH CONFIGURATION

```
version 11.3
!
hostname FRSwitch
!
frame-relay switching
!
interface Serial0
 no ip address
 encapsulation frame-relay
 no fair-queue
 clockrate 1300000
 no frame-relay inverse-arp
 frame-relay intf-type dce
 frame-relay route 101 interface Serial1 100
 frame-relay route 102 interface Serial2 100
 frame-relay route 103 interface Serial3 100
!
interface Serial1
 no ip address
 encapsulation frame-relay
 no fair-queue
 clockrate 1300000
 no frame-relay inverse-arp
 frame-relay intf-type dce
 frame-relay route 100 interface Serial0 101
 frame-relay route 102 interface Serial2 101
 frame-relay route 103 interface Serial3 101
!
interface Serial2
 no ip address
 encapsulation frame-relay
 no fair-queue
 clockrate 115200
 no frame-relay inverse-arp
 frame-relay intf-type dce
 frame-relay route 100 interface Serial0 102
 frame-relay route 101 interface Serial1 102
 frame-relay route 103 interface Serial3 102
!
interface Serial3
 no ip address
 encapsulation frame-relay
 no fair-queue
 clockrate 115200
 no frame-relay inverse-arp
 frame-relay intf-type dce
 frame-relay route 100 interface Serial0 103
 frame-relay route 101 interface Serial1 103
 frame-relay route 102 interface Serial2 103
!
!
end
```

show Commands

```
FRSwitch#show frame route
Input IntfInput DlciOutput IntfOutput DlciStatus
Serial0101 Serial1100 active
Serial0102 Serial2100 active
Serial0103 Serial3100 active
Serial1100 Serial0101 active
Serial1102 Serial2101 active
Serial1103 Serial3101 active
Serial2100 Serial0102 active
Serial2101 Serial1102 active
Serial2103 Serial3102 active
Serial3100 Serial0103 active
Serial3101 Serial1103 active
Serial3102 Serial2103 active


FRSwitch#show frame pvc

PVC Statistics for interface Serial0 (Frame Relay DCE)

DLCI = 101, DLCI USAGE = SWITCHED, PVC STATUS = ACTIVE, INTERFACE = Serial0

   input pkts 10           output pkts 10          in bytes 604
   out bytes 632           dropped pkts 0          in FECN pkts 0
   in BECN pkts 0          out FECN pkts 0         out BECN pkts 0
   in DE pkts 0            out DE pkts 0
   out bcast pkts 0        out bcast bytes 0          Num Pkts Switched 10

   pvc create time 01:07:59, last time pvc status changed 00:04:06

DLCI = 102, DLCI USAGE = SWITCHED, PVC STATUS = ACTIVE, INTERFACE = Serial0

   input pkts 22           output pkts 18          in bytes 1420
   out bytes 1076          dropped pkts 2          in FECN pkts 0
   in BECN pkts 0          out FECN pkts 0         out BECN pkts 0
   in DE pkts 0            out DE pkts 0
   out bcast pkts 0        out bcast bytes 0          Num Pkts Switched 22

   pvc create time 01:07:51, last time pvc status changed 00:09:26

DLCI = 103, DLCI USAGE = SWITCHED, PVC STATUS = ACTIVE, INTERFACE = Serial0

   input pkts 55           output pkts 62          in bytes 3480
   out bytes 4004          dropped pkts 1          in FECN pkts 0
   in BECN pkts 0          out FECN pkts 0         out BECN pkts 0
   in DE pkts 0            out DE pkts 0
   out bcast pkts 0        out bcast bytes 0          Num Pkts Switched 55

   pvc create time 01:07:42, last time pvc status changed 00:44:17

PVC Statistics for interface Serial1 (Frame Relay DCE)

DLCI = 100, DLCI USAGE = SWITCHED, PVC STATUS = ACTIVE, INTERFACE = Serial1

   input pkts 10           output pkts 10          in bytes 632
```

```
    out bytes 604              dropped pkts 0           in FECN pkts 0
    in BECN pkts 0             out FECN pkts 0          out BECN pkts 0
    in DE pkts 0               out DE pkts 0
    out bcast pkts 0           out bcast bytes 0            Num Pkts Switched 10

    pvc create time 01:02:53, last time pvc status changed 00:04:17

DLCI = 102, DLCI USAGE = SWITCHED, PVC STATUS = ACTIVE, INTERFACE = Serial1

    input pkts 8               output pkts 15           in bytes 516
    out bytes 1004             dropped pkts 0           in FECN pkts 0
    in BECN pkts 0             out FECN pkts 0          out BECN pkts 0
    in DE pkts 0               out DE pkts 0
    out bcast pkts 0           out bcast bytes 0            Num Pkts Switched 8

    pvc create time 01:02:53, last time pvc status changed 00:04:17

DLCI = 103, DLCI USAGE = SWITCHED, PVC STATUS = ACTIVE, INTERFACE = Serial1

    input pkts 10              output pkts 15           in bytes 632
    out bytes 984             dropped pkts 0            in FECN pkts 0
    in BECN pkts 0             out FECN pkts 0          out BECN pkts 0
    in DE pkts 0               out DE pkts 0
    out bcast pkts 0           out bcast bytes 0            Num Pkts Switched 10

    pvc create time 01:02:53, last time pvc status changed 00:04:17

PVC Statistics for interface Serial2 (Frame Relay DCE)

DLCI = 100, DLCI USAGE = SWITCHED, PVC STATUS = ACTIVE, INTERFACE = Serial2

    input pkts 20              output pkts 22           in bytes 1136
    out bytes 1420             dropped pkts 0           in FECN pkts 0
    in BECN pkts 0             out FECN pkts 0          out BECN pkts 0
    in DE pkts 0               out DE pkts 0
    out bcast pkts 0           out bcast bytes 0            Num Pkts Switched 18

    pvc create time 01:02:52, last time pvc status changed 00:47:37

DLCI = 101, DLCI USAGE = SWITCHED, PVC STATUS = ACTIVE, INTERFACE = Serial2

    input pkts 15              output pkts 8            in bytes 1004
    out bytes 516              dropped pkts 0           in FECN pkts 0
    in BECN pkts 0             out FECN pkts 0          out BECN pkts 0
    in DE pkts 0               out DE pkts 0
    out bcast pkts 0           out bcast bytes 0            Num Pkts Switched 15

    pvc create time 01:02:52, last time pvc status changed 00:04:18

DLCI = 103, DLCI USAGE = SWITCHED, PVC STATUS = ACTIVE, INTERFACE = Serial2

    input pkts 20              output pkts 19           in bytes 1164
    out bytes 1176             dropped pkts 0           in FECN pkts 0
    in BECN pkts 0             out FECN pkts 0          out BECN pkts 0
    in DE pkts 0               out DE pkts 0
    out bcast pkts 0           out bcast bytes 0            Num Pkts Switched 18

    pvc create time 01:02:52, last time pvc status changed 00:44:18

PVC Statistics for interface Serial3 (Frame Relay DCE)
```

```
DLCI = 100, DLCI USAGE = SWITCHED, PVC STATUS = ACTIVE, INTERFACE = Serial3

    input pkts 63          output pkts 55         in bytes 4034
    out bytes 3480         dropped pkts 0         in FECN pkts 0
    in BECN pkts 0         out FECN pkts 0        out BECN pkts 0
    in DE pkts 0           out DE pkts 0
    out bcast pkts 0       out bcast bytes 0          Num Pkts Switched 62

    pvc create time 01:02:51, last time pvc status changed 00:44:22

DLCI = 101, DLCI USAGE = SWITCHED, PVC STATUS = ACTIVE, INTERFACE = Serial3

    input pkts 15          output pkts 10         in bytes 984
    out bytes 632          dropped pkts 0         in FECN pkts 0
    in BECN pkts 0         out FECN pkts 0        out BECN pkts 0
    in DE pkts 0           out DE pkts 0
    out bcast pkts 0       out bcast bytes 0          Num Pkts Switched 15

    pvc create time 01:02:51, last time pvc status changed 00:04:12

DLCI = 102, DLCI USAGE = SWITCHED, PVC STATUS = ACTIVE, INTERFACE = Serial3

    input pkts 19          output pkts 18         in bytes 1176
    out bytes 1104         dropped pkts 2         in FECN pkts 0
    in BECN pkts 0         out FECN pkts 0        out BECN pkts 0
    in DE pkts 0           out DE pkts 0
    out bcast pkts 0       out bcast bytes 0          Num Pkts Switched 19

    pvc create time 01:02:52, last time pvc status changed 00:09:32


FRSwitch#show frame lmi

LMI Statistics for interface Serial0 (Frame Relay DCE) LMI TYPE = CISCO
    Invalid Unnumbered info 0 Invalid Prot Disc 0
    Invalid dummy Call Ref 0  Invalid Msg Type 0
    Invalid Status Message 0  Invalid Lock Shift 0
    Invalid Information ID 0   Invalid Report IE Len 0
    Invalid Report Request 0   Invalid Keep IE Len 0
    Num Status Enq. Rcvd 303   Num Status msgs Sent 303
    Num Update Status Sent 0   Num St Enq. Timeouts 34

LMI Statistics for interface Serial1 (Frame Relay DCE) LMI TYPE = CISCO
    Invalid Unnumbered info 0 Invalid Prot Disc 0
    Invalid dummy Call Ref 0  Invalid Msg Type 0
    Invalid Status Message 0  Invalid Lock Shift 0
    Invalid Information ID 0   Invalid Report IE Len 0
    Invalid Report Request 0   Invalid Keep IE Len 0
    Num Status Enq. Rcvd 43    Num Status msgs Sent 43
    Num Update Status Sent 0   Num St Enq. Timeouts 229

LMI Statistics for interface Serial2 (Frame Relay DCE) LMI TYPE = CISCO
    Invalid Unnumbered info 0 Invalid Prot Disc 0
    Invalid dummy Call Ref 0  Invalid Msg Type 0
    Invalid Status Message 0  Invalid Lock Shift 0
    Invalid Information ID 0   Invalid Report IE Len 0
    Invalid Report Request 0   Invalid Keep IE Len 0
    Num Status Enq. Rcvd 75    Num Status msgs Sent 75
    Num Update Status Sent 0   Num St Enq. Timeouts 172
```

```
LMI Statistics for interface Serial3 (Frame Relay DCE) LMI TYPE = CISCO
    Invalid Unnumbered info 0 Invalid Prot Disc 0
    Invalid dummy Call Ref 0  Invalid Msg Type 0
    Invalid Status Message 0  Invalid Lock Shift 0
    Invalid Information ID 0   Invalid Report IE Len 0
    Invalid Report Request 0   Invalid Keep IE Len 0
    Num Status Enq. Rcvd 284  Num Status msgs Sent 284
    Num Update Status Sent 0  Num St Enq. Timeouts 0


FRSwitch#show int s 0
Serial0 is up, line protocol is up
  Hardware is HD64570
  MTU 1500 bytes, BW 1544 Kbit, DLY 20000 usec,
      reliability 255/255, txload 1/255, rxload 1/255
  Encapsulation FRAME-RELAY, loopback not set, keepalive set (10 sec)
  LMI enq sent  0, LMI stat recvd 0, LMI upd recvd 0
  LMI enq recvd 310, LMI stat sent  310, LMI upd sent  0, DCE LMI up
  LMI DLCI 1023  LMI type is CISCO  frame relay DCE
  FR SVC disabled, LAPF state down
  Broadcast queue 0/64, broadcasts sent/dropped 0/0, interface broadcasts 0
  Last input 00:00:02, output 00:00:02, output hang never
  Last clearing of "show interface" counters never
  Queueing strategy: fifo
  Output queue 0/40, 92 drops; input queue 0/75, 0 drops
  5 minute input rate 0 bits/sec, 0 packets/sec
  5 minute output rate 0 bits/sec, 0 packets/sec
      584 packets input, 10652 bytes, 0 no buffer
      Received 310 broadcasts, 0 runts, 0 giants, 0 throttles
      7 input errors, 1 CRC, 0 frame, 0 overrun, 0 ignored, 0 abort
      425 packets output, 12423 bytes, 0 underruns
      0 output errors, 0 collisions, 53 interface resets
      0 output buffer failures, 0 output buffers swapped out
      154 carrier transitions
      DCD=up  DSR=up  DTR=up  RTS=up  CTS=up
```

APPENDIX G

Log File Location

With CiscoSecure ACS version 2.1, the logs are located in the directory structure shown in Figure G-1. The current file of each log type is `active.csv`, and each day that CiscoSecure is active at midnight, it copies the active file to a date-named file and starts a fresh `active.csv`.

Figure G-1
CiscoSecure directory structure and log file locations.

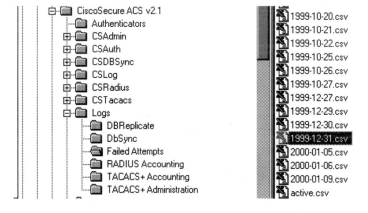

The next four pages are formatted so that facing pages represent a single report.

Failed Attempts

Date	Time	Message-Type	User-Name	Group-Name	Caller-ID	Authen-Failure-Code
12/31/99	11:15:31	Authen failed	UserLevel	Group 1	192.168.60.2	T+ enable privilege too low
12/31/99	11:16:08	Authen failed	midlevel	Group 10	192.168.60.2	CS password invalid
12/31/99	11:44:05	Author failed	superuser	Group 15	192.168.60.2	
12/31/99	11:45:51	Author failed	superuser	Group 15	192.168.60.2	
12/31/99	11:47:13	Author failed	superuser	Group 15	192.168.60.2	
12/31/99	11:53:56	Author failed	UserLevel	Group 1	4102801001/4102801000	
12/31/99	11:54:52	Author failed	superuser	Group 15	192.168.60.3	
12/31/99	11:56:53	Author failed	superuser	Group 15	4102801001/4102801000	
12/31/99	11:58:13	Author failed	superuser	Group 15	192.168.60.4	

Administration Log

Date	Time	User-Name	Group-Name	cmd	priv-lvl
12/31/99	11:42:38	superuser	Group 15	aaa accounting network start-stop tacacs+ <cr>	15
12/31/99	11:42:38	superuser	Group 15	aaa accounting system wait-start tacacs+ <cr>	15
12/31/99	11:42:39				15
12/31/99	11:47:09	superuser	Group 15	show running-config <cr>	15
12/31/99	11:59:13	superuser	Group 15	configure terminal <cr>	15
12/31/99	11:59:22	superuser	Group 15	interface Loopback 2 <cr>	15
12/31/99	11:59:24	superuser	Group 15	shutdown <cr>	15
12/31/99	11:59:28	superuser	Group 15	no shutdown <cr>	15
12/31/99	12:00:07	superuser	Group 15	copy running-config tftp <cr>	15

Failed Attempts (Cont'd)

Date	Time	Author-Fail-Code	Author-Data	NAS-Port	NAS-IP-Address
12/31/99	11:15:31			tty26	192.168.200.193
12/31/99	11:16:08			tty26	192.168.200.193
12/31/99	11:44:05	Command unknown	service=shell cmd=copy running-config tftp <cr>	tty26	192.168.200.193
12/31/99	11:45:51	Command unknown	service=shell cmd=configure terminal <cr>	tty26	192.168.200.193
12/31/99	11:47:13	Command unknown	service=shell cmd=show running-config <cr>	tty26	192.168.200.193
12/31/99	11:53:56	Service denied	service=ppp protocol=unknown	Async5	192.168.200.193
12/31/99	11:54:52	Command unknown	service=shell cmd=show privilege <cr>	tty26	192.168.200.193
12/31/99	11:56:53	Service denied	service=ppp protocol=unknown	Async6	192.168.200.193
12/31/99	11:58:13	Command unknown	service=shell cmd=show privilege <cr>	tty26	192.168.200.193

Administration Log (Cont'd)

Date	Time	priv-lvl	service	NAS-Portname	task_id	NAS-IP-Address	reason
12/31/99	11:42:38	15	shell	tty0	114	192.168.200.193	
12/31/99	11:42:38	15	shell	tty0	115	192.168.200.193	
12/31/99	11:42:39	15	system		116	192.168.200.193	reconfigure
12/31/99	11:47:09	15	shell	tty0	118	192.168.200.193	
12/31/99	11:59:13	15	shell	tty0	133	192.168.200.193	
12/31/99	11:59:22	15	shell	tty0	134	192.168.200.193	
12/31/99	11:59:24	15	shell	tty0	135	192.168.200.193	
12/31/99	11:59:28	15	shell	tty0	136	192.168.200.193	
12/31/99	12:00:07	15	shell	tty0	137	192.168.200.193	

TACACS+ Accounting Log

Date	Time	User-Name	Group-Name	Caller-Id	Acct-Flags	elapsed_time	service
12/31/99	11:43:57	superuser	Group 15	192.168.60.2	start	.	shell
12/31/99	11:47:21	London	SOHO800 Group		start		ppp
12/31/99	11:49:21	London	SOHO800 Group		stop	120	ppp
12/31/99	11:50:30	superuser	Group 15	192.168.60.2	stop	392	shell
12/31/99	11:53:56	UserLevel	Group 1	4102801001/4102801000	start		ppp
12/31/99	11:54:45	superuser	Group 15	192.168.60.3	start		shell
12/31/99	11:55:27	superuser	Group 15	192.168.60.3	stop	42	shell
12/31/99	11:55:43	UserLevel	Group 1	4102801001/4102801000	stop	108	ppp
12/31/99	11:56:52	superuser	Group 15	4102801001/4102801000	start		ppp
12/31/99	11:57:51	superuser	Group 15	192.168.60.4	start		shell
	12:00:59	superuser	Group 15	async	start		shell
12/31/99	12:08:45	superuser	Group 15	192.168.60.4	stop	654	shell
12/31/99	12:20:03	London	SOHO800 Group		start		ppp
12/31/99	12:22:04	London	SOHO800 Group		stop	120	ppp
12/31/99	12:22:07	London	SOHO800 Group		start		ppp
12/31/99	12:22:50	superuser	Group 15		NAS Reset	1558	
12/31/99	12:22:50	London	SOHO800 Group		NAS Reset	43	

Date	Time	service	bytes_in	bytes_out	paks_in	paks_out	task_id	NAS-Portname	NAS-IP-Address
12/31/99	11:43:57	shell					117	tty26	192.168.200.193
12/31/99	11:47:21	ppp					119	Serial0:22	192.168.200.193
12/31/99	11:49:21	ppp	432	562	28	29	119	Serial0:22	192.168.200.193
12/31/99	11:50:30	shell					117	tty26	192.168.200.193
12/31/99	11:53:56	ppp					127	Async5	192.168.200.193
12/31/99	11:54:45	shell					128	tty26	192.168.200.193
12/31/99	11:55:27	shell					128	tty26	192.168.200.193
12/31/99	11:55:43	ppp	4373	2459	87	57	127	Async5	192.168.200.193
12/31/99	11:56:52	ppp					129	Async6	192.168.200.193
12/31/99	11:57:51	shell					130	tty26	192.168.200.193
12/31/99	12:00:59	shell					138	tty0	192.168.200.193
12/31/99	12:08:45	shell					130	tty26	192.168.200.193
12/31/99	12:20:03	ppp					181	Serial0:22	192.168.200.193
12/31/99	12:22:04	ppp	1240	1394	44	46	181	Serial0:22	192.168.200.193
12/31/99	12:22:07	ppp					235	Serial0:22	192.168.200.193
12/31/99	12:22:50						129	Async6	192.168.200.193
12/31/99	12:22:50						235	Serial0:22	192.168.200.193

APPENDIX H

Table H-1 provides the reader with a list of vLabs offered by MentorLabs. Go to *www.mentorlabs.com* to check out the hands-on labs available that match this book's examples. Some of these labs will be available when this book is released, and the balance will be implemented over the next few months.

In addition to the labs defined in Table H-1, there are more labs available under the BCRAN banner available from MentorLabs.

TABLE H-1

MentorLabs vlab numbers

Description	Chapter	vLab Number
Asynchronous dial-in to an external serial port modem	1	2391
Chat scripts for modem initialization	1	2404
Asynchronous dial-in to an external AUX port modem	1	2405
Advanced terminal operations	2	3261
System controllers	2	2407
Asynchronous PPP connections	3	2394 2395
Asynchronous PPP multilink connection	3	3622
ARP experiment—highlight DDR address resolution needs	5	0922
Asynchronous DDR connectivity	5	2408
ISDN—BRI-to-BRI single neighbor DDR connectivity	6	1179
ISDN—BRI-to-BRI multiple neighbor DDR connectivity	6	2416
ISDN—BRI-to-PRI single neighbor DDR connectivity	6	2398
ISDN—extending DDR with dialer profiles (Cisco 7XX Lab)	6	2390 2371
IP routing—static routes with route redistribution into RIP	7	1180
IP routing—snapshot routing for RIP and IGRP	7	2409

Description	Chapter	vLab Number
IP routing—OSPF demand circuits	7	2410
IP routing—ODR and EIGRP	7	2411
Asynchronous and ISDN connections to an ISDN PRI interface (Cisco 7XX Lab)	8	2390 2371
WAN—HDLC connectivity	9	0921
WAN—channelized T1 connectivity	9	1181
WAN—X.25 connectivity	9	2383
WAN—multipoint Frame Relay with static address mapping	9	2413
WAN—multipoint Frame Relay with inverse ARP and fixed CIR traffic shaping	9	1183
WAN—point-to-point Frame Relay with BECN traffic shaping and data compression	9	2417
Backing up fixed WAN connections—backup interface and dialer profile	10	2387
Backing up fixed WAN connections—dialer watch and floating static routes	10	2418
Advanced security with TACACS+ and command-level authorization	11	3624
Protocol translations—X.25, LAT, and TCP/IP	12	3627
Network address translation—overlapping IP addresses	13	3628

GLOSSARY

16550 UART The fastest type of UART that is currently available

AA Accidental Administrator: A person responsible for their network whose primary duties and training are in other fields

Adaptive Speed Learning (ASL) Courier V.32bis and V.32terbo modems detect improved line conditions and shift upward again to the next higher speed. The modems at both ends of the connection adapt independently, each detecting and adjusting to line conditions. ASL keeps the modems always operating at the highest speed and constantly ensuring data integrity.

ADSL See xDSL

AIM Advanced Integration Module: New series of add-on boards available for certain routers, like the 2600 series

AMI Alternate Mark Inversion, an older line encoding technique for T1 circuits

analog signals Continuous, varying waveforms, such as the voice tones carried over phone lines. Contrast with digital signals.

answering mode A state in which the modem transmits at the pre-defined high frequency of the communications channel and receives at the low frequency. The transmit/receive frequencies are the reverse of the calling modem, which is in originate mode.

AppleTalk Apple Computers LAN protocol

application (application program) A computer program, such as a word processor or spreadsheet, designed to perform a specific function

APPN Advanced Peer-to-Peer Networking: part of IBM's LAN protocols

ARQ See automatic repeat request

ASCII American Standard Code for Information Interchange: A 7-bit binary code (0's,1's) used to represent letters, numbers, and special characters such as $, !, and /. Supported by almost every computer and terminal manufacturer

ASL See Adaptive Speed Learning

asymmetrical modulation A transmission technique that splits the communications channel into one high-speed channel and one slower channel. During a call under asymmetrical modulation, the modem with the greatest amount of data to transmit is allocated the high-speed channel. The modem with less data is allocated the slow or back channel (450 bps). The modems dynamically reverse the channels during a call if the volume of data transfer changes.

asynchronous transmission Data transmission in which the length of time between transmitted characters may vary. Because the time lapses between transmitted characters are not uniform, the receiving modem must be signaled as to when the data bits of a character begin and when they end. The addition of start and stop bits to each character serves this purpose.

ATM Asynchronous Transfer Mode: Relatively new scalable WAN and LAN networking technology

auto answer A feature in modems enabling them to answer incoming calls over the phone lines without the use of a telephone receiver

auto dial A feature in modems enabling them to dial phone numbers over the phone system without the use of a telephone transmitter

automatic repeat request A general term for error-control protocols that feature error-detection and automatic retransmission of defective blocks of data; see HST, MNP, and V.42

B8ZS Bipolar 8 Zero Substitution

baud rate The number of discrete signal events per second occurring on a communications channel. Although not technically accurate, baud rate is commonly used to mean bit rate.

B channel or bearer channel A 64 Kbps ISDN channel used to carry voice and data calls.

BGP Border Gateway Protocol: The dynamic routing protocol used between ISPs to manage extremely large routing tables.

binary digit A 0 or 1, reflecting the use of a binary numbering system (only two digits). Used because the computer recognizes either of two states, OFF or ON. The shortened form of binary digit is bit.

BISYNC Binary Synchronous Control: A protocol developed by IBM for software applications and communicating devices operating in synchronous environments. The protocol defines operations at the link level of communications (for example, the format of data frames exchanged between modems over a phone line). Also see protocol, HDLC, SDLC

bit See binary digit

bit-mapping A technique that lets one decimal number (in this case, a number between 0 and 255) stand for up to eight separate binary settings

bit rate The number of binary digits, or bits, transmitted per second (bps). Communications channels using telephone channel modems are established at set bit rates, commonly 300, 1200, 2400, 4800, 14400, and 28800.

BOD Bandwidth on Demand: A protocol used with MPPP to add additional dial-up connections as necessary, to increase bandwidth

boot flash Flash memory used to store an emergency copy of IOS. If installed, it will take the place of a Boot ROM.

bps The bits (binary digits) per second rate

BRI Basic Rate Interface: Low-speed ISDN connection providing up to 128 Kbps of data, two phone lines, or both. It consists of two B (bearer) channels and one D (data) channel.

buffer A memory area used for temporary storage during input and output operations. An example is the modem's command buffer. Another is the Transmit Data flow control buffer used for flow control and to store copies of transmitted frames until they are positively acknowledged by the receiving modems.

byte A group of binary digits stored and operated upon as a unit. A byte may have coded value equal to a character in the ASCII code (letters, number) or have some other value meaningful to the computer. In user documentation, the term usually refers to 8-bit units or characters. One kilobyte (K) is equal to 1,024 bytes or characters, and 64K indicates 65,536 bytes or characters.

call indicate A call originating tone defined by ITU-T recommendation V.8

carrier A continuous frequency capable of being either modulated or impressed with another information-carrying signal. Carriers are generated and maintained by modems via the transmission lines of the telephone companies.

CCITT Formerly an international organization that defined standards for telegraphic and telephone equipment. It has been incorporated into its parent organization, International Telecommunication Union (ITU). Telecommunication standards are now covered under Telecommunication Standards Sector (TSS). ITU-T replaces CCITT. For example, the Bell 212A standard for 1200 bps communication in North America was referred to as CCITT V.22. It is now referred to as ITU-T V.22.

CCO Cisco Connection Online: Cisco's Web site

CCP Console Command Processor: part of the PPP protocol negotiations

CDDI   Copper Distributed Data Interface: FDDI LAN technology over copper wire instead of fiber optics cable 100 Mbps

CDP   Cisco Discovery Protocol: A proprietary Cisco network protocol used by Cisco routers to discover other Cisco routers on the networks

Central Office (CO)   The facility to which devices such as telephones, fax machines, modems, and terminal adapters within a specific geographic area of a public telephone network are connected

Central Office Switch   A device, located at the telephone company's central office, to which devices such as telephones, fax machines, and modems are connected

Cert/CC   Computer Emergency Response Team/Coordination Center: A publicly accessible group dedicated to network security

CHAP   Challenge Handshake Authentication Protocol: High-security method of authenticating dial-in users in PPP

character   A representation, coded in binary digits, of a letter, number, or other symbol

characters per second (CPS)   A data-transfer rate generally estimated from the bit rate and the character length. For example, at 2400 bps, 8-bit characters with start and stop bits (for a total of 10 bits per character) will be transmitted at a rate of approximately 240 characters per second (CPS). Some protocols, such as USR HST and MNP, employ advanced techniques such as longer transmission frames and data compression to increase CPS.

Class 2.0/EIA-592   An American standard used between facsimile application programs and facsimile modems for sending and receiving Class 2.0 faxes

CLI   Command Line Interface: The test-based interface common to all IOS-based routers

CO   See Central Office

COM port   See serial port, EIA-232

CPS   See characters per second

CRC   See cyclic redundancy check

CSU   Channel Service Unit: A device that manages a digital connection to a digital phone line

CSU/DSU   Channel Service Unit/Data Service Unit: A type of digital modem used for switched and leased data lines

cyclic redundancy check (CRC)   An error-detection technique consisting of a cyclic algorithm performed on each block or frame of data by both sending and receiving modems. The sending modem inserts the results of its computation in each data block in the form of a CRC code. The receiving modem compares its results with the received CRC code and responds with either a positive or negative acknowledgment. In the ARQ protocol implemented in U.S. Robotics high-speed modems, the receiving modem accepts no more data until a defective block is received correctly.

data communications   A type of communication in which computers and terminals are able to exchange data over an electronic medium

data compression   When the transmitting modem detects redundant units of data, it compresses them into shorter units of fewer bits. The receiving modem then decompresses the redundant data units before passing them to the receiving computer.

Data Compression Table   A table of values assigned for each character during a call under data compression. Default values in the table are continually altered and built during each call; the longer the table, the more efficient throughput gained. If a destructive Break is sent during a call (see the &Y command), causing the modems to reset the compression tables, you can expect diminished throughput.

data communication equipment (DCE)   Term applies to modems that establish and control the data-link via the telephone network

data encryption   A means of implementing security whereby data is encrypted and decrypted on the fly over WAN lines

Data Encryption Standard (DES)   Available in 40 bit and 56 bit. Method of providing secure connections through data encryption until it was broken in July, 1998

Data Link Connection Identifier (DLCI)   Identification number for Frame Relay circuits

Data Link Switching Plus (DLSW)   A transport legacy protocol for networking.

data mode   The mode in which the fax modem is capable of sending and receiving data files. A standard modem without fax capabilities is always in data mode.

data service unit (DSU)   A device that manages a digital connection to a router

data set   Another way of saying modem

data terminal equipment (DTE)   The device that generate final destination of data

DCE See data communication equipment

D channel or data channel A channel in ISDN lines used to set up calls and carry out-of-band information about the calls. In PRI lines, the D channel is 64 Kbps. In BRI lines, the D channel is 16 Kbps.

DEC Net Digital Equipment Corporation's LAN protocol

default Any setting assumed, at startup or reset, by the computer's software and attached devices, and operational until changed by the user

demarc or demarcation point The physical location where the phone company's responsibility for voice and date lines ends within a given building

Dial-on-Demand Routing (DDR) Protocol for creating dial-up WAN connections, which are automatically initiated on an as-needed basis

Dialed Number Identification Service (DNIS) A telephony standard that can be set on high-speed data lines

digital loopback A test that checks the modem's EIA-232 interface and the cable that connects the terminal or computer and the modem. The modem receives data (in the form of digital signals) from the computer or terminal and immediately returns the data to the screen for verification.

digital signals Discrete, uniform signals. In this book, the term refers to the binary digits 0 and 1.

DIP switch DIP stands for dual in-line package.

Domain Name Service (DNS) Internet protocol that resolves host names to Internet protocol addresses (i.e., www.btg.com resolves to 204.176.115.69)

DRAM Dynamic Random Access Memory: See main memory

DS0 A data circuit carrying 56 Kbps or 64 Kbps of information. It may be its own line, or one channel in a DS1 (T1/E1). It can also be referred to as a 56 or 64 Kbps leased line.

DS1 A high-capacity data line; also referred to as a T1 or E1 line

DTE See data terminal equipment

dual-tone multi-frequency (DTMF) The standard used by all touch-tone digital phones. When pressed, each numbered button on the phone generates two tones, one for the row and one for the column on the keyboard.

duplex Indicates a communications channel capable of carrying signals in both directions; see half-duplex, full-duplex

Dynamic Host Configuration Protocol (DHCP) A network protocol used to automatically configure client machines on a network

E1 Digital leased line that has 2048 M bps of throughput available. Consists of 32 64 Kbps channels. Channels can be ordered as needed from the phone company.

ED Early Development: IOS releases, which deliver support for new features and platforms in their regular maintenance updates

echo See local echo

EIA Electronic Industries Association, which defines electronic standards in the United States

EIA-232 A technical specification published by the Electronic Industries Association that establishes mechanical and electrical interface requirements among computers, terminals, modems, and communication line

electronically programmable ROM (EPROM) ROM used to hold programs that cannot be changed once they have been loaded into the ROM chip. On Cisco routers, EPROM memory is used to store a scaled-down copy of IOS for emergency boot-up and to allow access to Flash to change IOS code.

EMI Electromagnetic Interface

Enhanced Interior Gateway Routing Protocol (EIGRP) A Cisco proprietary dynamic routing protocol

equalization A compensation circuit designed into modems to counteract certain distortions introduced by the telephone channel. Two types are used: fixed (compromise) equalizers and those that adapt to channel conditions. U.S. Robotics high-speed modems use adaptive equalization.

error control Various techniques that check the reliability of characters (parity) or blocks of data. V.42, MNP, and HST error-control protocols use error detection (CRC) and retransmission of frames with errors (ARQ).

ESF Extended Super Frame: A frame format currently in use for T1 circuits

Ethernet Most prevalent LAN technology, 10 Mbps

Ethernet hub See hub

expansion bus A series of slots inside a computer that allow for adding feature cards

Exterior Gateway Protocol (EGP) A dynamic routing protocol

facsimile (fax) A method for transmitting the image on a printed page from one point to another

fax mode The mode in which the fax modem is capable of sending and receiving files in a facsimile format

file transfer protocol (FTP) A TCP/IP application that allows users of an Internet to send (put) and receive (get) files

flash memory A form of memory that can be electronically erased and reprogrammed without the need to remove it from the circuit board

fast Ethernet New faster replacement for Ethernet, 100 Mbps

Fiber Distributed Data Interface (FDDI) Digital fiber optic LAN technology, 100 Mbps

firewall A network security device that governs and logs network access between different public and private networks

First Customer Ship (FCS) An initial release of any product to the general public

flash memory Memory that does not lose its information when powered off. Used like a small hard disk to store router OS; available as a SIMM or a PCMCIA card, depending on the router using it

flow control A mechanism that compensates for differences in the flow of data input to and output from a modem or other device

Frame Relay Access Device (FRAD) A network device specifically designed to work on a Frame Relay network

frame A data communications term for a block of data with header and trailer information attached. The added information usually includes a frame number, block size data, error check codes, and start/end indicators.

Frame Relay Wide-area network technology that can provide redundancy of data path and cheaper long-haul connections. It does this by creating private paths through a large packet-switched network.

FTP See file transfer protocol

full-duplex Signal flow in both directions at the same time. In microcomputer communications, it may refer to the suppression of the online local echo.

general deployment (GD) IOS releases considered stable

GNU GNU's Not Unix: The Free Software Foundation's GNU project

half-duplex Signal flow in both directions, but only one way at a time. In microcomputer communications, it may refer to activation of the online local echo, which causes the modem to send a copy of the transmitted data to the screen of the sending computer.

handshaking A sequence that two modems undertake while connecting to agree on the parameters of the conversation that will ensue. During handshaking, the modems negotiate the speed of the connection, whether error control and date compression will be used and in what form, and so forth.

hardware flow control A form of flow control that uses electronic signals to start and stop the flow of data

HDLC See High-Level Data Link Control

Hewlett Packard (HP) Manufacturer of computer and network hardware and software

hexadecimal or hex It is a number system with a base of 16 (e.g., 0,1,2,3,4,5,6,7,8,9,A,B,C,D,E,F).

High-Level Data Link Control (HDLC) A standard protocol developed by the International Standards Organization for software applications and communicating devices operating in synchronous environments. The protocol defines operations at the link level of communications (for example, the format of data frames exchanged between modems over a phone line). See BISYNC, protocol, SDLC

high-speed serial interface (HSSI) High-speed WAN connection supporting speed up to 54 Mbps

High-Speed Technology (HST) U.S. Robotics' proprietary signaling scheme, design, and error-control protocol for high-speed modems. HST incorporates trellis-coded modulation for more efficient use of the phone channel at speeds of 4800 bps and above. HST also incorporates MNP-compatible error-control procedures adapted to asymmetrical modulation.

Hypertext Transport Protocol (HTTP) Internet standard protocol for WWW connections

hub An active hardware device that connects multiple Ethernet devices together onto the same physical network

Hz (Hertz) A frequency measurement unit used internationally to indicate one cycle per second

IBM (International Business Machines) A very large multinational computer company

in-band Call information sent through the same channel as the call itself. When a voice call is placed on a POTS line, the tones or clicks used to indicate the number you are dialing are carried on the same line as the call itself.

Industry Standard Architecture (ISA) The most common type of computer expansion bus. Other types include Extended Standard Architecture (EISA) and Microchannel Architecture (MCA).

inter-exchange carrier (IXC) Phone company providing services between LATAs

Integrated Services Digital Network (ISDN) Digital phone and data service available to business and homes

inter-LATA Any phone service that occurs between LATAs

Interior Gateway Routing Protocol (ICMP) A dynamic routing protocol proprietary to Cisco

International Organization for Standardization (ISO) An international body that works to standardize network protocols and many other things

Internet Control Message Protocol (ICMP) A higher-level protocol, such as TCP, that rides on top of IP, the Internet Protocol. ICMP controls aspects of network connections. To debug network connections, the ping and traceroute programs send ICMP packets.

Internetworking Operating System (IOS) The operating system of most Cisco routers

Internetwork Packet Exchange/Sequenced Packet Exchange (IPX/SPX) Network protocol used by the Novell netware

Internet Protocol (IP) The main low-level networking protocol that is used on the Internet

Internet Protocol Control Protocol (IPCP) Part of the PPP protocol negotiation

Internet service provider (ISP) Any company providing Internet access to dial-in or leased-line users

interrupt request (IRQ) A number that must be assigned to devices that plug into your computer's expansion bus

IP Internet Protocol

IPX Novell's Internet Packet Exchange protocol

intra-LATA Any phone service that exists within a LATA

IRQ See interrupt request

ISA See Industry Standard Architecture

ITU-T International Telecommunication Union-Telecommunication sector (formerly referred to as CCITT): An international organization that defines standards for telegraphic and telephone equipment. For example, the Bell212A standard for 1200 bps communication in North America is observed internationally as ITU-T V.22. For 2400 bps communication, most U.S. manufacturers observe V.22bis.

jumper A switch composed of pins and a shunt. The shunt's position on the pins determines the jumper setting.

Kbps Kilobits per second, or one thousand bits per second

LAPM See Link Access Procedure for Modems

Layer 2 Forwarding Protocol (L2F) The underlying link-level technology for both Multichassis MP and Virtual Private Networks

light-emitting diode—LED TTL devices used to indicate modem status

Link Access Procedure Balanced (LAPB) A method of WAN data encapsulation

Link Access Procedure for Modems (LAPM) An error control protocol incorporated in ITU-T Recommendation V42. Like the MNP and HST protocols, LAPM uses cyclic redundancy checking (CRC) and retransmission of corrupted data (ARQ) to ensure data reliability.

Link Control Protocol (LCP) Part of the PPP protocol negotiation

Local Access and Transport Area (LATA) Geographical areas created by the breakup of Bell Telephone

Local Area Network (LAN) A data network contained within a small area such as a home or a building

Local Area Transport (LAT) DEC Net remote terminal protocol

local echo A modern feature that enables the modem to send copies of keyboard commands and transmitted data to the screen. When the modem is in command mode (not online to another system), the local echo is invoked through the ATE1 command. The command causes the modem to display typed commands. When the modem is online to another system, the local echo is invoked through the ATF0 command. This command causes the modem to display the data it transmits to the remote system.

main memory The memory in the router used to load the OS and perform many generic functions

Maintenance Operation Protocol (MOP) A network file transfer protocol

management information base (MIB) SNMP configuration files specific to individual pieces of equipment; often used by network management software such as HP Open View

MB Megabyte, or one million bytes

media access layer (MAC layer) Sublayer of the data-link layer that deals with framing and local addressing

media access layer address (MAC address) Also known as Ethernet address; a set of six two-digit hexadecimal numbers burned into an Ethernet product by its manufacturer

metropolitan area network (MAN) A data network spanning multiple sites within a given metropolitan area

Microcom Networking Protocol (MNP) An asynchronous error-control protocol developed by Microcom, Inc., and now in the public domain. The protocol ensures error-free transmission through error detection (CRC) and retransmission of frames with errors. U.S. Robotics modems use MNP levels 1-4 and Level 5 data compression. MNP Levels 1-4 have been incorporated into ITU-T Recommendation V.42. Compare to HST

MI/MIC Mode Indicate/Mode Indicate Common: Also called fixed or manual originate. Used when equipment other than the modem does the dialing. In such installations, the modem does not respond to AT commands, but when taken off the hook, immediately goes into call originate mode.

MNP See Microcom Networking Protocol

modem A device that transmits/receives computer data through a communications channel such as a radio or telephone lines. The Courier is a telephone channel modem that modulates, or transforms, digital signals for a computer into the analog form that can be carried successfully on a phone line. It also demodulates signals received from the phone line back to digital signals before passing them to the receiving computer.

Modem ISDN Channel Aggregation (MICA) A Cisco modem/ISDN integration technology

multilink PPP (MPPP) Method of extending PPP so that multiple connections can be added together for a higher bandwidth and lower latency; must be supported at both ends

Multichassis Multilink Point-to-Point Protocol (MMP) Cisco protocol that allows multiple connections from a single site to terminate in multiple access servers while still looking like one single larger connection

Multirouter Traffic Grapher (MRTG) A free program that graphs statistics taken from routers; available at http://www.ee.ethz.ch/~oetiker/webtools/mrtg

National Association of Security/Securities Dealers Automated Quotations (NASDAQ) A U.S. stock market that is home for many high-tech companies

Network Address Translation (NAT) A technology used to hide multiple machines behind a single IP address. It can also be used as a firewall.

network file system (NFS) A method of sharing files over a network; standardized by SUN Microsystems

network management system (NMS) Any product that helps you manage your network (for example, HP Open View)

network module (NM) Type of plug-in module used in 2600 and 3600 routers

network processor module (NPM) Type of plug-in module used in 4000 series routers

Network Terminal One (NT-1) A type of digital modem for ISDN service. The telephone company supplies this everywhere in the world except North America. It is the physical box on-site that converts U-loop onto S/T-loop.

Network Time Protocol (NTP) A protocol used for synchronizing date and time for computers and routers

nonvolatile random access memory (NVRAM) User-programmable random access memory whose data is retained when modem power is turned off; used in Courier modems to store a user-defined default configuration loaded into random access memory (RAM) at power-on

Numbering Plan Area/Network Numbering (NPA/NXX) The first six digits of a ten-digit phone number

octothorpe The proper name for the symbol #

online fall back A feature that allows high-speed error-control modems to monitor line quality and fall back to the next lower speed if line quality degrades. The modems fall forward as line quality improves.

Open Shortest Path First (OSPF) A dynamic routing protocol

operating system (OS) The software that tells the router or computer how to work

originate mode A state in which the modem transmits at the pre-defined low frequency of the communications channel and receives at the high frequency. The transmit/receive frequencies are the reverse of the called modem, which is in answer mode.

OSI Reference Model for Networking A seven-layer network design promoted by ISO

out-of-band Call detail information that is not sent through the same channel as the call itself (i.e., a voice call is carried on an ISDN B channel, but the call setup information—the number to dial, type of call, duration, etc.—is carried on the D channel)

packets per second (PPS) A measure of router speed

parallel transmission The transfer of data characters using parallel electrical paths for each bit of the character, such as 8 paths for 8-bit characters. Data is stored in computers in parallel form but may be converted to serial form for certain operations. See serial transmissions

parity An error-detection method that checks the validity of a transmitted character. Character checking has been surpassed by more reliable and efficient forms of block checking, including XMODEM-type protocols and the ARQ protocol implemented in Courier modems. The same type of parity must be used by two communicating computers, or both must omit parity. When parity is used, a parity bit is added to each transmitted character. The bit value is 0 or 1 to make the total number of 1's in the character even or odd, depending on which type of parity is used.

Password Authentication Protocol (PAP) Low-security method of dial-in user authentication in PPP

Personal Computer Memory Card International Association (PCMCIA) A standard for PC cards for notebook and laptop computers, as well as certain routers; also, People Can't Memorize Computer Industry Acronyms

plain old telephone service (POTS) Analog phone lines found in homes and small offices

Plug and Play ISA A variation of the standard ISA bus that attempts to automate the troublesome process of resolving the IRQ and COM port conflicts that can arise when new devices are installed in ISA-bus computers

Point-to-Point Protocol (PPP) A protocol used to send data over serial lines. PPP provides error checking, link control, and authentication, and can be used to carry IP, IPX, and other protocols. PPP is superseding SLIP as the leading dial-in-protocol.

Primary Rate Interface (PRI) High-speed ISDN line riding on a T1 or E1 digital leased line. All channels are 64 Kbps bearer channels except for one, which is a data channel reserved for call setup and other things.

programmable read-only memory (PROM) Usually refers to a hardware chip that contains software that cannot change unless reprogrammed using special equipment

protocol A system of rules and procedures governing communications between two or more devices. Protocols vary but communicating devices must follow the same protocol in order to exchange data. The format of the data, readiness to receive or send, error detection, and error correction are some of the operations that may be defined in protocols.

provisioning Another way of saying setting up telephone lines

Public Switched Telephone Network (PSTN) The collection of all the telephone companies and their networks

Q921 Data-link layer ISDN signaling channel protocol

Q931 Network layer ISDN signaling channel protocol used for call setup and disconnect

Quality of Service (QoS) A method of guaranteeing bandwidth to latency-critical network applications such as voice-over-IP

Radio Frequency Interference (RFI) Electrical noise that can interfere in the transmission of data

random access memory (RAM) Memory that is available for use when the modem is turned on, but that clears all information when the power is turned off. The modem's RAM holds the current operational settings, a flow control buffer, and a command buffer.

read-only memory (ROM) Permanent memory, not user-programmable. The modem's factory settings are stored in ROM and can be read (loaded) into RAM as an operational configuration.

Reduced Instruction Set Computing (RISC) A type of computer chip design that is fast for processing certain tasks

redundant power supply (RPS) The ability to add additional power supplies to a router, making it more resilient with regard to power problems

remote access A feature that allows a remotely located user to view the modem's configuration screens and change the modem's configuration. Password protection may be available.

Remote Authentication Dial-In User Service (RADIUS) A protocol invented by Livingston Enterprises (recently acquired by Lucent) for authenticating dial-in users across multiple dial-in servers

Remote Copy Protocol (RCP) The Berkeley network file transfer protocol

remote digital loopback A test that checks the phone link and a remote modem's transmitter and receiver. Data entered from the keyboard is transmitted from the initiating modem received by the remote modem's receiver, looped through its transmitter, and returned to the local screen for verification.

remote echo A copy of the data received by the remote system, returned to the sending system, and displayed on the screen. Remote echoing is a function of the remote system.

Remote Network Monitoring (RMON) Network-monitoring suite of protocols

remote office (RO) Medium-sized office that has a WAN or MAN connection back to a larger corporate network

Request for Quotation (RFQ) A document created by an end user and sent to a vendor asking for a price quote on specific products or services

Resource Reservation Protocol (RSVP) Part of a suite of protocols used to deliver QoS

result code Another way of saying status message. The modem sends result codes to your terminal (for example, to indicate the status connection).

RJ11 The Universal Standard Order Code (USOC) standard for wiring a single-line, two-wire phone network interface, typically passing tip and ring signals, from the public switched network

ROM See read-only memory

Routing Information Protocol (RIP) A dynamic routing protocol often used because WIN NT and UNIX systems can understand it to discover network paths

Santa Cruz Operations (SCO) Manufacturer of UNIX for Intel platforms

SDLC See Synchronous Data Link Control

SDSL See xDSL

Serial Line Internet Protocol (SLIP) A simple protocol that permits sending IP data over a serial line. SLIP is being superseded by the Point-to-Point Protocol (PPP).

serial port A computer port that enables the transmission of data characters, one bit at a time, using a single electrical path. Also know as a communications port, or COM port. On IBM-Compatible PC's, this is a port for asynchronous, serial data transmission and, in the case of modems, for data reception. Data is transmitted one bit at a time (serially) to devices such as a modem, a serial mouse, or a serial printer.

serial transmission The sequential transfer of data characters, one bit at a time, using a single electrical path; also see parallel transmission

shared memory Specialized memory available in some routers to keep transient information, such as packet data

shunt A small, plastic and metal piece used to cover sections of pins on a jumper. The shunt interconnects certain pins that, depending on the way the shunt is placed, determine functions.

Simple Mail Transfer Protocol (SMTP) The Internet standard for the exchange of electronic mail

Simple Network Management Protocol (SNMP) Network used to monitor and manage devices on a network

Single In-Line Memory Module (SIMM) A memory module that connects to a computer system with a card edge connector

Small Computer Systems Interface (SCSI) A computer peripheral bus, usually used for hard drive and CD-ROM readers

small office/home office (SOHO) Small office that has a WAN or MAN connection back to a larger corporate network

software flow control A form of flow control that uses XON and XOFF characters to start and stop the flow of data

SPID Service Profile Identifier, used for validating ISDN connections

S-Register An area of NVRAM that is used to store a modem setting

Standard Network Access Protocol (SNMP) Type of Ethernet framing

S/T loop ISDN service, made to run short distances from an NT-1

STAC Method of on-the-fly data compression

start bit The signaling bit attached to the beginning of each character before characters are transmitted during asynchronous transmission

stop bit The signaling bit attached to the end of each character before characters are transmitted during asynchronous transmission

Superframe Format (SF) Switch See Central Office Switch

Switched Multimegabit Data Service (SMDS) A type of WAN connection. Usually higher speed than a T1 circuit that provides Lan-like functionality

SYN IP packets used to initiate (or synchronize) a network connection

Synchronous Data Link Control (SDLC) A protocol developed by IBM for software applications and communicating devices operating in IBM's System Network Architecture (SNA). The protocol defines operations at the link level of communications, such as the format of data frames exchanged between modems over a phone line. See BISYNC, protocol, HDLC

synchronous transmission A form of transmission in which blocks of data are sent at strictly timed intervals. Because the timing is uniform, no start or stop bits are required. Compare to asynchronous transmission. Some mainframes only support synchronous communications unless their owners have installed an asynchronous adapter and appropriate software.

T1 Digital leased line that has 1.544 Mbps of throughput available; consists of 24 64 Kbps channels. Channels can be ordered as needed from the phone company.

Technical Assistance Center (TAC) Cisco's technical support system

telco Abbreviation for telephone company

Telecommunication Industry Association (TIA) A device whose keyboard and display are used for sending and receiving data over a communications link; differs from a microcomputer in that it has no internal processing capabilities; used to enter data into or retrieve processed data from a system or network; see EIS Terminal

terminal mode An operational mode required for microcomputers to transmit data. In terminal mode, the computer acts as if it were a standard terminal such as a teletypewriter rather than a state processor. Keyboard entries go directly to the modem, whether the entry is a modem command or data to be transmitted over the phone lines. Received data is output directly to the screen. The more popular communications software products control terminal mode as well as enable more complex operations, including file transmission and saving received files.

Token Ring   Network topology standardized by IBM and the IEEE

throughput   The amount of actual user data transmitted per second without the overhead of protocol information such as start and stop bits or frame headers and trailers; compare to characters per second

Transmission Control Protocol (TCP)   The main higher-level networking protocol used on the Internet to manage data connections

transmission rate   See bit rate

Trivial File Transfer Protocol (TFTP)   A method of file transfer that does not require passwords; usually used to back up router configuration information and IOS images

U Loop   ISDN service brought to the home by the phone company; made to run up to 18,000 feet from the phone company CO to the end-user location

Universal Asynchronous Receiver/Transmitter (UART)   Chip that transmits and receives asynchronous communications

unshielded twisted pair (UTP)   Twisted insulated copper wires bundled into an unshielded cable, commonly used in telephone and wiring systems. Grades of UTP include DTP (Datagrade Twisted Pair) and DIW (Distributed Inside Wire).

User Datagram Protocol (UDP)   A higher-level protocol, such as TCP, that sits above IP, the Internet Protocol

V.8   ITU-T recommendation that defines procedures for starting and ending sessions of data transmission

V.17   An ITU-T standard for facsimile operations that specifies modulations at 14.4 Kbps, with devices that transmit or receive at higher speeds

V.21 Modem   An ITU-T standard for modem communications at 300 bps. Modems made in the United States or Canada follow the Bell 103 standard; however, the modem can be set to answer V.21 calls for overseas.

V.22   An IUT-T standard for modem communications at 1200 bps, compatible with the Bell 212A standard observed in the United States and Canada

V.22bis   An ITU-T standard for modem communications at 2400 bps. The standard includes an automatic link negotiation fallback to 1200 bps and compatibility with Bell 212A/V.22 modems.

V.23 An ITU-T standard for modem communications at 1200 bps with a 75 bps back channel; used in the U.K.

V.25 An ITU-T standard for modem communications. Among other things, V.25 specifies an answer tone different from the Bell answer tone. All U.S. Robotics modems can be set with the BO command so that they use the V.25 2100 Hz tone when answering overseas calls.

V.25bis An ITU-T standard for synchronous communications between the mainframe or host and the modem using the HDLC or character-oriented protocol. Modulation depends on the serial port rate and setting of the transmitting clock and source, &X.

V.27ter An ITU-T standard for facsimile operations that specifies modulation at 480 bps, with fallback to 2400 bps

V.29 An ITU-T standard for facsimile operations that specifies modulation at 9600 bps, with fallback to 7200 bps

V.32 An ITU-T standard for modem communications at 9600 bps and 4800 bps. V.32 modems fall back to 4800 bps when line quality is impaired, and fall forward again to 9600 bps when line quality improves.

V.32Terbo Modulation scheme that extends the V.32 connection range: 4800, 7200, 9600, 12000, 14400, 16800, 19200, and 21600 bps. V.32 terbo modems fall back to the next lower speed when line quality is impaired, and fall back further as necessary. They fall forward to the next higher speed when the line quality improves.

V.34 An ITU-T standard that allows data rates as high as 33.6 Kbps

V.35 An ITU-T standard trunk interface between a device and a packet network, using signaling of at least 19200 bps

V.42 An ITU-T standard for modem communications that defines a two-stage process of detection for LAPM error control

V.42bis An extension of ITU-T V.42 that defines a specific data compression scheme for use with V.42 error control

Versatile Interface Processors (VIP) Network interface modules for high-end routers

V.Fast Class (V.FC) A proprietary modulation scheme developed by Rockwell International for data communication speeds up to 28.8 Kbps

virtual private dial-up networking (VPDN) Encrypted dial-up connections that use the Internet to carry sensitive data

virtual private networks (VPN) Encrypted network connections that use the Internet to carry sensitive data

voice interface card (VIC) Plug-in cards used in 2600, 3600, and AS5300 series routers to route voice over IP

WAN interface card (WIC) WAN modules for certain CISCO routers

Weighted Fair Queuing (WFQ) Part of a suite of Cisco protocols used to deliver QoS

wide-area network (WAN) A data network that spans a large geographical area

Windows Internet Service (WINS) Hostname to IP address resolution protocol used by Microsoft file sharing

word length The number of bits in a data character without parity, start, or stop bits

X.25 A packet-switched WAN technology

xDSL Digital Subscriber Line: A new high-speed data service just becoming available to home and businesses; can use existing telco local loops

Xmodem The first of a family of error-control software protocols used to transfer files between modems. These protocols are in the public domain and are available form many bulletin board services.

XON/XOFF Standard ASCII control characters used to tell a device to stop/resume transmitting data. In most systems, typing <Ctrl>-S sends the XOFF character. Some devices, including some modems, understand <Ctrl>-Q as ZON; others interpret the pressing of any key after <Ctrl>-S as XON.

Ymodem An error-correcting File Transfer Protocol that is related to but faster than Xmodem

Zmodem An error-correcting File Transfer Protocol that is related to but faster than Xmodem or Ymodem

INDEX

About the Author

Bill Burton is a Senior Instructor/Consultant at Chesapeake Network Solutions, Inc. where he primarily teaches Cisco courses: BCRAN, BCMSN, CIT, and SNAM. Bill actively consults in the wide area network field.